369   9841

Moley, Raymond
AUTHOR
The American Legion Story
TITLE

Moley, Raymond

The American Legion Story

DATE DUE

GAYLORD			PRINTED IN U.S.A.

The American Legion Story

by RAYMOND MOLEY, Jr.

With a Foreword by

J. EDGAR HOOVER

DUELL, SLOAN AND PEARCE

New York

369

First edition

DUELL, SLOAN & PEARCE
AFFILIATE OF
MEREDITH PRESS

Library of Congress Catalog Card Number: 66-22236

MANUFACTURED IN THE UNITED STATES OF AMERICA FOR MEREDITH PRESS

VAN REES PRESS • NEW YORK

To

My father, a steadfast friend;

My mother, of rare generosity;

The U.S. Navy, in which I have had the honor to serve.

Foreword

THE American Legion is truly an American institution—in origin, purpose and operation. Born from America's struggle to maintain liberty in World War I, the American Legion has become an inextricable part of the American story. Every patriotic citizen, from Anchorage to Miami, from Honolulu to Boston, salutes the brave men and women of the Legion—men and women whose exploits in war and peace have placed their fellow countrymen eternally in their debt.

The American Legion's influence has been positive, constructive, and beneficial. These are the men who know the horrors of war. They know that liberty—if it is to have meaning—must be defended, not alone by lip service but by the very lives of its adherents. For almost half a century, The American Legion has worked unswervingly for the principles of free government, for protecting the rights of our citizens, and for a deeper and abiding moral and spiritual strength. "For God and Country"—these words of its motto symbolize a faith not only for the past but for the years ahead.

Legionnaires have long been in the forefront in the fight against atheistic communism—an enemy which would destroy everything we hold dear. The American Legion has encouraged a factual study of this enemy—to know what it is, how it operates and what we as a Nation must do to defeat it. The Legion has encouraged a vigilant public opinion and a struggle against communism within the framework of law and order. Its work in the security field has truly been exemplary.

In addition, Legionnaires have taken America's youth to heart. Highly effective youth programs, such as Boys' State and Nation, the National High School Oratorical Contest, American Legion Baseball, have touched the lives of thousands of our boys and girls. Here is an affirmation of good citizenship—a belief that every person in a free society has not only rights and privileges but also duties and responsibilities. Many of our national leaders today have been influenced by the positive Americanism of The American Legion.

Above all, The American Legion is a symbol for other citizens— a symbol meaning faith in liberty. Americans see in The American Legion an organization of devoted men and women, working for country above self, for service to others over selfish, partisan and narrow interests. This is an influence which is felt not only nationally, but in every state, city, town and hamlet in these United States.

The American Legion Story by Raymond Moley, Jr., is an excellent book. It sets forth with skill and precision the history of this great organization. American citizens in all walks of life should know more about The American Legion. To read Mr. Moley's narrative is to relive the history of our Nation in the twentieth century.

J. Edgar Hoover

Preface

THIS book is addressed not only to Legionnaires but to a larger audience as well—Americans and others who may wish to understand one of our most influential free institutions by considering its foundations, history and objectives.

The American Legion exemplifies, on the record and in continuing performance, qualities vital to private and public organizations from which our nation derives much of its strength. Preeminently, the bedrock support upon which the Legion's structure and undertakings rest is the individual. This is as it should be in our Republic. Tens of thousands of Legionnaires and members of the Auxiliary are dedicated to service, carrying out programs directed toward the welfare of millions of their fellow citizens. Under a constitutional, representative system individuals formulate, legislate and administer Legion programs.

This condition is in striking contrast to that of members of arbitrary, monolithic organizations or of citizens of totalitarian states. This condition is a denial of various theories that hold men to be neither capable of changing their circumstances nor responsible for their acts. The unfinished American epic mocks economic determinism, dialectical materialism, the Freudian ethic or what have you. We choose to believe that peoples are not kelp beds in a sea of history, that individuals are not strands of seaweed moved by inexorable tides.

Yet much current thought is grounded in a morass of deterministic dogma. Abroad, where such nonsense is most energetically espoused, doctrines must be altered as unforeseen events occur. Break the misshapen bone and reset it. And, when the mended limb fails to fulfill its function, break it again. Periodically, Marxist-Leninist-Stalinist-Maoist doctrines undergo revision, and if there is any inevitability in history it is the ability of the totalitarian mind to delude itself about reality.

Constitutional democracy and liberty for whole peoples are the difficult, elusive, dynamic achievements and goals of modern men. In the United States, free men and free institutions are the guarantors of traditional principles of liberty. Threats that challenge these principles are familiar—apathy and ignorance, the denial of opportunity and the avoidance of controversy, intellectual cynicism and small betrayals of our heritage, "the insolence of office" and the arbitrary exercise of power.

To a high degree, The American Legion is active in countering these threats by constructive programs and forthright advocacy. And so this book seeks that wider audience whose understanding is essential to encouraging the Legion's valid and wholesome influence in American life. Legionnaires and equally dedicated Americans will preserve and advance our ideals by supporting institutions that establish their positions and set their course by the fixed stars found in the imperishable documents of human liberty.

In expressing my gratitude to those who have contributed directly to this book, I must assume full responsibility for certain judgments, interpretations and, I am sure, shortcomings. Above others, an illustrious American, my father, Raymond Moley, deserves my abiding gratitude for wise counsel, assistance and encouragement over the years. C. D. DeLoach, chairman of the Public Relations Commission of the American Legion, was a driving force behind the writing of this book. He has offered valuable contributions, enthusiasm and a steadfast friendship. Charles Duell and Charles Pearce have done likewise. I acknowledge a substantial debt to the special history subcommittee, of which Sam L. Latimer, Jr., was chairman and Lemuel W. Houston and Al Weinberg members, who read the manuscript and otherwise participated in the production of the book, and to those other Legionnaires who reviewed sections to offer valuable suggestions and whose interest and assistance have been unfailing, L. Eldon James, in whose commandership this book is published, Donald E. Johnson, National Adjutant E. A. Blackmore, William G. McKinley, Albert V. LaBiche, Walter E. Alessandroni, Raymond L. Olson, Madison B. Graves, and Thomas V. Hull. These men gave of their time, as did James C. Watkins, Robert E. Lyngh, Rod Anderson, Robert

B. Pitkin, Maurice T. Webb, Lawrence Fairall, George H. Maines, Randel Shake, Bertram G. Davis, James R. Wilson, Jr., C. W. Geile, William F. Hauck, H. Armand de Masi, Roscoe Turner, and Clarence H. Olson.

Numerous past National Commanders and other Legion officers mentioned in the text and appendix have contributed. They include James F. O'Neil, Alvin M. Owsley, Louis Johnson, Paul H. Griffith, George N. Craig, John S. Gleason, Martin B. McKneally, Charles L. Bacon, James E. Powers, E. Roy Stone, and Daniel F. Foley. Thomas W. Miller gave generously of his advice and friendship.

Similarly, I am indebted to the following Legionnaires for any success this book may have: Aldo R. Benedetto, Harold A. Cummins, Louis J. Greco, Robert L. Dunn, Donald W. Hynes, Norward W. Mansur, Arthur McDowell, Norman W. Stewart, James W. Doon, LeRoy D. Downs, Paul R. Greenaway, Owen E. Grinde, William D. James, Bryce W. LaPoint, Phillip A. Thomas, Frank A. Kelly, Gabriel Ditore, Paul DiFulco, Edwin E. Gamble, Charles L. Anderson, Ben B. Ballenger, Roscoe D. Curtiss, Ward W. Husted, Duane T. Brigstock, Franklin Sickle, William E. Christoffersen, and Sexson E. Humphreys.

I also appreciate the interest and aid of Marjorie Wilson of *Newsweek*.

For certain background material I relied upon numerous publications of The American Legion, its commissions and committees; *The American Legion Magazine;* Proceedings of Annual National Conventions; Digests of Minutes, National Executive Committee; and Reports to the Annual National Conventions. Marquis James's *History of The American Legion* (William Green, New York, 1923), Richard S. Jones' *History of The American Legion* (Bobbs-Merrill, New York, 1946), and Roscoe Baker's *The American Legion and American Foreign Policy* (Bookman Associates, New York, 1954) were most helpful. Both Martha Leslie and Dorothea Johnson of the Cleveland Public Library were generous throughout the preparation of this book. I thank, too, Loreen Seasock for alert secretarial work.

Finally, I recognize my obligation to countless individuals who have offered learning with open hands over the years. How am I to thank men like E. J. Whitcomb in my home town, Santa Barbara,

California, who opened a world of interests to me and gave me values I grew to understand and consider worthy of any sacrifice? How am I to express my gratitude to the United States Navy, with which I have been proud to be associated, and numerous organizations and institutions that have benefited me? My debt cannot be measured.

Raymond Moley, Jr.

Contents

Illustrations

xv

The American Legion Story

1

The Living Legion—for God
and Country

THIS is the story of an American institution. It is a story of what
individuals have done and can do in a free society. The chief
purpose of the following chapters is to describe the significant history
of The American Legion—not as something separate from the history
of the United States, apart from the mainstream of life in this Republic, but as a dynamic, consistent force in national affairs. For the
Legion's story is a human story, an integral part of any full account
or appraisal of our country's progress in the twentieth century.

The American Legion's history now spans a period of between
four and five decades, years of perhaps transcendent importance for
the United States and the world. Yet its contributions to community,
state and national achievements have not received adequate recognition. The influence of men and events is difficult to measure. The
surface of history does not reveal all the forces that truly shape it.
It is like an ocean that reluctantly discloses the submerged currents,
gradients, upheavals, and organic activity of its vasty deep.

Contributing to The American Legion's formation stands an array
of circumstances—an initial comradeship of those who served in the
first world war, their obligations to those who fell and to their widows
and orphans, the desire to serve the nation in peace as in war, the
emergence of the United States as a world power, a durable nationalism, the development of our constitutional and democratic institutions, and a realization among those who served of American

3

involvement in world affairs. These rank as immediate factors. Behind them, in the reaches of history, is a heritage of venerable traditions—from Pericles' Athens to Magna Charta and the Common Law of England to the liberties for which the Continental Army fought and the "rights of Englishmen" for which Edmund Burke so eloquently spoke. The American Legion's inception, development and activities owe their extraordinary character to this precious legacy.

Since 1919 The American Legion has reflected the Union, indivisible. The first world war galvanized the Union with a sense of national purpose that had been frequently neglected for a century, since the War of 1812. Unlike the Grand Army of the Republic and the United Confederate Veterans, which were sectional, The American Legion gained a national character. As an association of Northern soldiers the GAR attempted to maintain the Civil War issues and to see to it that justice, as they saw it, was forthcoming. This veterans' group exercised a political power of enormous scope from Grant to McKinley. The UCV, from Reconstruction days, functioned as efficiently through the South. The American Legion underlined ideals weakened in the divisive period of the Civil War and its aftermath. Within The Legion, North and South united under specific principles, and a bond grew up that runs through every state, to our territories and even to American communities abroad.

The Legion is, to anyone who studies its activities, resolutions and policies, an embodiment of strong, valid principles with the untorn continuity of high purpose for almost half a century. Maitland, in his *History of English Law,* speaks of this "seamless web" in history. The support of towering principles has been fundamental to the best efforts of the Legion—in national and international issues, in community affairs and in matters touching the welfare, health and rehabilitation of its own and others. It has emphasized the individual and the responsibility of the individual to the nation. The Legion's history is a seamless web going back to the original constitutional paragraph drafted at the Paris Caucus, a paragraph of extraordinary inspiration.

Any appreciation of The American Legion should recognize the awareness of its leaders and membership through the formative period that their creation was to be a departure from customary veterans' groups. Early they dispelled the fear of political alliance with either the Republican or Democratic Party. At the outset, and given written form at the Cleveland Convention of 1920, the principle of nonpartisanship was established from post to National Headquarters —a keystone in the arch of Legion undertakings. Ever since, the Legion has never hewn a party line, and has clashed with every Administration on at least one major issue. Within the Legion, compliance with its constitutional provisions and the resolutions and decisions of National Conventions and of the National Executive Committee rule out sanction of any political party. By promoting local and national policies without regard to party, The American Legion has kept its independence. With few exceptions Legion leaders have emphasized this principle, for to become a force behind or an appendage of any political party would destroy the essence of the Legion. Not only would its membership shrink but its identity and influence as well. Thus, Legionnaires who gather at 17,000 posts around the world and at department (state) and National Conventions may direct their efforts toward broad national problems, for these are their major areas of concern.

Union men, businessmen, farmers and industrialists, white-collar workers and men in government, the self-employed and men from all the professions find common ground in Legion gatherings. A Legionnaire at the post level may see his proposal adopted as a resolution at the National Convention and, through the Legion's legislative efforts, pass the Houses of Congress. Without concern for sectional support, the "big city vote" or the "farm bloc," without regard for attacks by pacifist, certain internationalist and academic, or extremist groups, The American Legion has since its beginnings compiled an astonishing record of judicious policies. By remaining apart from party politics at all levels, Legionnaires have been in a position to place the Legion on record for policies which, though unpopular or annoying, are considered to be in the best interests of the country.

For nearly five decades Legion emphasis on security through adequate military forces, counter-subversion measures, the teaching of communist and fascist intentions, and the promotion of patriotism has drawn intense fire from many quarters. At times, men and women deemed responsible have found it expedient or sophisticated to attack Legion warnings and proposals. Segments of the press and the academic community have neglected, ignored and scorned Legion positions for various reasons. And so, at times many Legionnaires, feeling slighted and frustrated, might have despaired, lamenting, "Wisdom cries out in the street and no man regards." Some struck back. Others chose to ignore this serious development, but most persevered. However, when unwelcome truths gain slight notice, when public figures mask malevolent facts, when men of learning indulge in wishful meditation on a present or potential adversary's intentions, when it is "smart" to regard patriotism as an out-of-date virtue, the Republic loses a measure of its strength. To counter these tendencies, The American Legion in recent years has more energetically exploited public relations. Consequently, a larger public and a growing number of notable figures recognize the judicious record of the Legion's resolutions on vital national issues. One is General Lucius D. Clay. In 1962 he remarked that it had often occurred to him that if the United States "had followed more closely the views and recommendations of The American Legion with respect to foreign policy over the years, our position in the world would be stronger than it is."

Here, only a brief recital of national programs is in order. It is important to realize that the multiplicity of Legion programs has not been directed at gaining consideration and benefits for its members to the exclusion of others. Legionnaires have labored for and directed their activities at Legion and non-Legion veterans alike; at veterans and those who have never served in the armed services; at all children, their own and others, whether healthy or stricken, gifted or benighted. Legionnaires have become expert in their programs, and they have learned that if they slacken their efforts they may see objectives they have gained or toward which they have worked being swept from view.

Rehabilitation, encompassing widespread local effort and legislative and administrative objectives for the welfare of war veterans and their dependents, has always been of primary importance.

The American Legion is prominent among many organizations that contribute to a more vital future citizenry and a more responsible contemporary society. Too many citizens tend to forget the zest, hopes, joys, and needs of youth. Yet American strength, the luster of her ideals and the promise of her future depend, in part, upon the attitudes and energies of successive generations.

Under the Americanism Commission are such undertakings as unparalleled support of the Boy Scout movement, the National High

School Oratorical Contest program, education and scholarship activities, the conduct of fifty Boys' State programs and the Annual Boys' Nation, sponsorship of The American Legion Baseball Program, the presentation of School Medal Awards, and other activities, such as the American Education Week conducted with the National Education Association, flag education, patriotic holiday observance, get-out-the-vote campaigns, cooperation with Boys Clubs, and the Counter Subversive program.

The commission under Daniel J. O'Connor will continue to contribute to the strength of the nation. O'Connor points out:

> The commission has, through the years, accepted and continues to accept, the challenge of promotion of positive Americanism and teaching our young people love of country and the rudiments of our governmental structure expressed through a democratic form of government.

Today, six hundred Legionnaires of the Americanism Council serve to advance the many programs administered by the commission. Of these programs National Adjutant E. A. Blackmore has said:

> They provide many outlets for wholesome, healthful activity for our young people, as well as the opportunity for them to learn of the principles and ideals upon which this nation was founded and through which it has risen to greatness among the family of nations.

National and post efforts in the child welfare field have also been energetically expended on the department (state) level.

Activities of the National Security Commission, the Economic Commission, the Foreign Relations Commission, the Legislative Commission, the Public Relations Commission, the Publications Commission, the Finance Commission, Divisions of the National Organization, and the Affiliated Organizations of The American Legion are all of major concern in the effective conduct of Legion affairs.

Legislative triumphs of The American Legion range from the field of rehabilitation to child welfare, from the establishment of the Veterans Bureau (later the Veterans Administration) to passage of the Legion-sponsored GI Bill of Rights. A leader in the Legion states that "the GI Bill was the most important single legislative accomplishment of The American Legion. Who can begin to measure its benefits and its impact upon the nation?"

In the realm of national defense Legionnaires' efforts and testimony have long been astute, if less successful. Only in recent years has the extent of national security requirements been generally recognized. In part, this development stems from efforts of Legionnaires who have made it their business to be knowledgeable in this complex field. Legionnaires of great ability who have contributed are listed in the appendix under National Security Committees and Commissions.

The American Legion's interest and influence in foreign affairs likewise will continue, for Legionnaires have long recognized the kind of enemy we face in communism and have displayed both an appreciation of the extent of the nation's commitments in the cold war and a growing understanding of the difficulties in successfully conducting foreign policy. National Commanders have shown a keen interest in promoting Legion determination that the United States pursue a firm and realistic foreign policy coupled with a powerful defense posture. Especially aware of America's obligations and commitments have been the post-World War II commanders—John Stelle, Paul H. Griffith, James F. O'Neil, S. Perry Brown, George N. Craig, Erle Cocke, Jr., Donald R. Wilson, Lewis K. Gough, Arthur J. Connell, Seaborn P. Collins, J. Addington Wagner, W. C. Daniel, John S. Gleason, Preston J. Moore, Martin B. McKneally, William R. Burke, Charles L. Bacon, James E. Powers, Daniel F. Foley, Donald E. Johnson, and L. Eldon James.

The Legion's deep mistrust of communism's protestations of good faith has been subjected to attack from numerous quarters over the years, and many of these critics were notable men and women. Some have changed their views. The influence of others has fallen into a decent oblivion. After World War II international communism clamped its ponderous apparatus on Eastern Europe, then swung into action on the streets of France and Italy and in the impoverished mountains of Greece. No longer could the most venerable powers of the West stand up to the new menace. Their empires around the world were becoming unhinged by the weight of anti-colonialism and the pressure of new nationalism. American Presidents and other public figures recognized the threat and acted. Public opinion backed the assumption of responsibilities of leadership among nations resisting communism and, wherever possible, supported men dedicated to liberty. The American Legion, long an advocate of firmness in confronting communism, has had much to do with continuing public support of the policy of containment and its enormous cost. Those who have guided the Legion in its foreign relations programs are listed in the appendix.

General Douglas MacArthur, a Legionnaire and always a champion of the citizen soldier, said of the Legion in 1952:

"One of the greatest contributions The American Legion has made to the nation has been in the strengthening of the potentialities of the citizen soldier. Since the Minute Men of 1776 formed the ranks of the Continental Army and brought victory to its arms in the American Revolution, the security of the United States has rested more than all else upon the competence, the indomitable will and the resolute patriotism of the citizen soldier. The professional has had his role . . . but in all of our wars, from the Revolution to Korea, the citizen soldier has met the full shock of battle, has contributed all but a fraction of the dead and maimed and has accepted the responsibility."

Those who make up the 2.5 million-member Legion of today shared a sense of purpose, sacrifice, comradeship, and unselfishness that is somehow absent in many civilian activities. In writing of the Battle of the Somme, where British and Commonwealth soldiers lost as many as sixty thousand of their number in one day, Brian Gardner observed, "There was a close bond between officers and men in most battalions on the Western Front, especially those of the New Army. They shared a secret horror that no civilian would ever fully understand." For the American soldier, sailor, Marine, and coastguardsman there are similar bonds, whether they endured the boredom of waiting, the dry taste of fear, the smell of the unwashed, the sight of people over which armies had marched, the naked white bone of the wounded, the useless anger toward friends, the arrogant order, the hard discipline, the frightening minutes going into a beach, or the longing for home.

How are we then to square the Legion's detractors' insinuations that Legionnaires are dangerous, even militaristic, because they are "anti-communist," "anti-pacifist" and advocates of great military strength, of firm foreign policies, and of a deep and abiding allegiance to their creed, "For God and Country"?

The vast historical library on the United States has, on the whole, neglected, dismissed or lampooned The American Legion and encouraged the creation of a stereotype. This travesty, this historical burlesque, has cultivated a false image which has been accepted by many people. It is interesting that some contributors have an almost unblemished record of grievous error on questions of great urgency and shaking consequence. I refer to (1) the national interest in diplomacy and war; (2) the nature and objectives of communism; and (3) the importance of national defense.

Strategies based upon the communists' good faith did not draw inspiration from Legion resolutions nor are they explained away by The American Legion. Policies based upon an underestimation of communism led to millions being swept into the communist orbit and, since the second world war, exacted a heavy price in American lives and national substance. The author of failure was not The American Legion. Through years when many intellectuals were raked by cynicism and doubt, when the public was barraged by subversive propaganda, the Legion remained steadfast in its idealism, unremitting in its adherence to judicious, though unpopular, positions on preparedness and foreign relations. Here, the Legion has been a sheet anchor in times of crisis. Its unrelenting activities and influence have been of far greater importance than is generally recognized. Perhaps the efforts of this mature organization with greater emphasis upon informing the public of Legion positions, policies and service will gain deserved recognition.

While there have been unfortunate events associated with the Legion and certain of its members, faulty judgment and irresponsible members are the occasional lot of any institution. Organizations of men cannot cancel all traces of the faults of men. Governments, religious organizations, political parties, citizen groups, unions, associations, and clubs—all are vulnerable to occasional criticism. Yet, in balance, they are a source of essential strength to the nation. To some extent the activities of these groups determine whether we shape our destiny or fall back crying that circumstances or fate or history holds dominion over us. Let us take off the 18-ounce gloves and question the cynic, the sophisticated critic of American culture and ideals and the detractor who proclaims that patriotism is passé. Before we give in to the barren philosophy of "determinism" or to the Freudian ethic, let us view the long shadow cast by those who went before us in this land, men who shaped a continent and a government and free institutions, so numerous they can only straighten our backs, reinforce our faith and compel us to persevere. Let us examine The American Legion. It is one of our great free institutions.

2

From Momentous Events

I T is said that the Humboldt Current has its source deep below the Antarctic where warmer water by displacement starts its slow northward flow. Along the coast of Peru winds sometimes blow the warm surface water away from the coast, and then the frigid Humboldt Current breaks to the surface.

There is a rough parallel to this phenomenon in the chilling events of the twentieth century. For the origins of the great happenings of our era must be sought in the recesses of modern history and the depths of the human soul. They require brief mention here since the momentous events they instituted are those from which The American Legion emerged.

The causes of World War I are several and date from distant history: the rise of the modern state and nationalism; the struggle for markets, empire and martial glory; the advance of the Industrial Revolution; the development of cynical philosophies and modern communications, by which whole peoples could be influenced; attention to new weapons—all these had a bearing on the outbreak of what became the first total war. In it the substance of nations was committed, entire peoples involved, and the essential soldiers and sailors enlisted by nationwide conscription which in modern history goes back to the *levée en masse* of the Napoleonic Wars. There was also a wide spectrum of onerous human emotions—rank, malignant hatreds, avarice, fear, and promiscuous desires. And, make no mistake, the saving virtues of man contributed as well—fierce love of liberty, devotion to justice and honor.

For years the nations of Europe had been choosing up sides. Periodically, intense German and Slav nationalism had endangered the general peace. Bismarck had forged a united Germany and inflicted a terrible defeat upon the French in 1871. The French were rankled by frustration and inflamed by *la revanche*—an unquenchable desire for past glory which involved striking Germany and recovering from that indignity. "Alsace!" was stamped in every Gallic breast. Bismarck had responded with the Triple Alliance—Germany, the Austro-Hungarian Empire and Italy. The mantle of the chancellor of "blood and iron" fell upon the narrow shoulders of Wilhelm II. But the Kaiser was not Bismarck. He lacked the genius of that exceptional figure who had shaped a powerful state and ambitious people from fragments, smashed France, and with masterful skill arranged alliances. Bismarck had left a people accustomed to martial glory and, equally ominously, to autocratic rule. The Kaiser was expected to carry on the traditions. Philosophers, military men and the press nudged him to the extremes of folly. Delicate balances were disturbed. Russia was alienated. France busied herself with treaties. By the overt display of strength and naval building the Kaiser alarmed Britain. In 1905 French and German ambitions clashed in Morocco. Austria, by annexing Bosnia and Herzegovina in 1908, brought Russia and Serbia to the point of unbridled fury. There, in the Balkans, rivalries had existed "cheek by jowl" for centuries.

In 1911 the Germans in a show of strength precipitated the Agadir incident when they sent the gunboat *Panther* to Morocco and were compelled to back down by the British. The Kaiser's threats, posturing and antics gradually destroyed Bismarck's security arrangements and stripped his nation of friends save for the tottering empire of the Hapsburgs.

All this was not lost upon European statesmen. Russia and France formed the Dual Alliance. Britain concluded the Entente Cordiale with France. Both were committed to Belgium's neutrality. Finally the Triple Entente of England, France and Russia confronted the Kaiser. He reacted with a scream, "Encirclement!" Britain, enjoying blue water supremacy, anxious to maintain her markets and *Pax Britannica,* was his nemesis. He and his generals were well aware of French plans and of Russian ambitions in Eastern Europe. But, when the time came, they would strike the heaviest blows. They regarded their gains of 1871 in the nature of unfinished business—and a bloody, unrewarding business it was to be. They spoke freely of *der Tag,* the day that war would transport Germany to greater glory. Unquestionably the German people, the most tractable and ambitious in Europe, were prepared. They possessed technical mastery and a positive taste for order, discipline and obedience. Many were mesmerized by passionate and morbid native philosophies, particularly the mystical scribblings of Nietzsche.

By 1914 Europe's vast pile of weapons was deliberately piled in frightening array. Mobilization by one great power would disturb the structure and bring it down like a matchstick house. There were those who prophesied. Bismarck had remarked that "some damned foolish thing in the Balkans" would start a war, and the Balkans had been labelled "the powder keg of Europe." The American Col. Edward M. House wrote to President Wilson, "The situation is extraordinary. It is militarism run stark mad," and sent a message in early summer, "It only needs a spark to set the whole thing off."

A telegram received in Belgrade read, EXCELLENT SALE OF BOTH HORSES. Had an American in 1914 known of this brief message, that it referred not to a livestock transaction but to the successful assassination of an Austrian archduke and his consort in a crowded street in Sarajevo, Bosnia, he could not have imagined the dread consequences of the act. It was the "damned foolish thing," the spark. A more appropriate simile than a powder keg blowing up describes what followed. Today we have more sophisticated devices than gunpowder, and what occurred was more in the nature of a nuclear detonation. For Europe was a critical mass needing only the swift introduction of an event to start the chain reaction. Happenings of tragic certainty followed the pistol shots. Austria, bent on humbling Serbia, checked with the Kaiser, since Russia towered behind her Slavic neighbor. The Kaiser casually gave Germany's full support to whatever might enter Franz Josef's head as punishment for the Serbs and promptly left the charged summer atmosphere for the cool waters of Norway aboard his yacht. Ultimatums and appeals flashed between capitals, rulers ordered mobilization and arms clattered throughout Europe.

The Kaiser suddenly had second thoughts. But, like the sorcerer's apprentice, he could not stop what his gossip, petty intrigues, intemperate outbursts, and vanity had helped to start. He was in no position to arrest the march of men and events. As Cyril Falls wrote later, he did not realize that making mischief makes war. The German generals moved swiftly. Contemptuous of democratic France, disparaging of British fiber, derisive toward plodding Russia, German leaders had prepared for a methodical and swift victory over their neighbors. The Emperor's reservations were quashed. What followed incinerated the European peace, shook the world and altered Western civilization forever.

Thus Europe went to war while all across America an optimistic people laughed and sweated in the growing season. In the long summer evenings you could hear the metallic clank of tools as they tinkered with new machines in back yards, the sound of water sprinkling lawns and the excitement of children before bedtime. For Americans the midsummer madness that engulfed Europe was beyond understanding and reason. Emotionally they were far removed from the consequences of what seemed the endless follies of Europe. And even had they the capacity to discern and judge interests and positions, causes and events, right and wrong, they could not have been persuaded to recognize any vital interest in the eventual outcome. Their President admonished them to be neutral in thought and deed. But when all the protestations are heard, all the evidence compiled and all the "ifs" considered, national interests were very much involved from the start and military intervention came when they appeared to be seriously jeopardized.

Since American Legion concerns have been those of the United States and are in part a product of World War I, an understanding of America and Americans at that time and the enormity, conduct, issues, and repercussions of that struggle is necessary. Further, to understand The American Legion, its ideals and principles, it is necessary to understand something of the history of the country whose sons eventually were to play an indispensable part in the outcome of World War I.

There is a common misconception that the United States entered the ranks of great powers in 1898 or even 1917. But if history has validity, if production is a measure or if international commitments are testimony, Americans who banded together in The American Legion were the offspring of a nation that had been a significant world power for many years. Had the United States avoided military involvement in World War I, her interests still were bound to momentous events in the world. This was true before Wilson observed in 1919 that "the isolation of the United States is at an end, not because we chose to go into the policies of the world but because by the sheer genius of our people [the United States is] a determining factor in the history of mankind."

Years before, when it might have seemed that our expansion had reached a barrier on the Pacific shore, when a destiny of continental dominion ceased to be manifest and only consolidation might have been pursued, there were other events that conspired and other men who acted to move the nation beyond the boundaries of the Pacific and Gulf Coasts. The strapping young Republic had not confined itself to its own back yard or even its own block. Its adventures abroad and its troubles with other world powers stretched back more than a century to its attempt to assert itself on the high seas and in the realm of international law. Americans were an optimistic and sometimes boastful lot, spoiling for a fight. And so on a number of occasions this nation of energetic people came into conflict with venerable states. The British were not the only power to "show the flag" successfully in distant places. American masters outstripped foreign sailors in the mid-1800's with their incomparable clipper ships. The U.S. Navy, too, became familiar with the Pacific—active in its western reaches and elsewhere. Its opening of Japan influenced the history of the world in decisive and continuing ways. Congress threatened war with Germany in 1890 over a challenge to American rights in the Samoan Islands. Americans, with the Monroe Doctrine, Navy and Marine Corps, and virtually undisturbed by the Old World, had a long record of influence in this hemisphere. With regard to the great powers, President Cleveland threatened war with Great Britain in 1895, when the British refused to arbitrate a Guiana Colony–Venezuela boundary dispute. The war with Spain three years later is frequently cited as the time when the United States entered the ranks of great powers by fighting Spain. This thrust American territorial interests across the Pacific to the Philippines, into the already familiar Western Ocean.

The United States not only moved far beyond the physical limits of the continental United States but pushed out the frontiers of industry, agriculture, research, science, medicine, and marketing. By 1914 Americans had an astonishing recent history behind them. By the 1890's the nation had grown from a population of less than that of Austria-Hungary to more than that of any European state except Russia. Whereas other newcomers to the fraternity of world powers —modern Germany and Japan—turned their energies toward expansion, the United States, its expansion virtually completed, turned inward to further triumphs of science, industry and business and the refinement of its institutions. Railroads linked all parts of the country, automobiles began their impact on the economy, and cities and factories, illuminated by electricity, drew more and more people from the land. It was generally a happy period of growing prosperity and national might. As the Progressive movement dominated American politics from 1901 to 1917, there was a shift to government intervention in economic affairs in the public interest and an attempt to re-examine American institutions to see if they squared with the democratic ideal. Progressive administrations struck out for fresh goals in local, state and national government.

And so in that hot August of 1914 the United States and its citizens were certain that they could pursue a peaceful course. But it was soon to become evident that as the greatest industrial power on earth, with its world leadership in the products so important in what is today referred to as total war—iron, steel, coal and foodstuffs— and its strong credit position, the United States could not take lightly what was to transpire in Europe. General war in Europe was not something easily to be put out of mind.

Most of Europe went to war with panache. Strange, when war had been dreaded for so long. After years of tension the news seemed like the refreshing wind before a storm that breaks the oppressive summer heat. An almost tangible sense of relief and celebration swept the capitals of the belligerents. The French marched into four and a half years of slaughter in their red pantaloons with flowers, bunches of grapes and bottles of red wine; British Tommies singing "Tipperary" had a holiday air one might associate with an outing to Brighton Beach; and the Germans swung into Luxembourg and Belgium with *"Die Wacht am Rhein"* on their lips.

The Germans had the brilliant Schlieffen Plan, which was to sweep like a scythe through Belgium and the lowlands and to roll up the

French. Russia could be dealt with later. The French and British were already bankrupt of ideas aside from the powerful blockade the Royal Navy was to impose. The Russians could think of nothing better than to point their massive columns toward Austria and Prussia.

The German attack through Belgium was a dark affair from start to finish, explained without reference to the obligation of their 1839 treaty on the grounds that "necessity knows no law." The Chancellor told the Reichstag that the French threat compelled Germany "to override the just protest of the Luxembourg and Belgium governments. The wrong—I speak openly—that we are committing we will endeavor to make good as soon as our military goal has been reached. Anybody who is threatened, as we are threatened, and is fighting for his highest possessions can have only one thought—how he is to hack his way through." Breaking the "encirclement" was everything; the Belgium treaty, a "scrap of paper," and the accepted principles of international law, nothing.

Von Kluck's drive through Belgium was grizzly enough with atrocities without the fabrication of atrocity stories which were later disproved and tended to cast doubt on all truthful recitals of Teutonic barbarism. It was not an Allied propagandist who dreamed up the parallel of the Germans to the Huns. The Kaiser himself admonished his legions to act like the Huns of Attila. The Belgians chose to fight and at Liège upset General von Moltke's timetable. Civilian hostages were shot when Belgian patriots were so unsporting as to fire from windows to resist the invader.

The French Plan 17 broke against Germans on the lower Rhine. French generals were almost mystics, even when their poilus faced hundreds of Maxim machine guns. For them *élan* (guts) and *offensive à outrance* would provide the answers, and they fashioned their doctrines accordingly: *"Attaque, attaque, toujours l'attaque"* of 1914 became *"Tout le monde à la bataille"* of 1917. For an inflexible doctrine brave soldiers were to pay an awful price. Obsessed by the Russians and the French right, von Moltke wavered and fatally amended the Schlieffen Plan, reducing the weight of what could have amounted to a roundhouse right knockout. The French with the British Expeditionary Force belatedly concentrated power on their left. As the Germans came within sight of the Eiffel Tower they swung eastward, hoping to roll up the French Fifth Army. Thus, the right wing of the mighty sweep through Belgium into the vitals of France—exhausted from unbroken days of marching and fighting, underfed and at the extremity of its supply lines and without its supporting artillery —presented its flank to the French Third Army and the BEF. At the bugle sound the Allies turned on their tormentor and slammed into the gray columns. The Battle of the Marne was decisive, largely because French Commander Joseph Joffre possessed what Voltaire saw in Marlborough, "that calm courage in the midst of tumult, that security of soul in danger, which the English call a cool head." The Germans fell back, and the race to the sea followed, which extended the front from the Swiss frontier to the Channel. Bitter and cruel battles ensued, in which hard-bitten British regulars sometimes were reduced to a thin line of gun pits. When the year was out, they still held them. This was the contemptible little army, so called by the British themselves, that a German leader said would be arrested by the police if it were to appear in Germany, a portent of the disdain those in control in Germany developed toward the United States.

The Allies on the Western Front and the Russians on the Eastern Front quickly experienced the devastating consequences of facing machine-gun patterns. The rapid-fire rifle had already damaged the efficacy of Horse Guards and Uhlans. The machine gun unhorsed the cavalry, made moles of the infantry, drove the cannon from the line to concealment, and frustrated generals versed in obsolete tactics and strategy. Americans and future Legionnaires two and a half years later were to find that these unimaginative generals and marshals had not yet solved the problem of reducing the effectiveness of the machine gun. The answer eventually came—a one-half-inch sheet of steel. Armor plate and the tractor tread led to the tank. Young officers like Fuller, Hart and Martel and civilian amateurs were the first to recognize its potential.

In the East the Russians did their share of dying and sustained severe mauling in 1915 as the Germans pounded deep into the front that stretched from the Carpathian Mountains to the Baltic Sea. The Serbs and the Austrians brutalized each other in a Hatfield-McCoy fashion.

Dreams of swift victory and triumphant homecoming were scattered with the late autumn foliage. The Western Front congealed, and an angry, jagged wound slashed across Europe.

Brief mention of the dreadful battles and human suffering endured in the years preceding U.S. intervention may illuminate certain important events and developments the consequences of which concern us to this day and have had an indelible effect not only upon the formation of The American Legion but upon several of its enduring programs.

With relentless monotony the killing proceeded on the Western and Eastern Fronts. The BEF, which had displayed a tenacity referred to in the bare-knuckle days of prizefighting as "bottom," had ceased to be after Ypres. And their place was taken over gradually by a generation of idealistic young men from throughout the Empire. The French soldiers who survived saw hundreds of thousands of their comrades die on the barbed wire, of shell and shot in the lunar terrain that stretched for a few miles from a line that was seldom altered, in "the glamorous aerial combat," and from all manner of disease. The front became an impasse of death. The years 1915 and 1916 are remembered for insensate attacks and mechanized slaughter. The words strike grief and horror in the hearts of thoughtful men—Verdun, the Somme, the Champagne, the Second Battle of Ypres (where poison gas was introduced), St. Mihiel, Soissons, Neuve-Chapelle, Loos, the Brusilov offensive, Isonzo, and Trentino.

Attrition—another word to ponder. It made those in command despair of swift victories and soldiers despair of survival. Attrition describes the first world war after its initial phase. Attrition faced both sides, on all levels in military and civil life. With it came the fruition of what we now recognize as total war, the twentieth century's contribution to the military lexicon. The war commenced to consume the manhood, substance and attention of the nations engaged.

Now the stranglehold of the British blockade tightened. British orders supplemented what was accepted in international law regarding contraband and the requirements of blockade. The British Grand Fleet anchored at Scapa Flow, its superstructures and guns hidden in the Orkneys' mists, and British squadrons steaming thousands of miles of ocean were those "far-distant, storm-beaten ships" that denied Germany many needs and kept the German High Seas Fleet glowering in Wilhelmshaven, Bremerhaven and Kiel. Germany countered with the U-boat, but its effectiveness was at first crippled by lack of experienced crews and the outraged cries of President Wil-

son. That the German High Seas Fleet might undertake a dangerous sortie was expected. It came in 1916. The British were waiting,
and the Battle of Jutland took place. In it German warships inflicted
the greater damage but were compelled to retire, never to challenge
the Grand Fleet on the open sea again.

In the East 1915 was the midnight of Russian fortunes from which
the ancient autocracy of the Tsars could never recover. Almost three
and a half million men from the length and breadth of Russia
marched to their graves in that frightful year. Italy joined the fray in
forbidding terrain against Austria, and as winter wore on the Serbs
were vanquished.

The Gettysburg of the war came in 1916 at Verdun. Already the
stencil for military operations on the Western Front, where the profligate slaughter was to continue to the end, was cut. Hopes for imaginative, "irregular" strategies had already been dealt a numbing blow
at Gallipoli the year before.

Verdun was the choice of the new German Commander Falkenhayn. This fortified area which, aside from its strategic importance,
held a ponderous, mystic sway over the minds and hearts of Frenchmen, "for the retention of which," as Falkenhayn observed, "the
French command would be compelled to throw in every man they
have." Joffre disregarded what proved to be accurate intelligence
and believed the Germans would strike elsewhere. As usual, his generals bent over their own suicidal offensive plans. Merciful weather
saved them. They reinforced the sector, and over a period of weeks
managed to hold the area. It was a French triumph of logistics rather
than arms. Falkenhayn's strategy to drain the life blood of France
also drained life blood from his army. Verdun was followed by the
great counter-offensive of the Somme, where British divisions broke
themselves against the superlative defenses of the Germans. In one
day they suffered 60,000 casualties. Thousands died attacking or
defending a few yards of front. This was indeed attrition on a grand
scale.

Generalship earned a dismal grade before and after. Military commanders, bereft of originality, ordered massive artillery barrages to
prepare the way for assaults to achieve breakthroughs which, from
the first, were doomed to the terrible adjective "limited." The means
to exploit an opening were absent. Troops could not survive the im-

pact of artillery, land mines, trench mortars, machine guns, and grenades and continue to negotiate the churned-up terrain. Their own barrage not only plowed up the battle area but alerted the defenders.

The general staffs' record was one of miscalculation, stubbornness in clinging to fallacious theories developed years before, failure to accept reasonable intelligence estimates, and refusal to recognize the supremacy of the machine gun and barbed wire once the front had coagulated. Most subordinate officers could recite by rote obsolete theories and held, perhaps with less zeal, the same faith as their superiors.

Meanwhile, America produced enormous quantities of supplies for the Allies and achieved an enviable credit position while waving neutrality placards and electing Mr. Wilson to another term in the White House. Prosperity verged on boom times and there was peace in the land. This, it seemed, was enough. Stern protests to the British for their usual high-handed conduct on the high seas did not match the ultimatums that went out to the German Foreign Office over sinkings by the U-boats. Woodrow Wilson had uttered a futile appeal when he urged Americans to be neutral in thought and deed. This angelic condition was unattainable in the President himself, let alone his closest associates, who entertained undisguised sympathy, if not commitment, to the Allied cause from the beginning. Grave incitements to war assailed him, but he was haunted by the specters of bloodshed, of his domestic program arrested, of his towering destiny as a peacemaker gone, and of democracy's demise in America from the shock of war.

Abroad, Mr. Wilson was regarded as a scolding schoolmaster and as a limitless source of gratuitous advice. But Wilson, obstinate to the last, saw himself as mankind's mediator, unable to see that neither side wanted his good offices, that the appalling sacrifices had to be justified. Reputations and careers had been swept away with millions of lives. The leaders knew that if some reward, some tangible gains were not to be found at the end of the bloody struggle, their own careers would be doomed. They were like gamblers in a frightful run of losses. How were they to stop? Their creditors, the people, had to be given something for a record of unsuccessful, profligate wagers. These men could not turn from the table with empty pockets. It was all very well for Mr. Wilson to admonish their behavior. But Mr. Wilson was not sitting at the table.

As 1917 approached, years of fierce and sanguinary war had left both the Allies and the Central Powers staggering. Months of unutterable slaughter, suffering and sacrifice had decimated hundreds of divisions. The Allies were bankrupt of both ideas and money, their armies very nearly bled white. Considering the indescribable slaughter, hardships and tensions they had endured, their soldiers must be counted among history's most steadfast. That French divisions were brushed by the evil wind of mutiny some months later is not surprising.

Britain's financial position was also perilous. Well might the English have recalled the lines from *Hamlet:*

> When sorrows come, they come not single spies,
> But in battalions.

Two great events of enduring significance to all Legionnaires occurred in 1917—American intervention and the Russian Revolution. The first led to the creation of their organization and several of their programs; the second, to a serious consideration and early recognition of one of the most challenging movements of modern times.

Gradually, provocation and propaganda stripped away most of the remaining vestiges of American neutrality. Sabotage, espionage and subversion in the United States by Germans and their agents compounded the U-boat sinkings of neutral vessels. In October 1916, pushed toward war repeatedly, his nation more partial to the Allies than ever before, Wilson concluded that the "business of neutrality" was over and that protection of the normal commerce of nations in the future required the end of war. When Germany announced unrestricted submarine warfare in January, it was clear that either neutral rights had to be abandoned or fought for. But still the President hung back. On March 1 the notorious Zimmermann telegram, proposing an alliance between Mexico and Germany in the event the United States joined the Allies, whereby Mexico would attack the United States and receive her lost territory north of the border, hit the front pages of every American newspaper.

Behind these events was the insane arrogance of the German military bordering on stupidity and self-delusion, so strong that it swept away realistic appraisals of the consequences of American entry. It was like a drug producing fantastic visions of power, whereby "no American will set foot on the Continent." The hallucination was reassuring and it was fatal. Their death struggle with the British had taught them nothing. Now another constitutional democracy was to be aligned against Germany. But, with evidence of Allied extremity, naval leaders in Berlin had insisted that their submarine weapon if freed of restrictions could throttle the British. By 1917 over one hundred U-boats, their crews trained and confident, were ready to launch torpedoes at all shipping not serving the Central Powers. British sea power could not check them.

At first glance what the Germans had announced seemed sheer madness. Weeks of foul weather lay ahead for the U-boat crews. Submarine operations on the North Sea and the Atlantic in February and March are grim ordeals at best, next to impossible at worst. The sea runs like a wild thing for days on end. At times visibility closes to a few yards. The gale winds strike like a Cossack's saber. Ice forms like poured concrete around hatches and valves, holds the periscopes in a frigid grip, covers the optics, and turns the deck into a narrow rink. But to suppose that this elemental conspiracy could check the submarine campaign underestimated the weapon and its elite crews. In aching cold crews slipped the moorings. Their exploits very nearly made good certain of the German admirals' boasts.

American reluctance to plunge into the European struggle continued until Congress declared war on April 6. The U.S. Army ranked fifteenth in the world, next to Persia. But the nation possessed all the ingredients needed to turn the tide of battle, given enough time. Initially, the Allies' financial problems were eased and much of their mental anguish. They believed that if enough supplies could be transported, if the sea lanes could be kept open against the increasing skill of U-boat skippers, victory might still be won without too many American troops. But the German effort was supreme, and it soon became clear that the Americans were their only hope for victory.

The American people entered the war with the same strange, carefree spirit that had pervaded Europe in 1914 but had long since been extinguished by endless casualty lists, hunger and despair. The United States turned its boundless energy and incomparable technology to the task of winning the war. After a period of adjustment, production and government purchases in the billions of dollars were directed by the War Industries Board. Other agencies established included the Food Administration, the Railroad War Board, the Fuel Administration, the Shipping Board and the War Labor Policies Board. In their enthusiasm state and local governments and citizens groups set up wartime organizations too numerous to mention. Shipments of food to Europe jumped from 7,000,000 tons in prewar years to 12,000,000 in1917–18 and to over 18,000,000 in 1918–19.

Mobilization of manpower and the training of soldiers, sailors and Marines moved at a desperate pace. During the nineteen months of war that followed, forty-three divisions of approximately 28,000 officers and men each were sent to Europe.

The Navy made its weight felt almost from the outset, when German U-boats were sinking ships faster than they could be built and it appeared that by October the U-boat might strangle Britain. The United States brought in fresh destroyers and, more important, an effective scheme to defend the convoys that sailed east of Cape Farewell after Admiral Sims had overcome the British Admiralty's opposition. The imaginative Americans developed other effective antisubmarine measures, including the great mine fields across the North Sea. The "bridge of ships" became a reality, with 200,000 men and 834 vessels assigned to convoy duty before the Armistice.

As Americans had learned in their earlier wars, an army could not be whipped into shape in a few weeks. The volunteers and draftees required intensive indoctrination and training. But the material was good. There were the tall, raw-boned men from the West, the big Midwesterners, the crack shots from squirrel, coon and deer country, the farm boys and the boys from the slums, the college boys and those who were too poor to finish grade school, con men and the boys from the Bible belt and the aristocracy. They were the men who were to fill the ranks of the Armed Forces and, later, The American Legion.

General John J. "Black Jack" Pershing, up from the Mexican border, was chosen to lead this future Expeditionary Force. With a handful of men he arrived in France and prepared for an American force of a million men. The first divisions to arrive were the 1st, 2nd (Yankee), and 42nd (Rainbow). Gradually port facilities, railroads, training camps and supply dumps were established. Troops, landed at Saint-Nazaire, were jostled into the famous 40-*hommes et 8-chevaux* (40 men and 8 horses) boxcars and trundled to training areas. Though few poilus or Tommies saw them, the words of those who did spread along the trench lines—of the "big divisions" and their laughing, joking, confident Yanks. It is said that this was the last of America's singing armies. Their sons were to be of the same breed—shrewd, resourceful and aggressive—but they did their soldiering with a wry, sometimes bitter, humor.

The aim of their strict and Spartan commander was to make an American army out of the divisions that were soon to swarm into French harbors. Allied generals were anxious to commit the fresh American units to the battle piecemeal, scattering them with abandon from Épinal to Ypres, but Pershing straightened his back, set his jaw and stood firm. The Allies exerted pressure by reducing the number of ships available to transport the AEF and its quantities of supplies. As the military situation worsened, Pershing put certain units at the disposal of Marshal Ferdinand Foch, and in October the 1st Division went into action in Lorraine.

There have been historians who have minimized the enormous impact of U.S. intervention and the contribution of American divisions. Perhaps they have relied on the memoirs of certain Allied generals, staff officers and statesmen who deliberately distorted the facts or were simply too far removed from their troops. That some had lost touch with reality was clear. In late summer, 1918, the French tried a cavalry attack at Soissons which was cut to ribbons—four years after British cavalry was lacerated as they charged with lances lowered against machine guns and artillery near Mons. Ensconced behind the lines, some never had so much as damp socks throughout the war and were blind to soldiers' problems.

By comparison, one topic of conversation in the trenches concerned the viscosity of the mud in various sectors. In the everlasting mud transport bogged down, mules disappeared and some men drowned. Add to this the rats, lice, trench foot, trench mouth, and other diseases, all of which the doughboy was to know, and it is little wonder that the Allied soldier had a different perspective. Without the arrival of Americans he could not have persevered much longer. And he knew it. He took little comfort from the pronouncements of his commanders who spoke for home consumption. French generals still spoke of their soldiers' *élan* as fate was about to foreclose on the Allies.

The French High Command ordered another offensive, and many poilus who followed their leaders' cry, *"En avant!"* baaed like sheep as they trudged through villages toward the carnage. Then mutiny swept and disabled the French divisions. This put it up to the British. The Third Battle of Ypres, in which a few yards' advance might require the death of ten thousand men, raged for over three months. The line changed four and a half miles. Now the British slumped. The French offensive, Caporetto, Passchendaele and other ordeals brought realization that salvation depended upon the big U.S. divisions arriving under Pershing.

"Our only hope lies in American reserves," said Britain's Chief of Staff. *"J'attends les Américains et les tanks,"* said Pétain.

In Russia the centrifugal forces of unrest and latent uprising, long held in check by the Tsarist regimes and their ruthless secret police, became ungovernable in 1917. Revolution deposed Nicholas II, and the Provisional Government continued the war. But the Germans conspired with the bolsheviks, and chaos ensued. Like a motor without a governor, the Revolution accelerated, fragmenting in all directions, until a new tyranny was clamped upon the people.

This freed Germany's strength in the East. Ponderously she swung these armies to smash into the Western Front. Hindenburg and Ludendorff visualized victory. German morale had improved, and Ludendorff formulated plans for a decisive offensive. His decision revealed an appreciation of the growing potential of the United States:

> Our general situation requires that we should strike at the earliest moment, if possible at the end of February or beginning of March, before the Americans can throw strong forces into the scale. We must beat the British.

The British had demonstrated the effectiveness of the proper use of tanks in the battle of Cambrai in November. In a small sector, without significant artillery preparation, British tanks broke through the German defenses and ranged at will until lack of reserves stopped their momentum. Though limited, the operation proved that stalemate was not an insurmountable problem. The tank was employed

later, and a British officer, J. F. C. Fuller, formulated brilliant plans
for its use in 1919. His 1918 study entitled "The Attack by Paralyza-
tion" was accepted by Marshal Foch for a projected spring campaign
and renamed "Plan 1919." The Cambrai lesson was not lost upon
certain young German officers—among them, Guderian and Rommel
—and, as we shall see in later chapters, upon certain future Legionnaires.

The great German offensive in March 1918 smashed into the
British and French on the Somme with a field-gray army five times
the Verdun assault force moving through a heavy fog. The British
reeled back and were able to hold only when starving German troops
turned to pillage. Ludendorff's second major blow fell in Flanders.
Emerging from the fog again, the German troops swept Haig's divisions to within a few miles of the marshaling yards of Hazebrouck.
Under the German flail the Allied front appeared to be a shambles.

American intelligence now overshadowed the stubborn guesses of
the British and French High Commands. It was convinced that the
Germans' heaviest assault would come on the Chemin des Dames
north of the Aisne. The French could not agree. There was nothing
to indicate the scale of the impending drive. But it was through this
quiet sector that Ludendorff would take dead aim on Paris. All traces
of activity were disguised from observation posts and aerial pho-
tography. Cleverly, the Germans moved four thousand guns and fifteen crack divisions into position. No sound betrayed their presence.
In late May they burst through, overran the French and British, took
Soissons, and reached the Marne. On war-room maps their spearhead
rested on a spot called Château-Thierry.

Staggered, the Allies looked to the Americans, for again the enemy
stood on the Marne and the flickering of the artillery could be seen
in the sky from Paris. Foch and Pershing arrived at a compromise
whereby American troops by divisions would fight in the line as long
as the crisis existed. The 3rd Division went forward to stem the assault, and the 2nd was pitchforked into the battle near Château-
Thierry. The French had felt that the Americans would not be ready
until 1919, that to send them to the Marne would be like sending a
boy to do a man's work. But they were available. A French officer
who expressed doubts about the 2nd's ability received the reply from
the division's Chief of Staff: "General, these are American Regulars.

In 150 years they have never been beaten." He failed to mention that 60 per cent of the Marines were fresh from college.

The 1st Division had distinguished itself a few days before. It had captured the strategic Cantigny objective and held it fiercely against repeated counterattacks. Now Marines and Regulars faced a field of summer wheat strewn with poppies. Behind it stood Belleau Wood. The 2nd was told to form a line and hold, and for five days the Marines stood off the thousands of German troops who came across the rough field. Berlin was informed the attack had met a "shock unit," and Clemenceau, with tears in his eyes, announced that the Americans had saved Paris. Now the Marines fixed bayonets and stormed Belleau Wood. The field was again a killing ground. Before they could gain a position in the edge of the trees they suffered greater casualties than the Marine Corps had taken since it was established in the American Revolution. The Marines and Regular infantry entered the dark, heavily defended wood into one of the horror stories of the war. The regiments were reduced by machine-gun and rifle fire, artillery and mustard gas in the gullies and on the tortured hogbacks. But they drove the Germans from the cover of the trees after three weeks.

The psychological consequences of this performance and that of doughboys in almost simultaneous operations were enormous. In war there is occasional talk of miracles. The Marne has been cited as the scene of two miracles in World War I—in 1914, when the Paris taxis shuttled troops, and in 1918, when American machine-gunners of the 3rd Division covered the retreat of the French Colonials and the 2nd threw up a thin line near a wheat field splashed with poppies and stopped the onrushing gray columns. The astonishing production and strength of the United States was called a miracle. But the real miracle was not so much that Americans finally trod French soil but that there were still French and British soldiers there to march at their side, that a war beyond the imagination of men before 1914 could have been endured for so long.

At Cantigny American fighting qualities dispelled only part of the German, French and British views of the unseasoned U.S. divisions. A German corps commander, however, did inform his superior, "I am under the impression that the troops should be given particularly firm commanders of strong character in order to overcome quickly the influence of the recent operation." During the Château-Thierry and Vaux operation, with the 3rd Division holding the river line to the east, a German commander observed that "should the Americans even temporarily gain the upper hand, it would have the most unfavorable aspects for us as regards the morale of the Allies and the duration of the war." But the situation was not regained as six German divisions were mauled attempting to regain that upper hand.

On the morning after Bastille Day German General von Boehn attacked toward Reims and ran into the "Rock of the Marne," the U.S. 3rd Division. Three days later, on July 18, Foch counterattacked in the Marne Sector with the U.S. 1st, 2nd, and 26th Divisions fighting beside Frenchmen. After Pershing had added the 3rd, 4th, 28th, 32nd, and 42nd, Foch wrenched straight the line from Soissons to Reims. With the fresh, tough Americans in the line and a promise of hundreds of thousands more to come, the realization that the German superiority on the Western Front had been erased gave heart to the Allies. The Aisne-Marne counterattack continued through August and September.

Pershing's dream of an American Army now materialized. The Germans had utterly underrated the capability of the British and U.S. Navies to counter the U-boat and convoy more and more men and matériel to the countries they had hoped to starve out and to the front they had hoped to destroy. With American troops arriving at the rate of more than a quarter of a million a month, Pershing launched his first offensive on August 10. Half a million men of the First Army smashed into the Saint-Mihiel salient south of Verdun. Although the Germans had prepared a withdrawal, the thirty-six-hour action to take the area was a hard experience for the Americans. One soldier described it:

> Bullets, millions of them, flying like rain drops. Rockets and flares in all directions. Shrapnel bursting the air and sending down its deadly iron. . . . Every minute looking for the next to be gone to the great beyond. A mad dash for 50 feet and then look for cover. A stop for a minute and then the barrage would lift to a farther point and then another mad rush. Always leav-

ing some of your comrades cold in the face of death. . . . The
field of dead a terrible sight. Both Americans and German. A
day never to be forgotten.

These events of September 12–16 gave another lift to the French
spirit, for the doughboys rubbed the old Saint-Mihiel salient from
the war maps. The verve, aggressiveness and growing skill of the
doughboy was recognized by friend and foe. For the Germans, hope,
that precious essential without which the will to win perishes, began
to drain away.

Pershing's concept of driving forward in a spearhead against the
strategic German complex of Metz was overshadowed by Foch's designs for a "grand offensive" along two hundred miles of front. The
confusion of the Germans was not exploited. Although the French-
man's will prevailed, the American displayed superior judgment. Strategic views advanced by Pershing and tactical theories meticulously
detailed by Fuller remained unused only to be fundamental in the
strategy and tactics of the German Army exactly twenty years later.

Instead the First Army swung around Verdun to the northwest
and ten days later assaulted on a 24-mile front facing the Meuse River
and the Argonne Forest. The Meuse-Argonne campaign was to be
one of the most frightening, sanguinary and decisive in our military
annals. It was conceded to be "the most difficult sector of the whole
front." There the doughboy survived or perished in a nightmare—a
"vast network of uncut barbwire, the deep ravines, dense woods, myr-
iads of shell craters, and a heavy fog." This was to prove the un-
excelled caliber of American troops. Those familiar with the epic
Meuse-Argonne campaign realize its dimensions. A few lines cannot
describe it. There was the fortresslike peak, Montfaucon; the deadly
heights of the Meuse; the weird, vast, booby-trapped Forêt d'Argonne, its defenses textbook tough. Barbed wire wreathed the expanse, and open spaces were laced with Maxim and Spandau patterns. The "first-class fighting qualities" of the Americans, their "won-
derful tenacity and endurance," became evident to Allies and Germans
alike. Divisions that did battle were New York's 77th, the 35th,
the 28th Pennsylvanians, the 82nd All-American, the 42nd Rainbow,
the 26th Yankee, the 91st, the 79th, the 37th, Illinois' 33rd, the 80th,
the 4th, the 32nd, the 3rd, the 29th, the Big Red One, the 2nd, the
5th, the 78th, the 89th, the 90th, and the 92nd.

Neither Foch nor the Germans expected the skill and aggressiveness, the prodigious feats of arms and tenacity, the progress and decisiveness Americans exercised in the seven weeks that followed. The Hindenburg Line stretched like a heavy chain anchored at Metz and tied to Lille. It was doubled and tripled most of the distance with the toughest, drop-forged links—across the approaches to the Sedan-Mézierès rail complex—across the 24-mile front the U.S. assault divisions faced in late September. Foch had in mind a mighty frontal assault, with the Americans holding most of their 94-mile front southeast of Verdun and maintaining pressure on the 24 miles just mentioned. Like a mailed arm the French and British would crash forward as the fist in Belgium struck into the Germans' right flank. The American Army was the shoulder from which the effort would hinge.

The Germans felt secure on the Meuse-Argonne with defenses to a depth of fourteen miles. Double garrisons manned the lines protecting the Sedan-Mézierès railroad upon which their provisions, reinforcements, communications, and survival relied. In four and a half years the concept of driving a salient to cut this vital artery had been neglected. The Germans had had time to turn its forbidding natural approaches east or west of the Argonne into a veritable legend of defense. In fact, behind the first barbed-wire entanglements and machine guns and the fortified artillery positions from the Aisne to the Meuse heights were the three barriers named after legendary Wagnerian figures. There was the Giselher Stellung, which included Montfaucon; the Kriemhilde Stellung, which was the strongest natural defense line in France, consisting of the whalebacks of the Romagne Heights; and the commanding, heavily defended Freya Stellung.

But Pershing thought in terms of breakthrough. Denied his objective of Metz, he chose to drive through the Meuse-Argonne by thrusts with exploitation of evolving flanks. His forces at the jump-off tapes seemed to merit their collective title, the "thin green line," for they were not as yet combat-seasoned. Experienced U.S. divisions were moving in behind them. Still, the Allies expected only a limited advance by the Yanks. In the monumental campaign Pershing staged, the Germans, after their initial surprise, punished the doughboys unmercifully and poured in divisions from reserve and from other sectors. But, despite frightful losses in some outfits and much confusion, doughboys gradually stabbed forward, breaking the German strength, confidence and resolve. A hundred gallant battles enabled Pershing to take dead aim on Sedan. By October 8, the Argonne Forest was cleared. Some of Pershing's army of 1,200,000 men, supported by artillery, American-manned French tanks and Mitchell's flyers in several hundred planes, had almost dislodged the Germans from the Hindenburg Line and driven them back toward the Meuse.

The whole German front was cracking. The Allies, particularly the British, had found new heart and an enormous aggressiveness. Several U.S. divisions contributed to the great offensive of 1918 in other parts of the front. There were the 27th and 30th with the British in the operations around St. Quentin, the 36th, 2nd and 93rd in Champagne to the west of the Argonne, the 37th and 91st bridging the Scheldt in the Ypres-Lys offensive, and the 88th driving toward the discarded target, Metz.

By the time Hindenburg urged armistice, the Allies were sweeping ahead in other theaters. After November 1, the Americans began their "race for Sedan." One of every ten who marched into the Meuse-Argonne drive became a casualty.

Throughout the thirteen major operations in which doughboys were engaged, American pilots flew with distinction. Seventy-one became Aces, and those who survived had been largely responsible for the development of American commercial and military aviation and the interest of America's youth in flight. Mitchell and scores of his pilots later joined The American Legion. Many contributed their knowledge and convictions to the Legion's immediate and impressive resolutions and its early efforts toward progressive legislation in aeronautics.

With Germany brought to the brink of starvation by the Royal and U.S. Navies, her armies suffering a rising tattoo of reverses, Pershing believed the Allies should demand surrender rather than armistice. But a few hours after the Americans reached Sedan, German envoys met Foch, and his armistice terms were accepted.

The word was passed from Army to Corps down the line to platoons and batteries and listening posts that fighting would cease at eleven o'clock. The noise of firing increased as exuberant soldiers heaved shells into the breeches of field pieces and fed belts into overheated Chauchat guns "to get in the last shots," or, more pragmatically, to spare themselves the task of sweating over heavy canisters and ammunition boxes as they dragged them back to dry dumps where they would deteriorate more slowly.

The din rose until 11 o'clock, when it ended with a crash that startled the soldiers. A great silence overwhelmed the front from Ghent to Belfort.

Then, depending upon the sector, the silence was frayed by a few ragged cheers or rent by wild shouting and the clatter of helmets. Bareheaded and unarmed, the enemies climbed over the top for the last time and stood in the pale sunlight blinking at each other.

Few men on the line or in the reserve, few civilians in the hysterical mobs at Times Square or celebrating in the capitals of Europe realized that for them the peace and tranquillity they and their fathers had known were gone. The Great War was a milestone on a different road in a violent century in which sensible men can only hope for qualified peace.

The insanity of the war was followed by the insanity at Versailles. The territorial arrangements for Europe and the economic conditions and political system imposed upon Germany were insane. Germany pulled back behind her frontiers bitter and vengeful, a candidate for future struggle, saddled with unwanted institutions and heavy reparations. This led to a national self-pity despite Germany's swift recovery and enormous U.S. loans that more than made up for the exactions of the Allies. Versailles and its aftermath soon gave expedient men in Germany ample excuses to pursue questionable policies with the support of the people. These men were found among the traditional governing groups, the military and industrial leaders as well as Hitler's underworld characters and brilliant misfits. One lesson of the war was lost upon them—the eventual British and American reaction to continued brutal behavior and deadly threats. Their failure to realize the strength and tenacity of constitutional democracy was as patent in 1939 and 1941 as it had been in 1914 and 1917. These fatal flaws in Germany autocracy and dictatorship were matched only by the terrible folly of the democracies' headlong drive for disarmament and failure to exercise their military might toward a satisfactory political settlement during World War II.

World War I destroyed some empires and accelerated the crack-up of others. The Austro-Hungarian empire was fragmented, and southeastern Europe became Balkanized.

World War I also ushered in a virulent and malignant international menace—communism. It is noteworthy that Legionnaires, many of whom served in Russia during its civil war and who saw something of the effects of communist propaganda in Germany and France immediately after the war, established their organization when communism became a real issue and were among the first to underline and attack the communist danger.

When he heard of the Peace Treaty, Foch observed, "This is not peace. It is an armistice for twenty years." France, despite her relief that the slaughter had ended, remained an unstable, haunted land, increasingly obsessed by fear of a revival of German strength and truculence. She nursed grievous psychological wounds and mourned millions of her best young men. Old theories, impaled on the barbed wire of the Western Front, were recovered and kept alive for another 20 years. Britain too suffered the consequences of losing large numbers of her future leaders.

The contribution of the United States to the Allied victory was discounted in some quarters even as fields unplowed in three years were readied for the spring planting in 1919. It was not long before certain politicians and writers abroad ascribed the defeat of Germany to causes suitable to the detractors' purposes and prejudices. But there are always those who resent others who have rendered vital assistance. After another great war another generation of veterans were to hear much the same talk. The best and final retort was made at an Oxford debate after a speaker had abused the United States and the presence of the GI's. It came like a rifle shot: "You were glad enough to see them in 1942!" In 1919 and 1920 some French and British leaders found it convenient to forget that less than two years before they had appealed for more and more American divisions; that they had informed Rear Admiral William S. Sims just before the first flotilla of American destroyers swept into Queenstown Harbour that England's fortunes were precarious, that six weeks' supply of food was on hand and that if U-boats continued their run of torpedo scores the British war effort could not continue beyond November 1917; and that after the big American divisions arrived

some of the old determination again flared among once mutinous
French and dispirited British units.

Men with a larger and more generous view expressed gracious
sentiment. Lord Northcliffe in writing to The American Legion in
June 1919 expressed a responsible British view:

> During the past two years I have had many opportunities of
> meeting all ranks of the American forces, and none realizes
> more fully than I do the great part they played in achieving our
> common victory. Those who are endeavoring to create misun-
> derstanding between the American and British commonwealth
> assert that the gigantic American effort is not fully appreciated
> by us. I am glad to have this opportunity of stating that the
> British people realize to the full the great part America has
> played, both in her workshops, on the sea, in the air and on the
> battlefield.

In the United States, government participation, intervention or
control in most phases of American life had been so great that the
suspension of many Federal activities was a severe test of an economy falling back on its own devices and of individuals relying suddenly upon their native intelligence and ingenuity. Americans did not
emerge from the war experience without blemish. War is a foul
stream. Few reach the far bank without foul stains. Enormous propaganda, inspired by the Federal government, foreign sources and
native groups had its impact upon the public. There had been governmental control or intervention in all media, the virtual suspension
of a free press, the liberal exercise of shameless deceit, and the dissemination of lies—all in the interest of "winning the war." These
activities by government or by citizens groups cannot be condoned.

Aside from these unfortunate consequences, the United States
emerged from the war optimistic and with her strength intact. The
war had conditioned the men who were to band together in The
American Legion and made them aware of broader interests that
would have been somewhat alien and strange to their forefathers.
The war experience was like a blow that strikes a compound in such
a way that the molecular structure is altered. The change is fundamental and it is impossible to rearrange it as it was before. In 1919
there was no going back.

It is important to consider something of this background—World War I, the historical legacy and the American society—from which The American Legion sprang. The early Legion was the product of a profound experience of wide dimension and of the American heritage. The Legion, as no other national organization, reflects the union, indivisible. The American Legion was the product of momentous events which reinforced the union with a sense of national purpose that had been frequently neglected for a century, since the War of 1812. The national purpose in the four decades after the Revolution was a fabric tough as homespun, but it wore thin, and the Civil War left it in shreds and tatters. The nation emerged from World War I with its national ideals and character intact—ideals and character somewhat lost sight of in the divisive period of the Civil War and its aftermath. The Legion embodied these ideals and character. Men from Georgia and Alabama had shared the common lot of fighting men side by side with New Yorkers and Nebraskans—they shook under the same barrage, ate the same food, laughed at the same jokes, took the same objectives, slept in the same hole, suffered the same fear and afflictions. Whereas the Grand Army of the Republic and the United Confederate Veterans were intensely sectional and gained enormous political power in their areas, within The American Legion North and South were united under specific principles. Bonds of union ran through every state, to our territories and to American communities abroad.

The Formative Time

3

A Gathering in Paris

HAD William Tecumseh Sherman observed World War I, his reactions might well have been those of shock and despair. For
the great Union general was the first fully to grasp the totality of
modern war and to pursue strategies for its successful prosecution.
Only order, lasting peace, prosperity, and freedom could justify its
enormous cost in lives and substance.

As we have seen in the preceding chapter, Sherman's doctrines
were not lost on Pershing and the few Allied officers and statesmen
with the wit to recognize the nature of total war, the folly in attempting to "outlast or destroy" vast conscript armies, the efficacy of mo-
bility and unorthodox operations, and the necessity to impress upon
peoples behind the armies the futility of war. A severe peace cannot
fulfill the last requirements. But those who saw clearly were submerged by the sea of inertia that ran through the minds of the highest commanders who led the combatants for more than three years
of brutal stalemate and attrition following the initial German offensive of the summer of 1914. Supreme commanders turned their
backs on Sherman's authentic genius and reverted to a desperate
grappling that resembled the heartbreaking war in Virginia of half a
century before.

But if the war into which the doughboys marched was a throwback
and a denial of Sherman's doctrines, the armistice bore out another
of Sherman's incisive observations. He might have called upon his
familiarity with Shakespeare and described the months following
November 11, 1918, as a winter of discontent. Following the Civil

41

War he remarked to his staff, "War's over. Occupation's gone," and some years later noted that to an army "peace and politics are always more damaging than war."

Elation, relief and celebration are short-lived things. These spontaneous reactions evaporated quickly after redeployment. And in their place moved a "great restlessness." To many the AEF had served its purpose. Europe's future could now be settled at a big table and on wall maps at Versailles.

Within weeks after the trenches had emptied, a corrosive compound found exposed surfaces in the AEF. Made up in parts of idleness, release from the compelling urgency of combat, impatience to return to families and postponed opportunities, and, now that no further battles lay ahead, an active distaste for military regulations and customs and what seemed the petty tyranny of the professional soldiers—this invidious mixture impaired the superb divisions under Pershing's command.

A foreign commander once observed that the genius of the American fighting man is grounded in his relentless questioning and initiative. By background and temperament individualism is there in unusual measure and no military indoctrination can seriously impair this quality once the enemy puts aside his weapons and picks up a pen to sign a cease-fire. Hence individualism, both the curse and making of American armies, was gaining the upper hand over order and discipline after November 11.

Two million Americans, from the channel ports to obscure German towns, faced the boredom, routine and wearing annoyances of billet life. In the tumultuous months since April, 1917, little thought had been given the day when victory would come. War called for instilling in fighting men anticipation of combat, the physical and mental tone required of them under fire, the suppression of a large part of their individuality. Occupation duty and peacetime status call for other approaches.

But it is an American habit to bear down on the moment, seize a swift "solution," follow a direct, if unwise, course to desired ends with alarming nonchalance toward long-range eventualities. This was true of President Wilson and of the military from its generals down to noncoms.

Consequently, when the lanyards had been pulled for the last time, the trench mud scraped from boots and most of the cooties exterminated at last, a good many indications sprang up revealing the absence of plans for occupying the time of hundreds of thousands of America's fittest young men.

Perhaps the great unrest could have been foreseen and avoided. But the General Headquarters' staff, comfortably settled at Chaumont, failed to anticipate the consequences of inactivity. No neatly bound operational plan was available. This led to grave morale problems, to dissatisfaction, disappointment, anger, and in some cases to flagrant disregard for military regulations.

Belatedly, GHQ recognized the deteriorating situation and met its responsibility. It is noteworthy that instead of turning the thumb screws available to most military organizations, Pershing and his staff sought the advice of Reserve and National Guard officers. A meeting of 20 officers from civilian life was ordered to consider ways in which the sagging morale of the AEF might be straightened. They met in Paris with Regular Army officers for two days, February 15 and 16.

It is likely that Theodore Roosevelt, Jr., a lieutenant colonel in the 1st Division and eldest son of the illustrious T.R., and Lt. Col. George A. White, a National Guard officer attached to GHQ, influenced the selection of these men. Over a month before, White had talked with Roosevelt about conditions in the AEF, and in the course of the conversation Roosevelt had brought up the idea of a veterans' association which should originate in the AEF, then organize in the United States, taking in all who served in the Army, Navy and Marine Corps. Roosevelt explained that such an organization, drawing its strength from nearly five million discharged fighting men, could preserve the unity of purpose and action which had been theirs during the war and could further in peace the ideals and objectives for which they had served. White observed later,

> There can be no question as to the fatherhood of the idea or as to the initiator of the chain of circumstances which led to the formation of The American Legion. The honor is Theodore Roosevelt's.

But the idea that a veterans' association would evolve following the war was one which unquestionably crossed the minds of many on both sides of the Atlantic. Others besides Roosevelt gave thought, time and energy to the concept. Senior Chaplain of the AEF Bishop Charles H. Brent had launched Comrades in Service some time earlier as an "experiment." It enjoyed a limited success. However, the fact that it was Roosevelt's enthusiasm, vision and practical ability to get underway an inclusive veterans' organization of great size and influence, makes another early record relevant here.

In 1919 George S. Wheat wrote of his conversations with Theodore Roosevelt, Jr., regarding the genesis of The American Legion. Roosevelt had fought with distinction from the Big Red One's sharp clash at Cantigny to the punishing ordeal in the Soissons sector, where he was wounded in the knee by machine-gun fire. His evacuation and convalescence took him to Base Hospital No. 2 in Paris in the summer of 1918.

One morning as Roosevelt hobbled along a walk he came upon a sergeant resting against a tree. The sergeant, William Patterson, gave Roosevelt a quick salute.

"Expect to get back soon, Sergeant?" Roosevelt said.

"Yes, sir. Anxious to go back and get the whole job over, sir."

"So am I. But what will we all do when the Germans really are licked?"

"Go home and start a veterans' association for the good of the country, sir," the sergeant answered.

Roosevelt professed that Patterson's was the first mention made to him of a veterans' organization, although the thought of such an organization had occurred to him in thinking of peace and postwar developments. Now he found that the prospect of a veterans' association was generally discussed among the men at the hospital. Doubtless the personable young Roosevelt had many conversations with fellow patients who soon would be veterans. It was there that he turned his energetic mind to details of such an undertaking and to solutions to problems entailed in its formation and survival.

The opportunity to put forth his views to a group of receptive and able officers representing ten infantry divisions, the SOS, GHQ and other AEF units, came during the two-day meeting in Paris. Among those ordered to the meeting were Lt. Col. Franklin D'Olier and Lt. Col. Eric Fisher Wood. Both left their divisions with a desire to

form a veterans' organization of some comprehensive nature, and
soon discovered that others at the gathering shared their hope.

The immediate mission from General Pershing—"to estimate the
situation and to make suggestions for the improvement of the welfare
of the enlisted personnel of the Expeditionary Forces"—was con-
scientiously and expeditiously carried out. The result was a series of
recommendations which included curtailment of restrictive regulations and emphasis upon comprehensive programs of recreation,
athletics, leave for travel, study, and entertainment. Further they
urged the sensible procedure that men be sent home in the order
in which they had arrived in France. This judicious procedure was
to be publicized throughout the AEF.

At the conclusion of this task Theodore Roosevelt, Jr., invited the
group to dinner at the Allied Officers Club in Rue Faubourg Saint-
Honoré, saying that he had an important unofficial matter to discuss.
All accepted the invitation. For most it was their last evening in
Paris before returning to their units.

That evening around the table were:

Francis R. Appleton, Jr., Lt. Col., Second Army, New York; G.
Edward Buxton, Lt. Col., 82nd Division, Rhode Island; Bennett C.
Clark, Lt. Col., 88th Division, Missouri; Ralph D. Cole, Lt. Col.,
37th Division, Ohio; David J. Davis, Lt. Col., GHQ, Pennsylvania;
Franklin D'Olier, Lt. Col., General Staff, Pennsylvania; William J.
Donovan, Col., 42nd Division, New York; David M. Goodrich, Lt.
Col., GHQ, New York; T. E. Gowenlock, Maj., First Army Corps,
Illinois; Thorndike Howe, Col., APO Department, Massachusetts;
John Price Jackson, Lt. Col., Peace Commission, Pennsylvania; W.
deLancey Kountze, Maj., GHQ, New York; R. W. Llewellen, Lt.
Col., 28th Division, Pennsylvania; Ogden L. Mills, Capt., SOS, New
York; Benjamin Moore, Lt. Col., 82nd Division, New York; R. C.
Stebbins, Lt. Col., Third Army Corps; R. C. Stewart, Maj., First
Division, Maryland; George A. White, Lt. Col., GHQ, Oregon; Eric
Fisher Wood, Lt. Col., 88th Division, Pennsylvania; and the host,
Theodore Roosevelt, Jr., Lt. Col., First Army, New York.

Roosevelt opened the after-dinner discussion with a forceful and enthusiastic proposal that a great inclusive veterans' society be launched.
For the most part, the twenty officers present were judicious men;
and their decisions that night and subsequently were the result of

responsible thought, searching debate, apprehension, and hope. Intractability, selfishness, opportunism, and horseplay were submerged by a serious comprehension of the importance of first moves and a willingness to compromise and to leave matters of specific policy to future gatherings. This general attitude prevailed over suggestions that a future association take a specific form or adhere to certain policy lines.

Of course, to say that those present were without ideas about the objectives a great veterans' society should advance would be false. These were men of strong convictions and opinion. It was only after much give and take, advocacy and persuasion that general accord was reached.

A number of purposes were advanced during the long evening and in further discussions of committee members. Some felt that a future organization should promote national preparedness through universal military training. The United States had, through most of its history, clung to the illusion that any emphasis upon a reliable, up-to-date military establishment would somehow soil the image of a peace-loving people, promote militarism and dispose the country toward war. On the pretext of avoiding hostilities and involvement in foreign conflicts, the United States shrank from equipping herself with warlike paraphernalia until it appeared, however inaccurately, to the German generals and admirals as a nation clad in a khaki loincloth carrying a broomstick. The doughboy divisions had seen little evidence that their country was an arsenal. Most of their artillery, tanks, planes, and machine guns were of British and French make.

Then there was the matter of the military establishment itself. As National Guard and Reserve officers, several present felt far from satisfied with the domination the Regular Army had exercised since President Wilson reluctantly delivered his war message. Inherent in preparedness, they said, was the overhaul of the army organization to accommodate leadership from the Guard and Reserve for future armies should the United States again become a participant in a general war.

Potential political power was naturally brought up. Had not Union soldiers swung great political weight in the North through the Grand Army of the Republic for decades following the Civil War? Had not fighting men done the same in the South through the United Confederate Veterans?

Concern about extreme radicialism was expressed. Among the soldiers and sailors of other nations there was ample evidence of their receptivity to the virus of revolutionary ideas. It had swept the Russian ranks with an intensity approaching that of the great influenza epidemic. Winston Churchill later likened the German delivery of Lenin in a sealed railroad car to the introduction of a plague bacillus into Russia. Grinding autocracy, the terrible shocks of war, the failure of the Provisional Government, and a long history of revolt, terror and bloody suppression led to a chaotic, revolutionary situation. While the Treaty of Brest Litovsk enabled Hindenburg and Ludendorff to shift a million men from the East to the Western Front it was not long before their own armies caught the strong infection they had so carefully introduced into Russia. Few armies were immune. On many sides—among fleet units of the Central Powers and in their deep trench positions, across the barbed wire among the French and among the Italians in the Isonzo sector, and across Eastern Europe the doctrines of revolution had spread. They were not whispered. They were shouted.

Now, since November, the specter of extreme radicalism materialized in other places. Even discounting the feeling that the bolsheviks' separate peace had amounted to a betrayal that freed crack German units rather than a reflection of the extremity to which the Russian soldier had been taken by archaic leadership and by sacrificial offensives urged by their allies; even minimizing the fact that thousands of American doughboys were billeted on Russian soil, there was cause for the concern of those at the Roosevelt dinner. Communism was abroad elsewhere. It stalked the streets of Berlin. It held Hungary in a momentary grip. It was seated in French cellars. It paraded over the debris of war in a hundred village squares. Urged by the Russian soviets its influence was evident, proven or suspect in extremist movements, strikes, propaganda, and soldiers' and sailors' councils which had sprung up in various countries among discharged men.

War profiteering and the subject of aliens in the United States who avoided military service on the grounds that they were not citizens were other sore subjects of discussion.

The more remarkable then that these twenty men put aside intense convictions concerning specific policies and vetoed all proposals that would commit future gatherings. They limited their decisions to the implementation of launching a great veterans' association, taking in all who served. This policy line, which was to be followed until representatives of veterans of all branches of the armed services met nine months later at Minneapolis to function in a representative democratic manner, made all intervening decisions provisional. Unquestionably this course was the mortar of the foundation that made for the strength and stability of what was to follow.

The group adopted steps for two organizational meetings—one in Paris, the other in the United States. Those present were to constitute a Committee of Twenty, devoting what time they could to promoting interest throughout the AEF and accomplishing whatever detail work would be necessary in the preliminary stages.

Three men, George A. White, Eric Fisher Wood and Ralph D. Cole, accepted responsibility as a Committee of Three to organize the caucus to be held in Paris of representatives—both officers and men—from each combat division, major unit of the SOS, GHQ, and other branches of the AEF.

Since Roosevelt was in a position to return to the States at an early date, he was designated "agent of liaison" with men in the United States. Until embarkation he was to observe developments concerned with the forthcoming Paris Caucus.

No one knew what attitude the High Command might assume toward their undertaking a caucus in Paris, but all were to correspond with the Committee of Three, forwarding suggestions and recommendations, and to bend their efforts to infuse enthusiasm in AEF units for the Paris Caucus.

Late in the evening, as they stepped from the club into the cold February air, the men who had that night made the first organizational moves toward The American Legion felt a sense of accomplishment. They were pointing toward another goal that embodied some of the stuff from which a dream for which they had fought was made, a dream that was to become rather vague and half-remembered, as most dreams tend to become. It was a dream of a better world and a stronger America that had recently inspired the exultation, sweat and sacrifice of a nation.

Soon the sharp edge of idealism would be ground dull for many who lacked realism, common sense and perseverance. But the claim that an entire generation suffered the traumatic experience of disillusionment and became "lost" is grotesquely inaccurate. Of the youth of Britain and the Commonwealth who were poured into the mud of Flanders by the hundreds of thousands, and the manhood of France, thrown into a military meat grinder for three and a half years, T. E. Lawrence wrote with some truth, "All the great words were cancelled out for that generation." Americans had been spared their Allies' extremity. Of course, the doughboys and sailors had buried their dead and brought home their cripples. Their eyes had been opened and they saw war for what it is. Theirs had been a painful experience. But most were tough enough to survive the awakening. Few could afford the luxury of despair. There were new challenges and old challenges. And new dreams. For dreams do not end merely because they do not come true.

4

Caucus at Cirque de Paris

EVERY soldier, sailor and Marine at one time or another makes a bid for membership in what might be called The Informal Order of Operators, Promoters and Scroungers. Many "wash out." Those who succeed know a discipline involving highly developed skills and take pride in their ability to get things done in the face of outrageously devilish circumstances, to move about with relative freedom, or to come by scarce commodities. To them the military establishment is a source of challenge, a test of nerve, reflexes, ingenuity, and perseverance. Asked why they indulge in this consuming and frequently pointless exercise of overcoming the military environment, they might reply as G. L. Mallory did in referring to the reason for climbing Mount Everest, "Because it is there."

Part of the story of the Paris Caucus was the exercise of this faculty by both officers and enlisted men. In fact, much of the success of that meeting is attributable to this proficiency. GHQ and many senior officers were skeptical of, if not hostile to, any congregation of doughboys in Paris. They took a dim view of exposing their troops to the temptations of the French capital. Better to keep them out of harm's way in their billets.

Promotion of the Paris Caucus, only a month away, was immediately undertaken by the Committee of Three. Eric Fisher Wood and Ralph D. Cole had the task of spreading information and arousing enthusiasm by writing to all commands as well as to the European and American press. Duties with his division precluded Cole's participation in this assignment—an early indication that the plans of a

50

group of Reserve and national guardsmen did not have the full support or cooperation of senior officers.

The paperwork struggle fell to Eric Fisher Wood, whose patient energy and devotion to detail and correspondence was a notable achievement and contribution to early organization.

George A. White had a more exciting time of it. He was to interpret, expound and explain to all combat divisions, Army and Corps headquarters, sections of Services and Supply, and miscellaneous commands the importance of Wood's letters and telegrams. This was no mean challenge. With the initiative and audacity one seldom sees in Army colonels engaged in unofficial matters, he assumed his role as "ambassador extraordinary with a roving commission." First, he concluded that the absence of one light colonel from the many thronged at Chaumont would go unnoticed. With a handful of questionable and antiquated travel orders, an old Dodge filled with government gasoline, an imposing red, white and blue GHQ sign, and, we can assume, the wary eye that is the mark of the true promoter, he set out.

From the first it became increasingly clear to White as he swung through France, Luxembourg and occupied Germany that the organization's survival in the AEF depended upon his powers of persuasion and Wood's publicity. Questions were crystallizing about the proposed veterans' association. Was this a GHQ scheme, a plot to promote compulsory military service or other militaristic ideas? Or was it a political move to swing the 1920 election to the candidate of the General Staff clique? "Some said it was Pershing. Some, curiously enough, said it was Leonard Wood," Marquis James wrote in 1923, "quite a few said it was political medicine-making of which Roosevelt was to be the beneficiary." There was also the hard question of whether the new organization was by, for and of the officers. While White and Wood managed to dispel the former suspicions, the latter died hard.

Tirelessly White and Wood persuaded and cajoled. That White was effective is borne out by the fact that the bitter Yankee 26th Division, in no mood to endorse a GHQ plan, since their National Guard commander had been removed, was at first unreceptive to White's proposals, discarded ideas for its own civilian organization, and sent more delegates to Paris than any other division when convinced that GHQ had no hand in the movement.

The drive to get as many units as possible to Paris with "a full quota of enlisted men on equal terms with officers" drew to a close. Optimism glowed. Suddenly, GHQ denied officers and men the privilege of attending the Paris Caucus under normal orders. No appeal availed. GHQ was firm. Delegates could obtain only three-day class-C leaves with travel and subsistence at their own expense.

Now the prowess of doughboy officer, noncom and private alike was challenged. Schemes concocted reflect their determination to get to the three-day meeting in Paris. Of course the "officer's tale" had to be countered. This meant gaining attendance of enlisted men. Financial problems naturally arose. Although some officers and enlisted men sold belongings to defray expenses, some had to fall back upon chance and cunning. The turn of cards and the roll of dice figured in a number of the leaves. Some reached Paris as orderlies; others were sent on the pretext of performing a military duty—to inspect new "smokeless field kitchens," to requisition rat poison and the like. One was dispatched to deliver "classified" documents to a nebulous Paris unit. He made his way across the French provinces clutching a briefcase stuffed with wastepaper.

To beef up the depleted representation of enlisted men due to the GHQ strictures, numbers from the Paris area were urged to attend as delegates of outfits to which they had been formerly attached. One, Pvt. Harold Ross, working on the *Stars and Stripes,* recalled later that he "fished out of his desk a letter of appointment as a delegate of the 18th Engineers." He found it with an accumulation of prospectuses of other organizations and, he said, he strolled over to the caucus not entirely convinced it would amount to much. Ross later became editor of *The American Legion Weekly,* then moved on to a brilliant career as the incomparable editor of the *New Yorker.*

Most who gravitated to Paris for the caucus were not drawn by a magnificent illusion, believers journeying to Mecca. It is safe to say that most were skeptical, many anxious to escape the drudgery of billet life, some with every intention of taking advantage of an opportunity to have a glorious time in Paris.

The month between the Roosevelt dinner and the March caucus hardly afforded White and Wood time to get the widest publicity.

The great mass of doughboys knew little, if anything, about the embryonic association. Those who were fortunate enough to attend and were serious about the proceedings came to make independent judgments upon the venture. The caucus' success can be attributed to these men.

The sharp, clipped rhythm of hobnails echoed in the halls of the old French residence at No. 4 Avenue Gabriel the morning of March 15 as the first arriving delegates walked to the drawing room. Soon the room was crowded. On the delegates' shoulders were most of the divisional patches. Like the tunes of glory, they were, to the fighting man, familiar and evoked memory. They were associated with violent events just as patches in future wars had their distinction and the power to stir the recollection of brothers-in-arms. The feeling grew that this was a representative meeting so far as the geography of Army organization was concerned. Delegates took seats beneath markers for the 1st, 2nd, 3rd, 4th, 6th, 26th, 28th, 29th, 30th, 32nd, 33rd, 35th, 36th, 41st, 42nd, 77th, 78th, 79th, 80th, 81st, 82nd, 83rd, 88th, 89th, and 91st Divisions; First, Second and Third Armies; GHQ; Headquarters, SOS; Advance Section, SOS; Intermediate Section, SOS; Base Sections 1, 2, 3, 4, 5, 6, and 7, SOS; Paris Command; and Troops serving with the French. Expectation gradually replaced the general feeling of reserve as the hum of conversation filled this foreign salon. Perhaps some of those present realized vaguely that they were there to organize. If the earth has raised a race of men talented at organization it is the American. The confidence of some that they could forge a satisfactory and lasting organization, like a village smith pounding out a horseshoe, perhaps equaled their self-assurance that they could win a fight. But these confident souls were in a minority. Most of the several hundred congregated at No. 4 Avenue Gabriel were curious and most circumspect. They were also very cold, for the March air penetrated the building. Many wore their military overcoats.

Chairs scraped on the once-polished floor as Eric Fisher Wood called the meeting to order and gained the delegates' attention. After summarizing the reasons for the caucus and its broad objectives, Wood turned the meeting to the selection of officers and order of business. The election of temporary chairman went to Lt. Col. Bennett Champ Clark of Missouri, that of secretary to Wood and of vice chairman to Lt. Col. Thomas W. Miller of Delaware and the 79th Division. Clark's chairmanship naturally helped to dispel the myth that Roosevelt aimed to benefit politically or that the organization was sure to be partisan, for as a prominent young Democrat and son of Speaker of the House, Champ Clark's party loyalty was not that of Roosevelt Republicanism.

The group that was to expand to almost a thousand delegates in three days adopted the parliamentary rules of Congress and vote by delegation. Now an energetic First Army man, Lt. Col. Lemuel Bolles, rose and moved that all considerations of rank be waived during the business of the caucus. Obviously this was necessary to counter the "officer's tale," to assure survival and growth and to assert American principles at an early date. Unanimous approval was a most unusual action in a rank-conscious Europe among men accustomed to the density of a military atmosphere. It was almost inconceivable on a continent encumbered by rusty conceits and calcified classes. But the action was uniquely American and natural. Throughout most of Europe the old distinctions and separations held, and where collapse occurred they were swept away only to accommodate other alignments, other classes. These men, sitting in their woolen khaki uniforms, knew where they came from. Whether they had breathed the wheat chaff of the Plains states, played on the pavement of the big cities or felt the early morning chill of the seaboard, they had within them the entailed inheritance of Locke and Mill, Madison and Adams, Jefferson and Lincoln.

Run your eye through a list of 463 of the delegates or the committees' composition. They are enlightening not merely because they are studded with names of men who were later to become illustrious in all fields, but because there are names that are not in the history books or chiseled in the stonework of buildings. Many returned to the hill country, the pace of city rooms, the mills, the schools, and the quiet communities across America. Many made their imperishable contribution in small, indispensable ways and are known to their Legion comrades as doing as much for the organization they helped to establish in Paris as others who moved on to become prominent politicians, Cabinet members, professional and business leaders, or literary figures. The gathering was an early indication of the cross-section the Legion was to become.

They were a vocal lot. Throughout the caucus the sessions on the floor were noisy and somewhat confused. After the severe discipline and obedience required of them in the Army, this collection of individuals was bent upon airing opinions, complaints, ideas, and plans. The Paris Caucus offered a convenient forum. But order was gained from potential chaos when Ogden Mills of New York moved that the caucus be organized for business by the appointment of four committees, reporting recommendations on permanent organization, Constitution, name, and place of next meeting.*

By Monday morning, March 17, committees had accomplished their work and the ranks of delegates had swelled, making a move to the Cirque de Paris advisable. The old playhouse's circular floor was lined with chairs, cards on slender standards marking out seating by divisions and units in the pit, the tiny boxes and around the balcony. The place soon had the incomparable look that comes with war—the ironic and rather incongruous sight of a building designed for gay entertainment made severely plain and matter-of-fact by the military—showy dress replaced by unrelieved khaki, the bright, excited faces of children by those of soldiers, some of them looking like old men with drooping mustaches. Men in uniform sat in straight-back chairs. Some wore their trench coats; others had hung them over railings above the gilded ornamentation along the balcony.

As the meeting got underway it was evident that a day and a night of committee work and talk had settled the previously tumultuous caucus. Many delegates had participated in committees, others had had their questions answered and their suspicions allayed. Talk and work had clarified purposes and procedure like chemicals introduced into a suspension leaving a clear solution.

Lemuel Bolles presented the report of the Committee on Constitution which had worked all night under the chairmanship of G. Edward Buxton, Jr., of Providence. Serving with him were Thomas W. Miller, Col. E. A. Gibbs, Maj. J. Hall, Col. C. L. Ristine, Pvt. H. W. Ross, Pvt. John T. Winterich, Lt. Col. John Price Jackson, Col. Milton J. Foreman, and the Subcommittee of Three who wrote the short preamble—Col. Frank A. White, Maj. Redmond C. Stewart and Lt. Col. W. H. Curtiss. As Buxton read the first paragraph of the draft

* See Appendix for committee membership lists.

constitution the restless shifting in chairs ceased and the words held the soldiers silent:

> We, the members of the Military and Naval Service of the United States of America in the great war, desiring to perpetuate the principles of Justice, Freedom, and Democracy for which we have fought, to inculcate the duty and obligation of the citizen to the State; to preserve the history and incidents of our participation in the war; and to cement the ties of comradeship formed in service, do propose to found and establish an association for the furtherance of the foregoing purposes.

Few such expressions of extraordinary inspiration have appeared in any language. What success The American Legion has had stems in large measure from this original paragraph drafted at the Paris Caucus. The wording of the final constitution written months later drew upon it and was more inclusive but hardly an improvement over this spare, direct prose.

Bolles went on to define membership as open to all who had served honorably. A comprehensive organization was laid out from a national organization to subsidiary branches for each state, territory and foreign country where members were resident and desired to associate. The document also envisioned the offices of National Commander, his associates and the National Executive Committee. A private moved for adoption.

It was then that Bishop Charles H. Brent, Senior Chaplain of the AEF, rose. He had come to see just what sort of association would be established, for already he had launched "Comrades in Service" on broad and effective lines within the AEF. Although its principles had been enunciated, the problems of organization were to be solved after the AEF returned to the United States. Brent had made it clear that he would sit in judgment and was willing to withdraw and consolidate his efforts with those of the Paris delegates if ideals held by "Comrades in Service" could be better served by the new organization. In addressing the caucus, Brent said:

> I was present on Saturday, at the beginning of this caucus, and I will tell you frankly that I was fearful at that moment lest you should create a great mechanism without adequate purposes. My fears have been wholly allayed and I see in the report of

your committee the ideals not only of the Army but of the nation adequately expressed, and I wish to tell you gentlemen that so far as I have any ability to promote this great movement, I will give you my most hearty support.

Brent's words threw the lot of his organization to the new association and assured vital and continuing support from another remarkable individual. This dramatic and magnanimous action also gave the Legion a great advantage in the AEF and in its early efforts in the United States.

Unanimous adoption of the Constitutional Committee's report was followed by recommendations of the Committee on Organization headed by William J. Donovan of the Rainbow Division. An Executive Committee of one officer and one enlisted man from each group recognized by the caucus should be named to forward organization and publicity. The report as adopted included a paragraph reflecting the irrefutable logic and wisdom that had prevailed at the close of the Roosevelt dinner:

No policy except in furtherance of the creation of a permanent organization having in mind the desirability of unity of action in organizing all the American forces shall be adopted or carried out by the committees.

Controversy over what title the association would bear was carried to the floor by the Committee on Name. "Legion of the Great War" and "Veterans of the Great War" were its first and second choices. Many had other ideas. Maurice K. Gordon of Kentucky moved the adoption of "The American Legion," and Joseph Mills Hanson, the historian, urged "The American Legion of the Great War." It was then that a portly medical corps sergeant, Alexander Woollcott, lifted his great bulk to point out that the word "legion" savored "slightly of the silk stocking." This drew fire from a 1st Division delegate who had fought alongside the French Foreign Legion at Soissons. Delegates seemed unwilling to give up their particular choices, and the debate wore on into the early afternoon as the crowd thinned. Finally, those who remained carried Gordon's motion without enthusiasm and with an understanding that the action was tentative and could be revoked.

There have been other American Legions, as Richard Seelye Jones has ably described. In 1780 an American Legion of Honor was established in Massachusetts. Troops under Mad Anthony Wayne were organized as legions instead of regiments after the Revolutionary War. Two American Legions sprang up before U.S. intervention in World War I. Arthur Sullivant Hoffman, editor of *Adventure* magazine, started an American Legion in 1915 after receiving a letter from E. D. Cooke in Costa Rica predicting that the United States would be at war within ten years. Cooke's idea, elaborated by Hoffman, that all former servicemen organize to serve their country when needed met with wide and prominent endorsement. Encouraged by General Leonard Wood and Theodore Roosevelt, Sr., an organization of between 25,000 and 50,000 members developed. It was incorporated in New York State as the American Legion, maintained files of technical and military abilities, promoted the Plattsburg idea of military training, and approached the government in 1915 and 1916 offering to aid in the preparedness program. In late 1916 the Administration took over its records for use by the Council of National Defense. Donovan, Goodrich, Mills, Drain, Hanson, and perhaps a few others at the Paris Caucus as well as Theodore Roosevelt, Jr., had belonged to this prewar Legion. The second was the 97th Overseas Battalion of the Canadian Expeditionary Force, made up of U.S. volunteers. To the chagrin of certain British brass, these individuals, with the words "American Legion" emblazoned on their badge, raised the American Flag every morning and at retreat played the "Star-Spangled Banner" on English soil until they were sent as replacements to Haig's battered divisions on the Western Front. Both groups generously surrendered the name to the new Legion in about 1920.

Late in the afternoon of the seventeenth, delegates gathered for the last session of the caucus. Under Milton J. Foreman a new Committee on Convention, appointed when its predecessor failed to reach agreement, recommended that a general congress of veterans should meet in the United States at 11 A.M. on November 11, 1919, at a place which the AEF Executive Committee acting with the American Executive Committee would select. Prompt acceptance followed.

Thus drew to a close the Paris Caucus where in three days a large group of unusually dedicated men managed to draw in a strong, free hand the outlines of an association that could be a force for years to come in advancing purposes and ideals they and hundreds of thousands of others like them chose to advance. They gave The American Legion from the start an idealism, flexibility, direction, and adaptability that persists as a towering achievement.

and adaptability that persists as a towering achievement.

5

From the Rhine to the Mississippi

BEYOND inspiration, success in most things depends upon experience, attention to detail and uncelebrated hard work. Men
may espouse grand designs which gain a momentary notice. It is
quite another thing to forward, to persevere, to implement, and to
prevail. Laws may be passed; charters proclaimed. But who are to
be the executors? The many men who gave generously of their talents, knowledge and energy to the beginnings of The American
Legion have never received proper recognition. There is a dearth of
records of day-to-day endeavor in unofficial matters within the AEF.
It is possible only to acknowledge what they did.

One of these men, looking back over the years, says,

> One of the reasons for success in organizing the Legion was the
> behind-the-scenes work of seasoned leaders who were thor-
> oughly experienced in the work of political organizations at
> home. These men steered the Legion away from any semblance
> of politics. They were dedicated to the fact that there must be
> no hint of politics of any kind and succeeded remarkably de-
> spite repeated hazards. There was equally a determination that
> the Legion should not be used for any selfish purposes and in
> that, too, they succeeded beyond all expectations.

Milton J. Foreman of Chicago, elected chairman of the Executive
Committee immediately after the caucus' close, spoke prophetically
to the group of the Legion's future:

> It is our duty as soldiers and sailors to unite into one organ-
> ization all persons who have been subject to military and naval

authority for the following purposes: To perpetuate the aims for which we entered this war; to form a concrete method for securing and enforcing proper care of the wounded, disabled and needy; by organization to impress on those who govern the country the broader point of view of those who served, and in general to be a great communal force for good.

In talking with Marquis James later, Foreman observed, "There I was the temporary head of an interim committee of a projected organization. Can you conceive of anything more diaphanous than that?"

George A. White, Eric Fisher Wood, Richard R. Patterson of New York, and Laurence Fairall of Iowa served as permanent members at large. White assumed the duties of secretary and he too was chagrined by his position: "If you want a clear mental picture of our situation just imagine yourself with The American Legion on your hands, its course not charted, its organization not begun, not a centime in the treasury and no method of raising a franc."

Foreman perceived that to work at a highly evolved organization in Europe would be effort wasted, that he and his associates should direct their effort largely at publicity and persuasion. The story of the Legion was spread among troops through the *Stars and Stripes* and divisional and regimental publications. Those who had attended the Paris Caucus rallied support. As the promise of The American Legion became established, units not represented in Paris came forth with leaders who participated in promotion activities. A short statement of early plans was run off at a French print shop after White failed to influence a general in charge of the Army printing plant at Chaumont who couldn't "see" the Legion. The statement emphasizes that the Legion "is going to be just what you and others who were in the service make it. The necessity of launching the movement early, for the benefit of those in service, is apparent, particularly to those who know of the abortive and frequently selfish efforts to form veterans' organizations at the close of preceding wars." It urged homeward-bound troops to get in touch with others who were interested as soon as they were discharged.

On April 7, the Executive Committee named a liaison group of 17, with Bennett Clark as chairman, to coordinate efforts with the organization Roosevelt was promoting in the United States.

Young Roosevelt's accomplishments in the early months of 1919 were prodigious. Beside him, a temporary committee worked indefatigably—Cornelius W. Wickersham, Henry Fairfield Osborn, Granville Clark, Leslie Kincaid, H. B. Beers, and, from the Paris gatherings, Richard Derby, Franklin D'Olier and Eric Fisher Wood. These men were not alone in their efforts to create a nationwide Legion, for they enlisted others in every state to serve as committeemen to develop state organizations and the machinery for election of delegates to the St. Louis Caucus. From the first Roosevelt knew that state committeemen must be carefully chosen, without partisan favor and frequently on the basis of solid reputations as selfless citizens untouched by political ambitions. As the Legion moved ahead of other veterans associations in promotion and publicity, stature and promise, the problem arose of lining up men who understood the tenets outlined in Paris and were not likely to prostitute the ideals and purposes of the Legion to personal advantage. Here Roosevelt's wide circle of friends, their counsel about contacts, voluminous correspondence, and extensive travel were invaluable. By the middle of April almost two hundred committeemen representing every state and the District of Columbia worked toward a caucus in St. Louis. Representation, so far as possible, was to be by election—two delegates for each congressional district in addition to a number of delegates at large. The committee stressed large attendance, for this condition could deny undue influence by willful minorities.

Rapid demobilization strained the resources and ingenuity of the temporary committee working out of rented offices in New York.

Besides benefiting from newspaper and magazine coverage, the Legion gained publicity from the distribution of thousands of one-page bulletins to YMCA and K of C huts and War Camp Community centers. Transports received bundles of Legion literature as they departed empty for France and again as they docked, swarming with shouting, waving, laughing, khaki-clad troops. A doughboy or sailor about to receive his discharge found the names of temporary state secretaries on placards in camps and bases throughout the country. Publications for servicemen and hospitals received ample Legion information. The government's Foreign Press Bureau in its "Home News Service" covered Legion activities on its wireless reports to the ships at sea and the AEF. If a doughboy had somehow escaped this barrage he found Legion information and, in thousands of communities, Legion activity when he returned home. Mayors received letters containing facts about the Legion and urging that they be given to the local press and welcoming committees.

On May 5, trains, puffing and wheezing, clanked to a stop in the big, begrimed station in St. Louis. Advance delegates from all parts of the country to the Legion's American caucus made their way along the platforms, past the steaming engines and railroad smells, through the vaulted concourse, to taxis which took them to the Statler and Jefferson Hotels. Their enthusiasm and determination was promising, like the Missouri spring—a contrast to a general feeling of letdown that had set in during the winter following the war. Next day they met in a small parlor in the Statler to formulate a working order of business for the caucus. These deliberations dispelled any suspicions that the temporary committee had "framed up the caucus" and belied the inevitable critics' suggestions that the Legion was an instrument of its earliest leaders, a mouthpiece of selfish interests. Theodore Roosevelt, Jr., spoke first:

> The idea underlying the formation of The American Legion is the feeling among the great mass of the men who served in the forces of this country during the war, that the impulse of patriotism which prompted their efforts and sacrifices should be so preserved that it might become a strong force in the future for true Americanism and better citizenship. We will be facing troublous times in the coming years and to my mind no greater safeguard could be devised than those soldiers, sailors, and marines formed in their own association, in such manner that they could make themselves felt for law and order, decent living and thinking, and truer "nationalism."

Secretary Wood explained in greater detail broad principles and purposes, then touched upon reemployment of soldiers, a legal department for handling insurance claims, allotments, disability, and other problems. The proceedings turned frequently to heated debate over such topics as universal military training, women's suffrage, prohibition, permanent headquarters, and the election of officers. Again and again the gavel struck. Roosevelt reminded excited delegates that the St. Louis meeting was to be a caucus, not a national convention. Finally the advance committee outlined an order of business, named

the committees to be organized and decided upon appropriate resolutions for discussion.

As full delegations rolled into town on Wednesday, the seventh,
advance delegates briefed them on the provisional nature of the caucus and assured them that nothing was to be "put over" on those
they represented. Certain loaded questions and issues that might have
blown the caucus into irreconcilable fragments were disarmed that
night and during the morning of the eighth.

Thursday afternoon the Shubert-Jefferson Theatre came to life as
eleven hundred excited delegates took their places beneath small state
placards. Improvised wooden tiers, occupied by the New York and
Ohio delegations and distinguished guests, flanked and backed the
large stage. Newspapermen and stenographers sat at tables while
temporary officers took chairs placed at random center stage. At two-
fifteen Theodore Roosevelt, Jr., called for order. Instead he received
a loud ovation. As the noise subsided Roosevelt asked for nomina-
tions for permanent chairman. Sergeant Jack Sullivan of Seattle was
on his feet and put up Roosevelt's name. The reaction of the crowd
was deafening. It drowned the second to the motion by Col. Luke
Lea of Tennessee and Roosevelt's first protests. The old cry, "We
want Teddy!" thundered.

"I wish to withdraw my name," young Roosevelt began, and, after
a long disturbance, continued, "I want the country at large to get the
correct impression of this meeting. We are gathered for a very high
purpose. I want every American through the length and breadth of
this land to realize that there is not a man in this caucus who is
seeking anything for himself, personally, but that he is simply working for the good of the entire situation . . . now, gentlemen, that is
my absolute determination to withdraw myself."

Further interruptions occurred as Sgt. Roy Haines of Maine nominated Lt. Col. Henry D. Lindsley of Texas, Sgt. W. E. Bolling of
Tennessee seconded Roosevelt's name and Col. Lester E. Jones of
Washington, D.C. praised Roosevelt and said, "I think it would be a
mistake to take 'no' from him." Delegates, disregarding the chair,
passed a motion for Roosevelt's unanimous election.

"Gentlemen, I resign," shouted Roosevelt.

"No!" cried the caucus, "No! No!" The mood of the delegates was
becoming set and stubborn. The clamor rose and fell, only to rise

again. Roosevelt, touched but obstinate, walked about the stage until the disturbance subsided. Then he said, "I want quiet for a moment. . . . This is something I have thought of and given my earnest consideration to, and I am positive I am right in it. . . . We must not have creep into this situation, in which we all believe, the slightest suspicion in the country at large. I do not think there is any suspicion among us here that any man is trying to use anything for his own personal advantage. . . . But I am going to stick by (my decision) because we have got to . . . create an impression all over the country today on which this organization will carry on and serve a great purpose for years in the future. . . ."

Amid the prolonged disturbance that followed, Lt. Col. Jack Greenway of Arizona, who had fought in Cuba with Roosevelt's father, told the delegates he knew that Roosevelt would not take the chairmanship. After further confusion Roosevelt forced a roll call between Lindsley and Jack Sullivan, who had been nominated during the tumult. Judge Lindsley was elected—a Southern Democrat, nominated by a Yankee from Maine, seconded by a Yankee from Ohio.

Thus Roosevelt turned back the almost overwhelming ardor of the caucus. He knew the gossip that was abroad, the wink of skeptics, the speculation of cynics. He knew that principles and the good of the organization towered over personalities. Yet many men compromise principle and lose judgment's balance in the presence of flattery and the tumult of acclaim. Roosevelt had only to stand silent. But Roosevelt submerged an ambition that might have been served by his Legion association. Without wavering he did what he knew was right. This was Roosevelt's finest moment.

Jack Sullivan, Seaman Fred Humphrey of New Mexico and Pvt. V. C. Calhoun, USMC, of Connecticut were elected vice chairmen; Eric Fisher Wood, secretary; and Gaspar Bacon of Massachusetts, treasurer. State delegations then appointed the standing committees' members, who turned to their uncelebrated tasks that evening and the following morning.

The second day's roll call triggered another dramatic episode as Wood came to the Soldiers' and Sailors' Council, a veterans group in the State of Washington, largely made up of IWW (Industrial Workers of the World) members. The IWW's lawless and violent behavior was well publicized and its allegiance to international communism and world revolution a source of concern, particularly in the western states. The Credentials Committee recommended exclusion. Sherman H. Curtin, the Council's delegate, desired to speak, but the caucus was vocal in its disapproval. Lindsley rose: "We are for a fair deal, and without a motion I ask you to hear this delegate."

"Give him a hearing!" shouted Roosevelt and others on stage. The mood of the delegates changed. "Give him a hearing," they echoed.

Curtin explained that he was out to rid the Council of the IWW. He and others were endeavoring to bring it into the line of American ideals, and they desired Legion backing. This drew applause. Then Sgt. George H. H. Pratt raised his voice, asking Curtin if the organization's constitution which Curtin had rewritten excluded officers. Curtin was shaken and the caucus became noisy.

"Answer 'yes' or 'no' " called Pratt. Curtin eluded the question. A Washington delegate pointed out that Curtin during a recent "demonstration of bolshevism in Seattle commanded a machine gun platoon on the right side of law and order." Over applause another delegate commended Curtin but declared that he represented a minority. "We can lick the majority," shouted Curtin.

Captain C. B. McDonald, intelligence officer at Camp Lewis, was asked to speak. "This man represents the element we were working against. . . . Personally, he is all right, but he is backing that organization, and he is here as the official representative of that organization. If he wants to be admitted, let him cut loose from it and come into this organization."

Curtin vowed to "clean out" the Council, stepped down and left the theater as the caucus affirmed the committee's recommendation to exclude the Soldiers' and Sailors' Council. Three years later historian Marquis James wrote that this caucus "established The American Legion for the Constitution of the United States and against forces making for its overthrow, and rejected thunderously the slightest commerce with bolshevism."

After the Name Committee's recommendation, "The American Legion of World War Veterans," was amended to "The American Legion," the caucus turned to the selection of a November convention site. Again delegates challenged a prepared report when the Committee on Next Meeting Place proposed Chicago. Already banners draped the theater—"Chicago wants you in November!" Grover F. Sexton of Illinois spoke, "When you consider the place of your next convention, Chicago will ask you, 'What do you want?' And in response to your reply, Chicago will answer, 'We will give you whatever you want.' "

A Pennsylvania delegate proposed Pittsburgh. It was then that John F. J. Herbert of Massachusetts held forth on the notorious mayor of Chicago, William Hale "Big Bill" Thompson, whose appeals to hyphenated Americans and diatribes against America's allies had brought unsavory publicity to Chicago and allegations that its first citizen was pro-German during the war. Herbert declared that Massachusetts stood ready to rebuke any city "for un-Americanism during the time when the soldiers of that city were offering their lives. . . . (Chicago) is now a most despised city. . . ."

Before Herbert had finished his attack on "Big Bill" Thompson and Chicago, delegates were tearing down the Chicago posters and banners. Confusion took over amid the noisy disturbance until John P. Cummings of Chicago gained the floor. Behind him stood the Illinois delegates, pale and frowning. Cummings protested the demonstration and asked that Illinois' soldiers and sailors not be insulted because of the record of one man: "Had the men who were serving the colors in France been in Chicago, they would have had no apology to offer for their mayor." Applause followed.

Anger among Illinois delegates drained away during the voting on proposed cities—Minneapolis, Indianapolis, Los Angeles, Atlantic City, Kansas City, San Francisco, and Chicago. Michigan and Nebraska cast their votes for Chicago "out of consideration for the soldiers of Illinois." Roy Hoffman cast Oklahoma's twenty votes for Minneapolis—"out of consideration for the soldiers of Illinois." After Minneapolis won in a runoff with Pittsburgh, Luke Lea, former Tennessee Senator and agile in parliamentary affairs, gained a resolution expressing the caucus' "admiration of the valor . . . of the thousands upon thousands of Chicago's sons." Herbert told the men of Illinois of the affection and honor he and the men of Massachusetts held for them, thus closing the session on a note of good feeling.

Perhaps the outstanding feature of the St. Louis Caucus was the self-restraint of many individuals who held burning opinions on a variety of issues—the League of Nations, the Army establishment, universal military service, and prohibition, to mention several. But Wilson was still in Versailles. More important, hundreds of thousands remained on active duty. That spring many still braced themselves against stanchions and bulkheads on the high seas; others who made the slow march from French mud into German mud still carried out occupation tasks; more served in billets, camps, naval stations, and yards on both sides of the Atlantic. Of course advance delegates had stressed the provisional nature of the caucus, for it hardly represented tens of thousands returning to civilian life monthly to face problems of unemployment and readjustment that became more aggravated as the weeks of 1919 passed. Many issues properly should await November.

Lindsley, after spending most of the night with the Executive Committee, called on Chaplain John W. Inzer of Alabama to address the caucus Saturday. With evangelical zeal Inzer delivered his "Don't-feed-the-baby-raw-meat" speech. He urged that delegates shun divisive issues, deal with principles and problems the nascent organization could handle, make a concentrated effort to conclude the caucus' work, and meet obligations to their unemployed and disabled comrades. Although the speech soared to impossible heights of idealism and optimism, it did stoop to these practical necessities.

The Executive Committee, heavy-lidded from the night's work, had drawn the lines of Saturday's business, considered expressions of dissatisfaction and cleared away misconceptions. First, an official publication, *The American Legion Weekly,* was established under Legion ownership and direction. Action on a statement of general principles and creed by the Resolutions Committee was suspended, awaiting the report of the Committee on Constitution and By-Laws. The caucus endorsed the Victory Liberty Loan and approved a demand that Congress investigate the trial, conviction and subsequent pardon of conscientious objectors.

The next resolution called for the deportation of aliens who had refused to perform military service during the war. Aliens by the tens of thousands, after taking out first papers, found that the United States expected its young men to fight its wars. They found, too, that they could avoid the call to arms by claiming foreign citizenship. Large numbers did so—comprising the most numerous exemption category—and many moved into jobs vacated by those who went to war as citizens. Their action and the fact that tens of thousands of veterans returned to find their former jobs thus filled were contributory factors to wide public endorsement of strong immigration measures adopted following the First World War. Veterans at St. Louis were familiar with this record. For them the death, suffering and sacrifices exacted by a war, presumably fought to rescue Europe from a demonstrably brutal tyranny, were very close. They had learned that beyond the gaiety of the soldier songs and propaganda there was a grim, heartbreaking reality. Only a year before the great German offensive was about to slam into the Somme, Flanders, Aisne, and Marne sectors. Less than six months before the terrible Meuse-Argonne fighting had been underway. Searing days and nights of battle were vivid in the minds and hearts of many at St. Louis. They had been pounded by artillery and trench mortar, by skillfully and long-emplaced machine-gun patterns, sought out by sniper scopes and gas. They had heard the steel-jacketed bullets strike their comrades, endured the cries of the wounded, felt fear and the last-straw moments of exhausted patience. The sod and mud had only begun to settle over doughboy graves. For many the peril of the sea and its hardships were only weeks away. And finally the entire military establishment had been the target of another killer—influenza. It is not surprising that the delegates took a strong line on those popularly known as "alien slackers."

The American Legion's significant programs of citizenship, its constructive efforts to educate the foreign born lay ahead and were to have profound results. We have only to regard the dedication of recent arrivals in uniform in World War II and Korea to discover the healthier attitudes that came with wide attention to this matter by the Legion and other groups. At St. Louis, however, these programs had not been formulated and there was bitterness. During the noisy approval of the resolution a delegate hitched himself forward between two crutches. Pvt. M. L. Sosnin wore two wound stripes on his sleeve and had one empty pant leg. Supporting himself on his remaining leg, he said, "I am Private Sosnin of Kentucky. I was born and raised in Poland. I came here and lived under the American Constitution. At the age of thirty-seven I left my business and my family to volunteer to fight for this country. If any of my former fellow-countrymen . . . or any other . . . is so despicable as not wanting to fight for the flag which gave freedom . . . I say, 'Kick him out!' "

The St. Louis Caucus had had its moments of excitement, turmoil, dispute, and elation so that the last hours seemed a time of grim plodding. Delegates were charged to instruct their state organizations "to see to it" that every disabled soldier, sailor and Marine be brought in contact with the Federal Rehabilitation Department. Other resolutions urged that the people of the United States provide reemployment for the returning servicemen and that the government undertake land reclamation projects.

Finally, the important Committee on Constitution under G. Edward Buxton, Jr., submitted its work. The committee had delegated responsibility of writing the draft preamble in three men, George N. Davis of Delaware, Hamilton Fish, Jr., of New York and Jack Greenway of Arizona. Inspired by the Paris document and aided by suggestions of others, they considered the task. Robert B. Pitkin, managing editor of *The American Legion Magazine,* wrote of this effort in 1959:

> Davis, then of Wilmington, and later Seaford, Delaware, and now—in his eighties—a resident of Hood River, Oregon, has recorded the work of the subcommittee: "After dinner (on the 8th) the subcommittee met and spent the evening in an informal discussion of the substance of what the preamble should contain, without making any attempt at phraseology. About twelve o'cock the subcommittee agreed to separate and go to their respective rooms where each one would attempt to put in writing the substance of the evening's discussions, and meet the next morning to agree upon and formulate a final draft of the Preamble. The writer (Davis) retired to his room and went into solitary action. From then until half past two in the morning he struggled . . .

His night's work is substantially the familiar and eloquent preamble that has guided the best efforts of Legionnaires since. Pitkin observed further:

> Fish and Greenway met with Davis in the morning, and said they had not been able to satisfy themselves with their night's efforts. They brought no drafts. On examining Davis' work they agreed to finish their task with that as a base. Greenway added the "100 per cent" before "Americanism." A delegation from

Washington, D.C., headed by Col. E. Lester Jones, visited the subcommittee with two suggestions that were accepted. (1) "To inculcate a sense of individual obligation to the community, state and nation" and (2) "To safeguard and transmit to posterity the principles of justice, freedom and democracy." Both of these will be recognized as refinements of statements in the original Paris document.

Before Fish, Greenway and Davis finished their work, they added "to maintain law and order" and made *all* the other changes by which the final preamble differed from Davis' draft —with one exception.

The three men then reported to the whole Committee on Constitution, which made one further change. It inserted "To preserve the memories and incidents of our association in the great war."

The full caucus listened in silence as Buxton read the preamble:

For God and Country, we associate ourselves together for the following purposes:
To uphold and defend the Constitution of the United States of America;
To maintain law and order;
To foster and perpetuate a one hundred per cent Americanism;
To preserve the memories and incidents of our Associations in the great war;
To inculcate a sense of individual obligation to the Community, State and Nation;
To combat the autocracy of both the classes and the masses;
To make Right the master of Might;
To promote peace and good will on earth;
To safeguard and transmit to posterity the principles of justice, freedom and Democracy;
To consecrate and sanctify our comradeship by our devotion to mutual helpfulness.

An observer wrote later of this reading, "It came at the opportune time, it summed up the spirit of our endeavors, it forecast a mighty future for us. It was adopted word for word."

Before the caucus adjourned, it considered the temporary Constitution point by point, laboriously. The designation of local units was changed from "billets" to "posts." Other minor alterations in the draft were adopted. Thus the caucus closed with the achievement of something substantial and durable—a constitutional document to serve as a guide in the pursuit of policies and in the exercise of devotion to principles.

For the last time Chairman Lindsley brought down the gavel and said, "This has been a momentous gathering; this is a splendid close. All those favoring adjournment vote 'Aye.' "

6

The Critical Days

THE transports from Brest entered the Narrows, passed the Statue of Liberty and docked at New York's piers. Tugs and harbor craft whistled, circled, blew throaty greetings, and waved flags, pennants and even laundry. Shouting, joking, laughing—from stem to stern, from gunwale to bridge—the big divisions of the AEF came home. The city cheered as they marched in their last formations. Up flag-draped Fifth Avenue, the air a stir of confetti and noise, the AEF passed into history and indelible memory.

And now the doughboy or sailor craved only to put down his duffelbag, turn in his rifle and bayonet, hang his uniform in a closet, and get on with civilian life. Dismantling the superb Army and Navy came with breathtaking speed and the alarming nonchalance characteristic of the United States after all her wars. By mid-April four thousand men a day gained discharge, sixty dollars and a ticket home. By midsummer only 20 per cent were still in uniform and only a fragment of the once seasoned, spoiling-for-a-fight units remained abroad.

Every home town welcomed her sons. But most veterans soon found that the nation they had left was not what it had been before the war. The age of innocence had slipped away just as had something of their reckless, carefree youth. Their countrymen too had lived through a dislocating experience. The totality of the war effort had interjected the Federal government into most facets of life from business to public opinion. Now, abruptly, war contracts and controls were terminated. And veterans found that no consideration of em-

73

ployment opportunities had anticipated their return. Unemployment awaited many in communities whose industries faced bankruptcy without government orders. The powerful War Industries Board had closed down, Wilson and his economic advisors expressing the belief that the American people knew their business and could make the necessary adjustments. With this, Wilson had sailed for France. Congress, too, failed to smooth the transition from war to peace. In March the U.S. Employment Service was cut back to 20 per cent of its operations.

It was largely the efforts of state and local agencies and civic organizations, strengthened by The American Legion, that eased what could have been a far more serious situation. For a slump of many months preceded postwar recovery.

In a *Life* cartoon of the time Uncle Sam speaks to a soldier, "Nothing is too good for you, my boy! What would you like?" The answer: "A job." To meet this unemployment problem and other needs of ex-servicemen thousands in the growing Legion gave tirelessly of themselves. What these men and women did throughout 1919 deserves recognition, for in most instances it was at the expense of their own personal affairs. What they did stands as a magnanimous task of extraordinary proportions. Implementing the principles and decisions of St. Louis and Paris—building an organization nationally and in our states and territories, raising membership and establishing posts, undertaking a vast instructive enterprise, financing, tending to the disabled and to the widows and orphans of fallen comrades, and forwarding preparations for the first National Convention—relied upon dedication, good sense and quiet service whether in cow towns and industrial centers or in State and National Offices.

In August Theodore Roosevelt, Jr., explained why he backed the Legion:

> It has been the policy of The American Legion, wherever I have come in contact with it, to play the game with all the cards on the table. The serviceman will not tolerate any other form of organization. He wishes, at all times, to be able not only to tell anyone what he is doing but equally to be able to find out anything that the organization, through some other branch, may be doing.

The Legion's democratic framework, characteristic of a constitutional republic, appealed to responsible veterans, to national figures and to the public. The national organization and Constitution developed since the Paris Caucus served as practical instruments. National Headquarters' and departmental officers, elected at St. Louis, served and drew strength from the local posts and individual Legionnaires, the sinew and the substance of the Legion. Representative democracy was to be practiced through delegates to state and National Conventions. Proposals and resolutions were to come initially from individual members subject to adoption at the annual National Conventions. The policies of National Conventions were to be carried out during interim periods by an elected National Executive Committee, National Commander, Vice Commanders, Adjutant, Judge Advocate, Treasurer, and a number of committees and divisions.

The Executive Committee of One Hundred at St. Louis had delegated its authority in a Committee of Seventeen which united with the AEF group to form the Joint National Executive Committee of Thirty Four which was to meet once a month. It elected Henry D. Lindsley chairman, Bennett C. Clark vice chairman, Eric Fisher Wood secretary, and Gaspar Bacon treasurer. The burden of day-to-day work fell to the Organization Committee of Five—Lindsley, Clark, Eric Fisher Wood, Franklin D'Olier of Philadelphia, and Dr. Richard Derby of New York—which met each morning at National Headquarters, 20 West Forty-fourth Street, New York.

D'Olier directed the enormous task of organization, his contacts and recognition of his work in every department literally growing by the hour. D'Olier's State Organization Division, working hand in glove with the National Speakers Bureau under J. F. J. Herbert, saw the structure of The American Legion, a framework of "national service in peace," rise quickly and surely in most states and territories.

The efforts of national officers were magnified many times at state and local levels. As with political parties, religious groups, unions, chambers of commerce, and the many other associations giving continuity, purpose and vitality to American life, the essential ingredients of The American Legion are application and energetic leadership at its broad base. State chairmen and secretaries drove for the establishment of thousands of posts, each requiring fifteen signatures and evidence that it would function along the constitutional lines of the national organization which issued the charters. The autonomy of the posts afforded them a wide latitude of independent activity in the affairs of their communities. Considerable assistance came from national speakers Herbert, Roosevelt and John W. Inzer and resident speakers of fifteen zones throughout the country. These men accepted engagements in localities where veterans desired information about the Legion. They stressed background, principles and objectives and answered such questions as: "What is The American Legion? What are its purposes, aims and ambitions, its right not only to existence but to take an important part in the community life and civil affairs of the United States?"

Department organizations worked out details for accepting charter applications. For example, Iowa set Monday, May 12, for filing. At midnight, Sunday, veterans at both Spencer and Council Bluffs were ready to sign and rank as Iowa's Post No. 1. At 12:05 A.M., Spencer's Maris DeWolf, E. T. Bjornstad and Rush Smith in a Ford car headed for Des Moines with their notarized document. The early morning train from Council Bluffs carried their rival's petition. The Spencer boys fared well for a time, then encountered bad roads. Hope faded. But with perseverance they reached Carroll as the Northwestern train pulled in. They abandoned their car, boarded the train, reached Des Moines, rushed to a taxi, and arrived at state organizer John Mac-Vicar's office five minutes before the special delivery from Council Bluffs reached his desk. Thus Spencer received Post No. 1, Council Bluffs No. 2, with Ottumwa, Hubbard, Cedar Rapids, Dubuque, and Carroll close behind. Within a month Iowa had fifty-one posts.

In July the NEC, at Roosevelt's suggestion, sent representatives into various states "to aid in hastening organization." The nearly one thousand posts of early July more than doubled by August. On September 1, there were 3,500, and a month later 5,670. Voting strength at Minneapolis was 684, based on a membership of 433,000 whose national dues were paid. Every state, the District of Columbia, Alaska, Hawaii, Mexico, Cuba, Panama, and the Philippines contributed to this total. Behind these statistics was D'Olier's masterly hand. He explained:

It is our business to make sure that the temporary state officers selected at St. Louis are functioning properly. We know here at National Headquarters how many men from each state went into the service. By checking . . . weekly reports from the states on the number of local posts organized we are able to decide, in all fairness to the states, whether they are doing their full share to enroll the potential membership in their territory. Reports from the state organizations on publicity, War Risk Insurance, and re-employment also keep us informed of the general progress of organization. If a state organization does not appear to be as active as we think it might be, then the Speakers' Division arranges to send to that state speakers who can stir up interest in the Legion.

This growth rested too upon other vital achievements and undertakings in what has been called the "critical time" between St. Louis and Minneapolis. The War Risk Insurance Division under Charles F. Sheridan and the Re-Employment Division under Richard Derby rendered direct service to national servicemen—in straightening out their affairs with the government and striving to improve job opportunities. A Legion representative in Washington expedited action at the War Risk Insurance Bureau. In the early summer Assisant Secretary of War Arthur Woods announced that the Legion through its local posts was proving effective in bringing ex-servicemen to desirable jobs. Consequently, the Re-Employment Division worked closely with Woods, who took charge of organizing the country's employment facilities. However, the shocking lack of government preparations for and the shameful plight of thousands returned from Europe became clearer as time passed.

To the energetic Thomas W. Miller and former Tennessee Senator Luke Lea, a tall and imposing man, fell heavy tasks in Washington including work toward incorporation of The American Legion by Congress. Identical bills of Democratic Senator Josiah O. Woolcott and Republican Representative Royal C. Johnson stated that the scope of the Legion's principles and work required its incorporation. An annual "full, complete and itemized report of receipts and expenditures of its national organization" and a Federal audit would be required. The bill, passed by both houses and signed by President Wilson in September, should have thrown sod upon the persistent fear of partisan political action, for it declared:

While requiring that every member of The American Legion perform his full duty as a citizen according to his own conscience and understanding, the organization shall be absolutely non-partisan and shall not be used for the dissemination of partisan principles or for the promotion of the candidacy of any person seeking public office or preferment.

From July 4, *The American Legion Weekly* under George A. White's direction served Legionnaires by informing them of the myriad activities undertaken at post, departmental and national levels. It provided guidance, outside opinion and editorial comment as well as articles, fiction and entertainment features. Its first issue celebrated the 143rd anniversary of the Declaration of Independence and declared that "the principles and ideals of that epochal document in human liberty are those of The American Legion, which *The American Legion Weekly* represents." It summarized the lofty hopes of Legionnaires:

> Out of their common experiences through the dark months of the war has grown a comradeship and a patriotism which is vitalized by their organization into this single concrete force which will stand always as a barrier against the forces of greed, ignorance and chaos. . . . Its voice is the majority voice of its members; its will the will of the many. . . . It has been democratic in its development. There are no titles recorded on its rolls. It is free of rank, of cast—and of partisanship. If it seeks in full measure to serve those who were in the service, it seeks in fuller measure to serve America.

Like its Constitution, this expression by the Legion's official publication is a touchstone of endeavor and purpose.

As returning soldiers and sailors joyously waved at the Battery with its towering buildings majestic in that spring and summer following the Armistice, many below decks did not see the heart-catching sight at the end of the voyage. These men and the tens of thousands of casualties still in France, their families and the families of those who would never return from French soil were the raw human tragedy of war. Comfort and succor surely awaited them. The government had surely made adequate provision for its disabled fighting men and the widows and orphans of its fallen defenders. These were general assumptions, shared by The American Legion. In early 1919 the Legion tabled all proposals of veterans' benefits since "it would be selfish for veterans to say what should be done for veterans."

Within weeks the mistaken beliefs that "a grateful nation" would meet its obligations with alacrity and compassion and that the Washington bureaucracy was up to such a task evaporated. As tens of thousands turned in desperation to The American Legion for help, shocking facts came to light in every state. Hastily, the temporary Legion Headquarters in New York set up its War Risk Insurance Division under C. F. Sheridan, which became the forerunner of today's great veterans' service chain.

Three government agencies, impaired by inadequate facilities, limited personnel and a growing indifference which single individuals could not penetrate, soon drew broadsides from the *Weekly*. Marquis James's series of exposés in the summer of 1919 led to the first great demonstration of the Legion as a force in formulating and gaining passage of legislation. James carefully exposed the incompetent bureaucracy of the Federal Board for Vocational Education which was charged with responsibility in teaching the war-disabled new skills and labeled its record one of "broken promises and betrayal of trust." Among other things he revealed a confidential order of the board to its field officers who examined applicants:

> The organs used in approving cases are the eyes and the brain. The ears and the heart do not function. Be hard-boiled. Put cotton in your ears and lock the door. If you are naturally sympathetic, work nights when nobody is there.

James's exposé and Legion pressure led to a congressional investigation and, as we shall see, further Legion action at Minneapolis.

At war's end a second agency, the U.S. Public Health Service, was responsible for medical care for the disabled. Its 1,548 beds for veterans were clearly an evidence of dereliction by Congress and the Executive Department. The Army had discharged 74,500 men for tuberculosis and mental illness alone by January, 1919. It held 120,-000 casualties overseas and many more at Army camps in the United States. Though a large percentage lay in tents, the cost of care cut deep into the Army's shrinking appropriations. The Navy and Marines, too, struggled to care for their disabled and diseased. Before long many of the discharged, thrown into makeshift arrangements, suffered the terrible oversight. Some with TB contracted after the gas attacks on the Western front and long exposure coughed their lives

out. The mentally ill were housed in jails, and other patients were led
to cots provided by Legion posts.

A third agency, The War Risk Insurance Bureau, suddenly found
itself delegated the responsibility of processing all veterans' claims on
top of its original task of handling marine and servicemen's insurance.
Unprepared and understaffed, submerged by paper in a basement
office in the National Museum, this bureau could process only a fraction of the claims of the disabled and of widows. These unfortunate
souls soon brought their plight to the doorsteps of Legion posts across
the country. James's revelations and the human suffering witnessed by
rank-and-file Legionnaires prefaced dramatic action by the Legion in
the months ahead.

The *Weekly* also provided guidance before the Minneapolis Convention. "Policies—not Politics" headed its editorial page. In those
early issues articles appeared on the future in the air, national preparedness, sports and scouting, the establishment and conduct of post
activities, and the dangers of communism and subversion. Here one
finds not a hysterical fear of revolution but an early recognition that
the activities of communists and their dupes in the United States were
subversive in "advocating the violent overthrow of government," in
open conflict with law and order. The Legion felt that its work and
the concepts of Americanism it supported were "an infallible antidote
for bolshevism." Recognizing the communist movement as autocracy
"by dint of conniving usurpation," editorials and feature articles during those summer months underlined the machinations of this "foe of
democracy." In a *Weekly* article Mayor Ole Hanson pointed out that
"in Seattle the Reds gained control of the central governing body but
the great majority of workers in Seattle, when the crucial time came,
stood for law and order." Six weeks after this article appeared, the
Communist Labor Party of America was founded in an IWW hall in
Chicago and the next day a rival group, the Communist Party of
America, was established. Both enjoyed the blessings of a foreign
power, Soviet Russia.

In 1919 the concrete beginnings of Legion support and assistance
in youth programs took place. Local posts improvised youth activities
in keeping with their conviction that deeds rather than words were
essential to the major purpose of "serving their country in peace and
war." Posts in several states fought the naturalization examiner's re-

The first caucus of The American Legion, conducted by veterans of the American Expeditionary Force, March 15–17, 1919, in Paris, France.

The famous St. Louis caucus, held in May, 1919. From these two meetings The American Legion was launched to become the world's largest veterans' organization.

Former President
Dwight David Eisenhower

The late General Douglas MacArthur

Former President Harry S Truman

*President Lyndon
Baines Johnson*

The late President John Fitzgerald Kennedy

On parade in Minneapolis, 1919—the first American Legion parade.

Ten thousand march at Portland, Oregon, August 23, 1965—the West Branch, Iowa, Drum and Bugle Corps on the line.

In the grand style: the kickoff of the thirty-sixth annual National Convention parade in Washington, D.C., August 31, 1954.

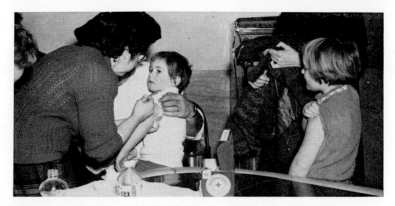

First aid is administered following the Alaskan earthquake on Good Friday, March 27, 1964, at Jack Henry Post No. 1, Anchorage, Alaska.

Representatives of The American Legion testify before the U.S. House of Representatives Committee on Veterans' Affairs.

National Commander Daniel F. Foley (1963–64) greets representatives of The American Legion's major youth programs: Boys' Nation, Baseball, Boy Scout support, and the National High School Oratorical Contest, all sponsored by the Americanism Commission; and the Sons of The American Legion, sponsored by Membership and Post Activities.

Mrs. Walter H. Glynn, National President of the American Legion Auxiliary, presents a Viet Nam Relief Fund check for $25,000 to General William C. Westmoreland at his headquarters in Saigon.

Members of the National Security Commission visit a launching pad at U.S. Air Force Missile Test Center, Cape Kennedy, March 15, 1963.

Yogi Berra scores, evading catcher Gene Mauch (later manager of the Philadelphia "Phillies") in an American Legion baseball game at Hastings, Nebraska, in 1942. The batter is Russ Steger, later to become an All-American fullback at the University of Illinois.

National Commander L. Eldon James, left, and C. D. DeLoach, center, National Public Relations Commission Chairman, confer with the President following signing of the GI Bill of Rights for cold-war veterans, March 3, 1966.

National Headquarters Branch of The American Legion, Washington, D.C.

The American Legion National Headquarters Building, 700 North Pennsylvania Street, Indianapolis, Indiana.

fusal of citizenship to a number of veterans. In a multitude of ways newly established posts commenced to serve the welfare of their communities.

The beginnings of The American Legion with its many unanticipated, attendant obligations and its ambitious publishing venture quickly marked the organization's ledger with red ink. Legionnaires who gave generously at the post level go largely unrecorded. Most gave without expectation of return or homage. In some communities property was given for the posts. The materials, time and labor that built other posts has been unrefunded in dollars and cents. From top to bottom thousands of Legionnaires paid their expenses connected with Legion work out of their own pockets, and in some cases depleted slender personal bank accounts for travel in building the early Legion.

The national organization, however, required a more businesslike approach. Shortly after St. Louis it was clear that the 25 cents dues for 1919 would not meet organizational expenses. Treasurer Gaspar Bacon and those at temporary headquarters huddled over the problem of solvency. In June the Finance Committee under John W. Prentiss estimated that the Executive Committee should have $250,-000 and inaugurated a national loan by voluntary subscription. The personal notes of Legionnaires—as individuals or by state organizations—enabled the borrowing of money at 6 per cent interest from banks across the country. Ninety-three note-signers and 146 guarantors made a total of $305,255 available. Up to the Minneapolis Convention $186,633.01 was required to finance the national organization and $178,882.31 to establish and operate the *Weekly,* making a total of $365,515.32. Receipts from dues and *Weekly* advertising came to $230,573.69, leaving a deficit of $134,941.63. The national loan, eventually paid off by membership dues set at Minneapolis at $1 per year, provided for this substantial deficit.

But already a disjointed, aggravating attack of insinuation and denunciation was underway against the Legion. It has resembled a sort of guerrilla war, flaring up across the wide area of Legion activities. And it continues to this day. It has been directed from many quarters and served by many groups. Radicals and pacifists have sniped from the ivy-covered buildings of our academic communities. The communists and fellow travelers have thrown their verbal grenades in the

city streets and served up Soviet propaganda with the salad at benefit dinners.

In 1919 Legion financing was attributed by these bedfellows
to "Wall Street." The whispered story blew from East to West.
Wall Street had slipped a million dollars to the right people to set up
the Legion. But this was hardly a presentable figure. The sum was
hiked until a radical journal on the West Coast put "the Legion's
blood-subsidy" at "conservatively $10,000,000." Strange that among
the first to battle the Legion were powerful men in the business and
financial world. Within a year National Commander D'Olier was to
receive an inquiry asking whether the Legion was "trying to make
suckers out of big business by taking their jack and refusing to
deliver."

As time passed the Legion was periodically hard-pressed for funds.
Legionnaires, not Wall Street, not big government, met the expenses
of the organization and a growing number of programs dedicated to
the best interests of their communities. As the Legion drove ahead
toward goals which were, for the most part, unselfish and honorable,
their enemies did not rest. Legionnaires have erred as all men do,
but never so grievously as those who have so energetically attacked
the Legion and its activities with a stubborn monotony.

Still, in 1919 there was an encouraging audience observing The
American Legion. The good will of most of the country was with the
Legion, and hundreds of publications greeted its principles and objectives with ready endorsement. To responsible Americans who
might have feared the sudden return of millions of servicemen to civil
life, who read with dismay and distaste of the enormous and immediate post-war dislocations and violence attending the soldiers' and
sailors' return in Europe and who saw the edge of bitterness among
many American veterans seeking work, an organization intent not
only upon resolving their own individual problems but upon contributing to the resolution of the larger issues facing the country was
a bracing development.

Dedication to national problems beyond their own, which were
neither few nor small, was not lost upon elevated national figures.
Woodrow Wilson wrote:

> I am happy to have this opportunity to address a word of greet-
> ing and comradeship to the men who have served in the Army,

Navy and Marine Corps and are now banding themselves together to preserve the splendid traditions of the service. . . . The spirit of their service, and the continuation of that spirit in The American Legion, will make it always an inspiration to the full performance of high and difficult duties.

Newton Baker, the self-effacing, brilliant Secretary of War, pointed out that he, who had been "permitted to maintain through these heroic years a close relationship to the great army," had the "kindest interest in everything that affects their welfare and the preservation of their great traditions." Secretary of the Navy Josephus Daniels admired "the continued mobilization for patriotic purposes of the Americans who served their country in the grim days of war" and felt that "it would be a distinct loss if the unity of spirit and the comradeship for better things should not be crystallized in such organized forces." American and Allied generals and statesmen acclaimed the beginnings of the Legion. Pershing underlined the Legion's opportunities and urged its members to carry on, inspired by motives which would benefit the country.

The vast majority of the press hailed the Legion. *The Washington Star* welcomed the Legion "as an agency for the promotion of the best in our national life." *The Grand Rapids Herald* observed:

> We need worry none concerning the policies to which the vast power of The American Legion will be given. Its members are men who offered their lives for their country. The country therefore means more to them than perhaps to others who made but small sacrifices in the war. The liberty which the people of America enjoy, the nation's law-giving institutions, the rights highly prized, are to the Legionnaire something bought at high price, therefore something not to be trifled with. Already there are evidences of the sturdy American stand which the Legion will take. . . . If ever again there comes a crisis in American affairs, a crisis either domestic or international, we can depend upon The American Legion.

The New York Times exclaimed, "Justice, Freedom, and Democracy, without partisanship! The idea is noble. It should prevail."

Consideration of public opinion toward future activities of the Legion was expressed with shrewd insight by Ivy Lee in the *Weekly:*

The Legion and those who are at any moment in charge of its affairs may do foolish or unwise things but if these acts are in perfect good faith and made public immediately, though they may be criticized, there will be ample time to correct them before any damage is done and the experience cannot but be helpful to the organization as a whole. . . . Complete information will be given to the press concerning each movement of the Legion. . . . (National Headquarters, state organizations) and the posts themselves are qualified to speak on every question. These men should and will make themselves heard, and it is believed that nothing will contribute more to the permanent success of the Legion than that these local posts will have an opportunity to make clear to the people of their neighborhood that they have come back from their country's service imbued with "100 per cent Americanism" and opposed to bolshevism, anarchy and disorder, and to every attempt to tear down the institutions of our country. That does not mean that The American Legion will be a "standpat" organization. It certainly ought to be progressive; not in the political, but in the truest sense of the word. Institutions of our country may and doubtless will require alteration and development. But there is one proposition on which every well-thinking citizen can stand—that whatever alterations undertaken must be by the orderly process of government and not through anarchy, riot and bloodshed.

The "critical days" of initial building and of articulating general concepts drew to a close. The time for implementing decisions to be determined by hundreds of delegates representing thousands of Legionnaires lay ahead. The Minneapolis Convention was at hand.

7

Achievement at Minneapolis

ELEGATES who look back almost half a century to the Minneapolis Convention remember it as a time of serious application. So large was the scope of problems and decisions facing them
that many recall that the relentless pressure of the workload transported them from November 10 through 12. To them it was a
convention of littered conference rooms, shirt-sleeved men working
through the nights with a determination that turned to grim, exhausting toil; of frequently tumultuous sessions on the floor, of remarkable
attention to practical details and the adoption of bold resolutions; and
of shocking news from Centralia, Washington. While there was adequate diversion for the city's twenty thousand guests it lacked the
organized entertainment and gaiety of future Legion conventions.
Half the delegates marched on Monday, the eleventh, as snow swirled
through their khaki ranks.

The resolutions of this first convention are in many respects fundamental—part of the bedrock upon which a modern democratic institution of principles and activities has risen as well as a part of the
foundation upon which the organizational structure of The American
Legion rests. All, with attention to explaining them in the context of
the time, in the experience and ambitions of Legionnaires, are followed in this and subsequent sections. Here, a brief recital of what
the 684 delegates resolved is important.

Adoption of the present Legion Constitution which includes strong
assurance of nonpartisanship followed approval of the work of the
temporary organization. The Committee on Legislation's report was

adopted, two paragraphs of which are the essence of the Legion's legislative activities. First, a committee appointed by the National Commander was to represent the Legion in Washington and establish a Washington office for the furtherance of the Legion's legislative program. Second, the National Adjutant was to send copies of all resolutions on national legislation to each State Adjutant for transmittal to each post. Local posts were to be directed to make efforts toward enactment of proposed legislation through Congressmen and Senators. Republicans Thomas W. Miller and John Thomas Taylor and Democrats Kenneth McRae of Nebraska and H. H. Raege of Texas served as the first National Legislative Committee. In 1920 the committee grew to one member per state, meeting twice a year, with the Washington staff reduced to Taylor and Raege.

"The first obligation"—the disabled—inspired a number of resolutions, both broad and specific. The convention charged the Legislative Committee to investigate all complaints or irregularities and injustices suffered by ex-servicemen at the hands of the War Risk Insurance Bureau and the Federal Board for Vocational Education. Congress was asked to act on pending legislation, to increase disability payments and rehabilitation allowances, to liberalize the rehabilitation act to include all disabled persons, to increase benefits to widows and orphans, and to place all ex-servicemen on the same basis as to retirement for disability as enjoyed by the Regular Army.

A second most important purpose expressed in the resolutions was the promotion in Congress and the country of a national defense program commensurate with the United States' position in the world and its requirements for national security. That The American Legion would pay close attention to this matter was inevitable. That its resolutions would, in almost every respect, become the basis of our military structure was not. For on the one hand there were those who really believed that the first world war was the war to end war, that national strength was prejudicial to peace as well as intolerable financially.

In 1919 and in the years following the Legion demonstrated an extraordinary vision. Legionnaires saw peace in the strength of free men and recognition of the evolving character of strength. They have held to the concept of flexibility of response. Adequate, up-to-date military strength would frustrate aggression. Legionnaires shared with their countrymen a profound revulsion toward war but harbored few illusions and false hopes. Their convictions first stemmed from the supreme test of general war. Overwhelming sentiment had grown among doughboys and sailors that unpreparedness had invited Germany's overt and covert acts that were the immediate pretext for American intervention. Doughboys who had fired only French and British machine guns and artillery felt that they and their fallen comrades had been obliged to fight a seasoned enemy without adequate training or matériel. They remembered training in the States with wooden guns. Should the international expressions and hopes for peace prove hollow, the United States could stand relatively formidable.

On the other hand, certain professional military men stood for a large standing army. Active distaste for the high-handed ways of many Regular Army officers at staff levels and in the War and Navy Departments was widespread among temporary officers and enlisted men of the Reserve and the National Guard. Many felt that the cavalier treatment accorded the Reserve and National Guard by-products of the academies was intolerable. The war had shown, if nothing else, that "national" armies composed of men outside the professional organization were requisite in conducting modern war. "The term GHQ," wrote George A. White, "brought to mind a hard, harsh institution bereft of soul, imagination or compassion, whose function it was to maintain a Prussian discipline and extract all joy of life from those who were in the Army. As a matter of fact, GHQ was a mild, if somewhat academic, sort of institution which did not entirely justify its hard name, and while I have no doubt that some of its personnel had their own ideas and hopes as to just what the organization of veterans ought to be and ought to do, it can be set down as a hard fact that GHQ had no voice or part in directing the course of The American Legion."

The resolutions at Minneapolis bore out this contention, for they drew the lines of a national defense organization consonant with concepts found valid in war and with a society whose shield and sword is the citizen soldier. The military policies adopted at Minneapolis opposed a large standing army as "uneconomic and undemocratic," called for universal military training but opposed compulsory military service in time of peace, and favored "a national military system based on universal military obligation, to include a relatively small Regular Army and a citizen army capable of rapid expansion sufficient to meet any national emergency." Strong emphasis was laid on civilian control. Finally a resolution stated that "the national citizen army should and must be the chief reliance of this country in time of war," and that the national citizen army "should be officered by men from its own ranks and administered by a general staff on which the citizen soldier officers and regular army officers shall serve in equal number." The Legionnaires also adopted a resolution that Congress "make the U.S. Air Service a separate and distinct department of our system of national defenses under control of a member of the President's cabinet appointed for that purpose alone."

Unquestionably the issue over which delegates clashed most vigorously was that of adjusted compensation. Marquis James, in a position to know, observed that "no one in touch with the National Headquarters could avoid being forcibly struck by the rapid increase and the crystallization of sentiment for a bonus, an adjustment of compensation, or something to square up matters in favor of the men who had fought the war." Chairman Lindsley arrived at Minneapolis convinced that a majority of veterans as well as Legionnaires favored adjusted compensation and that they were morally and economically right. Delegates were divided. Some bore instructions to oppose anything that could be construed as a "bonus or gratuity." Others regarded adjusted compensation as a "rectification" in small part of the economic balance between the man "who fought for a dollar a day" and the man "who stayed at home and drew wartime wages."

Following a statement requesting a law providing reclaimed land for veterans and loans for building homes, the Committee on Legislation's report resolved:

> That while The American Legion was not founded for the purpose of promoting legislation in its selfish interest, yet it recognizes that our Government owes an obligation to all service men and women to relieve the financial disadvantages incidental to their military service—an obligation second only to that of caring for the disabled and for the widows and orphans of those who sacrificed their lives, and one already acknowledged by our Allies—but The American Legion feels that it cannot ask for

legislation in its selfish interest and leaves with confidence to the Congress the discharge of this obligation.

Luke Lea moved for adoption. A dozen delegates rose, some to offer amendments stipulating a sum based on length of service; others to oppose any action whatever; most to explain their constituents' desires or to express their own convictions. Frederic W. Galbraith, Jr., suggested that a dollar a day be paid in government bonds. A disabled soldier endorsed this plan, saying it was "not fair or right" that the disabled receive all the consideration. Too many others had suffered irreparable financial loss. Protests against a bonus were expressed with equal energy. Brought to a vote, the resolution passed, leaving to Congress the initiative to act. Already Congress had in its hopper many proposals to give the citizen soldier some financial adjustment, so that there was reason to believe that prompt action was at hand.

If it was impossible for many Legionnaires to envisage a world made safe for democracy on the moral, spiritual, social, and economic chaos of 1919 Europe, it was equally impossible to square constitutional ideals and American aspirations with most recent developments in the United States. Foremost among disturbing trends were the criminal activities of communists, syndicalists and anarchists and the growth of the immigrant population. The first involved law and order and their enforcement by constituted authority; the second, an evaluation of immigration policies and problems posed by large numbers of aliens.

On the eve of the Minneapolis convention Henry D. Lindsley expressed the responsible approach toward communism and other violent philosophies that has been followed since:

> The American Legion represents concretely the determination of these five millions of men that those who would destroy the flag for which they fought shall not live under its protecting folds. It represents the further determination of these men that our country shall continue to be the land of law and order, and that the Constitution of the United States shall be supreme in its power over every man and woman who remains in this country. It, through its members, recognizes the great truth that there is but one way in which a democratic people can correct evils of government, and that this way is through orderly changes as

determined best from time to time by the people themselves. . . .
The American Legion stamps class-selfishness as wrong and as
shortsighted as individual selfishness. Made up, as The American Legion is, of men from every class and in every walk of
life, it will set its face against the supremacy of any class in our
American life.

Already it was clear that the Legion was to be an organization of
men made to stand and fight against groups, ideologies and propaganda dedicated to overthrowing constitutional government and de-
stroying its attendant institutions. To defend this heritage that traces
its genesis to the earliest aspirations of men, that grew on the shores
of the Mediterranean, in Europe and on British soil long before the
American Revolution, and that generations had struggled for, Americans from the Thirteen Colonies to those of 1917 and 1918 had
taken the fatal or crippling wound. Because it has always been the
lot of free men to fight for freedom, and because The American
Legion early recognized that peace in the twentieth century would not
mean the absence of conflict, that other malignant ideologies could
replace the autocratic tyranny and martial ambitions of Imperial Germany, and that Legionnaires felt perhaps most sharply the obligation
they had to those who fell in battle and the generations yet to come,
the Legion took an early lead against lawless, destructive and growing threats to free institutions. It was promptly listed for liquidation
by communists and syndicalists and for ridicule and denunciation by
radical and pacifist elements in American life.

The Minneapolis Convention's resolutions called for positive steps
by the Legion within the law and by Congress as the legislative branch
of the Federal government. To understand more fully the Legion's
positions at its first convention regarding communism and matters
pertaining to aliens and to immigration, as well as its outstanding
and constructive contributions in the years following, vital considerations are presented in the next chapter. It was with these considerations in mind and with an appreciation of the importance of
education and emphasis upon the American heritage that the Legion
resolved to establish a National Americanism Commission to combat
"all anti-American tendencies, activities and propaganda," to work
for the "education of immigrants," to inculcate "the ideals of Americanism in the citizen population," to promote "information as to the

real nature and principles of American government," and to secure "the teaching of Americanism in all schools." The Legion advocated taking measures to frustrate the "insidious propaganda of bolshevism, IWW-ism," and clearly anti-American doctrines. For four years the national organization, departments and posts implemented these policies until the Americanism Commission was formally established.

The convention also called upon the government to increase the powers of the Department of Justice and change it "from a passive evidence-collecting organization to a militant and active group of workers whose findings shall be forcefully acted upon" by the government. The war, Mr. Wilson and George Creel's Committee on Public Information had conditioned many to strike out at suspected espionage, subversion and sedition with a disregard for law and order the Legion never countenanced. The previous month Congress had empowered the Secretary of Labor to deport without jury trial aliens who "believe in or advocate" the violent overthrow of government, who sought unlawful destruction of property or belonged to an organization teaching such tactics. At the time the Communist Labor Party was estimated at from 10,000 to 30,000, the Communist Party at from 30,000 to 60,000 and the Socialist Party, entertaining more moderate methods for achieving a revolutionary panacea, at 39,000. There were quite enough firebrands among the "rag-tag collection of communists and syndicalists" to justify concern and positive action by the government.

But The American Legion did not participate in what has been labeled "the Red Scare" or the "national hysteria" by many historians and sociologists. On the contrary, *The American Legion Weekly* described the communists as "not much of a menace." However, their acts of terror and violence and advocacy of the overthrow of government required law enforcement. Preservation of law and order in the face of lawless acts including murder and the wrecking of property called for dealing with this political Mafia.

The American Legion, dedicated as it was to service to "God and Country," early considered education's many aspects in its resolutions and in its national, state and local programs. The World War I draft revealed that more than 24 per cent of those registered were illiterate. Twelve million of some 27 million children were not regularly attending school when the Legion in 1919 launched a campaign for better schools, better pay for teachers, greater community interest in education, higher professional standards for teaching, and the strengthening, or passage in states where they were absent, of compulsory education laws and anti-child-labor laws. Writing in the *American Legion Magazine* forty years later, Robert B. Pitkin observed:

> Between 1919 and 1925 The American Legion led the biggest revival of general public education since the inspiring work of Horace Mann eighty years earlier.

Associated with the general problems of illiteracy, unemployment and labor unrest and the bitterness toward draft evasion, pacifism and hard-core subversion and terrorism was the vast problem of immigration and aliens. Over fourteen million Europeans came to the United States between 1900 and 1917. This influx was simply too heavy to be properly accommodated and assimilated. Responsible men in cities and states where hundreds of thousands of aliens crowded saw that the economy was severely tried with a burgeoning labor force of foreign-born, few conversant in English, many illiterate and a majority unskilled. Prolonged indigence or poverty awaited the hopeful line of arrivals. Politically, the unfortunate immigrant too often was the life blood of the big city machine, where the boss, in exchange for benevolence, gained the allegiance of foreign-born voters. Finally, from these hard-pressed ranks a small minority lent their talents to organized crime and the violent, radical movements already mentioned.

To Legionnaires, returned to a tight labor market, the fact that only 155,000 of over 13,000,000 aliens, a shade over 1 per cent, had become naturalized citizens by virtue of military service revealed failure at assimilation. Resolutions at Minneapolis called on Congress to "pass laws for the deportation of all first-paper aliens who have renounced their intention of becoming citizens, and to make it impossible for first-paper aliens who surrendered their papers to evade military service to acquire citizenship," to cut off immigration for five years and to amend the Fourteenth Amendment to read "that no child born in the United States of foreign parentage shall be eligible to citizenship unless both parents are eligible." Deliberate evasion or avoidance of military service on various grounds aroused the strongest feelings among those who had served and who felt that availability in time of war should accompany citizenship. Hence, delegates found relaxation of regulations and "honorable discharge" of conscientious objectors unsatisfactory. During the war some aliens had signed the affidavit:

> I hereby withdraw my intention to become a citizen of the United States, which withdrawal I understand shall forever debar me from becoming a citizen ... and I do hereby claim relief from liability to military service in accordance with the law. ...

The convention, besides asking for the deportation where possible of draft-dodgers and others convicted of offenses against the successful prosecution of the war, urged Congress to require aliens to acquire knowledge of English and to see that a course in citizenship be introduced into every public school.

Congressional action was soon to follow. Consular reports of early 1921 indicated that fiscal year 1922 promised two million immigrants. Congress, with Legion backing, passed the three per cent act and, after many months, the Act of 1924 which divided immigrants into two classes, quota and nonquota. Persons born in Mexico, Canada, Central and South America could enter subject to examination as to health, sanity, pauperism, criminal record, and anarchistic beliefs. The quota of 2 per cent applied to foreign born of countries represented in the United States in 1890.

Oriental immigration presented peculiar problems of long standing. A Federal statute of 1875 barred Japanese and other Asians from naturalization, although American-born children gained citizenship. California in 1913 forbade aliens ineligible to citizenship to own farmland—a law declared constitutional by the Supreme Court in 1923. Intense anti-Japanese feeling stemming from economic and cultural causes had persisted on the Pacific Coast for years. In 1907 by the "Gentleman's Agreement" Japan was to prevent future immigration of laborers. With the war dark suspicions of Japanese collusion with Germany fed distrust. Japan's bold take-over of former German spheres of influence in China and the western Pacific and the Zimmermann telegram, suggesting the possibility of unleashing Japan, "the yellow peril," against the United States from Mexico, added to adverse sentiment toward "Imperialist Japan" and her people.

The Minneapolis Convention called for abrogation of the Gentleman's Agreement and the exclusion of Japanese from the United States "on the same principles as adopted in the case of other Oriental races." Congress acted accordingly in 1924.

In the confusion and competitive atmosphere of conventions the big prizes are usually hard-won things, requiring timing, strategy, backing, zeal, and that indispensable ingredient, the ability to stay, which the British admired in bare-knuckle days as "bottom" and Americans frequently describe as "guts." Between May and November a trio of Indiana Legionnaires, Dr. T. Victor Keene, Walter Myers and Robert L. Moorhead, determined to put Indianapolis in contention as permanent headquarters. Advised by Stoughton Fletcher of the Fletcher American National Bank, they gained the aid of Charles Coffin of the city's Chamber of Commerce and ten individuals who pledged $500 each to cover a hotel suite, publicity, entertainment, and other expenses. The infighting was heavy as several cities struggled for the recommendation of the Committee on Permanent Headquarters. When Minneapolis won by a single vote in committee, the Hoosiers' chances were kept alive when the chair cleared the way for a floor fight. A snowstorm conspired against the host city by giving Indiana Legionnaires the opportunity to pass out straw hats to shivering delegates and to comment on the weather. On the first ballot Washington, supported by large Eastern delegations, led Indianapolis, Minneapolis, Kansas City and Detroit, but in a run-off Indianapolis prevailed.

Triumphant, the Hoosiers returned to Indiana and campaigned for the five-square-block Memorial area in the heart of Indianapolis. There, the original headquarters was completed in 1925 and a new National Headquarters was built after World War II.

Minneapolis saw the start of an exceptional movement—that of The American Legion Auxiliary. Already women had begun to organize and had arrived at the first Convention with a proposal for a "Women's Auxiliary." They came away with a constitutional article. It limited membership to wives, mothers, sisters, and daughters of Legionnaires, of those who died in war service and of deceased veterans, and women who had themselves served in the war.

Immediately women undertook the task of turning a few legalistic lines into a working force. Three months later a convention of

Hawaiian chapters was held. A subcommittee under E. Lester Jones and the Legion's Organization Division promoted enthusiasm and assisted in chartering 1,342 units in forty-five states with 11,000 members before the 1920 Cleveland Convention.

Late Wednesday afternoon the election of national Legion officers came as the last order of business. The 1919 roll call and those of subsequent years followed the pattern of political convention balloting with similar enthusiasm, maneuvering and high drama. For the office of National Commander the field had narrowed to two strong contenders—Franklin D'Olier and J. Hanford MacNider of Iowa, whose distinguished record with the 2nd Division and the Legion was generally admired. The roll call commenced with Alabama, giving six votes to MacNider. Alaska followed with four votes for D'Olier. Arizona passed, and Arkansas gave ten votes to D'Olier. When the list of states, with New York passing, was finished, D'Olier had 321 votes to MacNider's 283. E. Lester Jones and Emmet O'Neal of Kentucky polled complimentary votes. Jack Sullivan declined consideration, while Henry B. Lindsley, nominated by Texas, reiterated his stand that he was not a candidate and expressed the hope that no National Commander would ever succeed himself. Tension had built up, for 352 votes were required to elect. Arizona was called again and gave its six votes to D'Olier. New York then announced thirty-nine votes for the leader and eight for MacNider, who was on his feet before the result was announced to move that the vote be made unanimous.

Five Vice Commanders were elected from 18 nominees: Allen Tukey of Nebraska, James J. O'Brien of California, Joyce S. Lewis of Minnesota, Alden R. Chambers of Massachusetts, and William B. Follett of Oregon.

Now the towering tasks of further organization and implementation of Legion policies had been thrust upon Franklin D'Olier and those who would work at his side. However, with the great responsibilities of Commander went unusual honor. For to many Legionnaires the office of National Commander is the most exalted tribute that can be bestowed upon a comrade. It is considered of great distinction— above any appointive or elective political office, save perhaps that of the Presidency. In this regard few have considered it as a stepping stone to state and national office. Few have tried and fewer have been able to translate esteem and popularity and fame gained as National Commander to political advantage. In his extraordinary way Franklin D'Olier was to set standards which have guided Legion leaders to this day.

8

The Centralia Affair,
Order and Challenge

TWELVE months had passed since the end of the war and the
long-abiding fear had drained from those with men in arms.
For townspeople across America November 11 was a day to be
circled on the calendar—a day of memorial and remembrance, of
cheers and celebration. Snow from a slate sky did not shade the
spirit of the Minneapolis parade. But more than a thousand miles to
the west in Centralia, Washington, Armistice Day 1919 was marked
by the crack of high-power rifles and revolvers, murder and violence.

The logging camps in that rugged area had for years been the
center of intense activity by the Industrial Workers of the World,
a marxist group dedicated to "one big union," overthrow of government, class war, destruction of all vestiges of capitalism, and seizure
of the means of production by the workers. "Where the Executive
Board of the IWW shall sit, there shall be the nation's capital," wrote
a pamphleteer after the Russian Revolution. Through the war the
IWW spiked logs, wrecked machinery, lit fires, and carried on widespread violence and subversion in the rich timberlands.

Shortly after the end of the war citizens had led an IWW organizer
to the outskirts of Centralia and told him not to come back. In the
fall, however, several IWW men dropped from a freight train, rented
a run-down hall, displayed red flags and inflammatory posters, and
commenced "organizing." Citizens met. Huber Grimm, city attorney,
suggested that he could draw up an ordinance to rid the town of this

activity if the state criminal syndicalism act could be invoked. Illness suspended Grimm's proposal as November approached.

There was no mention of the IWW at a Legion meeting prior to the parade nor, as suggested by radicals of the time and in certain more recent accounts, threats to raid the IWW hall. These and accompanying facts were developed during the many weeks following that November afternoon. At two o'clock civic organizations and The American Legion contingents of Centralia and Chehalis left City Park and marched down Tower Avenue. The Chehalis group, marching platoon front, had passed the silent, red-draped hall when one of several halts was called. The Centralia Legionnaires, in front of the hall, were ordered to close up by Warren O. Grimm, commanding the column.

Suddenly a shot cracked the cool afternoon. It and two others in fast succession came from the hall—a prearranged signal for other IWW gunmen to open fire. High-power rifle and revolver bullets slammed into the ranks of the unarmed Legionnaires from concealed positions in the ramshackle Avalon Hotel, across the street and to the rear of the Legionnaires, in a blistered old rooming house ahead of the column, and on Seminary Hill a quarter of a mile east. Grimm fell, his viscera shredded by a dum-dum bullet. Caught in the pocket, the veterans broke for cover or the source of the first shots. It was only a few strides to the hall and through the door. Arthur McElfresh, back from overseas with the 161st Infantry, was hit in the temple by a high-power bullet fired from Seminary Hill as he sought cover. He was dead moments later when a Red Cross nurse ran to his side during the height of the firing. Eugene Pfitzer was shot through the arm in front of the hall and Bernard Eubanks took a bullet in the leg on the curb not far away. As Legionnaires broke into the hall and seized several armed men, an IWW gunman who ran from the hall shot down Ben Cassagranda. Earl Watts fell within a few feet of the mortally wounded Cassagranda.

It was at this moment that Wesley Everest escaped from the rear of the hall, firing at his pursuers, reloading as he ran. Alva Coleman grabbed a revolver from an occupant of a house along the line of chase but was hit and passed it to Dale Hubbard, a powerful athlete, who reached the Skookumchuck River where Everest, after attempting to ford, had returned to the near bank. When Hubbard ordered

Everest to put down his gun, Everest opened fire. Hubbard fell. Everest then pistoled the dying Legionnaire twice before other ex-servicemen rushed in and overpowered him.

By now gunmen in the four-way ambush not captured in the hall and an icebox in the same building had fled their positions. Of the three who had fired from Seminary Hill, one Loren Roberts gave himself up, another was captured at his home and Ole Hanson made good his escape. Of those who were positioned in the Avalon, one man was taken and another escaped. Two men fled the rooming house and were later taken at their homes. Legionnaires moved the captured men to the local jail before a forming mob, intent upon invoking lynch law, could gain control. By sundown the sheriff despaired, and only the stubborn work of Centralia's Grant Hodge Post saved his charges from a summary procedure. Legionnaires and a few responsible citizens battled to protect the jail.

But the angry mob had purpose and methods other than singling out and beating a few defenders. It seized the municipal electric plant, turned out every light in town, rushed the jail, and abducted one prisoner—Everest. In the morning his body was found swinging from a bridge over the Skookumchuck. This mob vengeance, deplorable from the standpoint of law and order, removed a desperate ringleader from the subsequent trial and provided radicals with a heavy propaganda weapon. Indeed the shrill cries of radical intellectuals gained inordinate attention from liberal scholars and raconteurs of the era following World War I. A fuzzy image of what happened that November day is found too often in accounts. The nature of the IWW obscured, Everest some sort of martyr and the Legionnaires the conspirators have been among the distortions. That three Legionnaires were killed in cold blood and a fourth under the gun of the cornered Everest, that Grimm left a wife and child, Cassagranda a wife of five months and an aged father, and Hubbard a wife of one month have been played down or ignored.

Ten members of the IWW, together with their legal advisor, who counseled their crime, were arraigned for the murder of Lt. Warren O. Grimm and a lengthy trial at Montesano, Washington, ensued. The defense attempted to convince the jury with assertions that the IWW hall was in a state of siege, that shots were fired only after Legionnaires had attacked it and that no firing from other points occurred.

These assertions were discredited by testimony from many witnesses, among them defense witnesses, defendants and Legionnaires and by expert witnesses who testified that from the angles of entrance, bullets in buildings adjoining the IWW hall had their source in the three positions mentioned above. Then the defense sought to cast the burden of blame for rifle fire upon the dead radical, Wesley Everest, and Loren Roberts, alleged to be insane. Toward the close of the trial the defense admitted that one of the accused, Bert Bland, had fired as well. Testimony of the defendants disclosed a cohesive understanding of the part each was to play and the ambush to be taken.

"We expected to be killed and we done this with the intention of protecting our hall. We heard they were going to raid it," Loren Roberts, one of the man stationed on Seminary Hill with a high-power rifle, explained. He went on to say that plans for the attack had been consummated three weeks before. Diagrams of all IWW positions had been taken from one of the accused.

The prosecution proved the essential truth that the attack was not a defense, but an ambuscade. Of the eleven defendants, seven were convicted of murder in the second degree and received twenty-five to forty years in the penitentiary. From this trial and other IWW activities it was clear that the IWW was made up largely of men with little education led by ruthless leaders of communist and terrorist persuasion.

The Centralia affair was of profound importance. When, late on the eleventh, news flashed into Minneapolis from the West of an ambush of unarmed Legionnaires, outrage mixed with apprehension stirred the convention. How would ex-soldiers in the rugged Northwest react to this shocking attack? Good sense counseled that anger alone would be useless; vengeance, a disaster. Already delegates had made it clear that they meant to fight terrorism and subversion. But it was paramount that law and order dictate policies and action. How well individual posts would conduct themselves in certain situations was yet to be seen. Consequently, how the men of the Centralia post met this crisis was of grave concern. What happened that chill November afternoon in Washington State and in the days and weeks following could eclipse the constructive endeavor of the Legion.

The following month *The American Legion Weekly* could declare:

The Legion has acted quickly and effectively and with full observation of law and order. If there have been incidents when veterans, impatient over official disinterest, have in the name of Americanism taken the law into their own hands, it must be recalled that these were the isolated actions of individuals. The Legion has understood that where individuals practice violence against even the Bolsheviks they lend countenance to the practice of violence against the state. There are other and more effective methods provided by American law and order.

The Weekly also warned that the Legion and its hundreds of posts must never become a "vigilance committee." Frederic W. Galbraith, National Commander in 1920, could write that "the Legion men curbed their natural human impulses of revenge and waited on law to take its course against the criminals. That the Legion must always do." On December 12, *The Weekly* pointed out that at the request of civil authority, which was unable to cope with the emergency, Legionnaires remained active in keeping order in Centralia:

Thrown into the limelight where the slightest faltering or misstep would have reflected nationally against The American Legion the men of Grant Hodge Post No. 17 handled a difficult situation with a firm, just hand. . . . Had it not been for the spirit of the men of the Legion in those (early) hours the jail would have been emptied and a score of bodies would have dangled from Centralia's telephone poles. . . .

This episode came, too, when elements of both labor and capital strove to gain a partisan in the Legion. During the early years these efforts had only isolated local successes which were promptly repudiated and condemned by the national organization. Thus, by hewing to an impartial course the Legion early acquired the respect and commendation of the highest spokesmen of organized labor and management. In 1919 it expressed the view that "labor is fast realizing, except for a few radical nests, that the IWW is the worst enemy of union labor as well as of government."

From the first, long before the Americanism Commission was put in operation in 1924, the Legion's approach to the challenge of communism was essentially positive for it encompassed a broad spectrum of activities designed to strengthen its members, its fellow citizens, those who sought citizenship, and, finally, the nation's youth. Communism would blunt its weapons against the spiritual and mental arms and armor of practical, optimistic, informed men. The Legion's approach in the early 1920's was put concisely forty years later when a Legionnaire pointed out that at that time the Legion maintained that communism "would never disorganize America internally if all Americans were (1) educated to the facts and meaning of their history, traditions, liberties and Constitution; (2) if they were trained in the ethics and morals of western civilization; (3) if they knew their rights and responsibilities as citizens; and (4) if they were informed and alert to the purposes and plans and methods of the international communist power plot."

Then as now, the Legion took a sane, constructive and utterly realistic course. It did not see the communist menace magnified. But neither did it turn its back on its criminal and subversive features and the requirement of government to take action to protect the Constitution. It was not to be taken in by those permissive souls who have been duped and, to their sorrow, if they are capable of pushing aside the veils they have drawn about them, must realize that even today the communist doctrine in the hands of a man of perhaps psychotic tendencies can strike down our highest officials with bullets.

So distorted have been many recitations of the post-war period and the effort to characterize American attitudes so contrived and studied, it is well here to recall certain events and developments that shaped those years and to realize that while intolerance was widespread it was not a "national characteristic." The fears of President Wilson that by engaging in war Americans would become a "militaristic" and incurably intolerant people were an apprehensive exaggeration. Not that the Federal government and Wilson himself failed to indulge in specious propaganda to inflame the public. George Creel's Committee on Public Information "mobilized" thought and attitudes with cavalier treatment of news and facts. This at a time when the truth was quite enough. Valid accounts of German brutality and arrogance throughout the war, the U-boats' deadly operations and the outrageous scheme disclosed by the Zimmermann telegram conditioned a righteous anger, to say nothing of the Black Tom disaster and other acts of German sabotage to industry and commerce in the United States.

Congress deemed necessary the Espionage Act, the Trading-with-the-Enemy Act, the Sabotage Act, and the Sedition Act to the requirements of national security. Labor, business, the consumer, and the man who went into the service gave up prerogatives from which they would never have parted in time of peace. The press kunckled under to a voluntary system of censorship. The executive branch strove to condition the public to exert a maximum effort to make U.S. strength decisive. There was deliberate and incessant cultivation through propaganda of hatred. Those who opposed or undermined the war effort or failed to do their part were objects of attack. Wilson was unsparing of those who identified themselves with the nations of their birth:

> Some Americans need hyphens in their names because only a part of them came over. But when the whole man has come over, heart and thought and all, the hyphen drops. . . .

Many Americans, in no mood to accommodate socialists, communists, German-Americans, syndicalists, and pacifists, became overzealous and denounced and harmed persons merely on a national-origin basis. Bitterness caused by strikes and draft evasion joined hands with fierce desire to destroy the enemy. Citizens grew accustomed to rash denunciation. And the Federal government abetted this unfortunate course. Consequently, intolerance engendered in war sloshed over into the early years of peace.

The public could hardly be expected suddenly to abandon violent attitudes toward the "Hun" who had killed and maimed millions of Allied soldiers and civilians and the bolsheviks who had pulled Russia out of the war to release the Kaiser's Eastern divisions for the Western Front and who then proceeded to introduce amid the wreckage of Europe their infectious doctrines. The astonishing fact is that with the vendetta promoted by the Federal government there was not more disgraceful persecution. The striking fact was not that there was behavior unbecoming a constitutional democracy but that there was not far more of it.

Americans, imbued with a love of liberty and a faith in law and order, had only to look across the Atlantic to see the deplorable moral, physical and political consequences of a sanguinary war. The long conflict had beggared peoples and made bankrupt treasuries, toppled governments and wiped out venerable institutions, spawned wretchedness and spread disease, made a shambles of international law and indiscriminately snuffed out the lives of millions, sparked civil war and raised the banner of communism. It cemented the foundation of vengeance. It mortared the bricks in place for a chamber of horrors for another generation.

Russia, an ancient and oppressive autocracy, had become the bivouac of a new group of rulers more ruthless and ambitious than the Tsars and their secret police. George Bernard Shaw's maxim that revolution never lightens the burden of tyranny, but only shifts it to another shoulder, proved true in this instance. Modern dictatorship coupled with a goal of world revolution and international communism gained the apparatus of the Russian state. The new Soviet rulers proceeded to smash institutions, strike down liberties, enslave thought, liquidate detractors, persecute groups, denounce the slightest deviations, and spread subversion amid the wreckage of Europe and across the world.

The incendiary doctrines of Marx had long been shouted in Europe and, to some extent, in the United States. Now Lenin gave them currency. By 1920 European systems of government and economics had been taken to test depths, where they were subjected to stresses that tried every vulnerable fitting. Communism flooded some areas and threatened others. In March of the year before, the Third International in Moscow had drawn up plans to promote civil war and world revolution. Governments of capitalist states and their economic systems were marked for the wreckers. High on the list of those to be subverted was the United States.

Legionnaires from the first were relatively well informed by their organization of these facts. They could also see enormous quantities in aid flowing to Europe to alleviate conditions that communism fostered. Furthermore, American antipathy toward Marxian doctrines existed long before the war. From the turn of the century the Socialist Party, whose platforms reflected the doctrines of Marx and the ideals of a social revolution and whose membership included many foreign-born, was led by naturalized citizens of Russian, Austrian and German origin. In 1905 extreme revolutionary labor leaders established the Industrial Workers of the World (IWW), in part against the American Federation of Labor and the concept of collective bargaining and in part for "one big union" that would seize the means of production by direct action and destroy capitalism by illegal methods. Communists and syndicalists thus set a course away from the more moderate, constitutional policies of the Federation and Samuel Gompers. Syndicalists, who had been active in the West in the Western Federation of Miners and then in the IWW, directed their appeals to unskilled laborers, who were largely unassimilated immigrants. Their doctrine was founded on the assumption that the workman was entitled to the entire product and that to gain this entitlement, direct action to make capital untenable was required. Engaging in sabotage while drawing wages was considered effective. The IWW under "Big Bill" Haywood proposed to "take possession of the earth and the machinery of production and abolish the wage system" by employing "direct action," that is, violence, sabotage and the general strike. For seven years the IWW spattered the West with strife, then organized foreign laborers in Lawrence, Massachusetts, and called the bloody general strike in that city in 1912. About this time structural steel workers in California attempted to wreck *The Los Angeles Times* with a bomb. Radical labor elements took a punishing blow when the accused brothers McNamara changed their plea to guilty and some thirty-eight labor chiefs were convicted as accomplices in the conspiracy. Public opinion against radical movements was strengthened when several persons were killed by a bomb that exploded during a parade at San Francisco favoring national preparedness.

Socialists, meeting on April 7, 1917, declared American entry into the war a "crime" which they would defy by "continuous, active and public opposition." Congress responded to the possibility of unbridled defiance and widespread sabotage and subversion with the series of acts already mentioned. Besides German activities, the anti-war pronouncements and activities of many socialists, syndicalists, anarchists, and communists were deemed a clear threat. The actions of many alien radicals in the labor movement during the war who were attracted to syndicalism and to communism led to violence, wrecking of property and revolutionary talk. This aroused the public against labor's objectives and served to place industrial leaders at a fearful advantage. Samuel Gompers and his AF of L with other conservative labor groups, however, adopted a manifesto "to stand unreservedly by the standards of liberty and the safety and preservation of the institutions and ideals of our republic." A month later the United States was at war backed by these labor organizations representing three million members. Subsequently a minority of socialists left the party to become active in supporting the war and interpreting its issues to aliens.

Unrest and turmoil increased following the Armistice fed by dislocations and the wrench of readjustment. Dissatisfaction and disillusionment stirred numerous Americans. To many intellectuals, accustomed to taking their cues from Europe, it became fashionable to sit about exalting the great experiment in Russia and ridiculing American ways. Intrigued by the Soviets' seizure of power, blind to the underworld character of communism, they toyed with the theories of violent mass action. To many "parlor pinks" modern revolution was perhaps an amusing academic exercise. Their behavior over decades, however, is symptomatic of dreadful maladies—intellectual myopia and irresponsibility. Dedicated communists smiled but they did not toy. Talk was useless without action; theories, pleasant nonsense without the commission of subversion, incitement of violence and attacks on constitutional authority. These were legitimate measures in serving as history's henchmen.

The more subtle techniques of international communism were in a development stage in 1919. In the United States an assortment of groups pursued their particular interpretations of "the class war," the aims of Soviet Russia and the cause of world revolution. The IWW was a ready-made movement responsive to direction from what was termed "bolshevism." International communism chose this strange assortment of malcontents to exploit unrest and to trigger the violence deemed essential to class war. It was naïvely hoped that a take-over of the labor movement was possible, accompanied by the spread of discontent and grievances, a paralyzing succession of strikes, and the inevitable overthrow of government. Returning soldiers and sailors, demoralized, embittered and faced by unemployment, would provide strong arms and the steady nerve required for the bloody work of revolution. All but a fraction of America's fighting men, however, returned with their patriotism strengthened. Many were in The American Legion.

The American Legion's strong and constructive resolutions in 1919 were spurred by numerous considerations. Through the year violence, terror and subversion were not confined to the IWW, and many crimes went unsolved. In April a bomb was found in Seattle's Mayor Ole Hanson's mail. He had been a strong foe of communist activities in Seattle, where the communists fought to control the municipal government. Next day a bomb addressed to Senator Thomas R. Hardwick, Chairman of the Immigration Committee of the Senate, blew off the hands of a servant in Atlanta. Sixteen parcels spotted by a clerk in New York found to contain bombs were addressed to Attorney General Palmer, Postmaster General Burleson, Judge Landis, Justice Holmes, Secretary of Labor Wilson, Commissioner of Immigration Caminetti, J. P. Morgan, John D. Rockefeller, and other government officials and industrialists. All told, 32 such packages were turned up. A few weeks later several bombs exploded, one in front of Palmer's Washington residence, blowing a man to pieces—possibly the bomber.

As special assistant to the Attorney General, J. Edgar Hoover prepared a legal brief on the newly formed Communist Party and Communist Labor Party based on quantities of evidence. It concluded:

> These doctrines threaten the happiness of the community, the safety of every individual, and the continuance of every home and fireside. They would destroy the peace of the country and thrust it into a condition of anarchy and lawlessness and immorality that passes imagination.

Hence, there was some foundation for what has come to be called "the Red Scare" by scribblers and even historians who find it difficult to resist, or convenient to use, a label. Radicals, of course, have encouraged this fraudulent characterization of a "national state of mind." The hysteria attributed to the American public by observers, particularly foreign, applied to a minority. There has always been a more responsible and more influential group that has not flayed out indiscriminately, nor closed the shutters of its mind. The American Legion in 1919 was of the latter. With a few exceptions at the local level, the Legion has fought communism in telling ways from its beginning, and this explains why it is so frequently marked for destruction by the minions of Moscow.

It is important to underline, therefore, that first Armistice Day in the Legion's history when, as a Legionnaire observed a few days later, "the leaven of sanity followed the cowardly shooting."

9

The First Obligation
and Early Development

ALVIN OWSLEY after his term as National Commander in 1922–23
described the objectives of Legionnaires through an apt parallel with the lasting contribution of Roman soldiers:

> They pacified whole peoples and subdued the civilized world.
> And yet today the very localities of most of their battles are
> unknown, and the nations they conquered are free and have
> forgotten them. The work of their swords is undone. It is the
> work of their spades that survives. The work of the humble en-
> trenching tool has outlasted that of the spear and the terrible
> short Roman sword. . . . Where a legion was encamped, there
> came peace and order and security. Farmers and tradespeople
> sought the shelter of the Roman law, within those sanctuaries.
> . . . These ordered camps were the origins of some of the proud-
> est cities of the Europe of today. It is a curious thought, that the
> works of war have gone down while the less considered labors
> of the soldiers in time of peace have endured and flourished
> wonderfully. . . . The sword casts a glamour over men's minds.

The American Legion's early growth cannot be attributed to any
one individual or any small group of dynamic personalities, since it
arose from the impersonal strength of principles and purposes served
by tens of thousands. It was fortunate, however, that its early leaders
were extraordinary men, capable of putting the institution they served
above themselves. National Commander Franklin D'Olier was one.

Marquis James, who worked at D'Olier's side, described him as "a quiet, serene, unruffled man with . . . an analytical mind; an admirable compromiser and conciliator; a tolerant and agreeable man, always willing to hear the other fellow's side and a wizard at converting people to his own side so adroitly that they were apt to be unaware of the change." D'Olier's judicious belief in a plural government for the Legion precluded his seeking a second term. His leadership to the second National Convention in Cleveland saw substantial accomplishments, the betterment of conditions of the disabled and needy veteran, projections of principles, the rise in the number of posts to 9,709— in every state and in 19 overseas possessions and foreign countries —and recognition by the public as an established national institution. While shaving in his hotel room in Cleveland, D'Olier gave a *Plain Dealer* reporter his definition of The American Legion: "The best insurance policy a country ever had."

The pretentious legislative program developed at the first convention as well as further organization required the talent and unstinting labor of the National Officers, their staffs and the NEC. Lemuel Bolles of Seattle, who rose from humble beginnings to prominence in the National Guard and early Legion work, undertook the task of National Adjutant. With George H. Rennick as Assistant National Adjutant and Robert H. Tyndall as National Treasurer he transfered the National Headquarters to Indianapolis. Russell G. Creviston assumed the work of Department and Post Organization, and C. F. Sheridan headed the Service Division, greatly extended its endeavors and presently turned over his work to Gerald J. Murphy of Vermont. Arthur Woods was chosen to coordinate a program for the National Americanism Commission. Other committees set to work, among them the Weekly Re-organization Committee under G. Edward Buxton; the Hospitalization Committee under Abel Davis; the Finance Committee under deLancey Kountze; and the Women's Auxiliary, War Risk, Legislative, Military Affairs, and Constitutional Amendment Committees. There were also the Board of Directors of The American Legion Publishing Corporation and a Memorial Committee for Dead in France. For a time the committee structure was in a state of flux as the young organization developed.*

A small staff operated in Washington—Thomas W. Miller, John

* Changes are reflected in the Appendix.

Thomas Taylor, Kenneth McRae, and H. H. Raegge. Taylor, who succeeded Miller as chairman a year later, when Miller entered the political wars, was a colorful, effective spokesman for twenty years, always ready to present the Legion's case, always a showman, always good copy for the newsmen. With an optimistic flair and the comfort of knowing that he served and was backed by thousands of posts, unseen in the austere corridors of Congress, Taylor, in spats and swinging a cane, confided to reporters who waylaid him after testifying at committee hearings on bills endorsed by the Legion, "The American Legion favors it. It is inevitable legislation." This, of course, was part of the game. The desperate struggles for numerous measures held imperative at Legion conventions were frequently lost or were not as successful as the Legion wished.

Raegge served with Taylor for a few years; Edward McE. Lewis for a decade; and then Francis Sullivan.

Of the urgent problems crowding Franklin D'Olier's attention he chose to strike at those of the disabled first. Their plight under existing Washington agencies had received full exposure in articles by Marquis James of the *Weekly's* staff, who described in an unexaggerated manner a situation disgraceful almost beyond belief. The performance of the Federal Board for Vocational Education, "charged with the task of rehabilitating disabled soldiers and by re-education enabling them to resume self-supporting stations in society, is a black record of broken promise and betrayal of trust" to those "who gave most and have received least" from the nation. The Board stiffened and lashed back at Legion exposures. R. G. Cholmeley-Jones, on the other hand, with an impossible task under the tardy War Risk Insurance Act suggested a conference to work with the Legion to help his Bureau of Risk Insurance achieve efficiency. There, chaos in handling claims and compensation had arisen as twenty clerks toiled under a paper avalanche in one room in the basement of the National Museum. The Bureau had expanded, but disorder remained. Cholmely-Jones considered The American Legion a constructive critic, and a December conference was convened. Legion commanders from the 48 states were summoned to the capital, and called for simplification and improvement of Federal machinery to carry out extended and enlarged benefits expeditiously.

It was clear to conferees that the first step was passage of the

Sweet Bill, increasing disability allowances and providing certain administrative reforms. But congressmen were disinterested, preoccupied with more publicized matters. The conference recessed on the second day to allow conferees to call individually on their congressmen and senators. That night, leaders of Congress gave the Legion delegates a dinner in the House basement. They did not anticipate a number of Legion guests. Raegge, who had lost a leg in the Argonne, took a streetcar to Walter Reed Hospital and returned with a number of disabled men. They occupied chairs scattered among the lawmakers and Legionnaires and, following discursive remarks by Senator Reed Smoot, "Uncle Joe" Cannon and other statesmen, chairman Miller introduced the disabled men.

The impact of their three-hour testimony (e.g. a private, his head in bandages, told of his struggle to support a wife on his allowance at $6.50 a month) cut like a torch through any reservations the congressmen may have had. They realized that the treatment afforded disabled men was intolerable. Many disabled, whose bravery and sacrifice were unquestioned, were becoming unnerved and despondent. Their plight had undermined their confidence in their government and had worn thin that essential for the good soldier and citizen alike—morale.

Within 48 hours the Sweet Bill was passed under a suspension of rules and without roll call—a procedure unused since the Civil War. Compensation of the disabled rose from a maximum of $30 to $80 a month. The Legion later obtained legislation raising vocational training allowances, an appropriation of $125 million for payment of death and disability claims and $46 million for hospital facilities. The conference's findings were also a forerunner of inspired effort the following year by the Legion under Commander Frederic W. Galbraith, Jr., which led to creation of the Veterans Bureau.

Much of Franklin D'Olier's time in 1919 was taken up by the problems of men back from the war—those experiencing the trials of returning to civilian life as well as those suffering from some type of disability. It seemed that times had not changed since the soldiers of Marlborough's armies reflected:

> When war's declared and danger's nigh
> "God and the soldier" is the people's cry,

When peace is once more made and all things righted
God is forgotten and the soldier slighted.

Sentiment among Legionnaires for some form of adjusted compensation grew after Minneapolis when Congress failed to enact one of some fifty-four bills before it. In February the NEC adopted a resolution, drafted by Fred M. Alger, Thomas Lee and Kenneth McRae, calling for a $50 bond for each month of service. Commander D'Olier directed a Committee of Nine headed by A. A. Sprague to meet in Washington. There D'Olier presented a tentative program to the House Ways and Means Committee to give veterans the following choice:

1. Land settlement
2. Aid in the purchase of homes
3. Vocational training
4. Bonds

Immediately, the proposal was subjected to searching debate. D'Olier questioned departments, and, subsequently, the special committee outlined the provisions incorporated in the Fordney Bill—$2 for every day of service for the home option and $1.50 for the other three. The NEC favored the bill 47 to 5. Now the issue became a leading domestic question, characterized at the time and in history as the "bonus fight," a term that still grates many Legionnaires.

Commander D'Olier, a wealthy Philadelphia businessman himself, led the organization against the enormous prestige and open attack of many of his friends on Wall Street who charged that the bill would "wreck the Treasury." But he countered, saying the Treasury would hardly topple from an expense comparable to three more weeks of war, that adjusted compensation for fighting men who drew monthly pay that a shipyard worker could earn in a day was eminently just. D'Olier withstood tempting offers and subtle pressures. An expensive attempt by financiers to discredit the Legion by forming a veterans' organization with the slogan "No bonus" failed. Former soldiers, sailors and Marines would not marshal to the banner of Wall Street, nor would D'Olier salute it. And so, crossing Wall Street one day, D'Olier remarked to Marquis James, "I don't feel welcome down here any more. There are a lot of people in this neighborhood who used to think I was a pretty decent, respectable businessman who knew the rules of the game and played them. Now they treat me as if I belonged to the IWW." And so the struggle was shifted to the committee rooms of Congress. D'Olier directed Executive Committeemen to canvass their states and assemble in Washington. There a resolution urging immediate action passed 47 to 2. With John Thomas Taylor, D'Olier drove for passage before adjournment, two weeks away. Victory seemed theirs when the House passed the bill 289 to 92, but the Senate Finance Committee failed to assemble a quorum. Congress adjourned, and the 1920 skirmish died out.

It is ironic that the Legion counts among its earliest and most skillful adversaries the leaders of business and finance who charged that "Legion schemes would ruin the country" and that before and since critics and detractors of socialist and Marxian persuasion have never tired of hurling the bent and blunted barb, "tool of Wall Street," at this broadly representative organization.

By the end of his term Franklin D'Olier saw the National Headquarters well established, the Legion and its thousands of posts growing, and many programs that were only projections months before under way. He served with quiet, tireless devotion and has served as an example for most National Commanders who forwarded the Legion's many causes. D'Olier possessed a humility in the highest office Legionnaires can bestow upon one of their own. It approached self-deprecation when he explained his amusement with the high compliments he received:

They say I am a great man—imagine it—that my name will go down in history. But I always get them there. I ask them who was the first National Commander of the Grand Army of the Republic. I've never found anyone who could tell me and I've never seen it in history.

Legionnaires flocked to Cleveland for the 1920 Convention, staged a rousing red-white-and-blue parade and set to work to resolve a number of far-reaching decisions.

As with most organizations, successful handling of internal matters had assumed a vital importance for the Legion. Political endeavor in a partisan context was still widely entertained as a logical development for The American Legion as the 1920 Cleveland convention convened. Ebullience tinged with self-confidence led many Legionnaires to believe that this new power should be used to political advantage—in locker-room terms, to block supporters and blitz opponents. The brisk atmosphere of a Presidential year gave this issue a prominence that makes memorable that September gathering. Views covered a wide spectrum. On the one side, there were those who felt a liberal attitude toward partisan activity was either inevitable or desirable; on the other were advocates of an iron ban on political activity. The Charter granted by Congress describes the Legion to be non-political and requires the Legion to report annually its proceedings and financial affairs. The Constitution of the Legion determines in detail its organizational structure, eligibility for membership, restrictions on political action, discipline of members and posts, financial requirements, and the duties of officers. After delivering recommendations to which the Committee on Constitution agreed—that National Commanders and Vice Commanders be ineligible for reelection, that the National Adjutant be elected by the Executive Committee upon nomination by the National Commander, that past National Commanders be life members of the Executive Committee without vote, and that districting the country into five areas be rejected—Committee Chairman Eric Fisher Wood, haggard from debate, came before the Convention as a heated session on the "Legion and labor" question ended. He spoke slowly. The Committee had "been unable to reach accord." A majority opposed any political restrictions. A sizable minority desired an amendment or interpretation on three issues: questionnaires to political candidates, desirability of striking the words "absolutely non-political" from the Constitution, and exemption of post officers from paid elective office. Wood's final report came on the last day, after arduous committee work. Henry D. Lindsley came forward to read the majority report which had gained an impressive 33 to 3 margin. It resolved that the Legion could support and promote policies and principles within the purposes enumerated in the preamble as interpreted by acts of the National Commander, and rulings of its NEC could "ascertain for the information of its members the attitude of candidates for public office" toward those policies and principles.

James L. Boyle of Maine summed up the minority stand:

> Our constitution is brief. It says The American Legion shall
> be absolutely non-political and shall not be used for the dis-
> semination of partisan principles or for the promotion of the

candidacy of any person seeking public office. It says each member shall do his full duty as a citizen according to his own conscience and understanding. What more do we want? Our constitution says we are non-political. Go no further.

Opposition to the majority report gained ground. A question of how Legionnaires could carry out Legion policies was answered by a shout, "As citizens!" The convention voted down the majority report 963 to 142. This crucial decision, now recognized as most judicious, left some doubts. One Legionnaire wondered:

> Do not the processes we know as politics (nonpartisanship) constitute the only avenue to government? Will the Legion ultimately deal with these problems under the terms of a sort of Legion common law—unwritten—the slow crystallization of practice, custom and precedent? Or will it be a written law settled upon at one stroke by a convention resolution? Or did the stroke at Cleveland settle it for good and all? The subject has its ramifications and this writer (Marquis James) is frankly in a state of doubt.

The American Legion's proclaimed neutrality in labor disputes was reaffirmed in Cleveland. Solid backing was given the new Army plan under the Reorganization Act of 1920 with recognition that Legion efforts in maintaining the Organized Reserve and National Guard would be significant. The convention advocated consolidation of all agencies dealing with the disabled under a Cabinet officer. It forwarded the idea of a separate department for the Air Service— twenty-seven years before this became a reality. It urged deportation of aliens convicted or interned as enemies of the government during the war and enforcement of sentences of persons convicted under the draft and espionage laws. The loaded issue of Japanese immigration and naturalization was the only feature of the Americanism Committee's report that brought on debate. Reaffirmation of the Minneapolis resolution, despite New York's objections, was grounded in dark suspicions of the Japanese government's wartime activities, economic concern on the West Coast and a widely held view that the racial, religious and cultural heritage as well as the Japanese allegiances made them somehow "unassimilable."

Frederic W. Galbraith, Jr., won election as National Commander on the second ballot against Hanford MacNider, John F. J. Herbert and Arthur Woods.

Galbraith's term is notable for the great victory the Legion won in its campaign for the disabled and his administration's work for adjusted compensation legislation and the extension of the Americanism Commission's efforts regarding education, propagation of the ideals of better citizenship and immigration.

Galbraith was certain that the War Risk Insurance Bureau (WRIB), the Federal Board of Vocational Training (FBVT) and the Public Health Service (PHS) should be stripped of their responsibilities regarding veterans. He made certain the Legion played the dominant part in getting the facts to the American people and instructed the *Weekly* and his Publicity Division to disseminate information that might shake up the government bureaus. Three years after the Armistice 15,000 veterans were in hospitals and 2,500 a month were being admitted. The government had not constructed a hospital since 1919, and half the 15,000 were not in government-controlled institutions. The shattered of World War I were to be found in state and local places as well as private homes operated for a profit. Neglected and destitute, bedridden and diseased, some sought refuge in insane asylums, poorhouses and even jails. Thousands of veterans had contracted tuberculosis in giving the United States some of her most illustrious victories. Many flocked to the dry climates of the Southwest, where some were compelled to sleep in the open. These were hardly the rewards of a grateful nation.

Galbraith, as he put it, "barnstormed the country." The National Organization and Legionnaires throughout the country stirred the public and the newspapers. Gradually Galbraith's campaign gathered momentum. President-elect Harding, every Congressman and every newspaper in the United States was apprised of the situation. Galbraith saw President-elect Harding and gained a promise for action.

A national conference under Charles G. Dawes was called. Four Legionnaires—Foreman, Roosevelt, Miller, D'Olier—were among the sixteen members. After several sessions the Legion's programs prevailed. The committee recommended unification of the hospital functions concerned with veterans. It recommended that the $18,600,000 which the Legion had pushed through the previous Congress for hospital construction be allocated immediately. The President forwarded the Dawes recommendations to Congress as the Legion continued its pressure. It had the necessary bills before Congress and with the activity of every department and post this legislation was passed. The money for new hospitals was appropriated, and the Veterans Bureau was created, replacing the FBVT, the WRIB and that part of the PHS concerned with veterans' hospitalization. To date it was the Legion's greatest legislative victory and it became Galbraith's monument, for in August of 1921 he was dead.

The progress of The American Legion in the United States in November, 1920, was far ahead of veterans' groups abroad. In fact, Legion departments in other countries aided those involved in veterans' movements by providing information of Legion organization. Galbraith believed that the Legion's overseas departments carried heavy responsibilities. He pointed out that their membership must represent America and in some degree was responsible "for our national prestige abroad or our lack of it." On the previous Memorial Day Legionnaires had seen to it that the grave of every American veteran in Europe was decorated. Galbraith also spoke of a probable "Veterans' League of Nations." Allied veterans' organizations had the same idea and formed FIDAC—Fédération Inter-Alliée des Anciens Combattants.

Galbraith was four-square behind The American Legion's joining FIDAC and lived to see two Legionnaires as officials of that organization. After the British Legion had been formed, they requested Galbraith to express his views on various matters in the London *Times*. Galbraith wrote that "The American Legion feels itself closer to Europe than any other group of Americans." He also said that The American Legion hoped to be a small part of FIDAC which might become powerful "only if its motives are pure, and whose ultimate aspirations shall be to make impossible a recurrence of horror for which the heart of the world still bleeds—war."

By June 1921 extremists for disarmament were in full cry. Galbraith responded with realism, and then expressed a high idealism:

> For the United States to disarm now or at any time before other nations likewise simultaneously disarm . . . would be foolhardy and dangerous. . . . The American Legion is an institution of service and the goal of goals to which it aspires is to do something that shall make impossible a repetition of the devastating

horror of war . . . I believe the time is near at hand when FIDAC will come to enjoy the same prestige in international affairs that it is apparent to me the American Legion enjoys in American public affairs. . . .

Other commanders shared Galbraith's idealism. D'Olier and John G. Emery carried it to France a few months later and Hanford MacNider persuaded FIDAC to hold its third international conference in New Orleans in 1922, where the principles governing the world veterans' campaign for peace were enunciated.

Already influential individuals and groups sincerely questioned the Legion's wisdom in its stand for adjusted compensation, calling the bonus ill-advised. Marquis James recounted Galbraith's standard response to those who were against the bonus but whose help was desired during Galbraith's tenure.

My friend, I am not asking you to help us get the bonus. I am asking you to help us care for the men who have stood between you and your business and destruction and who are now wounded, sick and afflicted and are now without money or care. The Legion is not talking bonus now. It is talking disabled. When it gets ready to talk bonus it will not ask your help. It will not need it. But now it is talking disabled, and it does need your help and must have it.

Thus, Galbraith gained support for the Legion's first obligation. Shortly before his death Galbraith prepared a statement for the *Weekly* announcing a campaign he wished to launch on July 4:

The disabled situation is almost cleared. . . . But there remain another class of disabled, the financially disabled who have waited patiently until their physically-incapacitated buddies should be cared for. Our next great legislative effort will be for them. Our adjusted compensation measure once passed the lower House of Congress by an enormous majority. We are preparing to renew the fight for it.

Galbraith, the brilliant administrator, now told his staff to clear the decks for the compensation fight. He said, "I've been observing the opposition for a long time. Their defenses will not last for sixty days." But time ran out for Galbraith. After eight months in office Galbraith was in Indianapolis for a meeting of the Finance Committee. The automobile in which he was riding missed a turn. He was hurled from the car and was killed. Frederic W. Galbraith left an early legacy to those who followed him and to all Legionnaires. He was as close to a President as any Legion Commander and is reported to have said to President Harding, "When The American Legion believes the President, whoever he may be, to be right it will support him. When it believes the President to be wrong it will try to put him right, and failing, it will oppose him with all of the strength at its command." "Galbraith," the President replied, "I can understand that sort of language. I think we will get on well together."

Galbraith's abiding conviction has been evident in other commanders since, when The American Legion has taken strong issue with the nation's Chief Executive. Part of his legacy is to be found too in the demanding pace that both he and D'Olier maintained and in his unqualified efforts to further the convention mandates of the representatives of every post.

John G. Emery was the unanimous choice of the NEC to carry on as National Commander. He was compelled to pick up the continuity of both the executive operation Galbraith had worked out in New York and the administrative organization under Bolles in Indianapolis. There was remorseless demand for his attention in the nation's capital, where opponents of the Legion's programs perhaps saw an opportunity for procrastination in the days after Galbraith's death. Emery quickly realized that Congress was delaying passage of the Sweet Bill to put off the battle over compensation, and he instructed Chairman Gilbert Bettman of the Legislative Committee to drive for the McCumber Bill, the compensation measure in the Senate. Now the opposition swung into action, led by the U.S. Chamber of Commerce. Apparently, the President had second thoughts about the compensation measure, for when it seemed that the McCumber Bill was certain of passage, the Senate received the "wreck the Treasury" letter of Treasury Secretary Mellon. Though filled with sonorous platitudes and inconsistencies, the Administration's will doomed the bill.

When it was certain that the disabled legislation would be enacted and that adjusted compensation would have to await another Congress, Emery made the pilgrimage to Europe, discussed in a later chapter. He returned to face the staggering problem posed by 800,-000 veterans without work. He assembled a committee under Roy

Hoffman which evolved constructive measures for departments and posts to use in their areas.

The third National Convention at Kansas City is remembered as a great spectacle of a hundred bands, the Meuhlebach and Baltimore Hotels transformed into barracks and billets, of parades and dancing, and the warm spirit of camaraderie that has become the hallmark of Legion conventions since. The convention was distinguished and Americans touched by the words of some of the famous soldiers and sailors of the Great War. Legion speakers according to the *Weekly* included:

> Foch, head of the military coalition that crushed the German war machine; Beatty, admiral of the British Grand Fleet; Diaz, generalissimo of the Italian armies and savior of Italy; Jacques, hero of heroic Belgium; Pershing, commander-in-chief of the A. E. F.; Rodman, admiral of the American naval forces in British waters; and Lejeune, head of the United States Marine Corps and sometime commander of the Second Division. . . .

All stirred the delegates, the foreign commanders expressing deep admiration and appreciation for the U.S. Armed Forces' role during the war. "Italy remembers and appreciates," said Diaz as he urged a closer understanding of the world's veterans. Jacques thanked America for what she had done for Belgium before 1917 and for the services of her troops and the friendship of her veterans. Foch, Marshal of France, was a legendary figure. He was met first with silence and then, as his horizon-blue-clad figure briskly stepped to the platform, by rolling salvos of applause. After giving a concise summary of the American war effort, he said:

> As for me, the great honor of my life will be to have guided along the road to victory the American Army of 1918, which was a true "Grand Army," beginning with its Commander.

If Foch's remarks sounded like a field order, they were greeted with enthusiasm. Now the simple words of Pershing and Lejeune touched the heart of every delegate and the hundreds of thousands around the country who read them. Both were noted as officers who "knew their men." They showed that they had survived the tumult and acclaim of victory in a manner befitting soldiers of this Republic. They had been leaders in a democratic army and they spoke to a democratic audience. They still knew their men. Pershing said to the former soldiers, sailors and Marines, "Today I am an ordinary buddy of the rear rank." Lejeune regarded the assembled Legionnaires with a flinty glance, looked down at his notes and in his characteristically blunt manner said that he had three claims to fame. He was a Marine. He had commanded the 2nd Division. He was a member of The American Legion.

The more than a thousand delegates at Kansas City deliberated long and hard. The convention reiterated its stand on adjusted compensation, asking that "Congress pass this measure without further equivocation or delay." It expressed gratitude over the creation of the Veterans Bureau and demonstrated that it did not consider that the mere passage of legislation was enough. As it has done throughout its history, the Legion manifested an abiding concern with programs, policies and national postures it has had a hand in shaping. The convention resolved that there should be no interference with the Committee of Hospital Consultants, headed by Dr. William Charles White, which had the authority to carry out the hospital program. It also resolved that the Legion "must be continually on guard to prevent any attempt to interfere with the work of the new Veterans Bureau by political interference."

Its strong positions on national defense are considered in a later chapter. Finally, the leadership of the Legion went to Hanford Mac-Nider. Another crucial year lay ahead.

The Green Years

10

Through Anxious, Haphazard and Prosperous Times

Fᴿᴏᴍ a distance of four decades a certain perspective is gained of a time in American history that has been stereotyped and extravagantly described for years—the 1920's. While there are elements of truth in the popular image, the 1920's were years of pronounced contrasts and a wide variety of thought, behavior, economic condition, regression, and progress.

For most Americans the 1920's was not a period of wild parties, bathtub gin, speakeasies, playing the stock market, living in Jimmy Walker's New York, growing a beard on the Left Bank, or even going to a football game in a raccoon coat, although more Americans than ever before acquired the means and inclination to do so. Most Americans remember the 1920's as a quieter time although they vicariously shared the lives of a great many people who are so closely identified with that decade. Accomplishment and achievement and hero-worship were all present in the 1920's. An aura surrounds those ten years, setting them apart. Many things were done on a big scale from business ventures to baseball, from automobile production to Lindbergh's flight, from wholesale violation of the law to transgression in public office, from making fortunes to going broke.

Americans turned away from Mr. Wilson's political party, not because they were strongly against the League of Nations but because they were weary of great causes, both foreign and domestic. Before European politicians revealed their complete cynicism and their de-

vious ways, perhaps a majority of Americans were for joining the
League. They soon realized that American statesmen were no match
for the vindictive and practiced politicians of other great powers.
European leaders were impatient with the American President, for he
had listed a large number of ideals for which good men should strive
but offered little in the way of practical implementation.

The American public had shared Wilson's idealism but now it was
weary from emotional strain and the production of the huge quantities of matériel that had disappeared in the furnace of European
war. Government regulations and restrictions had worn its withers
raw. It would not be put back in the traces of domestic progressivism.
And it would not be saddled with world responsibility.

Change was inevitable. The public turned to the more benign Republican Party under Warren G. Harding and Calvin Coolidge and
got back to the business of continuing the advances of science and
technology. Quickly, inventories were piled up, and then there was a
setback. The long passage of months in which American business
wallowed in the doldrums lasted for two years, from 1921 to 1923.

The industrial recession imposed terrible uncertainty and hardships upon unemployed veterans. In 1921 every sixth man who had
served in the Armed Forces was without work. The American Legion
undertook promotion of local and state efforts to alleviate the situation but to little avail. Its posts maintained employment bureaus
and established messes and barracks for the hungry and homeless. By
early 1922 Commander Hanford MacNider had devised a nationwide
campaign which would be inaugurated on a specific date, designated
as American Legion Employment Day. Community meetings were
to pledge to care for their own. Legionnaires persuaded governors to
issue proclamations, mayors to call meetings and a score of national
organizations, including the Chamber of Commerce, Kiwanis and
Rotary Clubs, and the YMCA, to induce their local units to join
the drive. The simple slogan, "The community cares for its own,"
worked. On March 21, the day after the drive began, reports flowed
in from every state. The Ford Motor Company increased its work
force 20 per cent and other large employers did similar hiring. In
three weeks half a million men were back at work and trade indications reflected a healthier economy.

As the Legion gained early strength, detractors and radicals attempted with some success to label the Legion "anti-labor." Strike-breaking in which ex-soldiers and sailors participated did occur in the early 1920's when the specter of unemployment haunted street corners. On this matter, as with the subject of partisan politics, The American Legion was firm from the beginning. D'Olier had said:

> The attitude of the American Legion towards Organized Labor is exactly the same as its attitude towards all groups of American citizens who are interested in a square deal for all, in the maintenance of law and order, and the protection of the institutions handed down to us by our forefathers.

Cordial relations existed between Samuel Gompers and William Green of the AF of L and Legion leaders, including Galbraith, Mac-Nider and Alvin M. Owsley. Still, the anti-labor story persisted. In isolated instances posts joined with local authorities to avert local civil war. For example, when the UMW sought to organize the open-shop counties in West Virginia, the Raymond Nowland Post resolved that its members unite with the constituted authorities to preserve order and to repel an invasion of Logan County by a mob armed with machine guns, rifles and pistols. MacNider repeated the Legion's position toward labor, and Gompers responded:

> That the pleasant relations between the Legion and the AF of L be extended to every post and local union of both organizations is my earnest and sincere wish.

The affair mentioned above was distorted and used in certain notorious accounts of the Legion to slander, vilify and abuse an organization which the authors felt was gaining stature in the country. Their scribblings galled Legionnaires, among them men from the ranks of organized labor. Some posts were made up almost exclusively of labor men. If an organization's strength can be measured by its enemies, The American Legion at this time was a force to be reckoned with. It had a wide assortment of critics. Some said, "There is no need of such an organization now that the country is entering the era of peace." Some feared that the Legion might become a powerful political force in a party or partisan sense. And there was vicious denunciation from a wide band on the political spectrum which included a growing number of pacifists, misinformed liberals, the legitimate intellectual radicals, a mongrel lot of communists, fellow travelers, and a handful of terrorists.

For a time patriotism had held revolution in various parts of the world in abeyance. American radicals and revolutionaries became a problem soon after Russia pulled out of the war and were most active in the early 1920's. As the recession lengthened there was considerable unrest and already some intellectuals were hooting and hollering from Europe. Most Americans, however, stayed on the job at home. Legionnaires faced too many hard problems in their personal affairs and those of their less fortunate comrades to despair or take very seriously the rising clamor from the sidelines in Europe.

It is sometimes refreshing to return to remarks from American history which reflect the finer qualities of our people. Such are the sentiments Lincoln set down as his train rocked toward Gettysburg in November of 1863:

> It is for us, the living, rather, to be dedicated here to the unfinished work which they who fought here have thus far so nobly advanced. It is rather for us to be here dedicated to the great task remaining before us—that from these honored dead we take increased devotion to that cause for which they gave the last full measure of devotion; that we here highly resolve that these dead shall not have died in vain—that this nation, under God, shall have a new birth of freedom; and that government of the people, by the people, for the people, shall not perish from the earth.

In his Second Inaugural, Lincoln spoke quietly of caring "for him who shall have borne the battle and for his widow, and his orphan. . . ."

It is well to remember in considering any period of American life that there have always been men who have remained true to their heritage and have exemplified these finer qualities by their works.

The American Legion continued to direct enormous effort to rehabilitation and other tasks. Even with the creation of the Veterans Bureau and the appropriation for hospitals, the Legion soon discovered that its purposes were being undermined by the Treasury Department and President Harding's personal physician, Dr. Charles E. Sawyer, who regarded the expenditure as a waste. A third of the disabled were being "farmed out" to private and public institutions "at so much per head." Under this contract system certain states and private individuals were making a tidy profit in caring for disabled men. Half the patients with mental afflictions were to be found in ordinary madhouses under custodial care. A distinguished specialist, Dr. Thomas W. Salmon, observed that hundreds were doomed to "irretrievable insanity" unless conditions were improved.

And so the Legion went back to Congress and obtained seventeen million dollars for the Veterans Bureau with which it was cooperating. Although Sawyer, whom the President had appointed to head the Federal Hospitalization Board, promised to improve hospital facilities, angry Legionnaires at New Orleans in 1922 voted to censure him, although some of their leaders were more diplomatic and cautioned against this move. While President Coolidge did not remove Sawyer in 1923, in December, with the agreement of Sawyer, he announced commencement of a program for twelve thousand hospital beds for the disabled. A year later Gen. Frank T. Hines succeeded Forbes as head of the Veterans Bureau. The Legion established a Service Division at its National Headquarters to handle individual cases, but the real work—the contacting of disabled men—was done at the post level. Volunteer service received aid and direction from fourteen full-time Legion employees who worked in the areas served by the fourteen regional offices of the Veterans Bureau.

In 1921 the Committee on Rehabilitation of Veterans assumed all services for the disabled, replacing the earlier Hospital Committee under Abel Davis. Albert A. Sprague, Davis, John M. Dickinson, Jr., and Joe Sparks contributed to the committee's success. In 1923 Watson B. Miller became its chairman and served until 1941. Miller and his associates perfected the organization and became highly expert in this neglected field. He recruited some of America's most brilliant medical minds to contribute their knowledge and understanding. Without pay they assisted his staff, already well versed in clinical procedure, pathology and causative determination. The Legion's nationwide organization included hundreds of capable men serving on post rehabilitation committees, giving direct aid to the disabled and making known the importance of the whole problem to the American public. This large effort fell under five regional committees, a committee of consultants, a field service, and a Washington office under the National Rehabilitation Committee.

The tangle of laws surrounding disability received early Legion attention, not only by providing legal advice without charge to thousands of veterans, their widows and their orphans, but by working with the Veterans Bureau in the codification of laws, the simplification of the administration and, in 1923, in urging that each House of Congress establish a Veterans Committee. Miller and Edward McE. Lewis of the Legislative Committee worked with Senator David Reed and Representative Royal Johnson, both Legionnaires, and with their opposite numbers on the Democratic side, Walsh and Rankin, in gaining passage of the World War Veterans Act of 1924. The new code liberalized the law particularly with regard to presumption of service origin for TB and neuropsychiatric disorders and granted general hospitalization rights to all veterans. The Bureau could now decide whether a veteran was entitled to compensation. The Legion received a request from the President after its San Francisco conference in 1923 for a "bill of particulars" about what the disabled needed. Commander John R. Quinn presented a careful paper to Coolidge, who transmitted it to Congress with his approval. Over the years the law was strengthened. Each year Congress entertained Legion suggestions, with representatives introducing bills and calling hearings of the Veterans Committee to which Legion leaders and expert witnesses presented their views. The procedure was conducted before Reed's subcommittee in the Senate as well. The Veterans Bureau, the Pension Office and a number of hospitals serving soldiers of earlier wars were finally merged to create the Veterans Administration. By 1940 the VA operated ninety-two hospitals with about seventy thousand beds and reasonably efficient management.

Compensation "for loss of earning power," established in 1917, received considerable attention in the post-war years. After much wrangling over this difficult problem, ratings came to be based largely on medical determination. Wide discrepancies arose. For example, certain "dead beats" managed to fake a condition before a medical board whereas certain others with legitimate, service-connected disability might receive very little by way of compensation. The problem was an insoluble one although great improvement came in time as medical boards standardized their procedures. Of course, the honorable title "veteran" will always be somewhat besmirched by individuals looking for a free ride—a dishonest claim against the government at the expense of fellow citizens, former comrades and their own self-respect.

The Vocational Training Program was another matter. Some 129,000 veterans received training at an expense of about three-quarters of a billion dollars. It was a hard lesson, not lost upon those who later would make provision for another generation of service people.

Earlier pages have described the background of the adjusted compensation struggle which was to require some of the energy of the Legion for many years. For two decades the Legion fought what is now popularly called "the battle for the bonus." As with other Legion undertakings, the large decisions and broad strategy of that fight were decided by the representative National Conventions. Once in the knock-down, drag-out fight, Legionnaires might have broken contact with their adversaries any number of times. Believing in the essential justice of adjusted compensation, they never faltered. They won their fight against four Presidents, against a Secretary of the Treasury, the banking interests, against the U.S. Chamber of Commerce, the NAM, and a host of organizations, societies and individuals, some intent upon discrediting the Legion. Many Legionnaires did not favor the bonus and the bonus fight did not consume more than a limited part of the organization's energies. Many Legionnaires felt that the bonus fight damaged the organization, and unquestionably it did in some quarters. But the many people who today link the Legion with the word "bonus" and robust conventions draw their information and intelligence from shallow sources. There will always be in any nation the vast army of the misinformed.

Legionnaires not only won the battle for the bonus but, through it, gained a very thorough knowledge of how to win hard legislative victories. It learned the many techniques required to enact laws. It gained from experience the essential skill of political infighting, the power of publicity and the bare-knuckle tactics needed to prevail against certain enemies. And it learned about its friends and its own weaknesses.

By March 1920 the Legion's position had taken three forms—the "leave it to Congress resolution," the fifty-dollar-bond-per-month resolution by the NEC and the Four-Fold Bill, discussed earlier. Neither party endorsed the bonus in 1920. The lines were finally drawn for decisive legislative battle after the House again passed the adjusted compensation bill in 1921. Serious objections were leveled at the bill by responsible men, including Legionnaires. The national debt stood at $30 billion and a cash bonus would add another $3 to $4 billion. Opponents, led by Treasury Secretary Mellon, and President Harding's special message asking that the bill be recommitted to the Finance Committee buried the bill for that session. When Congress voted a billion dollars for farm aid and granted a half-billion dollar loan to the railroads, Legionnaires knew that this was ammunition for the next engagement. They had won the National Defense Act in the 1920 Congress and the Veterans Bureau reorganization and the hospital program in 1921. With more veterans elected to Congress they were ready for fray.

In 1922 the bonus became a national issue. After much debate the Ways and Means Committee amended the Four-Fold Bill by making the adjusted service certificates take the form of a paid-up insurance policy which would have a loan value after two years, requiring no immediate cash outlay by the government. Secretary Mellon, who had anticipated a deficit of $24 million, gave the Legion an opening when a surplus of $313 million appeared on June 30. The bill passed the Senate 47 to 22 and went to the White House. Harding, who had been noncommittal, vetoed the measure, but the House overruled the President 258 to 54. Two-thirds of the Senators were needed to overcome the veto, but the vote was 44 to 28. Twenty-four senators were "incapacitated" or chose to evade the vote. The Legion had lost another round.

Many angry delegates who assembled in New Orleans had trouble digesting the French dishes, so bitter and upsetting was debate in committee rooms. They voted to carry forward the campaign and then turned to other pressing resolutions. Now the votes for and against the bill in the Senate were publicized in Legion circles and a number of anti-bonus senators were beaten. The Legion's national legislative staff and thousands of posts were learning the business of practical politics. No action was taken in the short session of Congress in 1923 and Commander Alvin Owsley, a fighter, was compelled to leave the unfinished struggle to his successor, John Quinn. A special committee headed by John R. McQuigg was to wage the fight in Washington alongside the urbane John Thomas Taylor. Legislative

Chairman Aaron Shapiro ordered Taylor to clear all contacts in Congress through himself, and internal strife arose when the committee backed Taylor. Quinn made peace, and under McQuigg the open-battle plan was launched. Harding's forecast of a $650 million deficit proved to be $960 million in error. The House passed the bonus bill for a fourth time in March, 1924. The Senate passed the bill in May, and the President promptly vetoed it. Finally, the House overruled the veto 331 to 87, and the Senate, 61 to 27, with eight absentees, in May 1924. Four years after the fight had been joined, the Legion won adjusted compensation.

In retrospect, the Legion both gained and lost prestige in the battle. Many Legionnaires have resented the coupling of the Legion with the bonus by writers from that day to this. Legionnaires could draw comfort from the probability that many subsequent programs had easier going because the Legion had demonstrated its power. The spleen of its enemies would not have been checked had there been no bonus fight. There would have been another *cause célèbre*.

While congressmen and senators in Washington ruminated, The American Legion was not idle in the states. A Legion success came in California where it gained comprehensive veterans' assistance in 1921. For servicemen whose education had been interrupted the state allotted half a million dollars, and its doughboys achieved a higher scholastic standing than their fellow students. California's experiment was a forerunner of the Legion's great triumph twenty-five years later—the GI Bill.

Legionnaires were not immune to the opinions held by the general public on aliens and immigration. The war had inflamed hatreds and suspicion that only time could dispel. Legionnaires felt a strong, righteous disapproval of aliens' avoidance of military service. Of the 7,000,000 aliens in the United States in 1917, 2,000,000 were of military age. Only 155,000 became naturalized citizens by military service. Legionnaires had seen almost that many of their comrades cut down in the war and several times as many return as cripples. It is not difficult to understand their feelings. Add to this the knowledge that while men who had fought returned to the United States only to join the ranks of the unemployed, aliens who had "sat out the war," claiming nationality of the imperiled countries for which the doughboys had fought, were generally well off and gainfully employed. Legionnaires held that first-paper aliens who had refused to serve in uniform on the grounds that they held another nationality lacked an essential qualification of citizenship—military service in time of emergency by the citizen. Then, too, there were aliens who were prominent in the post-war wave of strikes and violence. Screening of those who poured into the United States left much to be desired. Seditious intentions, criminal background and devotion to revolutionary concepts were not checked as thoroughly as physical health at points of departure. The flood since 1917 had doubled the alien population by 1920. It seemed to Legionnaires that assimilation required more attention, and at their conventions they not only advocated stemming immigration but advanced highly constructive measures to naturalize the foreign-born already here. As early as 1919, posts in such places as Stockton, California, fought to obtain citizenship papers for veterans when the U.S. Naturalization Examiner had denied them. Posts established naturalization classes and encouraged aliens to become citizens. Some held warm ceremonies for successful students.

Responsible Legionnaires recognized that there are legitimate means to work toward peaceful change in constitutional democracy. When five socialist members of the New York State Legislature were expelled in 1920, Theodore Roosevelt, Jr., vociferously objected and defended the constitutional right of these men to represent their constituents. He agreed with former Justice Charles Evans Hughes, who declared:

> This is not, in my judgment, American government. . . . I count it a most serious mistake to proceed not against individuals charged with violation of law, but against masses of our citizens combined for political action, by denying them the only resource of peaceful government; that is, action by the ballot box and through duly elected representatives in legislative bodies.

In the early 1920's the Legion despaired of assimilating certain nationalities. This was a reflection of feelings generated in the war, particularly against individuals who were believed to entertain radical philosophies originating in Germany, eastern Europe and Russia. It also applied to Oriental races, particularly the Japanese. Kaiser Wilhelm's long tirades about the "yellow peril" had had some effect, and events surrounding the Zimmermann telegram from the German Foreign Minister to his Ambassador in Mexico suggesting that Mexico be encouraged to attack the United States if the United States entered the war against Germany were magnified into a complicated scheme which included "a Japanese invasion" of American territory. There were also economic reasons for Japanese exclusion in the West. Japanese were highly competitive, highly efficient farmers, and a large increase in their numbers was regarded as a threat to native American farmers in western states. Japanese in America chose or were compelled to live apart. Few of the older members of families sought citizenship and taught their young people Japanese customs, language and traditions.

Today we see more clearly, from the elevation gained by time and strengthened ideals, that notions of half a century ago were in error. The myth that the Japanese race was inherently inassimilable is now made doubly absurd as we realize that the Japanese are among the most adaptive races in the world and have gradually taken on the forms of constitutional democracy. Most important, Americans of Japanese ancestry have been among the most steadfast of our troops in recent wars.

If the Legion at first adopted resolutions that now seem unrealistic they were based on convictions that had a foundation in erroneous ideas. Also, the economic problems following World War I did not appear to recommend an unrestricted influx of foreign groups. Jobs were scarce, and the eventual prosperity that included labor was in part attributable to immigration laws that the Legion supported. There were some areas of growing distress away from the farm. For example, around the pits in the great coal-producing areas machines and falling prices cut back the work force from half a million to a hundred thousand. Over two thousand men perished in the mines each year. A mournful ballad describes the conditions and plight of these Americans: "The dangers are many, the pleasures are few. . . . It's dark as a dungeon way down in the mine. . . ." Already strikebreakers and gunmen of the operators fought against union organizers, and miners found a champion of Old Testament proportions with a thundering command of language and a granite-hewn face—John L. Lewis. But in the 1920's the miners' lot was a hard one, and it has been said that for them the 1930's was a case of "the bottom falling out of the bottom."

As the 1920's progressed, labor was to share in prosperity, although its history during the decade is a checkered one. Unionism declined and this brought shouts of protest from union officials. Yet the workingman enjoyed a 26 per cent rise in his real earnings. Businessmen and industrial leaders did gain the upper hand and many saw fit to undermine the cause of organized labor, frequently with various profit-sharing arrangements and other benefits.

While most of the country recovered from the recession after 1923, the farmer found himself in an abiding depression. Figuratively, it was as if the strong northeast trade winds he had been enjoying had ceased altogether and only a steady offshore breeze prevailed. In the lee of the land he was becalmed. There was agricultural discontent through the Middle West and the South. One-family farms were disappearing. Mechanization and business management added to the overproduction. The farmer was a victim of his own efficiency and the genius of his country. It was at this time that a number of "solutions" were offered to solve the farmer's dilemma. George N. Peek, who sold farm machinery, trenchantly observed, "You can't sell a plow to a busted customer," and began his fight for farm parity which was to be taken seriously by the public only after the passage of some years. It is ironic that the farmer, who had contributed so much to alleviate the food shortages of the war and who had fed Europe's starving millions in its aftermath, was the inheritor of fundamental and chronic difficulties, not a participant in the great prosperity that came to others after 1923.

For years the population had been shifting from the dirt roads and plowed fields to the paved streets and crowded neighborhoods of American cities and towns. Industrial society now surged ahead, producing enormous quantities of consumer goods. Soon, Americans appeared to be more richly endowed than ever before. There was the assembly line, mass production, clattering and hum in factories across the land. Everything an industrialized society might desire seemed on the rise. There was an outpouring of automobiles, parts, electrical equipment and gadgets, heavy transportation and building equipment, and a vast array of consumer goods. There was supersalesmanship, the growth of advertising and, most important, consumers with money in the bank or satisfactory credit ratings to keep the lines moving. All this called for a boom in highway construction, real estate, and unprecedented growth in public utilities, and entertainment and recreation for millions—a motion picture and a radio industry, parks, play areas, race tracks, dance halls, and bootlegging. As the great illusions of the war slipped away or sank beneath a morass of disappointment and indifference, new illusions took their place. True, businesses failed, but with every failure there were men anxious to rent the vacated site and launch a new enterprise. The extraordinary prosperity buoyed up the people—the businessman as well as the laborer, the consumer as well as a majority of those elected to public office. Most of the public wanted as little government interference in their affairs as possible and a balanced Federal budget. The great prosperity was made possible by the swift advance of the industrial revolution in the half century after Appomattox, the abundance of the land, the resourcefulness of the people, and the ingenuity of business leadership. As national income increased nearly 40 per cent, the gross national product rose proportionately from $69 billion to $104 billion from 1921 to 1929. Capitalism, it seemed, could provide Americans with the necessities and luxuries of life and go on to supply these items in abundance to foreign markets and to needy populations abroad. For the time being at least, the Progressives and reformers had had their day. They had left their mark in many communities and in the Federal government as well, but there was the inexorable return of the old system which the "good government" disciples had temporarily displaced. The bosses received another reprieve, patronage—a new lease on life. As long as the people were happy, there was no point in disturbing the fine edge.

Meantime, the exodus of those who are remembered as the expatriots gained proportions. Europe was to know them year after year as they drifted about the continent. The American economy which they denounced and indulgent parents whose society and customs they ridiculed picked up the tab for most. There was something synthetic about these young people who wailed about their era while celebrating with the means their era provided. A few were genuine. They struggled and did tough artistic work that required strong mental backs. The times produced a creativity, originality and new vitality in all artistic forms. Innovation and dedication produced enduring novels, poetry and painting. The 1920's showed that liberty is a source of both material and artistic achievement. Profound, moving and exciting works came forward in architecture, engineering and music. The dry sonority of the jazz band influenced serious composers. Architecture and engineering, with new materials and methods in the hands of a few men with genius and many with great talent advanced a tradition of an earlier time. The creativity in all these endeavors was an American Renaissance. It glittered.

Liberty produces spiritual achievements whether from the pen of a genius composing bars of music or in the hearts of common men going about their everyday tasks in a society based on liberty under law or in a tyranny where they struggle for that liberty. Though deeming themselves spectators of a chaotic business era, the intellectuals in the United States shared the prosperity. Education turned upward—there was the expansion of universities, colleges, high schools with all the buildings and impedimenta that go with such expansion. Perhaps it would be fair to say that America, suddenly in possession of a new array of creature comforts, transportation facilities, automobiles, ideas, publications, artistic and engineering advances, faced its greatest problem in learning to get along with its new wealth and going after solutions in those areas where whole groups of individuals did not share in the material advantages of that decade. Perhaps education would provide some of the answers. And millions of conscientious men and women made it their business from one end of the country to the other to see that their children were afforded its advantages.

While most expatriots loafed, sipping absinthe, or champagne and the political philosophies of marxism and socialism, or gnawed on garlic sausage and an indigestible disillusionment with the war, mankind and modern life, carping about the drawbacks of modern America, the vast majority of Americans were living with these imperfections and some were attempting to do something about it. Legionnaires through their new organization worked for a better America. The American Legion exemplified much of the individual and group virtues upon which the strength of a Republic must rely.

Since the national organization drew its leaders, strength and mandate from, and, to a large extent, owes its image to, the tens of thousands of Legionnaires throughout the country, great importance must be ascribed to the local post and individual Legionnaire. The Legion's purpose, according to the Preamble of its Constitution, is "To inculcate a sense of individual obligation to the community, state and nation." Although many individual Legionnaires and posts were from the first engaged in a wide array of what is now regarded as Americanism activities, it was not until 1924 that the National Americanism Commission was established. In its first report the Commission identified its purpose as building nationalism and patriotism, "the undying devotion and belief" in America. Aspects of the Americanism Commission's activities having to do with communism are dealt with in later chapters. Here, its many varied undertakings that took root in the 1920's require attention, specifically those directed at youth and the community. The National Organization in the 1920's recognized the importance of solid community relations, and today it is still attempting to strengthen them, since it recognizes they will become more and more significant. The general duty set forth in the Preamble was first assigned to the Americanism Commission and a Community Betterment Division. At the grass roots, posts not only undertook activities and campaigns suggested by the National Organization but pursued programs of their own inspiration. The Legion urged posts to develop programs to advance Junior Baseball, flag education, organization for disaster relief, National Education Week, adjustment of compensation claims, and an increasing number of worthwhile activities. Posts also raised funds for selected charities by holding Legion festivals, granted use of Legion halls to other organizations, sponsored young people's dances, aided in agricultural and home economics extension work, staged entertainments, and undertook a myriad of other projects for the betterment of the communities.

In those early years before the giant earth-moving equipment and the bulldozer rumbled onto the scene, strong backs were needed in places other than on the gridiron. An Iowa post, rather than raising money, appealed for aid in manpower to build a swimming pool. One hundred and ten farmers responded and dug the hole—250 by 135 feet. Men and boys of the town built the forms and poured the concrete. Posts built Boy Scout Camps—fully equipped with kitchens, headquarters, shelters, swimming pools, and sanitary systems. Activities included donation of iron lungs, the endowment of hospital beds

and rooms, fire-fighting equipment, and drives for Christmas toys for
the less fortunate children of many communities. Posts established
airports, landscaped their town with trees and lawns, built playgrounds and camping areas, and did those many things that characterize the happy, healthy American community. The American
Legion, where it approached the fulfillment of its principles and ideals,
became a mainstay in the "good life" which American communities
enjoyed.

By 1925 the Commission had articulated its objectives more specifically and identified Americanism with good citizenship. It urged
Legionnaires to consider every statement in the Preamble to the
Legion Constitution "for herein is found the catechism of our work.
Americanism demands a vigilance and an open mind." The produc-
tive liaison with the National Education Association had its start in
1921 on the initiative of Henry J. Ryan, who had succeeded Arthur
Woods as chairman of the Americanism Commission and his successor, Alvin Owsley. It has been continued to this day with the support of the Congress of Parents and Teachers and the Department
of Health, Education, and Welfare.

To Pennsylvania posts went the distinction of initiating the School
Award Medals based on "the desire to encourage serious attitudes
among school children." The program became national in 1926 with
Auxiliary and NEA participation—honor, courage, scholarship, leadership, and service being the basis of thousands of awards to outstanding students. The first national youth program was a 1922 essay
contest with fifty thousand entries for boys between twelve and eighteen. The first prize of $750 went to Ah Sing Ching, a Hawaiian
youngster. The number of contestants grew to more than 300,000 by
1925, when the Legion decided to put the program in the hands of
departments. Ohio alone reported over 100,000 entries in 1937.

Both the Legion and the Auxiliary began to support the Boy
Scouts, the Girl Scouts, and 4-H Clubs, and numerous programs devised locally by the posts outside the national framework but of particular importance in a host of communities. After voting approval
and support of the Boy Scout movement in 1919, Legion posts began to sponsor Scout Units and, in 1922, organized guidance and
cooperation came when Scouting was included in the activities of the
Americanism Commission. Every post, district and department was

urged to appoint a Boy Scout chairman. Sponsorship involved time, talent, expense, and frequently stamina on the long hikes, and always patience. The number of Legion-sponsored units rose from 741 in 1925 to 1,500 in 1930. Where Legionnaires were successful in the Scouting movement, hundreds of thousands of boys who were to become effective citizens, many serving in the future battles to which the United States became committed, were given a deeper understanding and appreciation of what the nation not only required but deserved of them.

The Legion's feud with certain intellectuals and academic circles was inevitable when it determined to promote the teaching of more history and civics in the 1920's. These subjects were being neglected in many school systems and, by Legion standards, were poorly taught in others. Here the Legion exercised a prerogative of free institutions —to attempt to alter the situation. Many Legionnaires were disturbed at the quality of textbooks, their lack of objectivity, balance and inordinate attention to the errors and weaknesses of public men, the mistakes and injustices committed by the government, and large helpings of distortion. The dispute gained considerable proportions and it still flares from time to time. This is to be expected in a democracy where many opinions, positions and prejudices circulate and strive to gain general approval. In the 1920's and 1930's Legionnaires sometimes took questionable positions. Few would object today to the inclusion in history of the facts that Washington kept slaves, that Lincoln sold whiskey, that Hancock had some interest in smuggling, or that Andrew Jackson used profane language.

But, besides undue emphasis on such facts, in 1922 there was serious distortion of American history in textbooks. The Legion brought together 26 associations, including the AF of L, civic groups, fraternal orders and patriotic societies, to sponsor a new history textbook.

Since the American school system is based upon separation from the Federal government and is handled by state boards of education and local school boards, most Legion activity has been conducted at these levels. In thousands of communities Legion posts have worked with school boards, parent-teacher groups, school superintendents, and others to promote emphasis on the American heritage and a reasonably favorable presentation of American history. Most Legion work was on the constructive side, strengthening students' knowledge. Naturally, there have been bitter charges and recriminations between the Legion and groups highly critical of the United States, some intent upon undermining the nation's institutions and even its strength and unity.

Other activities of an educational and Americanism nature in which the Legion has been a moving force has been the promotion of CMTC and ROTC programs since 1920 against fierce opposition of groups opposed to such military training and discipline; cosponsorship of National Boys and Girls Weeks since 1928; and participation in National Music Week and, since 1927, in National Constitution Week. Among other programs inaugurated by the Legion, in cooperation with other organizations, was the Flag Code, drafted in 1923 at a conference under the direction of Americanism Chairman Garland W. Powell. After use by millions of Americans and adoption by twenty-eight states, Congress twenty years later established the Code by joint resolution in 1942. Other associations joined the Legion in celebrating Constitution Day, Army Day, Navy Day, "I Am an American Day," and the birthdays of the nation's heroes.

A National Memorials Committee of the Legion was established to arrive at policy concerning erection of appropriate monuments and other memorials. The Battle Monuments Commission, a creature of Congress, was proposed by the Legion to meet the problem of memorials to be erected in France. England and France had already enshrined an unknown soldier when Congress took action to construct the American Tomb in Arlington Cemetery. The Legion worked for the plan, took part in the burial services on Armistice Day, 1922, and subsequently proposed that a permanent sentry stand guard at the Tomb at all times.

Marquis James relates an event at the dedication of another Legion-sanctioned memorial, the austere Column in Kansas City, dedicated at the 1921 National Convention. The Disarmament Conference was being held in Washington and city fathers decided it would be dramatic to have two white doves of peace fly to Washington with a peace message. No one thought of obtaining white carrier pigeons in Washington, but two small boys trapped a pair in a Kansas City park for the purpose.

Posts promoted a host of activities that appeal to children and adults alike—fishing, marble-shooting, horseshoe-throwing, fiddling, bowling, rifle-shooting, duck-calling and cotton-picking contests, as well as athletic championships. They promoted ice carnivals, festivals and amateur and professional boxing.

Legionnaires fulfilled their high purposes as vital citizens, sometimes undertaking the sort of thing that had not been seen since the days when their communities were on the frontier—building and repairing churches and even private dwellings of persons whose homes had been lost or heavily damaged by disaster. In certain places, to meet the acute hospital needs of veterans, the Legion constructed makeshift hospitals and even completed two substantial buildings—at Kerrville, Texas, and at Battle Creek, Michigan—where states were persuaded to help with funds. The Minnesota American Legion Hospital Association was formed in 1922, and in Arizona the Legion carried a heavy share of the burden when tubercular veterans swarmed to that climate in the 20's.

Legionnaires made music, too. Their enthusiasm would have warmed the heart of Meredith Willson's Music Man—hundreds of bands and thousands of drum and bugle corps gaining esteem throughout the country and contributing much to local, state and national parades, and the now famous Legion parades at every National Convention.

At an early date the Legion felt strongly that young people should be given the benefit of healthy outdoor activities, team sports, zest for the game, a competitive edge, and the virtues of good sportsmanship. Legionnaires' objectives were several. One approach was close to that of Knute Rockne's, "If you go hunting with your boy, you won't have to go hunting for your boy." Rockne also pointed out, "I want every boy on the upbeat."

A Legionnaire recently spoke of the Legion's best-known athletic program, Legion Baseball:

> The American Legion perhaps set the pace for providing an outlet for organized play in which almost one million boys across the nation now play baseball each year under American Legion sponsorship. With encouragement and some financial support from the major leagues, The American Legion developed teams and leagues in each of the states with scheduled contests and elimination playoffs leading to a "Little World Series" which,

through the levels of state, regional, sectional and the final series, has attracted scouts from all the professional teams. While a high percentage of current professional baseball players in the major leagues have sprung from Legion-sponsored teams, The American Legion insists that its interest in Legion baseball was not to develop major league players, but rather to expose the boy to the experience of learning to play by rules, to know how to win or lose with dignity and to be receptive to the simple processes of discipline, for when the umpire says: "Strike three. You're out!" there is little chance for argument and discipline is invoked. It's the type of discipline one doesn't learn in the schools, the church, nor the home, and the boy is willing to abide by the rules. This is an approach to injecting rules of fair play and learning how to get along with others that The American Legion has adopted to pass on to the young man of the day.

However, Legion Baseball had humble beginnings. A good many returning veterans had the idea of encouraging youngsters to participate or excel in athletics in 1919. One Legionnaire who visualized Legion work in this field was George H. Maines, who spoke of the Legion's sponsorship of "a junior activities program to teach American youngsters to care for their health through sports activities." T. R. Roosevelt, Jr., at a luncheon at the St. Louis Caucus thought it "a solid Americanism program" and urged Maines to pursue the matter. The cooperation of Ban Johnson, czar of organized baseball, was obtained. Many posts began to promote Junior Baseball in their communities, for athletics were recognized from the St. Louis days to be a field in which Legionnaires could convey wholesome and instructive adult leadership in "many civic and personal values."

Affluence in all manner of athletic facilities and highly sophisticated protective equipment are made available to a large percentage of our youngsters today. In 1919 boys went forth to play as a sort of mob of young Don Quixotes. The "playing fields of America" were mostly slum lots and cow pastures. A rousing game required only a bat taped with adhesive, a beat-up ball repaired by a parent's stitching and a few enthusiastic youngsters. Many Legion posts improved these conditions.

To most boys there were players whose names were legendary. They had heard their fathers tell of them and their awesome feats on the diamond. Their names—Grover Cleveland Alexander, "Chief"

Bender, "Three Finger" Brown, and "Old Hoss" Radbourne, who pitched seventy-two games in 1884, Tris Speaker, "Cap" Anson, Napoleon Lajoie, Honus Wagner, Walter Johnson, "Cy" Young and many others—quickened the breath. Still running the baselines was Ty Cobb, fast as a barracuda, his cleats flashing through the hot summer dust toward bag and infielder. Great managers were regarded as national heroes or villains, depending upon where you lived.

The "Black Sox Scandal" rocked the baseball world in 1920. Baseball was in need of an overhaul, and stern measures were taken. Unquestionably, the interest of individual Legionnaires and the initiative of numerous posts in supporting athletic activities, including baseball, did much to afford organized baseball the opportunity to come back, almost without pause, to national prominence and respect. The game quickly recovered to experience a golden time.

In 1924 the world's largest baseball, seven feet in diameter, was rolled across the country to dramatize Legion Junior Baseball and the CMTC's. Babe Ruth participated in Boys' Day in the American League and, by 1925, 750 junior teams had been organized. Connie Mack of the Philadelphia Athletics was a staunch supporter of Junior Baseball, and in 1926 the Americanism Director, Dan Sowers, took charge of the program on a national basis. In 1928 Judge Kenesaw Mountain Landis, Commissioner of Baseball, announced that each League would give $25,000 to sponsor American Legion Junior Baseball. The Legion had received $20,000 as a share of a World Series game in 1922 when an extra game became necessary.

Later, Babe Ruth, always a backer of organized, supervised amusement for youth, felt that The American Legion "deserved a lot of credit for interesting youngsters in baseball," thus reducing juvenile crime. He wrote in 1928:

> So I decided that I'd give the Babe Ruth cup to the kid getting the most home runs during the season. I understand there will be a lot of other cups too, given by fellows like Hornsby and Cobb and Connie Mack who are just as much interested in kid baseball as I am.

He added that with The American Legion back of it the movement was "one of the greatest kid stunts that ever was thought of." By that time 5,000 teams had been organized.

With substantial achievements and numerous programs underway, the Commission reported in 1929:

> We have given a great deal of our time and spent a great deal of our money to reach the youth of our country, the youth which is always the bearer of progress and upon whom we must depend for the perpetuation of American institutions, which have done so much not only to make our nation great, but in reality to establish equality of opportunity among men.

The first twenty years of child welfare endeavor by the Legion was characterized by an individual, case-by-case approach. This was given momentum after the 1922 Convention, when Mrs. Donald Macrae, Jr., of the Auxiliary, called the attention of the delegates to the seriousness of the problem of hospitalized veterans who worried about the welfare of their families. Since The American Legion had committed much of its finances and energies to rehabilitation, until it was able to turn to this matter, the Auxiliary and the Forty and Eight were ready to take on child welfare as a primary responsibility. The National Child Welfare Commission traces its origin back to the assassinations in Centralia, Washington. The 1920 National Convention approved the recommendation for establishing a suitable memorial for the dead Legionnaires—work in the child welfare field. A temporary committee was made a permanent National Child Welfare Committee in 1924.

After a brief experiment with billets for children the Legion realized that another approach was called for, since most children of deceased veterans had a mother or some close relative who assumed a personal responsibility for them. The 1924 Convention resolved that billets should be used as "temporary clearing houses until other forms of child care could be found suited to each individual child." By 1927 Legion publicity had raised a five-million-dollar Endowment Fund. Its earnings were limited to rehabilitation and child welfare. A full-time staff commenced work in Indianapolis in 1924, and in 1925 the Legion began a program of direct financial assistance for individual children of veterans to keep families together in periods of emergency. This was a form of aid still unique in the social-work field. The Forty and Eight contributed $25,000 during the first year. As much as $90,000 annually has been spent on direct aid in the years since. With pride, the Legion feels that it has been a pioneering influence, a forerunner of state aid laws and the Aid to Dependent Children Provisions of Social Security. Through the Legion's effort other legislative gains have been achieved on the Federal and state levels. Child Welfare Director Randel Shake observed in 1960:

> With all the changes in our way of life and living, the first forty years of The American Legion's child welfare effort stand as glittering proof of a democracy's ability to move with the times and adapt its principles to needs of the day without weakening those principles.

Throughout the 1920's the American Legion Auxiliary * rose from 11,000 members in 1920 in 1,342 units located in 45 states to 331,-409 members by the end of 1929. Their endeavor was indispensable to the Legion's programs. *The American Legion Auxiliary Bulletin* commenced publication in 1927 and became the *National News of the American Legion Auxiliary* in 1936.

The stubborn question of politics persisted in the 1920's. There was some concern before the Presidential election of 1924 among Legionnaires that certain of their leaders were taking the organization close to the brink of partisan politics. MacNider was organizing the Republican Service League to campaign for the national ticket. Other prominent Legionnaires were close to President Coolidge, and Democratic Legionnaires, including George Berry of Tennessee, William Ritchie of Nebraska and William Doyle of Massachusetts wondered whether James A. Drain, candidate for the Legion's leadership, was engaged in any way with the Republican Presidential campaign. A committee visited Drain and he quickly "cleared the air."

In addresses to the National Convention public figures spoke and National Commanders conveyed the growing activities, responsibilities and problems of the organization. John R. McQuigg in 1926 reported progress in rehabilitation, child welfare, legislative activity, the growth of the Legion Endowment Fund started under Commander Drain, the favorable response to the change of *The American Legion Weekly* to a monthly publication, warned of the flood of pacifist propaganda in the country, directed attention to the importance of posts and their service to communities. This format was followed in later years at the

* Presidents of the Auxiliary are included in the Appendix.

Paris Convention, discussed in the next chapter, and when Commander Edward E. Spafford emphasized the constructive, educational aspects of Americanism in San Antonio in 1929. This reflects a growth in positive Legion action to strengthen all segments of the nation with less relative emphasis upon underlining subversive threats.

The Forty and Eight (*La Société des 40 Hommes et 8 Chevaux*) was established in the 1920's. A "fun-making body" that amused itself in a "less dignified fashion than comported with the ritual of a post meeting," its officers took French titles from the local *voiture* to its Voiture Nationale. While it was devoted to good works, its horseplay and antics at National Conventions gained headlines over the serious work conducted by Legionnaires perspiring in committee rooms and on the convention floor. This secret organization eventually became a source of some embarrassment to The American Legion. Its rules excluded the colored and Oriental races from its membership, and, as is brought out in a later chapter, this became intolerable to Legionnaires who recognized that Legion membership is composed of all nationalities, creeds and color.*

As the years of the 20's rolled on, reformers were able to work their nostrums in certain distressed areas that persisted despite opulence all around them. And when public responsibility was shamelessly neglected, there were openings for individuals with the burning urge for reform. Fiorello LaGuardia was one. A self-confident, honest and fighting administrator, LaGuardia had flown in France under Mitchell. His opportunity came after years of Jimmy Walker's casual, permissive and flamboyant exercise of the powers of mayor of New York. Amid the glitter of that vital city idle, silent men and hungry women and children still huddled. From a distance of more than a quarter of a century LaGuardia's contributions and accomplishments stand out. His high-pitched insistence that new measures for social welfare were necessary would seem rather tame today. In the 20's it was another thing. And this comic, restless and extremely able man with a penchant for preposterous hats and a zest for ridding his community of "bums, hoods, and crooks,"—in fact, the whole unsavory lot that directs and lingers on the fringes of the underworld— left his most lasting mark, a new progressivism. It included, most

---

* In 1960 the Legion severed its relations with the Forty and Eight and disavowed the organization.

important, the cultivation of an awareness in the community of the need for an alert citizenry, a distinction he shared with Al Smith, unemployment insurance, child welfare legislation, and wages and hours laws.

The boom of the 20's gradually gained a dangerous size and velocity. It was like a great ocean swell influenced by the changing moon and a prevailing wind. The expansion of the 1920's depended on the buildup of vast credit and an emotion of supreme confidence. There was widespread borrowing and alarming speculation. The fascination of taking risks, the "easy-come, easy-go" attitude were not new hallmarks of the American character. Perhaps they were always present in the swarms of people who landed on our soil in the eighteenth and nineteenth centuries. The 1920's merely gave more people a chance to express their proclivities. Debt became fashionable. And what was practiced by individuals was certainly permissible for state and local governments. Everything from automobiles and homes to roads and ornate public buildings could be handled through a bank. Thoughts of the day of reckoning were something that might disturb an occasional night's sleep, like overindulgence, a heavy meal. Speculation on the stock market became widespread and alarming without realistic controls and their strict enforcement.

As the swell of prosperity rolled toward the end of the decade, few anticipated the submerged shoals ahead. The great economic wave suddenly crested like the ocean's swell that runs toward the beach and, unbalanced, broke.

On October 29, 1929, the stock market crashed. A clanking of gates and a slamming of doors echoed in every business community. Men and women who a few days earlier were blissfully in debt were now without a job and in debt. Confidence and optimism slowly drained from the public like the contents of a cracked beaker. As we shall see, although the Administration attempted to be optimistic and industrialists and stock brokers attempted to tell the people that they were witnessing a "readjustment," the people came to regard the economy not as a temporarily bedridden patient but as a generous provider in need of intensive treatment and long convalescence. President Hoover struggled valiantly. He was no stranger to the task of dealing with poverty and suffering, but it seemed that some of the heart had gone out of the people and the habitual American asset of confidence was, for the time being, impaired. Hoover spent interminable days conferring, urging and considering. He gained enactment of legislation for the Reconstruction Finance Corporation (RFC) and the Home Owners Loan Corporation (HOLC) which were later to be effectively employed under Roosevelt.

The American Legion was to find that it faced new challenges and that several of its programs were endangered. Strange, that while the lives of most Legionnaires and most citizens were a denial of the stereotypes of the 1920's and refute the popular notion of the 1920's as a relapse into chaotic living, they were to encounter and weather the privations and hardships of the 1930's that are more accurately cast in the public mind.

11

A Decade of Declining Defense

FOLLOWING the Armistice the victors slumped back with a gasp, the words "never again" echoing in their throats. Among the Allies and Associated Powers a passion for peace took hold that could tolerate neither retention nor development of reasonable military defenses. It overwhelmed the wisdom of preparedness in Western democracies. And through the 20's and 30's a curious fever of irrational, wishful thinking sapped their resolve. While the Anglo-Saxon countries sought security by disarmament arrangements, France, haunted by the war's lacerations, fears of the future, desire to punish Germany, and longings for the goods of life, repudiated theories of the "offensive" which dominated its military thought before World War I and became captive to "defensive" or "Maginot-Line" thinking at the exclusion of any practicable, modern military planning. England commenced to "postpone" defense measures, figuring from time to time that ten years of peace lay ahead and that little need be done for the time being. The United States recoiled from the behavior of its former comrades at the peace tables, and while it fulfilled vast humanitarian and reconstruction tasks in Europe, it turned its back on its military responsibilities.

These, among other factors, were essential parts of the twenty-year tragedy between the two world wars. Few exerted their influence to check these regrettable emotions or to correct these erroneous national positions. To do so was politically unsound and invited hysterical abuse.

The American Legion chose to take an unpopular course. National

151

security became its second most important endeavor, after care of the disabled. The Legion put forward through the 20's and 30's a national defense program of astonishing perspicuity when the interminable "ifs" we are accustomed to find in most histories are considered. Indeed, our historians, sociologists and political scientists have given little if any credit to the Legion for this record of prudent, reasonable and vital activity, perhaps because so many academic men were so mistaken through the period; because some were duped by foreign propaganda; because others were among or associated with the Legion's most vicious detractors; and finally because most witnessed their sacrosanct ideas made a shambles by the second world war and its aftermath.

The American Legion assumed that there would be future wars. It held that U.S. security hinged upon strength, that should war come, strength might prevent attack, and that if attack came, preparedness would greatly reduce the toll in lives and substance. No grasp of history was needed for the returned soldier, sailor, Marine, or airman to understand that while raw courage was a fine thing, if it lacked the support of training, adequate arms, leadership, sound planning, strategy and tactics, and logistics, brave men would fall unnecessarily. Legionnaires who did not know their American history were told by their new organization of their forebears who had fought for the Republic. Since the Revolutionary War U.S. military strength at a war's onset has been of fig-leaf proportions. Hardships, death and disease from inadequate preparation had always been the American fighting man's lot—against the British in 1812, in the Mexican mountains in 1845, in 1861, when civil war confronted an army of sixteen thousand, and in the disease-ridden campaigns of 1898. Legionnaires gained their instruction in the vivid ordeal of the Western Front and the Atlantic and in other areas.

President Washington, who encountered every shade of difficulty with the Continental Army, remarked to Congress in 1790 that "to be prepared for war is one of the most effectual means of preserving peace." Some years before Frederick the Great had noted that diplomacy without arms is "music without instruments." Yet in the period between the two world wars the United States and Britain— among nations best able to find fulfillment in these proven concepts —followed a diametric course.

Legionnaires could take their lead from history and their own experience. They supported disarmament but maintained that to go below certain standards was foolhardy. They rejected pacifism when pacifism lured large and influential groups at home and abroad. Arbitration and international cooperation should be strengthened, but not at the expense of adequate defenses. Commander Franklin D'Olier emphasized in 1919:

> The question before the country is not how large an army we should provide with or without the League of Nations. Rather it relates to the size of the force to be maintained during a period of uncertainty during which we face certain known obligations and a still larger number of uncertainties.

At Cleveland in 1920 the Legion resolved a fundamental policy it was to pursue for a generation:

> The examination of young men called under the Selective Service Act demonstrated a high percentage of physical disability and also illiteracy ... indicating the necessity for a system of compulsory universal training ... we recommend the adoption by the Congress of a system of compulsory universal training, which shall include physical training, educational training, and Americanization, as well as efficient military training to form a foundation for future extended military training in time of war.

From the start the Legion was both deliberately and naïvely given the label of "militarist" by pacifists, radicals and subversives. As we shall see, the Legion fought stubbornly but unsuccessfully for its UMT program while the shouts, "Disarm!" echoed down the years, to be joined almost twenty years later by the cry, "Peace at any price!"

Immediately after the Minneapolis convention the Legion began promotion of the proven concept of reliance upon a trained Reserve and National Guard to supplement the Regular Army and insisted upon their participation in staff functions. Meanwhile the Regular Army drove for an increased peacetime emphasis upon its numbers. In Senate committee hearings staff officers presented their case. General Pershing, now returned from France, gave testimony to the facts that 95 per cent of those who led troops in France and 95 per cent of U.S. troops were citizen soldiers, that despite limited training they had performed with great distinction and that our future defense might be entrusted in part to them. The bill for a large standing army was doomed.

Members of the Legion's first Committee on Military Policy, led by Allan Tukey, gained attention on Capitol Hill. Galbraith and Foreman testified while Henry L. Stimson of New York drafted proposals for the organized Reserves and Foreman wrote clauses governing the National Guard. Two men, Sen. James W. Wadsworth and John McA. Palmer of the Army's War Plans Division, were invaluable allies. Although Palmer lost his place on the Army staff, he gained the confidence of senators, for a quarter of a century worked with the Legion on defense matters and served as a general in the second world war. Senator Wadsworth worked out a new bill on the citizen-army plan. Now it became obvious that a contest lay ahead with the Army staff, unwilling to share its planning prerogatives and backward in recognizing a broad base of readiness. Legion action offers a good example of thorough, representative and selfless effort to achieve a legislative goal, a performance that was subsequently followed in the wide variety of undertakings, both nationally and at departmental levels. A Defense Conference at Indianapolis of department representatives examined the new Wadsworth Bill line by line, then suggested changes and amendments. To relieve the first committee, on the line for weeks in Washington, Thomas W. Miller was appointed chairman of a replacement group: Wm. J. "Wild Bill" Donovan, Ranson H. Gillette and H. C. Stebbins of New York, L. R. Gignilliat, head of Culver Military Academy, H. L. Opie of Staunton, Virginia, Frank Warner of Nebraska, and Benson W. Hough of Ohio. These men appeared before both House and Senate committees through the spring of 1920. The Legion position was spread through the states by the earlier committee and other Legionnaires. Thousands of veterans wrote members of Congress regarding the measure. On June 4 it was passed into law. This legislation, hailed by the Legion as "the first military policy this country ever had," authorized a standing army of 290,000, a National Guard of close to 500,000 and a substantial Reserve, military supplies and equipment, and a first-class Navy. Annual training was to keep the Reserve forces current, and military courses in colleges were to supply young officers. Reserve and National Guard officers were to share responsibilities on the Gen-

eral Staff. The act exceeded Legion hopes, with the exception that
UMT was excluded.

But to the dismay of the armed services, The American Legion,
certain legislators, and many citizens, its promise was unfulfilled.
Congress turned to other matters and failed to appropriate enabling
funds. The summer days of peace in 1920 were beguiling. War was
becoming less real, like a wound half forgotten or a memory already
below the surface of consciousness. Peace, a return to the old, un-
complicated, happy days, a prospect of the future stretching long and
undisturbed took hold of most Americans. This did not allow for
serious attention to the possibility of future international disorder.

To avoid a monotonous recital of the Legion's stubborn struggle
to realize provisions of the 1920 act as well as others dealing with
national security and related matters and the Legion's Universal Draft
proposal, only highlights follow. When it became apparent that the
ground had been cut from under the Defense Act, the Legion attempted desperately to save its intent by shoring up the Armed Forces
and their Reserves with more modest personnel requirements—137,-
000 for the Regular Army and an increase in the air arm; a Reserve
Officers Training Corps to train 5,000 officers annually; a Citizen
Military Training Camp of 50,000; and a National Guard of 190,000,
to be increased to 250,000 by 1936. This 1924 appeal was coupled
with demands for sound procurement, development and maintenance
of matériel for these forces and a war reserve for three field armies.
In 1927 the National Convention repeated defense resolutions and
asked that Congress enact legislation to retain enlisted men in a reserve status for a stated period to provide for "prompt passage from
peacetime to wartime organization." The San Antonio Convention in
1928 marked a signal year for Legion defense proposals. Since the
National Defense Act was "not being efficiently coordinated," it recommended that the Secretary of War appoint a committee "composed
of representatives of each component to make a study and recommendations upon a complete coordinated plan of training" under the
act. The plight of the Reserve forces had grown since Congress had
slashed the first budget estimates for the National Guard by one
third, $5 million for the Officers Reserve Corps to a mere $100,000,
and the allowance for the Enlisted Reserve to zero. This cutting was a
yearly congressional exercise. Then, too, the General Staff, jealous

of its authority, attempted by a rider to an appropriation bill to limit Reserve officers' service on the War Plans Division and other staff agencies to two weeks a year. The Legion managed to eliminate that proviso, but bad blood remained between Regular and Reserve forces. As Richard Seelye Jones observed in 1946:

> Members of the latter groups, subject to military discipline when on duty, their selection and promotion in the hands of the regular establishment, were not well situated to protest, argue or debate. In the Legion they had a continuing spokesman, an enormous organization ready to sustain the fight it had begun in 1920.

The Legion's Universal Draft proposal, initiated at Kansas City in 1921 as a basic policy of national defense with universal service and a plan to "take the profit out of war," has been known by various names through the years. The previous year a committee was appointed to pursue the objective of Universal Military Training (UMT). Wade H. Hayes of New York, chairman, and Frank Knox, future Secretary of the Navy, spent hours in congressional committees presenting the Legion case, but to no avail. Now a commission was authorized to study a Universal Draft which would enable government to draft in emergency "all persons capable of military and industrial service, and land, material, plants and capital suitable for preparation and prosecution of war." In 1923 The American Legion saw its own bill for the Universal Draft Act introduced in Congress. It provided the President with broad powers in time of war to draft persons into service without exemption on account of occupation, to place resources and industry under government control and to stabilize prices. This would place the burden of war more equitably upon all citizens, take profit out of war, expedite the prosecution of war, and eliminate the slacker, the Legion held. National Commander John R. McQuigg declared: "[The Universal Draft] is the one right way to carry on a war, and . . . will prove in time to be the greatest peace measure this country or the world has ever known."

National Commanders John R. Quinn in 1923, James A. Drain in 1924, and Edward E. Spafford in 1927 spoke out strongly in defense of the measure, and characteristically hundreds of Legionnaires gave countless hours to promotion of a concept in which they be-

lieved. But wrangling continued to the end of the decade. Besides
the pacifists' and radicals' steady refrains there was a strong ob-
jection that it would be unconstitutional to conscript labor and capital
at any time. A brief break in the overcast occurred in 1928, when
the Legion managed enactment of the Snell Resolution under which
President Hoover appointed Cabinet members, senators and representatives to a War Policies Commission to study the concept and
a possible constitutional amendment. The Legion was prematurely
confident:

> After eight years of consistent effort The American Legion has
> gained its first objective—and The American Legion always
> takes its objectives—its fight for justice; equal service for all
> and special profit by none in time of war, will be won in the
> end.

The Legion was pleased with the testimony of an outstanding array
of leaders from all walks of life, but gave little attention to the pacifist
groups that had appeared. "[The pacifists] argued that preparation
for a universal draft in time of war is useless, for as we have ratified
the Kellogg-Briand Pact (outlawing war), why talk about taking
profits out of war when there can be no war?"

Briefly the Legion entertained false hopes that the interests of
national security would prevail. They were expelled in a matter of
months. And while the pacifists were to carry the day, their more
profound self-deception was to hold them in an unremitting, malarial
grip for years.

At San Antonio in 1928, a signal year for Legion defense proposals, the Legion made its position clear in one resolution urging
caution:

> We endorse the principles expressed in the recently approved
> multilateral treaty outlawing war as an instrument of National
> policy (the Kellogg-Briand Pact), but we desire that The Amer-
> ican Legion make it clear to our people that the approval of
> this treaty does not, therefore, permit of any reduction in the
> very modest military establishment maintained by our Nation
> for purely defensive purposes.

From the beginning The American Legion maintained that the
Navy stood as the first line of defense, requiring bases, personnel,

ships, and backing from a powerful Merchant Marine. In 1921, with disarmament forces gathering on the legislative and diplomatic firing lines and the Washington Naval Conference only months away, the Naval Affairs Committee made its first report at Kansas City. The convention adopted its view that regardless of international agreements America should have:

> ... an adequate navy for the maintenance of our country as a world power and the protection of those policies which are distinctly American. ... If the American people are led to believe that its first line of defense is ready and adequate when, as a matter of fact, it is not, such propaganda is ... fatal in time of stress.

After the Washington Treaty established a 5-5-3 naval ratio for the United States, Britain and Japan in 1921, The Legion expressed the opinion many times that the accord was one not merely to reduce naval expenditures but "to make war less probable between the nations participating." This required building up to treaty strength, which "would have made war between any two of the countries improbable and highly hazardous." Bitterly, the Legion explained in 1944:

> The United States, richest of all the signatories, not only failed to build new ships to carry out the letter and spirit of the treaties (the Washington and London Treaties), but did not even replace existing ships as they became over-age and obsolete. This condition was permitted to continue through the years that our country was enjoying unprecedented prosperity and at a time the Treasury was reporting tremendous surpluses of receipts annually. All this over the protests of American Legion convention after convention, warning that this practice would involve the country in war, went unheeded by Congress and the people alike.

The Legion's first Naval Affairs resolutions in 1921 called for naval bases on both coasts and a complete surface fleet; submarines fit to accompany the battle fleet; an adequate air branch for the Navy "for patrolling, spotting and scouting, and for offensive operations—fighting, bombing and torpedo attacks; aircraft carriers and both operating and secondary bases for destroyers, submarines and aircraft; and a Naval Reserve. The 1922 convention described naval necessities: a "real naval base on the West Coast," a personnel allowance of 105,000; and more support for the Naval Reserve Force. In the months since the Washington Conference the Navy had spent its limited appropriations on battleships because they are most difficult to build in emergency. But in 1923, naval air, submarine and cruiser power were emphasized, since battleship construction had been suspended for ten years.

The Legion's early warnings, however, were not taken at face value with harrowing consequences in the initial phases of the Pacific War eighteen years later. Dereliction in the United States Congress and the British House of Commons led to Japanese advances in the North, Western, Central and South Pacific areas and consolidation of their empire from the Kurile Islands to the approaches of Australia and the Indian Ocean. All this was made possible by Japanese sea power. To dislodge the Japanese from conquests made during and after the lightning initial phases required enormous naval strength coupled with overwhelming Marine Corps, Army and Air Corps forces, sudden death on a hundred beaches, maimed and diseased men in a score of jungles, and the loss of a thousand good vessels. No one should accept accounts of the second world war that minimize a wide culpability for Pearl Harbor and the early episodes of the Pacific War or emphasize "beneficial" results of our early, grievous setbacks without considering these facts.

At conventions in 1924, 1925 and 1926, apprehension rose. The Legion felt that the British–United States–Japanese ratio had become 5-4-3, that our Navy strength might decline further and that the trend should be reversed with dispatch since "our navy stands as the nation's first arm of defense against foreign aggression and . . . such a Navy, properly manned and equipped, is our best and cheapest guaranty of national peace and security." Past National Commander John R. McQuigg at the NEC meeting and at the Philadelphia convention in 1926 called attention to "the flood of pacifist propaganda that had been released all over the country." Under the NEC he headed a committee and prepared substantial arguments "for reasonable military instruction and preparedness and answering the arguments and contentions of pacifism." Then the 1927 convention declared:

"The mere pendency of negotiations for naval limitations does not justify our Government in reducing its Naval forces below the standard set by the Treaties of 1921."

In 1928 full Legion support was thrown behind the pending Naval Construction Bill and its convention requested Congress to authorize construction of aircraft carriers and modernization of operational fleet units. Each department was urged to appoint a Committee on Naval Affairs to "make America Naval-minded." The Legion, oppressed by Congress' failure to implement the 1920 Act and, from recent experience, fearful of the consequences of the Geneva Disarmament Conference of 1926, spoke out in its 1928 *Annual Report:*

> Unless America is adequately prepared to insist on peace there will be no peace. If adequately prepared for our own defense, no combination of powers will have the hardihood to force us into war. Deliberately to strip ourselves to a condition of immediate helplessness, trusting on high purpose to solve humanity's wrongs and grudges, is to invite utter destruction. If we persist in this we shall be living in a fool's paradise, with an awakening ahead of us more bitter than that of 1914.

The Legion had entertained hopes that President Coolidge might reverse the trend. In close touch with Legionnaires since 1925, he had shown favor toward Legion proposals and in adopting the Legion's program for advance home-front planning had appointed Hanford MacNider Assistant Secretary of War to develop plans of this nature. Coolidge took up the cause of an up-to-date Navy by asking Congress to authorize seventy-seven new ships. The cries of the pacifists reached a new pitch. Propaganda and pressure doomed his responsible appeal. The American Legion, beaten on Capitol Hill, met in anger at San Antonio that summer of 1928. There it defined principles which were irreconcilable with those of a number of esteemed organizations sincerely dedicated to peace and other groups seeking to promote U.S. weakness through disarmament. Bitter words added to a burning, mutual hostility. As the above quote makes clear, the Naval Affairs Committee forecast the possibility of terrible consequences. From dark prophecy it went on, "Congress was asked for seventy-seven ships and (we) got none. Fifteen cruisers sought were not authorized. Japan and Britain are both building ships that can both outrange and outrun U.S. ships." It pointed out that in the seven years since the Washington agreement, the U.S. laid down 19 warship keels, Great Britain 55, Japan 127: "The U.S. sank the most modern part of its Navy under the (Washington) treaty."

Almost every doughboy who embarked for Europe stepped from U.S. soil to the deck of a foreign merchantman. In France and elsewhere he relied, almost exclusively at first, upon the Allies and American cargoes delivered by Allied vessels for his weapons and supplies.

The days of U.S. supremacy in speed and excellence on the seas was gone. That brief, half-forgotten period of greatness, when American masters and the clipper ships they sailed upon were unmatched, was a heritage, an unexercised talent, a wasted sinew. In World War I an enormously expensive shipbuilding program of good volume and poor fabrication eventually met a share of our armies' requirements.

Since World War I our Merchant Marine has been a source of constant concern and wrangling. The Legion in its national defense resolutions has considered a powerful Merchant Marine desirable in peace, imperative in war. Its support of this view has been vital.

In 1920 Commander Galbraith declared that "the growth, maintenance and prosperity of American shipping must be close to the heart of every patriotic American citizen," and the following year the Committee on Military Affairs reported, "We believe that the best interests of our country require that the Navy and Merchant Marine be closely united and commend the uniting of the heads of the Navy Department and Shipping Board under one roof." Subsequent National Conventions in the 1920's deplored the decline of the Merchant fleet, urged post interest, favored the Ship Subsidy Bill and chartering naval auxiliary vessels from "well-established merchant lines," promoted the concepts that at least 50 per cent of U.S. trade be carried in American flagships, and that the Merchant Marine be built up to a size "commensurate with the size of the Navy and proportionate to the size and wealth of this country."

But emasculation of the Merchant fleet was underway. The American flag was again disappearing from the blue-water trade routes. The American seaman was again on the beach. By 1927, when Legionnaires gathered in France, deterioration had progressed to an alarming point. The Paris convention resolved that the inadequacy "constitutes a great menace in the event of a national emergency," and advocated "proper recognition and support of our government . . . to serve the requirements of our industry and agriculture and at the same time be an auxiliary to our Navy as a guarantee of peace." In 1928 the situation was grave and the Legion resolved:

> We protest and express our disapproval of the contemplated sale by the United States Shipping Board and Merchant Marine Fleet Corporation of the three Atlantic Lines; namely, The United States Lines; American Merchant Lines; American Palmetto Lines, and do strongly recommend and urge that these lines be maintained and operated for the promotion and expansion of the United States Merchant Marine.

Stubbornly the Legion asked for the preservation of the Auxiliary Fleet in 1929, 1930, 1931, and 1935. Still, the Merchant Marine shrank. Insufficient appreciation by Congress and a combination of economic factors, both domestic and foreign, conspired to reduce the American Merchant fleet until it stood fourth in tonnage, sixth in speed and seventh in age among the world's maritime forces.

The first significant Legion resolutions concerning aviation came from the Legislative Committee and were adopted at Cleveland in 1920. Based upon committee study, they underlined the need of Federal legislation aimed at manufacture, flying and landing of aircraft and the fact that lack of such legislation resulted in dangerous confusion and retarded the development of aircraft which "is of vital importance to the national defense." Licensing of aircraft for air worthiness, licensing of pilots and their reexamination, and specifications for proper landing fields were all recommended. The Legion has maintained that only eighteen years later under the Civil Aeronautics Authority, created in 1938, were these early demands met "although some sort of control had been exercised previously by the Bureau of Aeronautics, Department of Commerce."

The Naval Affairs Committee in 1921 recommended "that great attention must be given in matters of research, experiment and development in connection with the aviation arm of our National Defense." Its most perspicacious recommendations, however, concerned specifics—twenty-one years before Navy pilots from the decks of the carriers *Hornet, Yorktown* and *Enterprise* changed the course of the Pacific War in the Battle of Midway:

> The use of aircraft for the purpose of patroling, scouting and spotting and for offensive operations, including fighting, bombing and torpedo attacks, and as a protection to our fleets is, because of the comparative newness of this branch of our National Defense, but in its infancy and for many years to come there must be extensive research and experimentation, with a view to its further development. We believe that the Nation should give all reasonable encouragement and where it is deserved and necessary should furnish financial aid to the efforts of scientists, inventors and makers of both heavier and lighter than air craft. While our naval aircraft during the late war was proved to be the equal of any other Nation, it is manifest that unless we carry on extensive research, experimentation and development, equal at least to that of other Nations, we will find ourselves outclassed in this branch of our naval power.

The New Orleans Convention of 1922 is remembered for its particular attention to aviation and the establishment of the Committee on Aeronautics which was "to so coordinate with the U.S. Army Air Service and other nationally-recognized institutions and organizations devoted to the interests of aeronautics, and through the medium of local posts, county and state organizations and national organization, to arouse the people in the development of commercial aviation, at such times and places as conditions and circumstances may warrant."

In 1923 the Legion described control of the air as "a practical necessity" in the future of the Nation. To this end a Merchant Air Marine, composed of a civilian force to supplement a highly trained Army and Navy fighting force, was suggested. The Committee on Aeronautics also recommended continued assistance to the National Advisory Committee for Aeronautics, sufficient funds for Army and Navy plane procurement, an expanded air mail system, and the construction of more air fields. A year later at St. Paul the Legion repeated its appeals, resolving that the country "must maintain its leadership as a world power but to do so it must develop a Merchant Air Marine comparable to those of the rest of the world." It complained that "the situation at present is not at all satisfactory from either the commercial or military viewpoint." Besides reiterating earlier proposals, it urged flight training for enlisted personnel of the Reserve Corps and encouraged departments "to cooperate in carrying out the aviation program of The American Legion within (their) jurisdiction."

The American Legion's early emphasis on naval aviation contributed to its enthusiasm at Omaha in 1925 and Philadelphia in 1926. For in 1925 two aircraft carriers came off the ways. Both were to steam in "harm's way," leaving a bloody wake across a page of history—the *Lexington* at the Battle of the Coral Sea, in which she was lost after blocking the enemy's great thrust in the South Pacific; the *Saratoga* off Guadalcanal all the way to Iwo Jima. Named after great battles, both gave the Nation victories to print in block letters across the sterns of future carriers. Ironically, in the same year, as the Legion called "for the strongest possible fortification of the Hawaiian Islands," naval personnel was cut from 86,000 to 81,-000. The Legion also expressed the hope that the President's Morrow Board would "reveal all the pressing needs which exist for the improvement, development and expansion of civil, military and naval branches of aviation," and offered the experience of Legionnaires to assist in formulating plans.

Posts which had installed landing fields in their communities were commended at Philadelphia in 1926, and post commanders were urged to advocate adequate air-landing fields. The convention also recommended that adequate air protection be provided for the Nation's great centers of population and industry. In Paris the following year the Committee on Aeronautics reported: "We believe the importance of aeronautics the world over is increasing from day to day. Already it has taken its place as one of the major arms of National Defense." It recommended greater U.S. emphasis on many aspects of aviation, including a thorough program of training younger men in all departments of aeronautics. In 1928 at San Antonio the Legion asked Congress to provide sufficient funds to keep aviation in the foreground of Navy policy and authorize the construction of aircraft carriers to bring the United States up to the tonnage allowed by the Washington Disarmament Conference. This convention called for an increase in the enlisted strength of the Army Air Corps, more military and naval aviation appropriations for primary training of pilots, more training hours, more and sufficient planes for school, military and naval purposes, more and better equipment for emergency landing fields, acceleration of aeronautical map making, and increases in Army Air Corps planes without taking appropriations from any other branch. All this was reaffirmed the following year.

The American Legion's national security program through a decade of declining defense had its foundation in the practical approach of men who devoted time to consideration of their common experience and effort toward realistic measures to ensure the safety of the nation.

Yet despite their contribution and the unrelenting efforts of thousands of comrades, dedicated public servants and conscientious citizens, preparedness suffered a downhill jouncing destined to last from 1919 to 1939. Heavy jolts in 1928 shook the efforts of the Legion and others aware of the dangerous course. "Disarm for peace!" had become the watchword of pacifists, including influential educators, an array of churchmen, foreign and domestic intellectuals, and numerous civic groups—all sounding their refrain in the ear of a Congress eager to please and to cut "unproductive" military expenditures. Women's groups, determined that their boys were not to be soldiers, carried the pacifist and radical line to Washington.

In vivid contrast was the 1925 Women's Conference on National Defense, sponsored by the American Legion Auxiliary. Mrs. O. D. Oliphant, president of the Legion Auxiliary, welcomed delegates from sixteen organizations. The Secretaries of War and Navy and staff officers addressed the conference, which became an annual event after 1926. Side by side with the Legion, the Auxiliary promoted the cause of National preparedness.

At the end of the decade Legionnaires could look back on their record with pride and regret, both well taken. For here there were sound, imaginative vision and a measure of accomplishment as well as frustration and neglect. It is an incontestable fact that were it not for the Legion the military position of the United States would have sunk even lower—our Navy, or what was left of it, tied with frayed lines in old anchorages; our Army further demoralized and perhaps beyond revival in crisis; more of our Merchant fleet rusting out; and air power regarded as little more than a novelty. Had the fighting men of World War I returned disillusioned, had they pushed aside vital

security matters to give their own personal affairs undivided attention, or had they been vulnerable to alien persuasion and never
banded together in The American Legion, it is not difficult to surmise
that the plight of the Nation and the enemies of the Axis would have
been immeasurably deepened after 1939.

12

Challenges, Foreign and Domestic

I N the years between the two world wars The American Legion
strove for international peace as well as security for the nation.
The last chapter emphasizes a fundamental Legion belief—a powerful United States is essential to ensure the nation against foreign
attack and to defend national interests. Without military strength,
the binding agent of security, efforts toward peace and understanding
may be as useless as sand and water without cement in pouring the
footings of a building. Therefore, Legionnaires focused attention on
three areas of endeavor, interrelated and dependent each upon the
others. Besides defense, Legion concerns have been directed at foreign relations and the strengthening of the nation against subversion,
which has derived much of its direction and inspiration from antagonistic systems abroad. All have been among the Legion's foremost activities since 1919. Here, it is important, first, to trace Legion activities for world peace through international understanding
and, second, to follow its continuing efforts to arouse its membership
and the American public as well as Congress and government agencies to recognize the threat of communism and other alien ideologies
and to take positive steps to counter them.

The American Legion's contacts with foreign veterans' groups and
distinguished leaders among the former Allied countries were warm
and cordial as early as 1919 and 1920. It was natural that unusually
auspicious relations with representatives of the British Commonwealth
sprang up and assumed an enduring quality at an early date. This
was true of the Legion's first association with Great Britain's vet-

erans. Both the Americans and the British were imbued with the Anglo-Saxon concepts of law. Both were accustomed to constitutional democracy. Both had a loathing of the chaos and scattered effort that accompanies a multitude of rival or antagonistic factions, whether they be associated with political life or community endeavor. Both experienced very similar problems following the war.

In establishing the American Legion as the dominant veterans' group in this country, U.S. ex-servicemen were ahead of their British counterparts. In a search for unity British veterans, after a gloomy time in 1919, managed to consolidate and emerge in 1920 as a united body—the British Legion. The British had taken a lively interest in The American Legion when they decided to "amalgamate" their various ex-servicemen's groups. British representatives studied the American Legion's structure and, in evolving the British Legion, adopted parts of The American Legion's Constitution and "approach to politics." Parallel and similar problems and questions beset the British effort. Possibly influenced by earlier American decisions, the group in Britain working for unity arrived at a more realistic appraisal and clear-cut definition of political action than did American Legionnaires. The British simply made a clear distinction between political action through the exertion of legitimate group pressure and political action through a direct, organic relationship with a political party. Ex-servicemen in Britain as in the United States were warned to avoid identifying themselves as a body with any political party. British Legionnaires in exercising their individual rights and responsibilities were admonished not to involve the British Legion in party politics. It was to be identified beyond all doubt as a nonparty organization. However, although both have functioned as nonpartisan organizations, The American Legion has more strenuously and effectively exerted influence.

Early, the British Legion was plagued by an unemployment problem similar to The American Legion's and felt that some government officials were prepared to "throw the disabled serviceman to the wolves." They quoted the soldiers' poet, Kipling:

It's Tommy this, an' Tommy that, an' "Chuck 'im out, the brute!"
But it's "Saviour of 'is country," when the guns begin to shoot.

By 1921 the British Legion had taken root and its Representative George Crossfield spent some weeks at Indianapolis studying The American Legion organization. The British Legion's motto, "Service, Not Self," reflects the same selflessness expressed in The American Legion's "For God and Country."

From the promptings of Miss Moina Michael of Georgia and the inspired efforts of the Auxiliary, the American ex-servicemen adopted as their emblem the poppy, derived from the poem "In Flanders' Fields" by a Canadian who had not survived the war, John McCrae:

> In Flanders fields the poppies blow
> Between the crosses, row on row. . . .
> We lived, felt dawn, saw sunsets glow,
> Loved and were loved, and now we lie
> In Flanders fields. . . .
> If ye break faith with us who die
> We shall not sleep, though poppies grow
> In Flanders fields.

At first the poppies were manufactured in devastated areas of France, shipped to the United States and profits from their sale on Memorial Day used for needy children. Then, hospitalized men in the veterans' hospitals produced them. Within a decade payments to these disabled men amounted to more than two million dollars and funds for use in rehabilitation and child welfare totaled ten million dollars. The British Legion has conducted a similar poppy program.

The British Legion felt that relations between ex-servicemen of the British Empire and their comrades in the United States required careful attention, for it believed that in crisis a bond between the two countries was essential, if not to maintain peace, then to wage war. There is no question that both the British and The American Legions were mistaken in their confidence that peace might be maintained and, perhaps wishfully, overlooked the complications of modern nationalism and the repercussions of exclusion of German veterans from an association of Allied veterans. In any event, the question of war or peace involved matters outside the control of veterans' organizations.

Clemenceau, the Old Tiger of France, once said that war is much too important to be left to generals. In retrospect, it might be said that lasting peace is much too important to be left to politicians. During the interwar years this was true, although a growing number of citizens in the Western democracies organized to promote international understanding. While their efforts were rudimentary and too often misguided, they contributed to a foundation of public opinion that has been important in the years since.

In 1920 Francis Drake, first commander of an overseas American Legion unit which was located in Paris, discussed talk abroad of a federation of Allied veterans with Legion leaders. While Cabot Ward and Arthur Kipling conducted conversations in Europe, Drake won Legion approval, and in 1920 war veterans of the United States, France, Great Britain, Belgium, Italy, Poland, Rumania, Czechoslovakia, and Yugoslavia formed the Fédération Interalliée des Anciens Combattants (FIDAC).

Meanwhile, the debate over the League of Nations raged in the United States, and the election of 1920 settled the matter in favor of abstaining from membership. The young Legion, conducting exhaustive campaigns for the immediate alleviation of the disabled veterans' plight, establishing its organization and attempting to finance its programs, took no official position on the League. There were also political overtones which did not encourage what would have been a dangerously divisive struggle within the Legion at the time.

However, the Legion did make its first important efforts toward international understanding at that time. The pilgrimage of Commander John G. Emery and two hundred Legionnaires to France in 1921 was inspired by the hope that greater unity among nations might be achieved through the union and cooperation of veterans throughout the world. Legionnaires found that France had not forgotten the khaki columns of the AEF, their decisiveness in turning the tide of the war and their countless gallant exploits. Representatives of the Legion made a profound impression on the French people. At the tomb of France's Unknown Soldier beneath the Arc de Triomphe Emery discovered that no wreath had arrived, but delivered a brief eulogy: "To him America pays the greatest tribute it knows how to pay—unknown hero of France our flag caresses you."

With that Emery draped the Stars and Stripes over the stones. The French press exclaimed, "Inspired!" Foch then walked under the Arc. When the Legionnaires moved to follow him, an aide reminded the Marshal that this was highly irregular. None but victorious troops by tradition pass under the Arc. The Marshal said, "The Americans never turn back."

Ceremonial pomp and the cheers of humble villagers met the delegation in its movements through France. After visiting all the terrible battlefields and unveiling the monument to the AEF at the ruined little village of Flirey, Legionnaires conferred with French veterans concerning their consolidation. As with the French political party system, there was a proliferation of veterans' organizations—5 large and 140 small societies. *Le Fanion,* a veterans' publication, advocated consolidation and the name Légion Française:

> They [American Legionnaires] leave with us the vision of a strong and compelling example, a French Legion which shall unite, in the same desire to serve, all the former combatants who are now loosely grouped in scattered associations.

The Legion delegation unveiled a plaque at Saint-Dié-des-Vosges commemorating the publication of the first map to bear the name America. Twenty-three years later, as American troops moved on the German-held town, Hitler's retreating army seized almost a thousand remaining male citizens, ordered most of the community evacuated, pillaged, and set fire to Saint-Dié. The flames gutted the town and the academic building where the plaque had been fixed. During 1945 and 1946 the Legion Auxiliary dispatched hundreds of packages, each addressed to a child in the town.

In 1921 the NEC ratified membership in FIDAC. Their action was endorsed a few months later at the National Convention. The FIDAC Congress of 1922 at New Orleans adopted a charter which reflected much of the idealism of the first world war: freedom of speech and press, unity against armed aggression, aid to commerce, progressive disarmament, opposition to communism, full publicity for treaties and their observance, establishment of an international court to outlaw war, no territorial aggrandizement, stability of monetary exchange, and the encouragement of international news reporting. Other FIDAC activities were adopted—a travel bureau, the encouragement of student interchange among universities and FIDAC awards to colleges advancing the cause of international understanding.

At this time Auxiliary President Mrs. Lowell F. Hobart and her successor, Dr. Kate Waller Barrett, were vitally interested and suggested a FIDAC Women's Auxiliary, which became a reality under the lead of Lady Edward Spencer-Churchill, Mrs. Hobart being named Organizing President at the FIDAC Congress in Rome in 1925 when its Auxiliary became official. Mrs. Joseph H. Thompson and Mrs. Lemuel Bolles were delegates. The Auxiliary actively promoted and perhaps outdid the Legion in promoting this program. Among its units were nine hundred FIDAC chairmen, scores of bulletins and other painstaking work for "peace and international understanding."

A listing of American presidents and vice presidents of FIDAC appears in the Appendix. Scores of Legionnaires, at their own expense, attended Congresses of FIDAC in European cities. A few, like H. Nelson Jackson of Vermont, gave years of devotion to advance FIDAC objectives. Others included L. R. Gignilliat and A. Piatt Andrew. National Adjutant Lemuel Bolles, too, was an advocate for keeping the cause of peace among the foremost considerations of the Legion. His boundless idealism was a reflection of what became a forlorn hope in the late 30's:

> I have met some of the best people and some of the worst people in at least four countries of Europe rather intimately. I mean England, France, Italy, and Poland. I know how much greater have been our opportunities in America, how much easier it is for us to be peace-loving people. It takes two to keep the peace, and the people of Europe have got to have American example and American leadership. I am not sure that everything we can do will create and maintain a peaceful world, but I am pretty sure that anything less will contribute to that self-destruction so innate within humankind. We had better keep trying.

FIDAC met annually, its main objective to promote peace through "friendship between peoples." In 1924 the Dawes Plan, concerned with the intractable problem of reparations, was formulated. Subsequently, many persons hoped that close contact might be established with the principal German veterans' groups. In fact, some German veterans appealed to FIDAC, expressing their "heartfelt desire for No More War." Unfortunately the continental members of FIDAC were unprepared to accept their recent enemy into their organization at this time. A number of ex-servicemen abroad attempted to resolve the scattering of effort toward international peace by establishing another organization which included the Germans and other ex-enemies in the Comité International des Anciens Combattants (CIP). The British Legion was a strong supporter. There was also CIAMAC, suspected of being under communist influence and from which FIDAC remained separated. CIAMAC, an international conference of associations of the wounded and other ex-soldiers, contained many of the more discontented ex-enemy veterans. Hence there were three competing international ex-servicemen's organizations. They were divided by nationalism, political theory and wartime status. By being exclusive the three groups were hardly equipped to advance the cause of peace.

American Legionnaires became FIDAC presidents, Thomas W. Miller in 1924 at London and Edward L. White in 1932 at Lisbon. There were American FIDAC Auxiliary presidents in 1928 and in 1936—Mrs. Adalin Wright Macauley and Mrs. Joseph H. Thompson. In 1930 FIDAC held its Congress in the United States. It was a hopeful time despite the widening repercussions of the great crash of 1929 and the first pressure waves of the depression. The Kellogg-Briand Pact which outlawed war as an instrument of national policy was being drawn up. President Hoover spoke to the assembled Allied veterans. He was well received, for a moratorium by the United States on the very nettlesome question of foreign debts had been declared.

It was not long, however, before the bleak savagery, medieval cruelty and terror and cynical disregard of good faith were to become full blown. Already the German state was coming under the overwhelming barrage of nazi propaganda, slipping under the influence of Hitler's limitless egotism and beginning to experience the discipline, order and comfortable loss of liberty that characterized a stage of the nazis' rise to power. Still, FIDAC members clung to hope. In 1933 its Executive Council resolved to consider the best means "of organizing a permanent and still closer collaboration with ex-enemy ex-service organizations." But a few months later, when ten thousand ex-servicemen gathered in Geneva to express the almost universal desire for peace, the Austrians and the Germans were not among them. Theirs was an ominous absence. Then Hitler and Ribbentrop considered that cooperation among veterans might improve Anglo-German relations, and a period of negotiations and discussions followed. But little came of this.

Among American disputes connected with FIDAC, one concerned the advocacy of withdrawal from the organization by Mrs. Julia Wheelock, a Legion National Committeeman from Italy. She struggled for disassociation from FIDAC because of fascist Italy's representation in the organization. However, numerous Legionnaires felt that it was important to keep open this avenue of contact with other nations. Among them was Father Robert J. White, a stubborn and determined fighter.

As international relations deteriorated, FIDAC continued its work, but the time had passed for more universal representation. German leaders moved with a glacial certainty and direction toward conflict. The cause of peace was severely stricken when Germany marched into the Rhineland in defiance of Versailles and of the Locarno Treaty, which guaranteed national boundaries and to which Germany had become a party of her own free will. Long years of futile negotiations ended with the takeover of Czechoslovakia in 1939. FIDAC was also a casualty.

The alien and immigration policies of the United States have been regarded by the Legion as both a domestic and foreign problem. These policies may have a bearing upon vital aspects of national life and, in several ways, they are directly related to American relations with foreign governments and peoples. Mention has been made of the trying economic circumstances which awaited hundreds of thousands of honorably discharged doughboys, the widespread resentment they felt toward the more than 92 per cent of aliens of military age who resided in the United States without serving in the Armed Forces, many of whom used their status to avoid bearing arms and who made the employment situation more acute after the war, and the veterans' anger toward the radicalism and violence that swept the country and was openly advocated by numerous resident aliens.

The Legion spearheaded the 1920 drive to deport sixty thousand aliens listed as "undesirable" in Department of Justice files. At that time the sabotage, espionage and subversive activities conducted by a wide assortment of foreign agents and radicals were widely publicized. *The American Legion Weekly* offered a simple solution after the first aliens were deported:

> Preachers of sedition, disciples of the venomous philosophy of bolshevism, they have been rounded up and sent, fare prepaid, to a land where common practice conforms to their utterances. They will be free hereafter to mingle with their own kind. They will be free to revel in the chaos and misery that are the inevitable products of their own disordered philosophy put into practice. They will not be fettered by the processes of sane, orderly government, of equal rights and equal responsibility.

Immigration took a startling leap upward from 1921 to 1922— from one to two million. Congress, with Legion backing, passed the Three Per Cent Act of May, 1921, the first restrictive immigration law in the United States. Since the economy required time for readjustment and could not handle the employment of many men who had served their country in war, Legionnaires felt with a majority of Americans that the overcrowded labor force might be spared the great influx. Legion officials favored a stop to immigration for five years. Among other problems arising from *en masse* immigration was not only the burden placed upon the economy but the difficulty of screening large numbers of individuals for disease, criminal background and subversive intent. In 1924 Congress cut back immigration and established a quota at 2 per cent based on the 1890 census and excluded those Oriental races ineligible for citizenship. Smuggling of aliens prompted a border patrol in 1925. The national origins' quotas of the 1924 act were to be effective in 1927, but the difficulty of accurately determining quotas postponed the date to 1929.

When Congress was urged to change the law, the Legion's legislative representative Taylor marshaled his organization's influence, strode to the capitol and refreshed Congress on the Legion's bitter feelings concerning aliens who avoided military service in time of peril. In 1929 the immigration policy was settled on a quota basis which the Legion defended in subsequent years on the grounds that in the grip of depression, with millions unemployed, the United States could hardly be expected to increase its labor force when there were already millions of men walking the streets in search of work and millions of families on relief rolls. It was pointless to import unemployment. But before the origins quota went into effect, the impact of the depression brought action by President Hoover, who instructed American consuls to employ provisions of the 1917 immigration act and refuse visas to all immigrants likely to become public charges. The administration of deportation laws reduced the number of aliens so that for a time departures exceeded entries. While the Legion and others were most concerned about persons advocating "the overthrow of our government by force, fraud or violence" and called for the deportation of all aliens who advocated such overthrow, even with watchful consuls and strict laws, numerous subversives and criminals slipped through. Citizens are familiar with some of the manifestations of organized crime, the presence of many foreign-born in certain "syndicates" and among underworld operations, and the enormous damage, trouble and expense they inflict upon the Republic. To jail one of them is an arduous procedure; to deport him, next to impossible.

The American Legion was somewhat naïve in its early hopes for resolving the problem of aliens and soon realized that it must put its influence behind constructive efforts to enable the foreign-born to attain and exercise the benefits and responsibilities of full citizenship. Post after post adopted enlightened naturalization programs which continue to the present. Legion posts set up hundreds of citizenship and naturalization classes with the cooperation of public school authorities, and Legion posts sponsored celebrations for those who successfully completed the courses and gained their final papers. This was the Legion at its best, building up the sinew and fiber of the Republic. Most graduates of these schools have been dedicated naturalized Americans who often held their citizenship more dear than their native-born neighbors.

The increased activity of communists and German-American Bundists concerned the Legion after the mid-1930's. But Legion proposals to have names, addresses, fingerprint records, and occupations of registered aliens placed in the public register were not followed by Congress. With war in Europe only months away, the Legion urged punishment of American citizens advocating the violent overthrow of the government. Then, in World War II, the additional concern of national defense and security arose. The dangers of sabotage, espionage and the advocacy of disloyalty became prominent.

After 1941, with a country fighting a world conflict, the Legion asked Congress to enact legislation to deport aliens who would not fight, to "amend treaties to deport naturalized citizens whose citizenship had been revoked due to subversive activities" and to provide that a country's refusal to accept its undesirables should deny its nationals admittance to the United States. The government did not adopt this proposal.

A 1943 proposal to improve Chinese morale by permitting greater immigration was opposed on the grounds that it "would be used as an opening wedge toward following through with similar rights for other groups." Then, as the war drew to a close, the Legion went on record advocating that immigration be ended until unemployment in the United States dropped to less than a million, all veterans had been afforded the opportunity of employment, and "all so-called members of imported foreign labor battalions, refugees, war prisoners, and/or those who have been given temporary sanctuary, employment or haven during the present state of war, shall have been returned to the lands of their origin." This reflected Legion concern that the employment problems of the post–World War I period would be repeated. With the end of the war the Legion feared that increased immigration would not only involve great expense that would be detrimental to the financing of rehabilitation and welfare of veterans and the economic well-being of many American citizens but would lead to greater labor difficulties "in areas where the foreign element is largest." Former National Commander Ralph T. O'Neil suggested that "immigration should be made truly selective and confined to the present quota or such reduced quotas as may hereafter be established, and that only such persons shall be admitted from any country who may be found to be assimilable and well disposed to the basic principles of our American form of government and way of life." American immigration laws had excluded persons diseased and mentally defective. The Legion objected to admitting fascists or communists as being perhaps a more serious threat to the well-being of the country than classes of persons already excluded.

In 1947 a proposal to admit nearly half a million displaced persons from Europe brought Legion protest. It would not be in accord with controlled selective immigration at a time when there was an acute lack of housing, Legionnaires said. These persons might better serve in the reconstruction of Europe rather than entering in competition for jobs with veterans and other unemployed people in the United States. Again, the Legion warned that many had been indoctrinated with the hatreds and prejudices of the communists, fascists and nazis. Some influential Legionnaires felt that greater immigration would allow hostile powers to build up a fifth column which might provide "the margin for disaster" in another war. The Legion also stood firm in its opposition to immigration or the assimilation of prisoners of war "who should be returned to their own countries in accordance with the Geneva Convention."

Firmly organized, The American Legion took a growing interest in foreign affairs. Its record has been idealistic and pragmatic, dedicated to the preservation of peace, understanding among nations and United States promotion of treaties and protocols which the Legion felt were not detrimental to national security. Through its first quarter century of activity it generally supported and at times influenced the government and the public regarding positions officially taken by the United States. The Legion approved an international court of justice in 1922 and gave its specific approval of the World Court in 1926. The deterioration of international relations after the onset of the depression brought about a reversal to this when both the League of Nations and the Court appeared inadequate to enforce international law and order. Agencies concerned with peace and foreign relations through domestic activities were centered in the Legion's World Peace Committee, later the Peace and Foreign Relations Committee. In 1923 at San Francisco the National Convention resolved to pledge Legion support to any "practicable and workable plans tending to promote permanent peace" stating that "war is an outlaw and its horrors constitute an indictment upon our civilization." The Legion resolved to support the American Peace Society with the admonition that this support was provisional upon the Society's refraining from opposition to an adequate national defense policy.

Some Legion positions were intimately connected with national defense and are discussed elsewhere. Others are perhaps more properly considered here, although they have a close identification with national defense. The use of poison gas in World War I was contrary to a solemn agreement by Germany, France, Great Britain, Austria-

Hungary, Russia, and Japan at The Hague in 1899. In 1926 the United States was represented at Geneva for discussions concerning international trade in arms and ammunition. One result of the gathering was the Geneva Gas Protocol, which called for elimination of chemical warfare. Conscious of the fact that in World War I the British had averted far greater casualties from gas by learning of the German clandestine production of this lethal weapon, the Legion opposed ratification on the ground that while gas had proved to be a highly effective weapon it was, according to the Association of Military Surgeons, "more humane and less destructive of human life than other methods of warfare." The Legion added the argument:

> The history of warfare shows conclusively that where the national unity of a nation is threatened, that nation will make use of every effective weapon at its command, regardless of agreements to the contrary.

Always in the background of Legion positions on international treaties was the underlying concern that the United States maintain a peaceful and cooperative attitude while looking to its own security and strength, the most lasting assurance of foreign and domestic tranquillity. Its attitude toward the Kellogg-Briand Peace Pact is one example:

> We endorse the principles expressed in the recently approved multilateral treaty outlawing war as an instrument of national policy, but we desire that The American Legion make it clear to our people that the approval of this treaty does not, in any way, guarantee peace, and does not, therefore, permit of any reduction in the very modest military establishment maintained by our nation for purely defensive purposes.

Through its departments abroad and visits to foreign countries The American Legion felt that it might improve international relations. Europe saw its first American Legion Convention in 1927 in Paris. National Commander Howard Savage of Illinois had won a close contest from J. Monroe Johnson of South Carolina the year before when General Pershing declined to be a candidate but accepted election as an Honorary National Commander. Savage led a small advance party to France. Then, over twenty thousand members of The American Legion, the Auxiliary and their families crossed the Atlantic. They exuded the zest, gaiety and enthusiasm of a large national group traveling abroad and thoroughly enjoyed this famous convention and the multitude of activities, associations and sights that distinguished it. The French government gave the Legionnaires a bedazzling official welcome, including honors and banquets.

Many prominent personalities addressed the convention delegates who conducted their official meetings at the Trocadero Palace. There were M. Gaston Doumergue, President of the French Republic, Marshal Foch and a number of others. Despite the gay, effervescent atmosphere of those September days of Paris in the 1920's, which many Americans wistfully recall, the Legion's activities were subjected to attack, crudely by communists in France and elsewhere, maliciously by an assortment of radicals and pious pacifists on both sides of the Atlantic. Legionnaires and the Auxiliary conducted serious deliberations and accomplished the high purposes of their visit. However, some American observers of the sort who never tire of belittling their country and countrymen filtered out this light from their colored reports. They delighted in recording that some Legionnaires had a riotous time and were jailed.

Others grasped the importance of the visit. A. Albert Petit wrote in the *Journal des Débats:*

> These true and valiant friends, we can think only of the friendship that must always last between Americans and Frenchmen despite all misunderstandings, all difficulties and all statistics. They are the messengers of concord and confraternity. They carry on direct diplomacy, namely, that of the heart. We know very well that this diplomacy is not all-sufficient, and is not competent for all purposes. So be it. But at least it answers one purpose that is very strong and very noble, and without which there could not be that understanding which is based not on signatures, but on trust and faith in the same ideal.

From the convention rostrum and in the French press there were tributes to the exploits and achievements of the AEF and praise of the Legion's emphasis on comradeship. There were convictions that the bonds between the United States and the former Allies were made of durable stuff and that together they would work toward peace.

The 1927 parade of The American Legion with troops and bands of all the Allied nations is remembered as a glorious climax. It was on a warm September day, Paris' avenues and buildings bedecked with color, when the greatest number of citizens of another nation paraded in a capital city. From formation in the Étoile Légionnaires moved from the Arc de Triomphe down the broad sweep of the Champs Élysées, past cheering crowds that thronged the sidewalks and leaned, waved and shouted from balconies and rooftops. French troops in horizon blue stood elbow to elbow along the parade route. Hundreds of thousands of Parisians, many shouting *"Vive l'Amérique!"* watched the marchers pour into the Place de la Concorde and swing past the reviewing stand. There with Foch and Pershing stood Haig of Great Britain, Diaz of Italy and other commanders. The line of march then moved along the boulevards from La Madeleine Church to the Place de l'Opéra and on, almost to the Seine, where it turned eastward to the Hôtel de Ville. It was the finest parade ever conducted by The American Legion. Paris newspapers said it reflected the strength, the discipline and the orderly freedom of the New World. Another generation was to pass before Paris was overwhelmed by the sight of parading Americans—when GI's of the second world war in their battle dress marched through Paris after its liberation.

After the excitement and convention sessions in Paris, Legionnaires struck out in all directions. Throngs toured the many battlefields of a decade before, the cemeteries where fallen Americans lay buried, French villages and cities, and the many sights for which France is known. For most, the European tour was a bittersweet experience. There was the warmth of Gallic reception everywhere for these men who had fought on French soil. Many former doughboys visited French war orphans who had been "adopted" by combat units—their support and education aided by numerous Legion posts through the Red Cross. A number of Americans, including John J. Pershing and Elsie Janis, had taken on the responsibility of providing for a French child as well.

The Commander's Tour of 250 Legion officials received official welcome and entertainment in half a dozen capitals. It traveled to Switzerland and Belgium, Nice, Monte Carlo, Metz, and Strasbourg. Visiting in Alsace-Lorraine was especially moving, for the AEF had proved itself on terrain that led into the territory, lost to France since the War of 1870. That Commander Savage and his party were received at Buckingham Palace by King George and Queen Mary, at the palace in Brussels by King Albert and Queen Elizabeth, and by King Victor Emanuel at his summer palace at Pisa underlined the importance attached to the tour.

The American Legion's journey to Europe did much to improve relations with a number of countries and increased the interest of Legionnaires in foreign affairs. However, it failed to impress the many German nationalists then gaining a following. Already, they were abusing the Treaty of Versailles to gain support of millions of dissatisfied Germans, and their subsequent actions indicate that they failed to comprehend the importance of the strong bonds of interest and friendship between the United States and their former enemies. Also, ruffled relations between France and the Soviet Union resulted, for The American Legion was already known to international communism for its strong attitudes against communism's creed and avowed ambitions. An organization that might bolster relations between the powerful American Republic and continental nations was marked for attack.

Hope for future tranquillity in Europe had risen with the signing of the Locarno Pact of 1925, which guaranteed the frontiers of Germany and her neighbors and the admission of Germany to the League of Nations a year later. Some members of FIDAC, including The American Legion, felt that these events would smooth the way for German representation in their organization. In 1927 German and Austrian veterans met with their former enemies in FIDAC, who made certain stipulations, including a "respect for treaties," a contingent of membership. The Germans evaded this inclusion until the American delegate, Henry D. Lindsley, confronted them with a resolution that bound them to respect treaties. The Texan, after other FIDAC delegates had been unsuccessful in their confusion and alarm to gain German inclusion of the words "respect for," had cornered the Germans with the skill of a cowhand running livestock into a corral. The Germans were compelled to accept the wording. But this was an inauspicious beginning for a more embracing FIDAC organization. As the years slipped away, the Germans and others came under the spell of men and ideologies incompatible with the objectives of FIDAC.

In 1930 the Foreign Relations Report encouraged the promotion of world peace and suggested that Legionnaires study the subject and attempt to establish "personal contacts" with other nationals. The Legion set up a "study program" in which Legionnaires considered significant international developments, among them the disarmament conferences, World Court discussions and FIDAC matters. This program stimulated the thinking of thousands of Legionnaires who in turn influenced other conscientious citizens. It provided groundwork for the considered opinions that the Legion has expressed through the years.

The ominous events that evolved in the world after the depression had set in were not lost upon Legion thinking, and at the 1935 Convention at St. Louis the delegates resolved that "deeply conscious as we are of the disturbing elements which say that war must come and that there is no hope for peace, we stand confident and unafraid in The American Legion in our belief that peace is possible and we offer all our efforts to its practical accomplishment." This is only one of many fond aspirations that expressed the desperate desire for peace in those twilight years before the darkness of the late 30's set in. The Legion's hopes found inspiration in false assumptions. Critical as various situations had become abroad, totalitarian aggression could still be arrested. While a number of people were convinced that Hitler was "half mad," few appreciated the extent of his lunacy. There was also the expectation that the Western democracies would eventually make a stand. But the low condition of military readiness and the absence of resolve among those who might have checked the German and Japanese advances, were not appreciated. Then, too, while German grievances had been wiped from the books, other dangerous developments had transpired in swift succession.

Through American efforts the punitive provisions of the Versailles Treaty were softened. The Dawes Plan and the Young Plan both served this purpose. And the American government had poured money into Germany during her times of great distress, equaling the reparations that were squeezed from her by the Allies. Then, in 1931, the Bank of England led a number of countries off the gold standard. In the summer of 1933 at Lausanne a conference decided to liquidate the German reparations debt for the final payment of three billion reichsmarks.

But already the more democratic and liberal parties in Germany were in trouble. German nationalism was strident. Before long Hitler and his followers were exploiting this development, subjecting the population to an incessant barrage of malicious, false, crude, but effective propaganda. Political instability took hold. The German people wearied of elections. The numerous parliamentary coalitions were mutually destructive. After much maneuvering, Hitler became Reich Chancellor under President Hindenburg, a man of advanced age, impaired health and declining faculties.

Hitler crossed over from constitutional power after this. He dissolved the Reichstag and then, following the Reichstag fire which his stooges described as a "signal" for a communist uprising, managed to get the failing President to sign a decree which suspended the most important civil rights "until further notice"—personal liberties, including freedom of the press, assembly, and association and guarantees of private property and the inviolability of home and communications. For certain crimes, hitherto punishable by imprisonment, death was decreed. This decree was followed a few days later by the emasculation of the Reichstag, its constitutional powers relinquished "legally" so that both the legislative and executive functions of the state would reside in one office. Hitler gained the measure which gave him a shabby vestige of legality. Here, the representatives of the various parties who granted Hitler their votes for fear of his seizing these powers through a *coup d'état* thus betrayed the constitution and the people.

To add to its long-standing concern with the totalitarian communist regime in Russia and its international manifestations, which are considered below, The American Legion now had other totalitarian sources of danger—fascist Germany and Italy and militarist Japan.

Hitler awaited only President Hindenburg's death to bring together the power of the President and the Chancellor. When Hindenburg died in 1934, an oath of loyalty to "render unconditional obedience to Adolf Hitler, the Fuehrer of the German Reich nation, the Supreme Commander of the Armed Forces . . ." was introduced. Whereas soldiers previously swore loyalty to a democratic constitution, they now swore loyalty to one man. Germany fast became a police state. The persecution of the Jews and of persons known to hold views contrary to those of the nazis was to be handled with a barbarian ruthlessness made more terrible through the order and thoroughness attributable to many Germans. Methodically, Hitler destroyed justice by adulterating the courts, made religion less compelling and with his henchmen concocted the hate campaigns based upon racial myths and moved against his objectives with outrageous pretexts.

In Japan, too, ambitious and powerful factions eliminated effective liberal leaders and moved their Emperor and nation toward disastrous adventures. In fascist Italy Mussolini was strutting his hour on history's stage, like a comic-opera character, to a ludicrous extremity. He was to manage, after base and frightful military blunders, to fall headlong into the orchestra pit—pulling scenery, chorus, props, and curtains with him.

But for years the Legion had seen little humor in the world situation. The intrigues and subversion of communism throughout the world were a grim reality. The American Legion had long been expressing its concern about European radicals and revolutionaries, dedicated to undermining the principles and institutions that were the strength of the United States. The 1924 annual reports attacked communism saying its advocates aimed to make the United States "a nation of weaklings and slackers, which is part of a great international scheme to allow anarchy and communism to domineer the world."

In 1930 the Americanism Commission made a prophetic observation:

> In the opinion of our committee, the history of the next half century will be given over the conflict between the political and social philosophies represented on the one hand by that movement known as "communism" and on the other hand by the stabilized institutions of politics and society as represented by the constitutional governments of the world.

In 1930 the House of Representatives created, by a vote of 210 to 18, the Special Committee to Investigate Communist Activities. After this committee was dissolved, the only committee in the House that could effectively concern itself with subversion was the Standing House Committee on Immigration and Naturalization. As fascism gained control in Germany and Italy, there were investigations of nazi and fascist propaganda. Momentarily, communism was neglected in this antisubversive activity. The American Legion was foremost in the effort to expand the activities of this committee to include surveillance of communist as well as fascist activities. In the debate in the House over creating a committee to carry on investigations, the word "nazi" was dropped, and "foreign" was substituted. Finally, the House created a Special Committee to Investigate Un-American Activities with John W. McCormack of Massachusetts as chairman. This committee continued until 1935, and as a result of its recommendations Congress passed the Foreign Agents Registration Act of 1938 with strong Legion support.

After the McCormack committee was discontinued, the problem of subversion went back to the Committee on Immigration and Naturalization. Under the continuous prodding of the Legion, Vice President Garner called upon Congressman Martin Dies to attempt to create an un-American activities committee. In arguing for the creation of this committee, Dies made it clear that the committee's purpose should be broader than an attack on nazi activities. It should also concern itself with communism. The purpose, he said, should be to expose and provide legislation opposing the concept which was common to both fascism and communism—dictatorship. Finally, the Dies resolution was adopted and a Special Commitatee on Un-American Activities was established. Through an unbroken chain of committees, which eventually resulted in a permanent standing committee, support in the House for this purpose has increased, by vote and appropriations.

Meanwhile, under the leadership of Senator Pat McCarran, chairman for a period of the Senate Judiciary Committee, the Senate actively labored in accumulating evidence and forcing action concerning the presence of communist-affiliated individuals in the government itself.

The Legion has always supported congressional investigating committees on the grounds that they bring to light conditions that recommend legislation, and the un-American activities committees have delved into subjects of primary Legion concern.

However, American society makes room for a wide range of conflicting opinion, and this accommodation has properly allowed strong differences of opinion on the work of these committees. Liberals and radicals of the left have attacked conscientious men serving on these committees and have viciously denounced groups and individuals that support them. The communists and fellow travelers have not been idle. They have exploited the condition that properly permits extreme liberalism under our laws. Through nefarious and clever propaganda and front organizations their views have been introduced into the ideology of numerous intellectuals. Some intellectuals, in awe of their European counterparts, have also fed upon the observations of foreign critics who have searched out the sensational, unsavory and sleazy in American life. While there has been some hysteria, it has not been a part of the reaction of informed groups and individuals concerned with the subversive threats to national security and interests, and as an affliction has not been as serious as the total blindness of some intellectuals, bureaucrats, public figures, and many citizens to communism's objectives.

As events abroad deteriorated, there was increased activity of communists and German-American Bundists in the United States. Allegiance to the Third Reich was celebrated publicly in American cities. The American Legion became alarmed when the German Embassy in 1938 announced registration of German citizens in this country, and the Legion asked that Congress take appropriate action to obtain and make public the names of persons who so registered, an act contrary to international law. John Thomas Taylor of the Legion's Washington office urged enactment of a House resolution to investigate un-American activities, condemned "all alien organizations which in our country promote loyalty to some other government or system" and urged Congress to "investigate and make public findings on organizations . . . which are militantly serving Germany, Italy, Russia, Spain or any other alien power or system." Taylor further urged "national legislation that will punish American citizens who advocate the overthrow of our government by force, fraud or violence, and deport all aliens who so advocate such overthrow."

As the problem of refugees from nazi Germany arose, Taylor expressed Legion opposition to waving immigration restrictions and suggested that the German quota be used to accommodate them.

In 1939, when the German American Bund was engaged in extensive activities, the Americanism Commission reported:

It is our purpose to re-inspire and, if necessary, dramatize the traditional initiative of the American people and the will to preserve our constitutional form of democracy. . . . We are returning to the traditional American way although it has been difficult to retain a mental stability in these hysterical times. . . . Let us be prepared to preserve our traditions within the walls of our country and to resist the enemies from without.

Thus Legionnaires emerged with credit from two decades of struggle with the problems of working toward greater international understanding and of alerting the country to external and internal threats. Between the two world wars the Legion and the Auxiliary strove for peace. Both supported FIDAC and were represented in its deliberations; both encouraged wider study and discussion of international affairs and supported international agreements to which the United States became a party. The Legion maintained that several of its domestic programs, particularly national defense, were conducted in the interests of peace. The American Legion was convinced that a nation prepared could better meet any future vicissitudes. Adequate defense might modify the ominous lines,

> No truce with time, nor time's
> Accomplice, death. . . .

The Legion was one of the first groups to devote time and study to the difficult subject of international relations, an area that stretched like an unexplored continent before twentieth-century men. International relations achieved a certain vogue and, gradually, a prominence. Most approaches were unsophisticated, unproductive and even harmful. But broad frontiers for thought and consideration were opened.

Many who undertook to venture into international relations accepted questionable and false premises and theories, then attempted to make facts fit the confines of their preconceptions. But reality did not fit the shoe. Vanity may force a size five on a larger foot. This is hardly conducive to comfort in walking on cobblestones. Wishful thinking may disregard facts. This is hardly prudent in twentieth-century politics.

The American Legion demonstrated a greater sense of reality than most organizations and agencies, but was not altogether free of questionable optimism. Being uniquely American, the Legion was bound to hold American viewpoints and share certain widespread American misconceptions. The American individual crowded into his philosophy concepts, ideas, hopes, longings, horse sense, and a soaring idealism, cracker-barrel wisdom, and a towering optimism. But generally the Legion's programs were pragmatic and had the stamp of hard thinking. The Legion put forth strenuous efforts to improve foreign relations while interjecting into its foreign affairs program considerations felt to be imperative to the future of the Republic, its ideals, its principles, and its heritage. It is difficult to evaluate the influence of The American Legion in our foreign relations. Certainly it was substantial, although every point of Legion programs was not fulfilled. Again, the imponderable "ifs" arise. If the Legion's influence from crossroads to the nation's capital had been absent, surely our history might have been different. The wide chasm between the Legion and those who shared its views and the growing number of people who became mesmerized by pacifist doctrines gained emphasis and attention where America's foreign policy is roughly shaped. That is, within the executive and legislative branches of the government and among the general population which elects Presidents and congressmen. Through its publications and membership the Legion kept before the nation the issues of national security and foreign threats. The hard measures inspired by the Legion did not go by unnoticed by communists, fellow travelers and fascists. The communists came to regard The American Legion as an enemy and slated it for early dissolution during a revolutionary situation.

The end of an era of shallow and permissive thinking about the communist experiment should have come with the conclusion of Hitler's nonaggression pact with Soviet Russia, which put both tyrannies in a position to attack and carve up the Polish state. But, as we shall see, grave miscalculations were to be perpetuated in certain American attitudes and official policy decisions, and The American Legion was to face many more years of trying and unfulfilled activities in the foreign relations field.

The Proving Time

13

Through Depression and Reform

D URING the thirty years following midsummer, 1914, four great
international events took place which shattered the equilibrium
of the Western world and changed the course of history for all time.
One was the war in Europe, which in its course engulfed the United
States. The second of these calamitous circumstances was the great
depression halfway between two wars. The third commenced in 1939,
when the outbreak of the second world war occurred. And the fourth
was the rise in Russia of international communism, with which the
United States and the free world has struggled to this day.

These upheavals have been closely interrelated. While the United
States believed that it enjoyed a prosperity during the years which
followed the Armistice, thought by many to be endless, there were
economic dislocations which were part of the heritage of the war
years. Agriculture never recovered from the effects of overextension
of its planting to provide food and fiber for America and for the
nations ranked with her in the war. In the euphoria which possessed
so many Americans in the later 1920's, abundant credit and industrial expansion directly encouraged a wild wave of speculation in
land, in securities and in commodities grown from a teeming soil.
The stock market crash which cost investors something like thirty
billion dollars in a few weeks was merely the registration of facts
which might have been anticipated by anyone who looked below the surface at the conditions of the U.S. economy and its dangerous relationships with those of the rest of the Western world. The direct impact of the decline in stock values was not to be felt upon the

economy until some months later, for there was a momentum inherent in our massive economy which kept industries moving until they ground to a halt in 1930 and 1931.

Two theories of the causes of the great depression have been explored in the years since. One ascribes the trouble to domestic excesses and neglect. The other holds that the American economy could have achieved a measurable recovery as it had from previous upsets but for the repercussions of a collapse in Europe which began with failure of the Kreditanstalt in Austria in May 1931. A sober look at these theories which characterized the political conflict between President Hoover and Governor Roosevelt in the Presidential campaign of 1932 should convince the observer that both had a part in promoting the economic illness which prevailed in various forms in all of the Western world.

Four years of systematic destruction and deterioration of plant facilities had left deep scars on the economy of Europe. The needs of war created means of production for materials which were in oversupply in peace. There was not only need to rebuild the means of peacetime production but shifts in the direction of trade. Russia was isolated by her revolution. What she had contributed before in commodities such as wheat had to be imported from the United States, Canada and Australia. Further, Britain and France had lost tens of thousands of their more inventive and imaginative young men. The less able physically and mentally were left in oversupply. In Germany the pressure of reparations and the loss of her markets and colonies led first to ruinous inflation and then to vast unemployment. Austria under the terms of the treaty was left a body without a head. Social unrest swept over the Continent, especially in Germany, Italy, the Balkans, and Eastern Europe.

In a vain effort to rescue domestic economies, nations turned to nationalism and erected barriers to free trade—embargoes, tariffs, exchange restrictions, and barter trading.

Americans, riding a great wave of prosperity, had not yet learned how to carry the responsibilities which go with a creditor nation. It had entered the war a net debtor to European nations to the extent of three billion dollars. After the war, exclusive of the Allied debts, it was a creditor in the amount of six billion dollars. By 1926 the United States and France held half of the world's monetary gold.

In this situation Britain found it hazardous to return to a gold standard. She tried in 1925 but was forced off gold again in 1931.

The stock market crash had been preceded by ominous warning signs. Farmers had not recovered. For two years there had been declines in the production of manufactured goods and building. After the 1929 crash degenerative forces set in which had been latent for some years. Production, commodity prices, profits, employment, world trade, and international lending fell away. Of all these related manifestations of distress the loss of employment became the most serious to the average American family.

In preceding years there had never been reliable estimates of unemployment. But in the census of 1930 an effort was made to provide a reliable figure. It was somewhere between 3,000,000 and 4,500,000. After that the number looking hopelessly for jobs went up rapidly until it reached something like 12,000,000 in early 1933.

This vast wave of unemployment brought about unprecedented demands for relief. Savings withered away. Credit was constricted. Private philanthropy could not meet emergency needs. And local governments, struggling with declining revenues from taxation, felt the pinch in their efforts to supply public relief. Relief had never before been regarded as a proper function of the Federal government, but now there was an increasing demand that regardless of its impact upon the Federal budget, some means must be found to provide through the still unimpaired Federal credit the help state and local governments required. President Hoover at first tried valiantly to stimulate private resources to come to the rescue. But these efforts were like so many sand bags against a tidal crest. Remorselessly, the wave of depression swept across the land through the winter of 1930–31. But with the coming of spring, there were signs of improvement in the United States. The Hoover Administration took heart, believing that recovery was on the way. Instead, ahead lay collapse in Central Europe and acute economic distress followed by political crisis in the United Kingdom. These happenings, according to Hoover, marked the turn for the worse in the United States. For Europe could neither find the money to buy our products nor pay installments on her debts.

For the perceptive observer it is clear that the 1920's were replete with signs, both domestic and foreign, of eventual trouble. The decade of the 30's was the inheritor of fundamental and chronic difficulties.

We have already noted the irony of the U.S. farmers' position. They, who had contributed so much to alleviate the food shortages of the war and who had fed Europe's starving millions in its aftermath, had become too efficient and found their surpluses caught on a plunging coaster to low prices. Many veterans, too, had failed to become participants in the great prosperity. They were among the first to be affected.

The many U.S. veterans who early became part of the "hard core," stubborn unemployment figure had their counterparts abroad. Graham Wootton tells of the British government's shabby treatment of veterans.* Thousands of British ex-servicemen were unemployed and unemployable, through premature age and "chronic ill-health," their constitutions undermined while "doing their bit" for Britain. Wootton points out that in the hour of need these men had been "the salt of the earth," and had been told from thousands of recruiting platforms, "Go out and fight and when you return the nation will see you have a place in the sunshine."

The same was true in other countries, with dire consequences. For the problem contributed to the rise of demagogues and tyrants, the resort to expediency and the sacrifice of liberties. The world's ex-servicemen's problems dated back to the post-war period, when so many men who had learned the skill of combat at the expense of uninterrupted training for civilian employment had difficulty finding work.

Despite the frantic efforts of The American Legion in behalf of all unemployed veterans, without which their plight would have been deepened several shades, their situation was not to be relieved as it had been less than a decade before. It was inevitable that the perilous decline should not only deeply concern the leaders of The American Legion but affect the lives of most members of the Legion, representing as they did a cross section of American life. But in the proceedings of the Louisville Convention, held early in the same month that the stock market sounded the alarm, there is nothing to indicate that Legionnaires anticipated anything excepting the continuation of prosperity and progress. A year later at Boston the Legion was honored by the presence of President Hoover and former President Coolidge.

* *The Official History of the British Legion,* London, MacDonald and Evans Ltd, 1956.

In his address the President reviewed at some length the state of the Nation, its participation in international affairs, and his sympathy and approval of the efforts the Legion had made in the cause of good government. He also reviewed the activities of the Federal government in behalf of veterans. He noted that it was spending $900 million on veterans' affairs, and that of this $600 million was for veterans of World War I. He warned, no doubt anticipating more requirements for veterans, about further calls upon the government. They should not "exceed the measure that justice requires and self-help can provide. If we overload the burden of taxation, we shall stagnate our economic progress and we shall by the slackening of this progress place penalties on every citizen."

From the AF of L came William Green. If anyone should have been sensitive to the fact of rising unemployment it was this man. However, he spoke to the convention without great alarm. He said that there were thousands of men out of work and seeking employment, noted that "distress, to some extent, is abroad throughout the land," expressed the hope of improvement, and referred to signs of some turn in the tide. But he warned that "this coming winter is going to be most difficult." Therefore, he suggested, the Legion and the AF of L should cooperate in establishing "official committees in cities and towns in the industrial sections of the land, in an effort to relieve distress."

While even this distinguished leader of organized labor sought to allay alarm while admitting that unemployment and distress might be ahead, the Legion sought to be prepared for further economic trouble. Accordingly, the convention created a National Employment Commission headed by past Commander Howard P. Savage. During the year that followed this commission worked on a three-point program: (1) to obtain work for the unemployed; (2) to urge the appointment by the President of a representative group to find the cause and cure for the economic situation; and (3) to stimulate work projects by Federal, state and local governments. National Commanders O. L. Bodenhamer in 1929–30 and Ralph T. O'Neil in 1930–31 called upon the Legion's ten thousand posts to take action in behalf of the unemployed. The Employment Commission did likewise. Honor certificates were given to posts performing outstanding work in this effort.

While this activity was proceeding, a 50 per cent adjusted service loan act was passed by Congress. The beneficial results of this were immediately apparent. Distress among veterans subsided. Emergency relief stations established by the posts found their work reduced. In April, 1931, reports from the departments showed that altogether there were 6,000,000 unemployed, of which 710,000 were veterans.

The commission worked closely with the U.S. Employment Service, and a plan evolved for an employment office in each of the Legion's departments. These offices working with the U.S. Employment Service established methods for maintaining contacts with the posts. In September, 1931, in part at least due to the Legion's efforts, a conference was held in Washington with representatives of the U.S. Chamber of Commerce, the AF of L and various government agencies. This conference adopted a broad program in which Legion posts would cooperate with other agencies in their communities to create the means of registering the unemployed and in seeking to obtain jobs for as many of them as possible; to prevent if possible migration in search of work since it was thought better to seek relief in home communities; to create projects for "made work"; to create sentiment to urge Federal, state and local governments to undertake public improvements which would create more jobs; to recommend to employers and the employed to arrange for staggered employment by a five-day week and a six-hour day; and to urge upon the Americanism Commission the need for legislation further to restrict immigration during the emergency.

The Legion had regarded the fight for a bonus as completed in 1924 with the receipt by veterans of an "adjusted service credit certificate," not immediately payable. However, accumulating distress raised the question in a vital way in 1930. Certain congressmen, including Wright Patman, a persistent advocate of inflation, urged a plan which would have used unsecured paper currency to redeem the certificates. The Legion's NEC faced consideration of what stand the Legion should take. Under overwhelming pressure from posts, it deliberated and advocated immediate payment.

The threat of this issuance of paper money aroused the Hoover Administration and a large element of the business community. Owen D. Young, chairman of General Electric, appeared as a witness before the Ways and Means Committee and proposed a compromise.

His plan was that the loan value of the adjusted service certificates be increased to 50 per cent of their face amount. This would cost, he said, about $500,000,000, which could be raised by the Treasury without difficulty. Commander O'Neil and the Washington Headquarters rallied Legion strength and the Young plan was adopted by Congress and passed over a Presidential veto. The Legion considered this a victory for a rational solution. However, in the face of an increasing economic paralysis, it was a fleeting victory.

Young's optimism that only 30 per cent of veterans would ask for loans proved false. Ninety per cent clamored for the benefits and then for complete payment. Many prominent Legionnaires, among them Sam Reynolds, Hanford MacNider, Monroe Johnson, Theodore Roosevelt, Jr., Ed Spafford, and Harry Colmery, worked to line up support before the 1931 Convention to defeat any resolution asking prepayment. They were confident of a large margin when a "bombshell" disrupted their plans. President Hoover suddenly announced that he would appear before the delegates, although he had deferred response to an official invitation. Newspapers quickly surmised that Secretary Mellon was behind this move. These Legionnaires feared the President might defeat his own purpose, and MacNider attempted to dissuade the President.

But Hoover felt he could not alter his public announcement. In a short address he pointed to the fact that the Federal budget was facing another substantial deficit largely due to a fall in revenues and more expenditures for public works to help employment. He urged the necessity of the utmost care in such expenditures. Also he noted that within the week the National Commander and the Employment Commission had visited him to offer Legion cooperation to relieve distress during the coming winter. He gratefully accepted, for by this time suffering was abroad in the land and earlier hopes for revival were fading. The President concluded his remarks with a moving appeal for the same spirit of sacrifice which had characterized the war "when you and I served our appointed tasks." In the report of Commander Ralph T. O'Neil the work of the Legion in behalf of employment and the alleviation of unemployment distress was placed second only to the Legion's concern for the disabled. He said that due to the Legion's efforts no less than 200,000 had obtained employment.

Colmery read the majority report of the Legislative Committee which concluded:

> That the American Legion in full possession of its limitless faith in the destiny of the nation we fought to preserve, calls upon the able-bodied men of America, rich and poor, veteran, civilian and statesman, to refrain from placing unnecessary financial burdens upon the nation, state or municipal governments and to unite their efforts as they did in 1917 to the end that the war against the depression be victoriously concluded, prosperity and happiness restored.

Past National Commanders James A. Drain and O. L. Bodenhamer and Legionnaires James Morris of D.C. and Wallace Williams of Maryland spoke for the resolution. Wright Patman, as a delegate from Texas, Ray Fields of Oklahoma and others fought for prepayment. The vote by roll call was 902 to 507 for the majority report, and although the press attributed the victory to Hoover, those who had worked for the resolution felt they would have won by a larger majority had the President not appeared. Legionnaires felt they stood on "the high ground of patriotic idealism." It proved a difficult summit to hold.

When the Congress assembled in December 1931, many bills were introduced for the full payment of the bonus, and finally the Patman Bill went through the House. Two days later the Senate, influenced by its revulsion to the Bonus army and the inability of the government to deal with it, rejected the measure 62 to 18. Now the Legion observed from their vantage point gained at Detroit the sad spectacle of the Bonus marchers.

The "Bonus Expeditionary Force," or BEF, in its trek from Oregon to Washington, D.C., grew to considerable size, attracted adventurers and agitators and caused two deaths. Most marchers were "down-and-out" veterans; the rest, a scattering of women and children and an undetermined number of malcontents, including a few zealous communist agitators. At the end of May the vanguard struggled into Washington and within a few days they numbered between ten and twenty thousand persons without means. They managed to survive in vacant buildings and jerry-built shacks along the Potomac on what was known as the Anacostia Flats.

The BEF proved a problem to many individuals, agencies of government and the Legion. The American Legion took no official part in what it regarded as a deplorable and futile odyssey, accompanied as it was by certain excesses, but Legion posts did feed marchers, a Legion band played during one of their parades in Washington and a Legion post buried a marcher at Arlington. The area and its inhabitants presented a problem to the government of the District of Columbia. The Chief of Police, General Pelham D. Glassford, told the campers that they would receive fair treatment if they maintained law and order, and he secured tents and blankets for them. A few communists and other troublemakers encouraged the veterans, and Anacostia took on the aspect of a semi-permanent slum. The main concern of all authorities was to get the marchers back to their homes, and Congress appropriated $100,000 to make loans to cover railroad fares. Congress then adjourned, leaving the responsibility with the District authorities and the President. While more than five thousand secured these loans and some went home, others arrived. An effort by the District commissioners to get the army out of town failed. And then the situation reached a climax. The police killed one Bonus marcher in self-defense and wounded others.

It was a particularly critical moment for the President. The political campaign of 1932 was already under way. Hoover directed General Douglas MacArthur to get the remaining individuals out of town. Troops used tear gas and scattered the BEF without resort to shooting or killing. The burning camp lighted the capital's sky that night, and by morning the BEF was disbanded. While the whole incident did not affect the bonus payment, it took its toll in the declining popularity of President Hoover.

Whether the political campaign in 1932 was a contributing factor to further distress is a matter which will be debated forever. In the fall of 1932 the markets, after a brief rise earlier in the year, began to fall again. In three years the GNP had dropped to the 1920 level. By the coming of the new year not only did employment fall farther, but the banks entered a crisis which was to reach its climax in February and March.

The 1932 Legion Convention in Portland was a nerve-racking affair. Sam Reynolds of Nebraska withdrew his name from consideration for Commander and took the floor to assail prepayment. Many present were of the Bonus army and he could hardly make himself heard. Delegates voted overwhelmingly in favor of immediate payment. But the bonus question was destined to be of secondary importance.

In the midst of a hotly fought Presidential campaign, no political preference was uttered by a Legion speaker at Portland, nor was either candidate in attendance. But politics was in the air. Commander Henry L. Stevens, as well as Reynolds, spoke of a subject which was to stimulate a major legislative struggle in the year that followed. In February, 1932, the House of Representatives had created an Economy Committee to consider and reduce the benefits for veterans in the interest of holding down the prospective budgetary deficit in the coming fiscal year. The Commander pointed out that this committee held its meetings behind closed doors, affording representatives of the Legion no opportunity to present their views.

The Economy Committee proposed an eighty-million-dollar reduction in veterans' benefits. Seven changes in the law were proposed—a need test, a reduction of compensation to veterans in hospitals, removal of the "presumptive service connected" clause from the Emergency Officers' Retired list, elimination of the per diem allowance for men awaiting hospitalization, abolition of the retroactive allowance for more than six months, modification of the procedure against the government in War Risk Insurance cases, and repeal of sections of law regarding the revival of insurance.

Legion officers had alerted posts, and as a result of a combined publicity drive and vigorous lobbying, these provisions were defeated in both the House and the Senate. However, the Commander warned, the fight would be resumed in the next session, since the House Economy Committee was planning hearings during the recess.

Since its establishment by adoption of Representative Lewis W. Douglas' resolution, the Economy Committee had had the full cooperation of General Hines of the Veterans Bureau. While Legion representatives were not permitted behind its closed doors, Hines had a hand in framing a number of its recommendations including the provisions of the law concerning veterans' disability.

The Legion had cause for dark suspicion and grave concern. The Democratic platform of 1932 recommended that the Federal budget be cut 25 per cent. Roosevelt in his campaign had come out strongly for economy and went into office committed to it. The budget directorship went to Lewis Douglas. Then, in the period before Roosevelt's inauguration, a stringent economy bill was prepared by Douglas, who had the assistance of Representative Swager Sherley, Dean Acheson and others. Since Roosevelt had been convinced that a strong move for economy would be a powerful stimulant to confidence and thus assist the cause of recovery, he agreed to make the Douglas Bill a major part of his program.

The bill was introduced on March 10, and, despite strong objections in Congress, was passed on March 20. This measure was called "An Act to Maintain the Credit of the United States Government."

It was estimated that this legislation would save something like $750 million. Of this, $470 million was cut from veterans' benefits and the remainder from an over-all reduction of 15 per cent in the compensation of government employees. Undoubtedly, in the haste with which the bill was prepared, adequate consideration was not given to the real and just needs of many disabled veterans. Douglas was among the first to recognize this. Through many weeks representatives of the Legion strongly argued their case before Congress. On Capitol Hill and in the country Legion spokesmen tangled with many powerful and celebrated individuals—those connected with the National Economy League, which included numerous men of great ability and wealth, leaders of the Chamber of Commerce and certain Congressional leaders. In asking for the bill Mr. Roosevelt had said that the Federal government had been on the road toward bankruptcy in piling up an accumulated deficit of five billion dollars in three years. He had yet to embrace the doctrine of the efficacy of deficit financing. In 1933, when economy was considered, veterans' benefits immediately came in for scrutiny. The most indefensible cuts involved benefits related to battle casualties and the tuberculosis and neuropsychiatric cases, although other reductions were heavy. Service-connected death compensation was to be severely cut back. While opposition in the House faltered, in the Senate the bill came under heavy bombardment. James Couzens of Michigan, Cutting of New Mexico and Steiwer of Oregon lined up with Bennett Clark of Missouri, who said that he wanted his vote against the measure inscribed upon his tombstone. But nothing availed to change the measure, and it passed the Senate on March 20. "Descriptions" were soon promulgated which clarified the full extent of the measure. For example, the one-legged veteran was cut from $60 to $20 per month. Certain TB and mental cases with presumption of service-connection received nothing. Now the Legion's Legislative Committee and Washington Headquarters went into action with Commander Louis Johnson. Johnson took up the regulations with the President on May 10. Ray Murphy, Taylor and Edward Lewis worked among congressmen while Watson Miller conferred with the President's experts to alleviate some of the injustices. Through the ceaseless labor of other Legionnaires at Indianapolis, on national committees and in energetic departments, and the humble but effective activities of Legionnaires who could make their convictions known only by letters from their communities, pressure was brought to bear on Congress and the Executive Branch.

Amendments to the regulations were worked out and issued on June 6. For example, the above $20 compensation was raised to $36. Meantime, congressmen, shocked at the power they had vested in the President, drove through a limitation on reductions to 25 per cent. This June 16 enactment set boards of review in all Veterans Administration offices and a central Board of Appeals.

Still, the act which took effect on July 1 was a severe blow, and The American Legion prepared for a long fight. Commander Edward A. Hayes laid out "four points" of attack: (1) restoration of rates for service-connected death and disability compensation; (2) restoration of some 29,000 "presumptive" cases disallowed by the boards; (3) restoration of the general hospitalization privilege of veterans; and (4) protection for the widows and orphans of World War I. Raymond Kelly became Legislative Chairman and Earl V. Cliff, Rehabilitation Chairman. They joined the fray in Washington "to educate Congress and the public." It should be noted that when Budget Director Douglas realized that in the administration of the legislation gross injustices were imposed, he wrote to Roosevelt and asked for review boards to assure restoration of compensation for service-connected disabilities.

The Legion fought a hard campaign. Within a year major elements of the Economy Act were discarded. Three of the four points were won. The widows and orphans bill, which had never been law, was destined to wait. Some 382,579 drawing partial disability allowances remained off the rolls and pending applications were not considered. Through Legion efforts and those of others who fought beside it the cause of all veterans was reaffirmed. The faith in the nation whose sons had returned from her wars impaired was vindicated.

In addition to restoring lost benefits, the law of March, 1934, liberalized the eligibility requirements for nonservice-connected hospitalization and instituted the procedure requiring veterans applying for such hospitalization to declare on the application their inability to pay for treatment in private hospitals. The Legion considers this basic legislation, and many of its provisions are applicable today. Three months later Congress enacted another Legion proposal which gave pension benefits to widows and orphans of veterans who had died from nonservice-connected disabilities.

The American Legion in its rehabilitation efforts and care for the disabled had continued to keep close track of the Veterans Bureau and then of the VA. Legionnaires responsible for reporting to the national organization became alarmed at an early date at the fact that U.S. veterans' hospitals had not met expectations. In its 1931 Convention report they spelled out their dissatisfaction, emphasizing that in the VA hospitals good medical practice was being suffocated by the weight of bureaucratic and political considerations. Bureaucracy was driving out many good doctors, and some hospitals had become havens for physicians unsure of their ability to make out in private practice. The Legion had the benefit of the services of many top-flight doctors within its membership who served as a national American Legion Advisory Board. However, conditions did not improve. In 1941 the Legion felt that VA medicine had continued to get worse and at its National Convention at Milwaukee it "took off the kid gloves" and adopted a resolution urging that VA medicine be reconstituted, VA doctors freed from bureaucratic control, that they be organized as a separate medical department, that an improved system of promotion and transfer of personnel based on merit be established, and that the light of outside medical practice be brought into the VA. The consuming occupation of war and the tight coils of bureaucracy perpetuated the unsatisfactory situation until the reforms proposed by the Legion were brought about in 1946.

The Legion's legislative attention with regard to veterans returned to the confused problem of payment of the bonus. Conventions in 1933 at Chicago and in 1934 at Miami reaffirmed the Portland resolution. The Patman measure was bounced about the capital with

House passage, Senate maneuvering and Presidential veto. When the Legion under Commander Frank Belgrano realized that the inflationary Patman Bill was a hopeless cause, it searched for another plan. Representative Fred M. Vinson, a Legionnaire, submitted a simple prepayment bill but was frustrated by Patman.

In January 1936 the Legion was determined to "go down the line for the Vinson Bill." Commander Ray Murphy urged smaller veterans' groups to cooperate, and the drive was on. After passage in the House, the bill, which provided payment by bonds that could be cashed or held to maturity in 1945, was rewritten in its final form by the Senate. Roosevelt vetoed the bill but knew the fight was over and before the final vote instructed the VA to prepare for payment. His veto lost 325 to 61 in the House and 76 to 19 in the Senate. Most bonds were cashed within the year.

The four billion dollars which adjusted compensation cost was soon to be dwarfed by rising Federal spending and virtually lost when measured against the astronomical costs of World War II and the domestic and foreign programs of its aftermath. Legionnaires feel that their somewhat inconsistent record regarding payment must be considered in the context of a period of swirling politics, inflation, government spending, and distress. Although its enemies have seemed never to tire of striking at the Legion with the "bonus stick," it is interesting that many of them have championed Federal spending for the sake of spending. They have advocated legislation which had none of the justification upon which adjusted compensation was based. And in most opponents of the Legion the real reasons behind their attacks are profound differences in fundamental principles and ideology.

Although many Legionnaires have been and are reluctant to acknowledge their significant achievements in certain areas as the result of political action, in the 1930's they had become highly proficient in the nonpartisan sense. They had suffered setbacks in the field of national defense and they were to be unsuccessful in attempting to provide military training in the CCC camps. But there were other sources of gratification. At Legion prompting, Congress had created the War Policies Commission, which included five Cabinet officials. In 1932, after hearing Legion leaders, prominent men in industry and labor, military officers, and spokesmen for civilian organizations, this body formulated a plan to "take the profit motive out of war." Its proposal that in the event of hostilities individuals and corporations should be taxed 95 per cent on all earnings above a previous three-year average was to be influential ten years later.

In the field of child welfare the Legion, by example and by political pressure, brought about improvement of conditions, particularly at state and local levels in the 1930's. Hence, conscientious Legionnaires might share the conviction of my father, who observed:

> Politics is not something to avoid or abolish or destroy. It is a condition like the atmosphere we breathe. It is something to live with, to influence if we wish and to control if we can. We must master its ways or we shall be mastered by those who do.

As if to heap additional suffering on communities hit by the ravages of economic catastrophe, the forces of nature struck frequently in the 1930's. The American Legion and its posts had dealt with natural disasters many times before, but in the darkness before dawn on September 3, 1935, Legionnaires of the Harvey Seeds Post of Miami moved into the largest disaster job organized Legionnaires had yet undertaken. Hurricane winds and tidal waves had ripped across the Florida Keys, inflicting heavy damage and snuffing out hundreds of lives between Miami and Key West. Among them were veterans, remnants of the Washington Bonus army, located in three Federal Emergency Relief Administration camps, who had been working on bridge and road construction. Out of 696, 256 were killed—a sad ending for men already beaten down by the catalog of life's misfortunes. Through four days Legionnaires in rescue squads risked their own safety to save lives and to minister to the desperate needs of their former comrades and others in the disaster area. They were aided by many other workers and women of the Auxiliary.

In previous disasters Legion posts had gained a reputation for mobilizing faster than other community organizations. There were notable examples in the Indiana tornado areas in 1923 and a mine disaster in Illinois in 1924. The Omaha Convention in 1925 resolved "that the National Americanism Commission be, and hereby is, instructed to perfect such arrangements as may appear most advisable whereby the American Legion may assist in emergency relief." Subsequently, many posts and departments made arrangements for disaster relief, including assignment of tasks, training in first aid and lifesaving, and many other essential preparations. Pamphlets instructed posts on organization of disaster relief units. Arrangements were made with other agencies for delegation of responsibilities. Negotiations brought about agreements with the Red Cross, the national agency charged with general disaster relief and with raising relief funds. Stephen F. Chadwick, Chairman of the Americanism Commission, described this 1926 liaison in 1937 when he pointed out Red Cross and Legion disaster relief coordination:

> The Red Cross recognizes that the disaster relief activities of The American Legion are of two kinds:
> First, those activities that The American Legion carries on under its own authority and because of its own type of organization, such as assistance in maintaining law and order.
> Second, those activities that The American Legion carries on in co-operation with the American Red Cross, such as assistance in meeting the emergency food, clothing and shelter needs of disaster sufferers.
> The American Legion recognizes the American Red Cross as the agency chartered by the Congress to represent the American people in carrying on disaster relief, and, therefore, as the primary agency. . . . This joint recognition of the place of each organization in the field of disaster relief permits of distinctive activities on the part of each and at the same time furnishes the basis for a cooperative plan of action that will best serve the interests of those who suffer from disaster.

In 1927 the Mississippi went on a rampage and the preparations of scores of posts from Cairo, Illinois, to the Gulf of Mexico paid off. For two months Legion posts up and down the river basin worked with other citizens to keep to a minimum the enormous devastation—building levees, evacuating threatened lowlands, rescuing hundreds of persons stranded when the river and her tributaries brushed aside man-made barriers. Sixteen days after work on the levee at Dorena, Missouri, started, it was taken out. Commander Clarence Dick of Aubra Township Post of Kentucky crossed the river in a gasboat and brought out refugees. More boats went into action and a refugee camp was established. After hours of lifesaving, Dick went into the backwaters and sidestreams and brought out five hundred more people in a steamer secured for the search. Six days later the levee above

Greenville, Mississippi, went out. The Beppo Arnold Post served nine thousand meals a day. Power boats from the Gulf were railroaded to the river and with barges, hauled by steamboats, they recovered thousands of persons.

Remorselessly, the devastation moved south, fingering out from the great river and its tributaries. Up and down the Mississippi and on a hundred rivers and streams that feed it, Legionnaires and their fellow citizens labored on, exhausted from days on the levees and in boats, their pants stuck to their legs with river mud and their shirts to their backs with sweat and grime, bone-weary, sunken-eyed. Arkansas and Louisiana, also in the path of the flood crest, suffered perhaps more devastation than Mississippi. When the Red River and the Bayou des Glaises broke through the levees, hundreds of thousands of acres of Louisiana were submerged. New Orleans, to save itself, dynamited the levee below the city while the main levees stood firm. Secretary of Commerce Herbert Hoover led government relief work, receiving full Red Cross and Legion support. When he appealed for boats, a Legion commander from Monroe provided forty to work with a barge fleet saving refugees. Forty towns were wiped out and 400,000 people left homeless.

Following the emergency, Legion representatives from six states met in Memphis under Roane Waring of Memphis and formed an American Legion Central Flood Relief Committee which aided the government and the Red Cross with rehabilitation for the homeless.

In the great disasters of subsequent years, the Legion continued to provide emergency relief and perfected its techniques for tornadoes, floods, earthquakes, and other natural disasters. An earthquake which struck Long Beach, California, late in the afternoon of March 10, 1933, triggered immediate Legion and Auxiliary mobilization. In that catastrophe between 150 and 200 persons were killed and another 2,000 injured. Though the Army, Navy and National Guard acted with dispatch, the Long Beach *Press* and other publications emphasized that American Legion workers were the first to mobilize.

At the 1934 National Convention in New Jersey, Legionnaires and members of the Auxiliary canceled their schedules and festivities to work day and night to aid the survivors of the steamship *Morro Castle* which burned off the coast. Other notable disasters in which Legionnaires distinguished themselves were the 1933 flood at Newport, Kentucky, the Nebraska floods in 1935 and the 1938 disaster on Loop Creek, Washington. The last almost demolished the town of Malott after a dam collapsed. Add to that list the March 1938 floods in southern California and the 1940 floods along the Arkansas River in Oklahoma. The Ohio and Mississippi floods of 1937, greatest in recent American history, saw scores of Legion rescue squads in action. Thousands of tons of food and clothing were distributed through Legion centers and more than a quarter of a million dollars raised and turned over to the Red Cross. Legionnaires manned thousands of boats and many flew airplanes loaded with supplies and communications equipment to isolated locales. The Auxiliary fed the hungry, sheltered the dispossessed, ministered to the injured.

Besides the above, Legion disaster workers reported rescue and relief operations in nine hurricanes and cyclones and a disastrous fire in Auburn, Maine, in the 1930's.

The auspicious progress made by the Legion, the Auxiliary, the Forty and Eight, and the Eight and Forty in the 1920's in the field of child welfare became an extremely successful undertaking in the 1930's. The Endowment Fund grew, at least one-half of its earnings allotted to child welfare and $10,000 budgeted to cover administrative expenses of the National Child Welfare Division in Indianapolis. At the department and post level, child welfare activities were greatly expanded and the country was divided into five area groups, with a Child Welfare chairman as the presiding officer. The Auxiliary appointed an Area Child Welfare Chairman as well to cooperate in the work within the area. Annual conferences with equal participation by the four groups mentioned above became important affairs. Every Legion post was urged to work within its community through a Child Welfare chairman. In 1937 a Legion publication, *Child Welfare Guide*, emphasized:

> An alert, efficient Child Welfare Chairman is able to compare the conditions and problems in the community with the facilities that exist for the prevention, protection and care of children, and if those facilities fall short of the needs, he does something about it. He brings the matter to the attention of others in his community whom he can interest, and soon there is enough interest to compel attention, and those in authority will improve conditions almost as quickly as public opinion demands it.

Mutual benefits were obtained by cooperative relationships between Legion Department Child Welfare chairmen and Post Child Welfare chairmen and those in charge of local, state and national agencies, and organizations related to child welfare. The Legion's aid, available to the family or child of World War I veterans, came to be expeditiously handled by efficient methods and knowledgeable personnel. By immediate attention to emergency situations a maximum benefit could be realized, and post chairmen assumed considerable responsibility in this area. The Legion retained responsibility for families and children in many such cases until Federal aid was "actually received by the families." The Legion also instructed its chairmen to recognize that "pauperization is a menace," and it regarded the disclosure of the identities of those it aided as "thoroughly unethical, highly destructive, and truly unpardonable."

National Convention mandates during the 1930's called for securing in department officers persons with experience in child welfare work, publicity of child welfare conditions in *The American Legion Monthly,* strengthening state child labor laws, Federal aid for physical rehabilitation, education and vocational guidance of physically handicapped, expansion of a minimum Child Welfare legislative program to include a public health record for every child and protection of the juvenile offender, raising of local child care and protection standards, spreading of information on maternal and child care, social hygiene and other related subjects, and strengthening its Child Welfare legislative library and research material.

The American Legion adhered to a policy of not relieving local communities and states of their responsibilities. It was ready to point out in 1937:

> The more than fifty-year battle to help get needy children out of poorhouses and jails, and to secure for them proper care and protection, is gradually reaching its accomplishment even though it has its setbacks in periods of economic depression.
>
> In the midst of emergency relief administration for the unemployed and destitute, children and their more personal needs are almost entirely forgotten beyond just the bare necessities of life that provide immediate food, a covering of clothing and shelter.

Throughout the troubled years of the 1930's The American Legion placed increased stress upon its youth programs under the Americanism Commission. Its sponsorship of Scout Units rose from 1,500 to 2,631. The Auxiliary's efforts paralleled those of the Legion. It was an ardent supporter of the Girl Scouts, the Campfire Girls and the Girl Reserves. And it supplemented the widespread Legion support of 4-H Club activities.

The Sons of The American Legion, founded in 1932, had as its purpose the development of good citizenship and an objective to carry on Legion programs after Legionnaires were gone. It flourished in several states and had a membership of 72,000 in 1941, when World War II began to produce another generation of veterans. This affiliate had its beneficial effects upon those who participated. In many communities it worked out its own salvation, developing many drum and bugle corps and drill and rifle teams. It established summer camps, Americanism councils and a variety of character-building activities. A high percentage of participants were to serve in the Armed Forces and its younger members to carry out other wartime tasks, including bond drives, scrap collection and civilian defense.

Outside the scope of the Legion's nationwide youth programs, thousands of posts demonstrated that they needed no national manual to improve conditions for their youth. Summer camps, bathing areas, fishing derbies, athletic contests, special programs in juvenile delinquency areas, teen-age dances in Legion halls, and a score of other activities were financed and supervised by conscientious posts for the benefit of their communities' youth.

American Legion Junior Baseball became the Legion's largest national youth program in the 1930's with upward to 400,000 youngsters participating. Of that period a Legionnaire has recently emphasized that while many professional ballplayers began to rise to prominence after gaining experience in Legion baseball and most youngsters enjoyed the pastime the Legion's objective was more ambitious:

> Junior Baseball was not just sport. The sport was bait which the young ballplayers readily took. The Legion from the start was insistent that, along with baseball, the local Legion coach would require his players to learn and live up to all the standards of playing the game that apply also to the game of life.

Still, the millions of American baseball fans have thrilled to the skill and dedication of many, many stars who began their playing days and found their enthusiasm on the dusty baselines and mounds of Legion sandlots. Bob Feller, the greatest pitcher of his day, has recalled that he "cut his baseball eyeteeth" on American Legion Junior Baseball in 1931. He began playing as a shy boy of twelve at Adel, Iowa, a town of 1,100 population and ten miles from his home in Van Meter. Feller was deeply influenced by Legionnaire Lester Chance who organized and coached the team. Chance brought Feller along until Feller switched to a Des Moines Legion team. Feller has emphasized that he gained friendships and valued experiences from those early days that have never left him and paid a tribute to Chance, one of thousands of men with similar dedication:

> Mr. Chance died three years ago. His last request was that his ashes be spread on the Adel diamond, on a direct line from home plate to center field. This was done by his sons-in-law. Even in death, he wanted to remain close to the program which had been a major part of his life. From such dedication American Legion Junior Baseball has flourished.

In his days of glory, Feller played before stands often crowded with Legionnaires and at such times, seeing the Legion caps all around, he would find himself "thinking back to the days when men wearing those same caps were building my baseball foundations."

As a Legionnaire Feller has devoted time to being chairman of The American Legion Division in Cleveland consisting of more than 120 teams. In 1962 he was honored by the Americanism Commission with a trophy for "the first American Legion baseball graduate enshrined in Baseball's Hall of Fame." The ceremony took place at Bismarck, North Dakota—a few hours' drive from the Legion monument at Milbank, South Dakota, which commemorates the inception of Junior Baseball with a statewide tournament there in 1925.

Only in 1934 did professional ball fail to support the Legion program. Frank Knox, New Hampshire Legion leader who became Secretary of the Navy, and Dan Sowers, a portly and aggressive Legionnaire, raised needed funds by private subscription.

During the 30's the number of nationwide baseball leagues, patterned after the Legion undertaking, increased, and numerous organizations and businesses aided Legion posts in sponsorship. Legionnaires have been anxious to point out that they "claim no monopoly" in promoting these programs.

The American Legion School Medal Awards increased from 1,046 in 1926 to 8,417 in 1936 and to 13,302 in 1943. Alumni groups of holders of this award organized in some communities to devote attention to aid to education. The Legion's essay contests were discontinued as a national program, but received a large response where adequately managed by departments in the 1930's. Ohio reported 100,000 essays submitted in 1937, and a dozen states held contests in 1939.

In 1938 The American Legion National Oratorical Contest was first held. It was started in 1923 by *The Los Angeles Times* and was conducted for a period of years by a group of papers. When it was discontinued, high school debating coaches and speech instructors were anxious to see this activity revived. The Legion found an immediate response to this program "designed to encourage high school students to study the U.S. Constitution and Bill of Rights which give them their freedoms." The competition, from the community level to the national finals, produces a winner who receives a four thousand dollar scholarship and addresses the National Convention. By 1939 the program had spread to twenty departments, and in 1942, forty-seven departments participated.

Another highly successful Americanism program originated in Illinois in 1935—Boys' State. It was adopted as a national program in 1936 when Ohio, Pennsylvania and West Virginia joined, and by 1940 it had expanded to thirty-four states. From the first Illinois experiment, conducted by Hayes Kennedy, the program has reflected an ambitious, difficult, but rewarding undertaking. The Legion explains:

> Boys are given the opportunity to learn government by operating government. They organize political parties and operate a pattern-type government of their own with every boy playing an active role. State, county and municipal elections are held on the legal pattern of the respective states. City and county governments are formed and operated by the boys, and a state government, complete with executive, legislative and judicial units, emerges and functions. The boys themselves perform

every operation and fill every position in government, elective and appointive.

Thus, in the crucial period between the wars The American Legion went far in its own programs and in its support of others dedicated to the moral, spiritual, intellectual, and physical strength of youth. Its programs and many of its actions were constantly under attack, as were those of other groups devoted to similar goals. For the period produced a plethora of nostrums, offered to cure all of society's ills. There was the spread of socialist and even communist ideas, since many felt that capitalism had brought about the world's miseries. Many American intellectuals clutched at ideologies antagonistic to American principles. Emphasis on state planning rose. American ideals came in for hard scrutiny and questioning. Numerous people suspected patriotism, and, in the terrible trial, liberties. They concluded that people, if given great liberties, may abuse them. Pacifism swept the academic community. It was inevitable that the Legion would have more frequent and bitter controversies with educational groups and numerous intellectuals. It continued to exercise an outspoken opposition to textbooks it felt undermined American principles. Individual Legionnaires and local posts, as private citizens and as organized groups, continued to have a powerful influence with local school boards. This situation brought about strained relations with the NEA and the U.S. Office of Education with which the Legion worked year after year. The Legion endorsed Federal aid when large grants-in-aid by Congress went to public schools where financial ability to sustain a satisfactory educational program was lacking. But it maintained the condition that such aid be free of Federal control. The Legion succeeded in increasing the emphasis upon American history and civics in the public schools, but not without occasional demands for dismissal of an educator with radical leanings, bitter publicity and recriminations. Of course, The American Legion collided with the pacifists on the issue of ROTC, as in 1936, when strenuous efforts were made in Congress to abolish compulsory military training in land-grant colleges. Its no-quarter conflict with those considered "un-American" is considered in previous chapters.

Legionnaires are emphatic in pointing out that they have never claimed a "monopoly on patriotism" and express appreciation of the fact that during the 1930's "an increasing number of organizations joined them in participation in flag ceremonies, observance of patriotic holidays, loyalty days, and national holidays." In 1939 the Congress of Parent-Teachers and Canadian educational groups joined in the work of observing American Education Week.

It was during the 30's, prior to the second world war, that The American Legion encountered severe criticism from its habitual detractors and suffered from some dissension within its ranks because of real, imagined or magnified conditions. One had to do with a certain amount of wild behavior during Legion conventions.

National Conventions of The American Legion came to lack nothing in pageantry, color, celebration, good times, stirring music, excitement, and general fun-making. Indeed, these aspects of the annual conventions too often obscured nationally important and sound deliberations of the thousand or fifteen hundred delegates. Serious Legionnaires regretted that hard committee work was relegated to the inside pages of newspapers while the gay, sunshine atmosphere of the conventions was splashed in headlines on front pages. Proposals for the forthcoming year and reports of hard-won victories were subordinated too frequently to rather sensational accounts of frivolity and even misbehavior. At a time when many Americans were pinched by hard times, Legionnaires felt that their beloved organization was suffering from the superficial aspects of their annual gathering and the reports of many hostile newspapermen and "yellow journalists" who covered them. Any convention offered Legion critics incidents upon which they gloated and related with relish as "typical of The American Legion."

National Conventions were well attended, by hundreds of delegates and alternates, thousands of other Legionnaires not accredited who came to attend the largest Legion gathering of the year and thousands more who flooded into metropolitan centers to view the famous Legion parades, reviews and competitions. For many Legionnaires and citizens alike these few days were the high point of festivity during the year, and some felt entitled to "let their hair down." This inclination was frequently encouraged by local authorities and businessmen who provided every outlet for a visitor's exuberance and the contents of his pocketbook. The press exploited the colorful, hilarious and, sometimes, very rowdy behavior. The so-called "Where's

Elmer?" parties were given inordinate publicity at the expense of the organized glamour of the celebration. Legionnaires moved from party to party in downtown hotels, the inquiry "Where's Elmer?" gaining them admittance. Since the American society does not condone such irregular antics in most communities, many of those who traveled to Legion conventions took advantage of this release from repressive local attitudes. Further, the participants were generally not so affluent as to make the daily pattern of their lives so carefree and festive. This is not something that was or is characteristic of Legion conventions alone. The drinking and noisy conduct at Legion conventions was and is part of practically all conventions of any size in the United States, including those of the service clubs, businessmen's and labor associations, professional meetings, and fraternal gatherings.

This festive mood and holiday spirit dated back to 1921 in Kansas City, mentioned previously, and Cleveland a year earlier. But Kansas City set the pace, and a fast pace it was. While Legionnaires marched with a rusty military precision and complete discipline, the onlookers knew no restraint. As the foreign dignitaries rode past and Marine General John A. Lejeune tramped by on foot, confetti mixed with straw and feathers pulled from pillows and even mattresses showered down upon them. So many people had poured into the city that, as Richard Seelye Jones observed a quarter of a century later:

> When the line of parade had been completed, bands and bugle corps invaded public buildings, and one enthusiast rode his horse into the principal hotel lobby. The celebration lasted all night, a circumstance assisted by the inability of many visitors to find a place to sleep. There were dancing, drinking and dicing. . . . In 1922 a similar spectacle moved the length of Canal Street in New Orleans, and in 1923 up the broad reaches of Market Street in San Francisco. St. Paul in 1924, Omaha in 1925 and Philadelphia in 1926 vied for records of entertainment for the multitude. . . . In 1928 the Legion met at San Antonio, Texas, in 1929 at Louisville, in 1930 at Boston, in 1931 at Detroit, in 1932 at Portland, Oregon, and in 1933 at Chicago. Each city was holding its first national Legion gathering and sought to outdo all others in hospitality. President Hoover was at Boston and at Detroit. President Roosevelt came to Chicago. The Century of Progress Exposition was in full swing. The crowds and enthusiasm surrounding the convention were the greatest yet recorded.

For 1934 the Legion chose Miami, Florida. . . . The 1935 gathering was at St. Louis. In 1936 the site of the second convention, Cleveland, became the first city to repeat with the eighteenth. For 1937 the invitation of New York City was accepted. . . . Two and a half million spectators witnessed the seventeen-hour-long parade. . . . Street cleaners swept up six and a half tons of paper after it was over. . . . The 1938 gathering went to Los Angeles, where the glamour of Hollywood was added to the hospitality of the great Southwest. In 1939 Chicago again welcomed the veteran hosts, and in 1940 Boston repeated the spectacle of ten years earlier. . . . The last prewar convention packed (Milwaukee) full to overflowing and witnessed another magnificent parade.*

The onset of war canceled convention plans for four years.

The Forty and Eight Society, noted among Legionnaires as outstanding in good works as well as in horseplay, gained inordinate attention at conventions. La Société, organized in 1920 in Philadelphia, went to Cleveland in a boxcar (the title Forty and Eight deriving from French railroad cars which carried forty men or eight horses). Before World War II its "wrecking crews" had initiated many outstanding Legionnaires into its 143 "voitures" in thirty-one states.

Annual events within the Legion were numerous—a dinner of the Founders of the Legion who had been present at the original Paris or St. Louis Caucuses, the annual farewell dinner to the retiring National Commander given by the Headquarters staff in Indianapolis, the National Americanism Commission's annual luncheon, and, throughout the country, departmental and post celebrations and observances.

The Legion's political strictures were almost universally observed, but in 1933 the NEC was called upon to enforce adherence to its National Constitution. This was a result of political activity and irregularities in the Department of New Mexico. After strenuous debate, in which the department was accused of repeatedly violating the prohibition against those holding elective public office serving as Legion officials and the assertion made that before state conventions, politicians paid dues for scores of members, some nonexistent, to gain additional delegates, the state's charter was suspended. It appeared that the old "tombstone-vote" practice of machine politics had

* *A History of The American Legion,* Indianapolis & New York, The Bobbs-Merrill Company, 1946, Chapter 22.

migrated from the bailiwicks of big city machines to the sunny climate of the Southwest, and it was feared that the Legion might die out in New Mexico. A controlling committee under a single coordinator went into the state to take over department records and provide administration. Two years later the suspension was lifted and the public standing of the Legion in New Mexico was thus salvaged.

The contests among candidates for the office of National Commander were always dramatic. This was true from early years when it took eleven ballots to select John R. Quinn over Wilder S. Metcalf of Kansas and James A. Drain of the District of Columbia at San Francisco in 1923, and when voting was deadlocked for twenty-two ballots before Howard Savage won over J. Monroe Johnson of South Carolina and several "favorite sons" in Philadelphia in 1926. As with most organizations, the Legion developed its internal politics and the most influential practitioners were referred to as "kingmakers." These men through active Legion work and popularity were usually named as delegates and with a wide acquaintance they gained influence in formulating policies and advancing candidates. Consequently, by the 1930's most Legion Commanders gained office in a manner roughly approximating the selection of Presidential candidates in our Republic. William H. Doyle of Massachusetts, Phil Collins of Illinois, Mark McKee of Michigan, Frank Belgrano of California, and Ben Dorris of Oregon acquired the reputation of being able to "line up the vote." Various state delegations came to conventions with a favorite son or already committed to one of a number of possible winners. Caucuses were held by states or sections which heard from candidates. Promises of important committee assignments and visits to certain areas were generally obtained. By the time of voting on the final day of a convention the choice of Commander was usually settled, although there were occasional lively contests on the convention floor. This procedure became firmly established, and candidates who "blasted the kingmakers" were doomed to failure. Usually they spoke of "returning the Legion to the blue caps," in other words, somehow removing the influence of those skillful and generally highly respected "politicians" within the Legion and leaving the election up to the individual delegates (whose Legion caps are blue, whereas those of Department officers are white and National officers, including the NEC, are red). Just as there are cries of anguish over the methods of selecting candidates for high office in our political party system, so the rumble of dissatisfaction may be heard among Legionnaires over their imperfect system to the present day. In both areas, however, men selected are as a rule outstanding at best, adequate at worst.

Although a general account of Legion organization and administration is the subject of a later chapter, it is appropriate here to mention significant facts that help to explain why The American Legion survived the lean years of the 1930's in a sound condition. By 1930 The American Legion had come a long way from the time when its first National Adjutant, Lemuel Bolles, trundled the early Legion records to the National Headquarters city of Indianapolis or even when Russell Creviston of Indiana took over in 1923. James F. Barton, who had gained considerable experience as Department Adjutant in Iowa, served as National Adjutant from 1925 to 1932. The notable record of Robert F. Smith of California as business manager of the *Legion Magazine* was ended by a mountain-climbing accident in 1932. This brought about Barton's move to become manager of the publication, which he skillfully directed through the depression and the "big years of advertising" from 1940 to 1945. The office of National Adjutant went to the able Frank E. Samuel.

The National Adjutant's duties and responsibilities became more difficult when Legion activities grew. It was the National Adjutant who directed all the Divisions of National Headquarters, managed the plans for each National Convention, served as ex officio secretary of key committees, and frequently substituted for the National Commander in fulfilling his myriad obligations. Samuel and his assistant Adjutant, Donald G. Glascoff of Michigan, handled the membership detail, which was accompanied by keen competition among various states. At the annual department commanders' and adjutants' conference in Indianapolis, trophies from eight past National Commanders were awarded among departments for prompt and thorough renewal and additional membership, and wagers between individual states were paid (for bets of Maine's best potatoes against Idaho's finest tubers or Washington's finest apples). When the National Aeronautics Commission met, Legion fliers carrying cargoes of membership cards arrived in Indianapolis by plane, winning various prizes.

The National Adjutant also had an assistant in Washington who managed the branch offices where the rehabilitation, employment, veterans' preference, and legislative work was done. The operating divisions in Indianapolis included administration, child welfare, national defense, Americanism, finance, emblem, and public relations. The National Headquarters also provided space for the part-time secretaries of a score of national committees. The library, a purchasing office and a Special Activities section conducted essential administrative work. A field service of traveling secretaries, originally devoted to rehabilitation and service work for the disabled and the inspection of hospitals, served as the contact with departments. The field service's work expanded and was destined to be an important attribute in the growing number of problems facing the Legion as World War II approached.

It is a tribute to the Legion that the men they called upon over the years, particularly in the stringent 30's, were of the highest caliber and, whether on a salaried or voluntary basis, gave unsparingly of their time and experience to important Legion programs. This was reflected too in the volume of contributions to worthwhile Legion undertakings by individuals and organizations, frequently with no official connection to the Legion. During a period when many of the most venerable organizations and financial institutions in the country not only went to the wall but crumbled, the Legion maintained a financial integrity and even improved a number of its trust and endowment positions. The endowment funds to finance work for the disabled and for child welfare, so ably handled by Commander James A. Drain at their inception in 1925 and for which Ignace Jan Paderewski had given the total proceeds of $28,500 from a concert tour, moved forward in the 1930's. The $19,000 that the Auxiliary and $6,000 that the Forty and Eight had given toward rehabilitation and child welfare in 1925 grew to a customary $25,000 and $10,000 annually by the end of the 1930's. Financially the Legion was able to improve its condition too by economies, its membership fees and the generosity of many people and organizations, Legion and non-Legion alike. Fund-raising campaigns for child welfare and disabled veterans' care met popular response, quickly acquired a net amount of slightly less than $5 million and began to yield a substantial income. The fund weathered the depression, and by the end of World War II stood at just over $5 million, having yielded more than $3,250,000 income.

Through the 1930's and the war the Legion's trust funds were in strong hands—the investment policy committee, established in 1936, the endowment board and the overseas graves trustees. Excellent management was clear by the endowment fund's record through those ruinous years. Dr. Carlton D. Culloch of Indiana served as the board's treasurer, devoting time he might have spent more profitably to himself in medical practice and government.

It is appropriate here to record that the Legion has been fortunate in the selection of those who served as its chairmen of the Finance Committee and Commission and as its National Treasurers—as chairmen, deLancey Kountze, Milton J. Foreman and Wilder S. Metcalf in the 20's, Samuel W. Reynolds and John Lewis Smith, Sr., in the 30's, Reynolds and William J. Dwyer in the 40's and 50's, and Harold P. Redden since 1955; as Treasurers, Gaspar G. Bacon in 1919, Robert H. Tyndall in the 20's, Bowman Elder, Neal Grider, Drain, and John R. Ruddick over 30 years since 1927, and William Francis Polen since 1958. As with so many others who served with distinction at the national level and contributed so much to the comprehensive activities of the Legion, limitations of space rule out definitive accounts of their individual contributions.

Another fund, the Overseas Graves Decoration Trust, which had its start when the Legion received many small checks from relatives of men buried overseas, continued to cover the expense of decorating every American grave abroad.

While industrial production rose slowly as the 1930's wore on, for a number of reasons capital expenditures continued at a depression rate. Confidence had been badly shaken, and it would be 1945 before a peacetime economy saw its leaders conducting large-scale, optimistic construction of new plants.

The 1930's were a time of tumult for the national economy. There were starts and halts in various government undertakings to alleviate the consequences of the depression. In the so-called "First New Deal" government was compelled to come to the aid of dispossessed millions. Demagogues sprang up with the promise of fantastic benefits. Huey Long, the Louisiana Kingfish, put forth a scheme to share the wealth and to "make every man a king." Dr. Francis Townsend's clubs flourished when he promised old people enormous benefits, and the unemployed in the big cities listened with rapture to Father

Charles Coughlin. Their footing was cut away by the more realistic measures of the First New Deal—benefits to the poor farmers, the Social Security Act and WPA programs. The Reconstruction Finance Corporation (RFC), originated under Hoover and directed by Jesse Jones's sure hand in the New Deal years, was most effective.

Roosevelt, with an especially cooperative Congress, was able to instill some of the confidence Americans had lost, and recovery continued until it suffered a sharp setback in 1937. During this time the President had moved from a conservative view of budgetary matters and limited Federal intervention to more radical and expedient views. All this alarmed many Americans, who saw the hand of "big government" reaching out to grasp powers and functions previously left to the states, communities and themselves. But trends were underway that were not to be arrested. The President was persuaded by the astute Edward Flynn, Democratic leader of the Bronx, that to perpetuate his administration it was necessary to win the big city majorities and the ranks of organized labor. This was accomplished by a flurry of measures including the National Labor Relations Act, the Fair Labor Standards Act of 1937 and other legislation, which were not struck down by the Supreme Court as the NRA and the AAA had been. Welfare legislation and government "policing" of the economy were continued, and the 1930's saw the almost glandular growth of Federal departments and bureaus which was to project the economic theories of Keynesian economics of deficit financing even beyond their author's intentions. What started as reform measures that would be incorporated by our society and emergency measures that would be cast aside as unnecessarily expensive after the crisis of the early 30's passed have been expanded. Hundreds of thousands entered the Civil Service, and bureaucrats, entrenched, burned with a desire to expand their activities. Ex-servicemen were afforded the greatest opportunity to obtain positions in the Civil Service due to legislation obtained as a result of Legion efforts in the face of stubborn opposition of Chief Executives, many vocal minorities and a large segment of the nation's press. For good or ill, big government became the order of the day. The second world war introduced unprecedented spending and further consolidation of Federal power, and with the further expansion of Federal activities the American public is becoming accustomed to even greater Federal service and

intervention and familiar with the pathology of a monumental bureaucracy and various features of the welfare state.

These national developments have had a profound effect upon
state, local and individual sense of responsibility and the ability to
perform those responsibilities financially. It is to the Legion's credit
that it has not succumbed to the belief that Washington can minister
to all the nation's needs and it would be incorrect to propose that
many public servants intend to do so. It is beyond the scope of this
book to discuss the pros and cons of big government. So long as
men and women are this side of paradise there will be a multitude
of opportunities to improve their communities, to take part in the
direction of their children's destiny and to contribute to the well-
being and needs of their neighbors and themselves. In a Republic these opportunities are in the nature of responsibilities and obligations.

Whereas the employment efforts of the Legion had been handled
by the Americanism Commission, when the second wave of depression hit, conventions from 1937 to 1940 made employment a
major activity and placed the problem under an Employment Committee which took over the established system of field secretaries.
A national director of employment was authorized to conduct this
activity. Among other things, the committee worked with government agencies and private industries to alleviate the difficulty many
veterans encountered in securing new employment because of the
so-called age bar for older workers. Certainly in the 1930's the
Federal government, however powerful it became, could not hope
to substitute its activities at the exclusion of vigorous endeavor by
the multitude of organizations and individuals that make up the
American society. In fact, it never can, and the proof is always evident when there is distress, disaster, emergency, or national crisis.

Hence, the work of the posts and of the Auxiliary for the disabled,
for children in need, for employment, for disaster relief, and for
public health continued and grew. The Auxiliary, its contributions
and undertakings paralleling and strengthening those of the Legion,
surpassed its goal of half a million by 1941, when its membership
reached 520,178.

As the 1930's closed, The American Legion and the Auxiliary
could take pride in their achievements. While slow progress and

failure in some areas evoked disappointment and regret, much of this was beyond the power of the Legion to determine. Its admonitions and warnings had not received the attention they deserved. As a result the Republic was destined to pay a heavier price in war. Still, many of the young men who were to fight the nation's battles were far better prepared than they would have been had there been no Legion posts and no Legionnaires putting forth an effort to strengthen the nation and its citizens.

At its conclusion a decade of apprehension, insecurity, fear, and hope made way for one of stark and bloody events, terror, chaos, and the panoply of war.

14

The Legion and Defense
in World Crisis

IF a nation turns away with distaste, fear or ignorance from the
work, expense and sacrifices necessary to ensure its security and to
fulfill its obligations, it will eventually confront hardships that dwarf
those it neglected. In fact, it may find itself unequal to the larger task
—without the means, without the time, without the stomach, and
without the faith to prevail. This was true in full or in part for all
who faced the Axis onslaught in World War II.

For Legionnaires the 1920's had been a frightful dream of defense
cutbacks. By 1930 the National Defense Act of 1920 was little more
than a memory of a hollow triumph, a bright spot in the dream.
Congress had denied it enabling funds. Each year appropriations for
the armed services diminished—from 1919 to 1939. But if the 1920's
had been a bad dream, now Legionnaires were on the threshold of a
nightmare. Ahead lay years of unfulfilled policies carefully drawn out
and advocated by The American Legion, years of abuse from generally respected groups and individuals, years of government failure
to heed Legion warnings and the obvious dictates of reason.

As the self-deceit of pacifism pervaded the nation, a parsimonious
approach to defense matters resulted in even more frugal outlays for
the Armed Forces. Once in the grip of depression, economy advocates
swelled the forces opposed to Legion preparedness proposals. Enemies appeared in depth from one end of the Legion front to the
other—from subversive groups and foreign propagandists to those

who saw the nation's salvation in economy and others who visualized world peace in further disarmament.

In 1931 the Detroit Convention declared:

> The American Legion is opposed to the disarmament of the United States either for economy, or as a claimed means to bring about world peace, or as an example which, it is hoped by some, other nations will follow.

C. B. Robbins of Iowa read the national defense report that year —a typical sample of annual Legion recommendations. America, in an unprepared state similar to that of 1917, had plans requiring three to five months to mobilize a million men and one and a half to two years to equip them. This adopted report called for a "navy second to none" and deplored our failure to build ships to the limit of international agreements, thus placing us third, behind Britain and Japan. It called for a Regular Army of 165,000, a five-year aircraft-building program, an increase in the National Guard to 210,000 and an Officers Reserve of 120,000, an emergency reserve of arms and ammunition, training of personnel in arsenals ready to instruct private factories in case of war, and placing educational orders with selected industries. Here, eight years before Hitler's Panzer columns gained lightning victories while his opponents clung to static defensive doctrines followed through much of the first world war, The American Legion recommended "that ample appropriations be made available for the development of mechanization." This proposal reveals a remarkable grasp by the Legionnaires who drafted and adopted it, a profound understanding of military concepts by a group of civilians and former citizen soldiers at a time when only a handful of professionals fully appreciated them.

The convention also called for an antiaircraft defense, developed to correspond with the five-year program for aviation. Also, it urged "that sufficient funds be provided with which to establish an ROTC Unit at each and every educational institution desiring it." Immediate measures were called for to provide an adequate system of supply, including a reasonable war reserve of munitions which "will correspond to the immediate needs of our mobilized manpower and will in addition tide over the period between mobilization and the

time when our industries will be able to supply the current demands
—the most important elements in this supply being munitions."

But the Army was on the decline, to a point where its enlisted
strength stood at 118,750. The Legion wryly observed in 1944,

> Whether it was a feeling of confidence inspired by the belief
> the veterans of the World War were still fit for duty, or a return
> to the feeling of false security which has been a dangerous Amer-
> ican characteristic, the fact remains that the lessons of the war
> were soon forgotten. The Navy fared no better than the Army.
> In a beautiful gesture, we extravagantly scuttled the advantage
> we had gained as a result of wartime naval construction and
> proceeded to sink battleships while rival maritime powers sank
> blueprints.

The situation, however, was graver than this. In 1930 President
Hoover and Prime Minister Ramsay MacDonald sponsored another
disarmament conference. Despite urgent appeals from National Commander Paul McNutt, Hoover suspended action on the naval construction bill, credited to the Legion the year before. The now familiar
propaganda, twisted and beguiling, poured across the country. A low
condition of American strength was favored by Britain and the Western democracies as well as their voracious, totalitarian neighbors
and the imperialistic circles in Japan. Duped, educators, religious
leaders and foreign experts sponged up alien persuasion, made it
their own and passed it on to their audiences.

When the Japanese diplomats returned from London with the short
end of a British-American-Japanese agreement to a 10-10-7 naval
strength ratio and an end to unlimited light-cruiser building, the
Japanese military were in a position to exploit this "indignity." In
1931 the Kwantung army seized Manchuria. Henry L. Stimson, long
a Legion national defense advocate, protested as Secretary of State.
But words without a ready sword were useless. The toothless League
of Nations could only bark, "Aggression!" Conservative Japanese
swiftly lost control and an attempt to regain it in 1936 led to the
assassination of venerable admirals and generals by young firebrands
of the Imperial Army. In 1932 the mainland of China was invaded.

National defense, reefed in the eye of depression, was further taken
in. The American Legion was alarmed and in 1932 called for the
War and Navy Departments to declare an "irreducible minimum" of

needs and government appropriations to meet them. By 1933 the Army and its Reserves stood seventeenth behind those of other nations including Turkey, Greece, Belgium, and Yugoslavia; a fourth those of Japan or Poland, a fifth those of Spain, and a fourteenth those of France or Italy. The National Defense Committee declared:

> We believe that America will never seek a war and that a war will never seek a prepared America. We believe in an America, peace-loving and intent on peace but strong enough to insure and enforce the peace. We know that the pitiably small army in existence at the start of every war has never kept us out of war.

The 1933 National Convention expressed a policy in the face of serious economic conditions that would have mitigated the enormous demands in blood and substance in World War II and Korea:

> The American Legion holds that national defense interests every man, woman and child in constant, equal and vital degrees and should therefore be a constant quality. It should be the last element of a nation's organization to be influenced by economic conditions. National defense must be absolutely and always divorced from politics.

There are times when "wisdom cries out in the street and no man regards it." The tenure of a fiery National Commander, Louis Johnson, had been such a time. He told the 1933 Chicago Convention that in many of its activities the Legion had passed through a critical year:

> We were subjected to the most merciless and most untruthful campaign of slander that ever beset an association of American veterans. What few shreds of criticism our enemies could honestly bring against us were magnified and distorted to a degree that made even them malicious falsehoods. . . . It must be realized that there are within this country many who would scrap our defensive forces and leave our Nation subject to attack from within as well as from without.

Johnson praised the work of the National Defense Committee under Milton A. Reckord and the Aeronautics Commission under E. V. Rickenbacker, which promoted aeronautics by coordinating its efforts with those of the former and with the Americanism Commission and the newly organized Sons of the American Legion. He appealed for an army and reserve force to protect the nation; a navy second to none, "competent to protect our commerce ... and guarantee the freedom of our sea-borne trade routes in time of war; and a Marine Corps ready for instantaneous service as an expeditionary force to meet a temporary emergency." This at a time when the Army stood at 12,000 officers, 118,750 enlisted men and 6,500 Philippine scouts; when the Navy ranked third in the world and could not replace its aging ships of the line, let alone conduct satisfactory fleet exercises; when the Marines were a very lean and hungry outfit.

It is significant that in 1933 the Legion called for motorization of the Regular Army and National Guard and the mechanization of "a reasonable number of tactical units." Local National Defense Councils were mentioned for the first time.

It is well to recall those ominous months and years of the 30's. On the heels of the depression events in Europe and elsewhere crowded one against the other toward chaos: Hitler's ascent to power and Germany's withdrawal from the League, his insidious economic measures and masked rearmament, his racial doctrines, then outright repudiation of the arms provisions of Versailles and reintroduction of conscription; Italy's invasion of Abyssinia in 1935 and Britain's economic sanctions against her; Hitler's reoccupation of the Rhineland; the Spanish Civil War, where totalitarian blades were sharpened; the German Anti-Comintern Pact with Japan; continuing aggression in the Far East; German annexation of Austria; and then agreement at Munich giving the Sudetenland in Czechoslovakia to Germany. For Britain and France Munich was the trough of a long wave of surrenders. Neville Chamberlain spoke of "peace in our time." But Hitler's contempt for Britain, her former might dissipated save for the Royal Navy, and for France, politically fragmented and spiritually stricken, made it certain that he would carve more off Europe as his appetite returned. A year later subjugation of Czechoslovakia came to pass and then the fatal move on Poland. Here Britain's honor was at stake, for she was pledged to fight beside the Poles. Lloyd George's admonition twenty years before, that Danzig and the Corridor "must sooner or later lead to a new war in the east of Europe," became a fact. That the Wilsonian ideal of a free and independent Poland should be the immediate pretext for the outbreak of the second world war and that those who went to her defense in 1939 and with the United States proclaimed self-determination as a war aim were later to witness Polish freedoms subjected to the tyranny of Stalin and communism is among history's most appalling jokes.

That the nation ignored The American Legion and others concerned with U.S. strength through this period was not a phenomenon of democracy in North America. Pacifism was epidemic in Britain and France, and their bleak performance stemmed from failure to maintain a striking force commensurate with their responsibilities. In 1930, only sixteen years after putting the BEF ashore in France, the pacifist socialist government in Britain could not muster half that force. Nor was the Royal Navy up to the requirements of defending British interests. It is not surprising that British governments to retain power treated preparedness gingerly, when a candidate for Commons was mobbed as he spoke for strength, when the electorate's opposition to increased military outlays was clear to all politicians.

There have been many incisive indictments of the League of Nations, a covenant of words, a cause of discontent, a body dedicated to the *status quo* without the military means to enforce its decisions and without the ability to adjudicate grievances. Its black hours came in the 1930's. The League's ideals were illusory from the beginning not because the United States failed to become involved but because its ideals were far from the ideals of many nations. The treaties and the new *status quo* were unrealistic. Their enforcement by the League might have been possible, if not just, had the victors given a cutting edge to this Wilsonian dream. But the League was an empty scabbard. *Pax Britannica,* which had maintained relative peace for a century after the Napoleonic Wars through the British Navy, flexible response and balance-of-power diplomacy, was gone. Words filled the void.

Certain observations require emphasis here. First, The American Legion, virtually alone among powerful pressure groups, influential organizations or departments of government, fully appreciated the dependence of the nation's security and interest upon strength distributed among the various armed services, the Coast Guard and the Merchant Marine. Professional military men were inclined to extol their own particular service at the expense of other branches, to promote certain weapons with undue claims over other arms. The Legion shared General Billy Mitchell's enthusiasm for air power but did not share some of his prophecies. Mitchell stated, for example, that to transport large bodies of troops and cargo by seacraft, as in the first world war, would be an "impossibility." Mitchell believed air power would dominate all sea areas when based from land and that no ships, whether they carried aircraft or not, could contest this supremacy; that aircraft carriers are useless against first-class powers; and that the diminishing effectiveness of antiaircraft guns could never be improved appreciably.

A careful study of Legion positions over the years leads to the conclusion that they represent a full awareness of the "totality" of modern war with regard to resources and a proper conception of the indispensable roles and the need for coordinated effort by all military arms and the Merchant Marine. Also, the Legion became more specific on defense while continuing to promote UMT as described in an earlier chapter. Finally, while it had long advocated reasonable defense measures, its failure to gain its objectives in the 1920's became high tragedy in the 1930's. For a while time remained to look to our national interests. It ran out before proper measures or deadlines were met. This, as war's alarums grew louder and more distinct.

Legion pressure had brought about the creation of the War Policies Commission in 1930, which heard exhaustive testimony from experienced administrators from public office, the military, The American Legion, industrial management, labor, and other interested parties. Among others, Bernard M. Baruch, wartime Chairman of the War Industries Board, supported the commission's proposals which closely followed what the Legion had long been advocating. He concluded that a proper plan would allow the nation to pass from a peace to a war status and back again with a minimum of confusion and loss and that it would reduce the cost of war 50 per cent and probably more. The commission's report to the President recommended that at the inception of war the government should fix prices and should confiscate 95 per cent of incomes above normal, and that a constitutional amendment giving Congress authority to fix prices be submitted to the states. The Sheppard-Hill bill, incorporating Legion proposals, was bitterly assailed by pacifists, many liberals, some educators, and of course the radicals. The Nye-Vandenberg resolution in 1932 created a special Senate Committee to go over the commission's work, investigate war profiteering, study the desirability of a government monopoly in the munitions industry, and inquire into the Legion's draft proposal. It credited its inception "to the long-standing demands of American war veterans speaking through The American Legion for legislation to take the profits out of war," and out of it came the exposé of activities of munitions makers. The Legion hoped for more. After bills to eliminate profiteering and to equalize the burdens of war seemed well along, it reported in 1936 that more "legislative progress has been made during the past year on universal draft legislation than in the years which have elapsed since 1921."

However, Congress and its committees could not reach agreement on specifics—as barefaced aggression moved unchecked in Asia and Africa and nazi diplomacy was accompanied by the tramp of jackboots and the grinding of armored columns. In the United States it was a time of false economies, when even modest shipbuilding brought screams of protest. The Legion's suggestion that military studies be given in CCC camps raised the frenzied barking of our watchdogs of peace, the pacifists and disarmament advocates. The American Legion could later observe that such training could have been used by many young men to preserve their lives and those of their comrades.

Legion efforts were conducted despite frustration on a front that took in the broad aspects of security, the Army, the Navy, air power, the Merchant Marine, and civil defense.

The Legion's resolutions in 1936 brought up the urgent need of antitank and antiaircraft weapons and the desirability of strengthened coastal defenses. And in the late 30's the Legion drove for an increase in the Army toward strength specified in the National Defense Act of 1920—in 1937 to 180,000 enlisted men and 15,000 officers and in 1939 to the full 280,000 men for the Regular Army and 426,000 enlisted men for the National Guard with appropriate officer strength. At New York in 1937 the Legion gave support to the War Department's revised industrial mobilization plan now under the management of the Legion's 1932 Commander Louis Johnson. As Assistant Secretary of War he devoted his considerable talents to war production planning, as had Hanford MacNider before him. Emphasis on this activity, urged by the Legion since its beginnings, proved out in World War II's industrial mobilization, rationing and price, wage and rent controls. Already Germany and national socialism were well along the road to war with conscription and open aircraft building. Britain had reluctantly abandoned her ten-year peace conjectures and had turned to the task of developing aircraft and radar. Ironically, the United States continued to provide Japan, which had abrogated the Washington naval treaty and was fortifying the mandated islands, with huge quantities of oil, scrap iron and machine tools over strenuous Legion opposition.

The American Legion's position on naval affairs deserves inclusion in any history of those tragic years but is habitually ignored by many scholars. In 1930 the Legion reiterated the resolution that our fleet be brought to parity with the world's strongest under a five-year building program *including aircraft carriers* "to the full limit allowed by the terms of the Washington Treaty." A Navy "second to none," the Legion felt in 1931, would support national policies and commerce and guard the continental safety and overseas possessions of the nation. The Legion "deplored" congressional failure to make "such authorizations for new ships . . . to reach London Treaty (1930) strength." A "treaty Navy and men to man it" was detailed at Miami in 1934. Funds to provide drill and active duty training for Naval and Marine Corps Reserves were emphasized, and those precise specifications, eventually adopted, to this day give the Navy its trained and ready man-power potential.

Doggedly, the Legion program was reemphasized—in 1935, 1936, 1937, 1938, and 1939—with the 1935 recommendation for a Merchant Marine Reserve of at least 92,000 enlisted men and 17,000 officers and provision for a strengthened U.S. Coast Guard "to meet the demands of . . . emergency."

Turning out a capital ship of the line takes years from keel to shakedown. Even after Pearl Harbor with unsparing effort a battleship's construction took over two and a half years, a fleet carrier's well over a year. The fate of the 1927 bill for 71 ships including 5 aircraft carriers and 25 cruisers was sealed after "peace societies" barraged the cautious Congress. A trickle of naval strength followed. Two cruisers came down the ways in 1934 and a *Brooklyn* class keel was laid in 1935, the result of the modest "cruiser bill" of 1928. Fleet Admiral King later wrote that from 1920 to 1933 "Except for cruisers hardly any combatant ships were added to our own fleet . . . and few were under construction." Battleships and destroyers were not numbered among those few. The first aircraft carrier, *Langley,* had led to completion of the *Lexington* and *Saratoga,* built on cruiser hulls in the late 20's. Finally, in 1934, the first "fast carrier," *Ranger,* came down the ways.

Pressures from the Navy, The American Legion, the Navy League, and a number of concerned individuals in public and private life gained ground. Chairman of the House Naval Affairs Committee, Carl Vinson, with President Roosevelt's cooperation made substantial beginnings to bring the Navy up to treaty strength. An eight-year replacement program was provided in 1934, although treaty strength was not to be achieved under the plan until 1944. Naval personnel was not increased until 1937. Many designs were approved, and some ships were put on the building ways at this time.

The Legion's vision became a constant, improbable dream. The refrain "a Treaty Navy and men to man it" was accompanied by a detailed program well within U.S. capabilities. The problem of bases and logistics was fundamental. The advice of our world-famous Admiral A. T. Mahan emphasizing overwhelming naval strength in the Pacific was overlooked; the recommendations of the Joint Army-Navy Board in 1905 that the battle fleet operate from a powerful base in the Philippines had never been instituted. Even after Japanese abrogation of the 1922 treaty prohibiting fortification of the mandated islands scarcely anything was done to ensure our Far Eastern responsibilities. The American Legion urged expansion and refinement of the fortifications and capabilities of Guam and the Philippines. This advice, shared by distinguished soldiers and sailors, was ignored, partially for fear of "irritating" the Japanese.

The United States and Britain, holding themselves bound by treaties disavowed and revealing a stubborn lack of urgency on the eve of war, saw fit to entrust their obligations in the Far East to lamentable defenses. Even greater urgency and detail marked the Legion's naval resolutions in 1941 as Pearl Harbor drew near:

> Our present program to build a two-ocean Navy with its own air arm capable of defending our interests in both the Atlantic and the Pacific against any possible grouping of aggressors should be carried through to completion as speedily as

possible. Naval auxiliary vessels must be provided in proportion to the increase in combatant ships.

Other resolutions emphasized what might be called "an advanced base strategy." Japanese buildup and fortification of bases in the Pacific were widening like concentric circles set in motion when rocks are thrown into a pond. The Legion recommended mutual agreement with the Philippine Commonwealth for "an adequate, well defended fleet base"; that Guam be made "an impregnable base for naval operations"; that "the major fleet base in the Hawaiian Islands be made impregnable and the outlying island bases and Samoa be strongly held"; that naval bases and naval air stations be "intensively developed in Alaska"; that the major base sites acquired from Britain "be completely developed as soon as possible"; that Puerto Rico be developed as a major fleet base; that joint agreements in the Western Hemisphere provide for effectiveness of our fleet in defending it and upholding the Monroe Doctrine; and that outlying bases be acquired to make Panama impregnable.

The "advanced base concept" was to be dearly bought. Logistically, too, the Navy was hamstrung, for it limped into the vastness of the Pacific on December 8 with only one transport and one oiler ready for operations.

The Merchant Marine Act of 1936 was to the Legion a realization of long-standing resolutions. The act declared U.S. policy "to foster the development and encourage the maintenance" of a Merchant Marine. "It is necessary for the national defense and development of . . . foreign and domestic commerce." But the three years remaining before World War II did not bring this asset up to a realistic level. The American Legion strove for a strong Merchant Marine and "a sound, well-rounded program of replacement of our merchant fleet," reflecting an evident appreciation of logistics.

In 1936 the National Convention advocated establishment of a Merchant Marine Academy and in 1938 called for strengthening the U.S. Maritime Commission by getting away from appointments based on political party affiliation to selection on a "geographic basis" and with "due regard to . . . special fitness, etc., understood to mean an expert knowledge of Merchant Marine and Naval Auxiliary needs."

Earlier resolutions were strengthened in 1939 for inclusion of officers and seamen into the U.S. Merchant Naval Marine Reserve. At Boston in 1940 proposals for a National Maritime Mediation Board and an expanded building program to provide auxiliaries for our "two ocean Navy" were prominent.

Furious shipbuilding efforts just before Pearl Harbor gave heart to the Legion, but it feared return to a traditional, casual attitude after emergency and warned:

> From experience of the past, it is not too early to contemplate the future of our Merchant Marine, and we strongly recommend a national policy which will help keep these ships under the American Flag, adequately protected and guaranteed for our own use in international commerce after the present emergency ceases to exist.

In 1943 and 1944 the Legion was specific. Its resolutions called for reaffirmation of the Declaration of Policy of the Act of 1936 and asked Congress to retain in service adequate "fast vessels" for our needs and a "laid-up reserve" for emergency; to ensure operation of American flag vessels on essential trade routes; to prevent Axis nations from rehabilitating their Merchant Marines since they served as potent instrumentalities for waging war; to encourage patronage of American flagships; to preserve shipbuilding facilities through a replacement program; and to continue maritime training. In 1944 the Legion appealed:

> We want no more "rush construction" to meet emergency demands, we want the American flag to fly at the mast head of the world's largest and finest merchant ships, we demand a fleet of merchant ships, ready to be used for commerce and in time of emergency to be an auxiliary to our Navy. Nothing short of that is safe, nothing less is sensible.

The need for research and development of new and more effective weapons received greater Legion emphasis as the early years of the 1930's slipped by. This applied to air power for both the Army and the Navy and became more evident as crisis abroad grew. Germans stalked out of the 1933 Disarmament Conference and asserted the right to rearm in defiance of the Versailles Treaty and a year later, after Hindenburg had died, Hitler announced the introduction of conscription and the revival of the German air force.

The struggle for American leadership in aviation has no more constant advocate than the Legion. Before Mitchell and other apostles of air power caught the attention of the public, sometimes proclaiming the efficacy of their creed at the exclusion of other military requirements, The American Legion at its first gatherings and in its first publications in 1919 spoke prophetically of the future in the air and the need of air power in a balanced defense structure. The Legion called for practical and acceptable measures—industrial and governmental efforts that would develop the airplane commercially— perhaps the most reasonable assurance that it would gain its potential place in the military scheme of things. The influence of the Legion by stimulation of interest by its posts in air fields and flying is incalculable. Nationally, in the 1930's it advocated:

Sufficient equipment "to perform their tactical mission" for the Army Air Corps in its five-year program (1931).

Further recommendations for naval aviation, stressed in the 20's:

Immediate expansion of the Air Forces "until they are on a parity with those of other nations" (1931).

Establishment of fields and tactical bases and the procurement of 800 planes annually to achieve a "balanced force of 2,500 military planes" (1935).

A "closely prosecuted" program of support from government departments toward solution of problems of aircraft design, construction and operations; construction of one or more rigid airships (later used effectively in antisubmarine warfare); modernization of all radio beam and other aids to air navigation, including "blind flying"; an increase in air routes and Air Mail service; and a study to bring up to strength the Air Corps Reserve (1936).

Flight instruction for upper classmen in ROTC (1937).

In 1938 the Federal government fulfilled a Legion proposal of eighteen years before that Congress enact legislation which would further the development of flying by licensing aircraft for "air worthiness" and pilots for fitness and setting forth specifications for landing fields. The Civil Aeronautics Act of 1938, the Legion felt, was a great triumph.

Air power was an outstanding cause of the 1938 Los Angeles Convention. Opposing a referendum on war and stating, "If an emergency threatening the territory of the United States arises we want to be so prepared on sea and land that battles for defense be fought as far from American shores as possible," the Legion raised its recommendation for an air force from 2,500 to 8,000 planes and an annual increment from 800 to 1,500. This proposal had been under consideration for more than a year by the National Defense Committee and the Committee on Aeronautics, and it received full Legion backing. It was not an immodest proposal especially in view of our enormous, if unrecognized, commitments merely in the Far East. In the forthcoming war 1,000 planes a day moved off assembly lines. Under pressure, Congress authorized an Army plane strength of 6,000 in April 1939.

There is no question that proposals of long standing by the Legion would have had the nation first in air power long before Pearl Harbor and even before the nazi invasion of Poland in September 1939. Consider that at war's outbreak the British could muster 1,982 operational aircraft; the French, 1,112; and the Germans, 4,162. However, in 1936 the German "first line" strength stood at only 1,000 the British at 700. The Hurricane and Spitfire, with outstanding speed, climb and hitting characteristics, were coming into service. The British and the French had a "first line" strength of about 1,000 bombers and 1,200 fighters, whereas the Germans, facing enemies on two fronts in 1939, had roughly 1,000 bombers and 1,250 fighters.

Concern in 1938 with the deteriorating international situation, neutrality legislation, the war profits bill, a war referendum, and a war tax bill led Legion officials to confer with War Department officials and to defer pressure for a universal draft bill, although Legion conventions continued to reaffirm the principle. Two seasoned Legion workers, Henry L. Stimson and Frank Knox, headed the War and Navy Departments.

War in September 1939 transfixed the public and Congress. The pacifists found themselves perched uncomfortably on the horns of a dilemma. Fascism's unspeakable drives must be checked or blunted, they screamed as their ideological loathing of military preparation gave them constant jabs. But it was already too late in Europe where their brethren's mistaken theories had very nearly swept away effective security arrangements. All too clear now was the plight of those who had failed to maintain up-to-date armed forces *and military doctrines*. The French found it impossible to drag themselves from the warm bed of defensive thinking. The fact is well established that had the British and the French, even in their psychologically unprepared state, applied the men and weapons they had to imaginative concepts to challenge nazi takeovers during the period of "armed appease-ment," Hitler would have had to pull back his legions. His generals knew this. But Hitler followed his insight into the temper of the Western democracies. He saw the tragic flaw of Franco-British inde-cision and played on it with the contempt of an Iago. While the West-ern democracies negotiated from their weakness, Hitler negotiated from a willingness to use what strength he had.

When the fatal time came, the Germans displayed a dazzling mastery of offensive tactical concepts and an appreciation of twentieth-century logistics although they enjoyed neither a preponderance of strength against the combination of France, Britain and Poland nor the extent of mechanization and motorization they might have had. Troops advanced on shoe leather with horse-drawn supplies. Poland, which exhausted the German Army and Air Force, was not a *real* test. The German generals knew that their strongest adversaries stood beyond the Rhine and they shuddered when they considered the possibility that the French and British might launch an offensive. But in a miasma of "Maginot Line" mentality the French generals scanned the terrain from which the attack should eventually come while their substantial superiority in troops and armor manned a wide, continuous front. This and the nursing of tired war plans went on through the "phony war." With Poland mopped up and replenish-ment complete, Hitler could wheel his Panzer divisions west while carrying out the assault on Scandinavia at heavy cost to the German Navy.

Ironic, that the nazis' enormously persuasive propaganda which swallowed the nerve of the Low Countries was to catch up national socialism's political and military leaders, eventually taking them into the vortex of disaster. Still, a train of victories lay ahead. By May 1940 German ground and air forces gained respite and a superiority over the Allied forces in the west. They struck with an unexpected, imaginative and bold offensive. So effective was the Mannstein Plan of operations that leaders of the divisions that overwhelmed French territory remarked that those spring days were the setting of little more than a field maneuver.

The French collapse recommends itself to the consideration of free men who would remain free. Not only were its military doctrines out of date but the country was eaten away by corruption and the communism of the *Front Populaire* government. General Gamelin wrote a few days after the German breakthrough in the Ardennes:

> The men mobilized today have not received, during the period between the wars, the patriotic and moral education which would have prepared them for the drama which was to resolve the fate of the nation.

Of course Gamelin failed to mention the grievous shortcomings of the French general staff. But he did head an army without the morale of a generation before. In 1914 there had been *élan*, roughly translated as guts. In 1940, before defeat, a French minister remarked, "There is no will to fight. There has been a general *défaillance*, a collapse of the whole nation."

These deplorable consequences are precisely those The American Legion programs of two decades sought to avoid. Legion activities from national security to Americanism (through education, patriotic endeavor, Boy Scout work, naturalization efforts, etc.) were to prove their value. Fortunately liberty, besides being a hard-won thing, dies hard. The British and Commonwealth peoples and numerous others whose soil was assaulted and even conquered by the Axis showed the common stuff of greatness. At supreme moments they rose to meet appalling reversals, just as Americans were to rise after Pearl Harbor, their ill-equipped manhood tried and found flint-hard, resourceful and manly, frequently with minds as fast as buggy whips. On all the seas, in a hundred battles and at a thousand desolate posts, the American revealed his stubborn resiliency. For this the Legion and the Auxiliary, by countering numerous groups, had contributed to those who forged a strengthened tradition and heritage.

But following the "phony war," when the Low Countries and France crumbled and Britain fell back across the Channel, the future was shrouded. A variety of legislation including Selective Service was enacted which the Legion accepted as a practical fulfillment of its universal service resolutions:

> The Legion may now take full credit for having laid the ground-work for the universal service plan that has been thrown together hastily in a hodgepodge of executive orders and piecemeal legis-lation . . . it was not until the emergency was upon us that offi-cials hurriedly tried to throw a plan together. But the fact that it is now adopted, in practically every phase, displays the wisdom of the Legion in having advocated it and in attempting to have it enacted into law years ago.

Now the Legion's wisdom in its struggle for training young men to defend national interests and policies with a reasonable prospect of survival came into focus. Because so many insufficiently trained doughboys went over the top with unfamiliar British and French weapons in their hands and supported by French artillery, Legion-naires had long been apprehensive. And justifiably so, for in the first American battles of World War II the GI, Marine and sailor were ill equipped. Americans should remember the plight of our lost gar-risons. They should remember not only Pearl Harbor but soldiers reduced to throwing rocks and swinging their rifles like clubs because national negligence denied them enough grenades and ammunition. They should remember submarines and their crews, lost because tor-pedoes were inferior and failed to function. They should remember that in North Africa's fierce fighting some GI's were given weapons still packed in Cosmoline. Under fire they could fight only by shoving single cartridges into the chambers because clips were defective. National folly had its tragic consequences. Improper preparation led to death and individual frustration. To "foul up" became a permanent term in American usage.

The United States and Britain, holding themselves bound to treaties Japan had disavowed, demonstrated a stubborn lack of urgency to the final, fatal moment in the Pacific. After two ruinous decades the Navy could not match Japanese tonnage in that vast expanse of ocean. In midsummer 1940 eight battleships were at last under con-struction. But completion dates were set for two in 1942, two in 1943, and four in 1944. USS *Washington,* commissioned in May, was the first dreadnought completed since 1921.

The Legion's 1931 proposal recommending "education orders" to industries "to enable rapid expansion in the event of war" had found a measure of fulfillment in the Educational Orders Act of 1938, authorizing two million dollars a year for five years, but this was very little on a calendar of catastrophe. The Legion has maintained that this tardiness resulted in unprecedented expense. Still, as time ran out, four months before Pearl Harbor, the Legion urgently stressed efforts toward a defense buildup through UMT and Federal regulation of war supply agencies. An unusual grasp of logistics was reflected in its emphasis on the ability to remove "geographical limitations on movement of forces and adequate provision for corresponding plans and material." The 1941 Milwaukee Convention described the Atlantic and Pacific as "our greatest assets or worst liabilities, according to our strength or weakness thereon." Finally, if it was to come to a fight, the conflict should be waged outside the United States. Implicit here is determination to carry the battle to an enemy —the assumption of offensive rather than defensive strategical and tactical thinking.

In arriving at specifics the Legion "made studies, conducted researches and conferred with responsible officials of the Federal government on matters concerning our National Defense." This approach in gaining information and opinions from many knowledgeable men through committee, post and convention effort is evident in most Legion undertakings through the years. However, success in sifting, evaluating and the most important exercise of judging and recommending national security policies has been the Legion's most outstanding achievement. This record has received small credit in history. And in the struggle for preparedness The American Legion lost. More important, the nation lost.

15

Endeavor Through Neutrality
and War

NATIONAL defense throughout the interwar period was inextricably locked together with a credulous diplomacy. Like two exhausted men, struggling one with the other to keep afloat, neither gaining buoyancy, the United States' military and foreign policies could not overcome the international rip currents of the 1930's. Eventually both went under with the breaking of World War II. As we have seen, the United States was not alone among the Western democracies in the folly, nor can any one factor explain the trend to war. Through the 1930's reckless and ungoverned tides in Europe and Asia cut a channel toward war. The French had grown accustomed to fear, the British to deferral and appeasement, the Americans to illusion, the Russians to patience and expediency, and the Axis powers to brutal ambition. Men are fond of slogans, generalities and scapegoats. The "Slave Treaty" of "grinding reparations" served for years to articulate German grievances—long after any shred of evidence to support this myth had dissolved. The United States had poured staples and money into the Germany economy as fast as the Western Allies could wrest payments from it toward the cost of the war. Led by a man "half-mad," with a deep sense of indignation and a willingness to believe that all their hardships were brought on by the Treaty of Versailles, German leaders and citizens saw promise in *Lebensraum,* living space, although neighboring states with the exception of Russia were more densely populated than the Reich. With fraudulent interpretations of history Hitler hysterically and Goebbels methodically exploited credulity. They harbored a total disregard for acceptable international morality and an undisguised contempt for statesmen anxious for peace. "Our enemies are little worms. I have seen them at Munich," screamed Hitler.

And while Goebbels professed, "Hatred is my trade," men directing the destinies of Western democracies groped for European peace, even at the expense of free men. For a time they could say as Hotspur does in *Henry IV,* "Out of this nettle, danger, we pluck this flower, safety." Certainly the Axis had reason to believe that the United States would not wreck their expansionist program nor give decisive support to their "enemies." The U.S. government had pursued an isolationist course and the election of 1933 was universally regarded as a triumph of isolationism. Americans supported their government.

The Legion supported government policies aimed at averting participation in European war, and the condition of national defense only strengthened this resolve. Although the Legion had taken no official stand during the League of Nations' disputes in 1919, it later felt that the League had been thoroughly discredited. Rather than a powerful deterrent to aggression, it is now clear that the League actually opened the way for the fulfillment of nationalist ambitions. It promoted weakness by lending a sense of false security to many member nations. It gave governments the excuse to justify their failure to maintain adequate defense establishments, burdens that would have been so unpopular that peoples, rather than shouldering them, would have turned their governments out.

In considering the shift of official American policy from neutrality and the corresponding changes in Legion policy, we must bear in mind first, the growing aggression of nazi Germany, fascist Italy and imperialist Japan; second, the vacillating and feeble policies of France and Britain; third, the official American policy toward growing threats to peace; and finally, Legion policy over those years.

Relentlessly, each year from 1931 to 1939 was marked by menacing military steps. A diplomatic jockeying accompanied these steps, culminating in certain agreements that accelerated the onrush of dangerous adventures.

Disagreements and division within the Legion sometimes occur, and in the 1930's there were irreconcilable differences concerning foreign policy. In 1935 Commander Frank N. Belgrano, Jr., declared:

> Those who practice the theory of splendid isolation are smoking the opium of self-deception. They may have pleasant dreams for the moment, but some day they will awake to a nightmare of tragic reality.

But across the land there was a deep desire for tranquillity. The Legion repudiated Belgrano—a move in keeping with American isolationism. Roosevelt and the Congress had held firmly to a policy of detachment from entanglements abroad, following what might now be called "the mainstream of American thought." Sources of potential irritation or responsibility were swept aside. These included fundamental but embarrassing policies and doctrines, suddenly regarded as "dangers to navigation" in the channel of international harmony. Soviet Russia was recognized in 1933, and a nonagression treaty with Latin American states was signed in Rio de Janeiro. A new arrangement with Cuba abrogated the Platt Amendment which had pledged the United States to guarantee a free republican government there. In 1935 Congress passed and the President signed the Neutrality Act. This provided: (1) an automatic embargo on the export of arms and munitions to belligerent countries immediately after a status of war was declared, (2) a prohibition of private loans to belligerents, (3) a prohibition against American ships entering the ports of belligerents or navigating in war zones on the high seas, and (4) a prohibition against American citizens taking passage on the ships of belligerents. This act reflected the determination of the United States to avoid participation in any foreign war and was passed in part because of evidence brought out in the hearings of Senator Nye's committee. In 1937 two new major features were added. One was the "cash and carry" plan for trade with belligerents; the other, legislation that applied the Neutrality Act to civil wars abroad.

As the threat of war increased and strong American sentiment favored assistance to victims of aggression and to our former allies should they be attacked, Roosevelt attempted to persuade Congress to lift the arms embargo. Congress refused to act. In 1937 the fantastic Ludlow bill for a constitutional amendment, providing that the

United States could not declare war except by vote of the people, gained support, but was defeated by a rather narrow margin in Congress. In 1937 there was a demand that the Neutrality Act be invoked against Japan. The Administration decided that this could not be done because the Sino-Japanese war had not been declared. However, a number of restrictions were placed upon trade which encouraged Japan's aggressive program.

In September 1939 war broke across Europe. Congress repealed the arms embargo, but still maintained the "cash and carry" policy and a restriction on financial dealings with warring nations. American shipping was ordered to keep clear of belligerent zones.

With some justice it has been said of Roosevelt that, like Mahmud II, "peace was on his lips, while war was in his heart." While he ardently promised that "we will not participate in any foreign wars," and as late as the end of the 1940 political campaign solemnly declared, "your boys are not going to be sent into any foreign wars," Roosevelt stopped at nothing short of acts of war to aid nations arrayed against fascism. A procession of belligerent episodes led to patrolling the Atlantic routes to protect British shipping, hardly behavior associated with a neutral power. Early in 1941 the President declared a national emergency, and late in the summer, the Atlantic Charter was adopted by Roosevelt and Churchill on a warship in the Atlantic.

During the period up to 1939 the Legion had generally supported the policies of the government. Legionnaires shared the national revulsion from war. In 1937, for example, the Legion declared its support of the government by "urging the United States to maintain a strict policy of neutrality regarding foreign affairs and further urging the United States to be kept from any alliance which might draw this country into war." In 1938 the Foreign Relations Committee of the Legion qualified its position on neutrality:

> We beg leave to say that it is now apparent that even the word "neutrality" is a relative term. It means one thing to one person and another thing to another. We have no particular recommendation to make at this time, but we do report that we consider a proper neutrality policy, whatever that may be, a perfectly proper part of the Legion's general peace objective.

In the early months of 1940, when Germany was moving into the Low Countries and Scandinavia, the Legion seemed to be convinced that neutrality was no longer possible, and Harry A. Sullivan, who gave the Foreign Relations Committee report, declared:

> The totalitarian powers, having proved their attitude toward neutral nations are, in essence, no better than international bandits, uninfluenced by the customary rules of honor and fairness recognized by non-aggressor nationalities, as evidenced by their non-provoked invasion of Czechoslovakia, Poland, Finland, Norway, Denmark, Holland, Belgium, Yugoslavia, Greece and other unoffending countries, and we strongly disapprove of any policy of compromise or so-called appeasement in American dealings with the Axis powers and approve only a policy of stern and unrelenting justice.

Legionnaires from the West were particularly conscious of our hazardous position in the Pacific. Among them were Stephen A. Chadwick, elected National Commander at Los Angeles in 1938, who shared the concern of Henry Stimson and urged the nation to prepare its Pacific defenses, and Senator Louis Schwellenbach, former member of the NEC, who revealed that "his one heated dispute" with Roosevelt concerned Japan. "The President," he said, "would not agree that Japan was arming against America with American supplies." Less than a month after war broke out in Europe, the Defense Committee again considered Japan, but the Chicago Convention issued no strong resolutions that might disrupt relations then in progress. Two months later the NEC benefited from the views of Paul V. McNutt, returned from the post of U.S. High Commissioner in the Philippines, and Major General Frank Parker, retired Pacific Commander, now a member of the Legion's National Defense Committee. In the period remaining before Pearl Harbor a division within the Legion widened as the organization avoided questioning the national policy toward Japan.

National Commander Raymond Kelly spoke for the Legion's policy of neutrality and preparedness in 1940. In May, Louis Johnson, as Assistant Secretary of War, spoke off the record to the NEC and accurately forecast events in Europe. In a future crisis only a balanced military structure could dissuade attack. And if such an attack came, only strength could assure an expeditious response.

Any appraisal of Legion proposals should consider that while they come from the National Conventions, a twelve-month effort precedes them. This is carried on at the NEC meetings, two or more meetings of the National Defense Committee and the National Convention, all benefiting from suggestions and resolutions of departments and posts. Before these policies are adopted they are debated and discussed in a thousand forums. In the final analysis they are usually not the product of a small group but the decisions of the whole organization.

This does not preclude the fact that policy decisions seldom reflect a unanimity of opinion or that some resolutions in the broad spectrum of Legion activities have not been somewhat arbitrarily muscled through certain conventions.

During the opening months of the European war the Legion was divided, as was the nation. In September 1939 Commander Chadwick counseled caution:

> Continuing our hopes and our prayers for a means of remaining at peace, informing our public officials that such is our greatest desire, let us counsel all citizens to avoid the thought, act or deed which might threaten or disturb the peace of the Americans. To a generation that knows war from its participation in it, this today is the greatest and most solemn mission of the American Legion.

The 1939 National Convention in Chicago will be remembered for the intense conflict of those who favored greater aid to the Western powers and those who sought to keep Americans aloof. It also marked the depth of isolationism within the Legion. With banners and shouts Legionnaires in the parade expressed prominently slogans associated with neutrality. Commander Chadwick recommended that the Legion withdraw from the *Fédération Interalliée des Anciens Combattants,* FIDAC, an organization to which the Legion had given unstinting support from the 1920's. This was the prelude to a great debate, and we must sympathetically understand the motivations of both sides. Many of those who had seen war's awful aspect and who had believed that their generation would bring an enduring peace were frustrated and disheartened when hopes dissolved in the acid of Europe's perennial hatreds and rivalries. Why, they asked, should

Americans turn back and run the risk of enduring the withering fire
of war again? Never again should the fine, tall youth cross the oceans
to die on old battlefields. Many who preferred detachment reasoned
that we might better lend our good offices to mediate the conflict. The
United States was still recovering from the great depression, and war-
making would frustrate our recovery at home. For, in 1939 and 1940,
unemployment was still at a high figure, and rising. We were militarily
weak, for the Washington government had ignored the repeated
urgings of the Legion to prepare for any eventuality.

There were others who with equal sincerity felt that the nations
of Europe threatened and then embroiled in war with Hitler's Germany were our natural allies. Their forms of government and ideals
were akin to ours. There was no question about public opinion so far
as Hitler's policies and actions were concerned. Americans were hor-
rified by nazi excesses and deeply shocked by Germany's rising
military fortunes.

In October, 1939, Commander Kelly announced:

> I pledge myself to make known to our fellow-citizens your
> mandates to keep our nation out of any armed conflict overseas.
> Attempting to cloak our neutrality with a biased belligerency
> must inevitably lead us straight into war.

However, events moved swiftly. Legion leadership in the interval
between conventions found that Kelly's fine sentiment would have to
be bent. Those for more active support of Hitler's enemies were gaining the upper hand against the staunch isolationists as the administration and Congress cast off the tattered garments of neutrality.

But another trough in the groundswell of isolationism came in
March, 1940. National officers thought that the United States would
"avoid involvement," for "neither the peace to follow these wars, nor
the conditions facing our country (would) be bettered by our participation."

At the height of the neutrality debate the Legion met in Boston
in 1940 and abandoned its sixteen-year position on neutrality. Without debate, delegates adopted the National Defense report which
urged "all practical aid to Britain and those aligned with her in their
fight for freedom."

We of the American Legion, as lovers of peace and human freedom, devoted to the principles of Justice, Freedom and Democracy, condemn aggression and aggressor nations. We condemn all war parties which are leading their own people to death and ruin, and the world to chaos. To those countries which have been ruthlessly and without just cause invaded, and particularly to our former comrades in arms in the invaded countries, we express our sympathy and the confident hope that soon they will break the chains of their present servitude. To the people of the Great British Commonwealth who are so heroically defending their shores and their freedom, and to the gallant Republic of China, we extend our friendship and our assurance of our sympathy. We urge that the government of the United States exercise all lawful means to prevent the shipment of war materials to the aggressor nations and that it continue to extend to all peoples who are resisting aggression the fullest cooperation consistent with our obligations, our security, our liberties and our peace.

Another resolution took note of foreign-directed propaganda and urged Congress to take steps to control this activity. This action was directed at Germany and Russia as well, since at that time Russia was regarded as an ally of Germany. In 1941 the Legion intensified its efforts toward defense production. It also condemned strikes and slowdowns in industries engaged in war production, and put its cause squarely before labor on grounds of national security. The Legion asked that the President "make available immediately to the Congress and the people of this country a full and complete statement of the facts which constitute danger to this nation." It added that people generally needed to be awakened from their peacetime complacency.

Commander Milo J. Warner made it his business to cultivate contacts with Roosevelt, Hull, Knox, Stimson, Chief of Staff George C. Marshall, and others in government. In February 1941 he, Franklin D'Olier and Frank Parker toured Britain, talked with its war leaders, observed civil defense measures, and learned from Churchill how desperately American aid was needed. Many Legionnaires were critical about this trip and a special session of the NEC was a forum of sharp division. In May Warner told mass meetings in Philadelphia and Newport that the Navy should convoy our merchant ships to Britain. He urged the necessity of defending our rights by force if necessary on the ground of freedom of the seas. Subsequently, the Legion came out for delivery of aid to Great Britain by employing units of the Navy.

A profoundly important dilemma was presented to the Legion when, on June 22, 1941, the German armies entered Russia. On the one hand there had been the Legion's firm position in opposition to communism. On the other hand, Russia was now an ally of Great Britain. This led to serious conflict at the National Convention at Milwaukee in September, 1941. There, forces for and against staying out of the war were mobilized. Secretary of the Navy Frank Knox, Mayor La Guardia of New York, General Marshall and others made fighting speeches for full aid to Britain. Opposed to them were former National Commander Hanford MacNider, former Ambassador Cudahy, Senators Bennett C. Clark and C. Wayland Brooks, and Congressman Hamilton Fish. Past National Commander Ray Murphy read the brief Foreign Relations report calling for united support of the President and Congress and repeal of the Neutrality Act. Hanford MacNider suggested an amendment calling on the President to explain his foreign policy:

> I hope I never hear again that our only safety is to get behind the fleet of some other nation. If this is our war, let's get in. If this is not our war, let's get out. Let the President and the Congress tell the people that this is our war, or it is not our war. Then there will be unity in America.

The atmosphere was tense. Frequently it was pointed out that it was impossible to separate Russia as an enemy of Germany and Russia as the home of communism. The decision before the convention narrowed down to lend lease aid to Russia. Tough debate ensued, and the controversy received widespread publicity in the press. There were those who advocated "America first," and they rallied anti-Soviet sentiment. It is possible that the tide had been turned on the evening preceding the vote on this question, for those who were opposed to the course of the government had held a mass meeting which heard speeches by Colonel Charles Lindbergh and other advocates of strict neutrality. Witnesses to the scene say that this swung the vote of the Legion toward approving lend lease to Russia. Delegates adopted a resolution, phrased in such a way that it did not mention aid to Russia specifically but gave general support to the President and Congress in their foreign policy. Lynn U. Stambaugh, the new National Commander, had opposed the policies of the government, but he promised faithfully to carry out the mandates of the convention. Thus, the Legion was finally committed to the course that led the United States toward war.

On the eve of American involvement in the War the Legion could take some satisfaction from the fact that the government was following a course long advocated by its conventions.

National Commander Milo J. Warner enumerated "action urged by The American Legion, which antedated any action by our government":

> Universal service; reduction of the selective service age bracket; increased training for men to man the expanded merchant marine; creation of the aircraft warning service; preparation for civilian defense; establishment of home guard units to supplant National Guard units called into federal service adoption of anti-sabotage legislation; prevention of work stoppage in national defense industries; curbing of profiteering and hoarding; and collection of scrap metal.

He stated: "Our members . . . are truly a crosscut at the very trunk of the tree of our American life. All of you are of the very blood and sinew of your own communities. Our solid phalanx knows no class, racial, religious or political demarcations. We as an organization have a duty, a destiny, if you please, to fulfill." Warner stressed that while public attention was devoted to national defense problems and world events, it was all the more important that the Legion look to the welfare of the disabled and their families and to its "farsighted child welfare program." He reviewed the twenty-two years of effort for an adequate national defense. He pointed out that the Legion at Boston in 1940 had called for giving all practicable aid to Britain and that the President and Congress had made the nation a supporter of England and China.

Great events had occurred during Warner's commandership. Hitler's "juggernaut" had overwhelmed many nations and he had turned on Russia. Warner called upon the President to "state precisely and clearly the situation and condition as it exists today. His statement . . . [could] burn away any fogs of obscurity or groping doubts of confused people or timid persons. Congress should act promptly in accordance with such statements." Warner emphasized that the Legion's duty lay in backing the President and Congress. He noted that a few months before the two "big-time dictators" fell out, that Hitler had attacked Russia and that this development did not call for any change in attitude toward the Communist Party in the United States. The convention criticized the government for its inaction and its continuation to tolerate the "fomenter of labor disturbances, Harry Bridges," who was under attack as a communist.

The convention reaffirmed the resolution on tolerance of the Americanism Commission, which recognized "a growing attitude of intolerance on the part of certain American and resident-alien classes toward the race, religion and political beliefs of other American citizens." This attitude was a threat to the rights of citizens, and the Legion resolved to illustrate to the communities in which the individual posts lie, the threat to America imposed by this setting of class against class. This resolution anticipated the possibility of intense feelings against nationality groups whose countries of origin might become enemies. It also had a larger connotation in that it showed that the Legion, "composed of all races, creeds and political parties, is best organized to combat this intolerance."

Further, the delegates directed that the Legion extend its free servicing of disability claims to veterans who served under Selective Service. This was a valuable reassurance to servicemen and their dependents, for it placed at their disposal the medical, legal and claims structure built up over twenty-three years. VA medicine was floundering in bureaucratic incompetency. The Legion knew that if war came, the VA would be unable to meet the nation's obligations to its casualties. The convention moved that the VA be torn apart and rebuilt, but, as mentioned earlier, this overhaul was destined to be delayed for five years.

While most attention was focused on catastrophes in Europe, Africa and the Atlantic, where American sailors were already dying, the blow came in the deceptive calm of a Sunday morning in Hawaii. In that serene early morning of December 7, as the color guards stood on the fantails of our ships standing in Battleship Row, the first Japanese planes appeared over the mountains that look down on Pearl Harbor, Henderson Field and Honolulu. Within hours one of the most devastating blows in naval history had been dealt. It is not the purpose of this account to allocate the blame and responsibility for the disaster. Many individuals were involved from the President, his Secretary of State and military advisors to commanders on the scene. Their performances over months before the attack have been debated elsewhere.

After the attack on Pearl Harbor, the Japanese swept almost all before them, their advances as spectacular as those of Hitler previously. Japan's war leaders realized that domination of Asia and the Pacific depended upon defeat of the Western powers and the seizure of their bases. Great convex defense lines would then insure the trade routes upon which Japanese superiority would rest. Hong Kong and Singapore, Wake and Guam, the Java Sea and Corregidor punctuated Allied reverses as Japan smashed forward to New Guinea and the Aleutians, into Burma and toward the heart of the Pacific, Midway. American fighting men endured with stubborn hope, insufficient supplies, and uncommon nerve. At times they were reduced to the rifle butt and bayonet. Men of extraordinary valor and trepidity bought time. Many perished, their lonely bravery unrecorded. Others were ordered to surrender when nothing but the radio message could reach them. Some survived, led by audacious commanders. While the nation rushed to make up for lost years when preparedness was frowned upon, other Americans and their Allies put themselves "in harm's way."

News of the catastrophe at Pearl Harbor reached National Commander Stambaugh as he arrived in Washington, and he immediately placed "all the Legion was and has" at the disposal of the President. He dispatched similar messages to the Secretaries of War and Navy, both long-time Legionnaires. Frank Knox of the Navy knew as much as anyone in America of the scope of the disaster to his service. At his request Stambaugh with his staff, Navy men and several congressmen prepared a speech, delivered that night on nationwide radio. Stambaugh's firm, moving message spoke of the work ahead, the sacrifices to come and the nation's ability to prevail. Within twenty-four hours the Legion and the nation had closed ranks.

There is a footnote to the great neutrality debate in which Hanford MacNider bucked the strong tide toward belligerency. MacNider went to his second war, and before sailing for Australia called his old comrade Ray Murphy. "So long, Ray, America First is on the way to war. What are the interventionists doing?" Thus with a jest the leader who lost at Milwaukee put service to his country foremost. After four years he returned with one eye impaired, having been wounded and having commanded up to 30,000 troops in battle. His example is only one of thousands. Of the 70,000 Reserve officers called into service between 1940 and 1943, a majority were Legionnaires. Legionnaires' sons and many of their daughters distinguished themselves by extraordinary conduct in battle and in the more usual, unheralded tasks of war.

America's entry into the war focused national attention, energy and devotion to a common task. The terrifying logic of The American Legion's preparedness proposals of more than two decades were now clear to citizens, some of whom had felt that the Legion was "militaristic" or that Legionnaires were alarmists. Now only monumental efforts could provide the nation with the armed forces and industrial mechanism necessary to prosecute successfully a war that spread across the world and the world's oceans. That irretrievable commodity, time, had been squandered. Initially, Congress set authorization and requests of $141 billion while the President called for an army of seven million, the greatest navy in the history of the world, and an air force of half a million men. Production for 1942 was scheduled for 60,000 aircraft, 45,000 tanks, 20,000 antiaircraft guns, and 8,000,000 deadweight tons of merchant ships; for 1943, 125,000 planes, 75,000 tanks, 35,000 antiaircraft, and 10,000,000 deadweight tons of merchant ships. Of the first $109 billion provided for war, $24 billion was earmarked for airplanes and engines, $24 billion for tanks, guns, ammunition, etc., and $10.6 billion for naval vessels. The days of Legion agitation for defense expenditures were temporarily recessed.

On two oceans Americans began to counterpunch with what they had. At first, Hitler's fortunes on the Atlantic rose against shipping necessary to check his precocious adventures—U-boats ravaged shipping routes almost with impunity. The Navy could provide little protection. To overcome this menace the United States required time, during which sailors' lives were snuffed out by explosives, incineration and the sea.

At the lower curve of Japan's anticipated outer line of defense the United States Navy and Marine Corps joined battle in the near approaches to Australia—in places now carved in memory and memorials: Coral Sea and Guadalcanal. Midway came between these two operations. This great American naval victory against the powerful Japanese Navy marked the end of Japanese hopes in the central Pacific. It ranks with the great victories of history.

American aid was beginning to be felt in Europe and North Africa as U.S. and British ships gradually began to cope with the U-boats. Hitler's advances were blunted at Stalingrad and El Alamein. Thus the fortunes of war were hinged at several places.

The offspring of American despair following Pearl Harbor was stupefaction, anger and remorseless determination. From this reaction grew the mightiest, most imaginative and ingenious military power the world had ever seen. It beggared the imagination and still defies description. Here it is important to convey something of the effort, the profound contribution of the Legion and of the War that produced a new generation of veterans and Legionnaires. A few pages cannot describe the enormity of the events of those years, for the gigantic upheaval can hardly be comprehended by describing lines on maps, relating numbing statistics or mentioning great battles. It is like attempting to grasp the consequences of an earthquake, tidal wave and flood by glancing at a seismograph or scanning the headlines of disaster.

It is to the lasting credit of innumerable Legionnaires whose names may not appear on honor rolls of World War II that they served in most communities as members of Selective Service Boards. The fierce criticism of conscription and widespread defiance of the draft so prevalent in earlier American wars was absent. This was due in large part to the high caliber, sense of justice and hard work of Legionnaires. Legionnaires were in the war effort on every hand, holding many of the highest public offices in Washington, government positions as "dollar-a-year men," and posts in state and local government. Legionnaires and members of the Auxiliary were among the farming families who when their sons and hired men went off to war, turned out food for half the world. Legionnaires went into the defense industries, some of them returning to jobs from retirement. And throughout the war years they increased their efforts in post activities from tending to the disabled to preparing youth to face the obligations of citizens.

Recruiting was another Legion activity, and the Legion gained credit for 275,000 men and women for the Navy. At the request of the Civil Aeronautics Administration the Legion recruited persons over combat-flying age for training as transport pilots and instructors.

Long before, the Legion had assumed leadership in organizing civil defense readiness. The primary mission of Commander Warner's trip to England concerned this precautionary requirement. Warner had Henry H. Dudley, later head of the National Defense Division, correlate data and prepare instruction booklets. Not until mid-1941 did Washington establish an office of Civilian Defense under Mayor La Guardia of New York, and Dudley assisted the government agency to do what the Legion had accomplished in part. Past Commanders D'Olier and Kelly served as regional directors in two corps areas, T. Simmes Walmsley as executive assistant to La Guardia, and Reed Landis, whose contribution to the Legion's aeronautics program had been outstanding, as another assistant. Dudley took on the job of director of the Veterans' Division in civil defense. Of course, in the confusion many organizations rushed to the foreground to participate in various wartime activities, and cities and states developed Defense Councils. The Army and Navy handled their own recreation and welfare programs. The nation's health and welfare matters were under Paul V. McNutt of the Federal Security Administration, and his office took over many of the state and local programs as the United Service Organizations. The Legion chose to remain outside this office and the activities of another large series of programs, the Participating Services, headed by Mrs. Franklin D. Roosevelt. Legion leadership believed that their organization could direct its manpower more effectively. Differences between the Legion and Mrs. Roosevelt became sharp while the Legion worked in close harmony with the President. Especially her interest in a scheme to send conscientious objectors abroad to fill positions under military government caused sharp Legion criticism. In turn, Mrs. Roosevelt attacked the Legion, and in 1946 was a modest financial backer of the American Veterans Committee, a body of World War II veterans generally critical of the Legion.

The Americanism Commission had expanded its commitments to disaster relief in 1940, and the Legion took measures to counter sabotage, organize air-raid wardens, fire wardens and auxiliary police, and provide a model State Guard Protection force to take up the mission of the National Guard which had been called into Federal service. Most states adopted "an emergency guard," with Legionnaires commanding most units.

When Civilian Defense became a task for a full-time director, Mayor La Guardia resigned and James M. Landis took over the job. Landis had high praise for the Legion, pointing out that it had established and managed schools for air-raid wardens in every state, that Legionnaires had enhanced their value by attending Army Chemical Bomb Defense courses and by becoming proficient in a wide range of technical work. Through these men thousands of volunteers were trained to protect their communities. Fifty-six air-raid wardens' schools in thirty-one states graduated 7,748 instructors who conducted 13,323 local schools, which trained 225,000 wardens. The bills were met from the Legion treasury.

Another specific task given the Legion was the Aircraft Warning Service. With the Army Air Forces, the Signal Corps and the American Telephone and Telegraph Company, the United States' borders and interior were manned by hundreds of thousands of "spotters." In the program 100,000 Legionnaires were active with many Auxiliary women, other organizations and individuals—totaling more than a million people.

Posts throughout the country undertook various special wartime projects. A million new records went to men in every war zone and, perhaps more important, those billets forgotten in the backwash of stirring events from Sitka to Ascension Island. The Forty and Eight Society supplied playing cards to troops. Posts provided hometown newspapers and the scores of items that make life more bearable.

The mutual respect and solid relations of the Legion and the Department of Justice and the FBI were particularly constructive in

1940. According to Don Whitehead,* The American Legion during the summer of 1940 considered a plan under which its eleven thousand posts would organize their own investigative staffs to counter subversion. This meant that each post would give special badges, a manual of instructions and credentials to selected members. Such a staff would investigate subversive activities and report to local law enforcement agencies. Attorney General Robert H. Jackson discussed this plan with American Legion officials. Jackson held that patriotic groups and individuals should not engage in investigative activities, a job for professionals, and he suggested that any data concerning subversion be turned over to the FBI.

As a result, some Legionnaires felt that they were being shut out of an important aspect of the national defense effort and began to campaign for a special Legion investigative force. It was at this time, says Whitehead, that J. Edgar Hoover offered The American Legion a counterplan designed to enlist the assistance of the Legion but at the same time to avoid the possibility of a vigilante movement. Hoover's plan envisioned a liaison between post commanders and Special Agents in Charge of FBI offices for discussion of national defense problems. If the Legionnaire had information about espionage, sabotage or subversive activities, he should furnish it to the FBI. However, any investigation would be made by the FBI, not by the Legion. The American Legion accepted this proposal in November, 1940. The plan became the basis for splendid cooperation, a model for citizen liaison with the FBI. The citizen should not conduct his own private investigations. This could lead only to chaos, misunderstanding and a violation of civil liberties. Very quickly a vigilante force might spring up, harming our security and damaging liberty. Spying would become a neighborhood pastime. Character assassination and rumor-mongering would be rife. However, the citizen has a duty to remain alert. If he possesses information of a security nature which he feels would be of interest to the FBI, he should report it immediately to the nearest FBI office.

During the war the FBI, with citizen cooperation, was able to control nazi, fascist and Japanese activities inside the country within the framework of law and order. Special Agents contacted thousands

* Don Whitehead, *The FBI Story,* New York, Random House, Inc., 1956, pp. 208–209.

of Legionnaires. Commanders and adjutants of local posts, as well as national officers, were advised of the FBI's jurisdiction. The essential factor of FBI-Legion cooperation was that men of unquestioned discretion and familiar with local conditions could be found in the Legion to help the FBI in conducting its difficult task "without publicity or even neighborhood gossip." Hoover credited the Legion with outstanding aid in detection and conviction in several thousand cases. Over the years since, Legionnaires have furnished much valuable information to the FBI. A Special Agent knows that if he needs help in a case, he can contact The American Legion with complete confidence.

The American Legion's national organization was compelled to carry on Legion programs understaffed, as the government and the military required many of its most outstanding men. Membership grew to well over one million, and the number of posts reached almost 12,000—both all-time highs. The Auxiliary also reached new peaks. More than 150,000 Legionnaires were back in uniform. Among civilian leaders were such prominent Legionnaires as Navy Secretary Frank Knox, Under-Secretary of War Robert Patterson, Manpower Director Paul V. McNutt, former Aeronautics Chairman Eddie Rickenbacker, and many others. More than 70 per cent of draft board members came from the ranks of the Legion. Thousands of others served on ration boards, appeal boards and state and local government agencies. Nearly 400,000 served as air-raid wardens, 300,000 as volunteer policemen and 50,000 as volunteer firemen. Legion posts trained 350,000 in its air-raid warden schools and trained thousands of drill instructors for the Victory Corps' High School program. Hundreds of Legionnaires served in the civil air patrol. Hundreds of posts conducted successful recruiting for the armed services.

The American Legion's endeavors regarding youth, patriotic observances, education, naturalization, and other firmly established programs described in previous chapters and those that follow were energetically maintained throughout the war.

Legionnaires managed to maintain their strenuous Americanism programs during the war including the sponsorship of some 3,000 Boy Scout troops and the conduct of Junior Baseball. The 1938 Legion program of national high school oratorical contests to promote study of the U.S. Constitution and Bill of Rights grew with entries exceeding 100,000 in 1942. Boys' State had spread to thirty departments with more than 15,000 high school boys attending Boys' States in 1942.

The Legion worked with the Treasury in bond drives and with the Red Cross in the blood-bank program. A highly successful aluminum drive, suggested by a local post, then an iron and steel-scrap drive and finally a wastepaper drive were conducted by the Legion.

Throughout the war the Legion occupied a unique position with regard to defense policies. Unlike the Army and Navy—the Federal departments that had to be most circumspect in their official statements for fear of bruising the sensibilities of the committees of Congress, organized labor, industrial management, and the public—the Legion could and did speak with blunt and effective language when its conventions, the NEC and its leaders considered straight talk essential to the war effort. The National Defense and Legislative Committees could promote bills in Congress that the armed services hesitated to touch. Thirty-five major statutes concerning the armed services were in whole or in part due to Legion effort. The Legion lobbied for the GI's. It was responsible for pushing through pay bills, family-allowance bills, uniform allowances, free postage, servicemen's voting laws, death gratuities, National Life Insurance, and other measures. Commander Roane Waring by national radio pushed for the eighteen-year-old draft, something the armed services could not do.

In 1942–43 the Legion was outspoken in its criticism of work stoppages and slowdowns. It also resisted efforts to curtail the size of the Armed Forces, pointing out that this decision could best be made by the High Command.

The Legion had anticipated the commitment of millions of Americans to battle and resolved that never again would the wounded and diseased experience the neglect of their country. Legion rehabilitation efforts had resulted in a large code of statutes and regulations, and, fortunately, had its champions in both the House and the Senate, and in Frank Hines, who had served for years as Veterans Administrator. Watson Miller, Rehabilitation Director, resigned to become Assistant Administrator of Federal Security. He was succeeded by T. O. Kraabel. Lynn Stambaugh, Rehabilitation Chairman, became National Commander in 1941.

Through the rigors of war the national organization labored with a skeletal staff. Those who knew him say that Frank Samuel, National Adjutant, who died of a heart attack in 1943, was a victim of overwork. His job, to which he had given ten years of tireless performance, with a complete sense of public and private obligation, was taken up by Donald G. Glascoff. The long term of John Ruddick as National Treasurer ended with his death in 1945. Since Comptroller Glenn Crawford was overseas. John Heizer became Acting Treasurer and Comptroller.

Preoccupation of the many Legion undertakings in the 1920's and in the first years of the depression postponed a constructive Latin-American policy, which the Legion expressed in 1923. The Good Neighbor Policy, enunciated by President Roosevelt, was not to achieve its desired emphasis until after the outbreak of war in Europe, when the activities of nazis in Central and South America were generally recognized. In 1941 the Legion gave official recognition to a positive program by adopting the Foreign Relations Committee's request that all Legionnaires study "the results of the recent conferences on Pan-America" since "the rapid advancement of the new spirit of mutual help and friendliness can be furthered immeasurably by an appreciation of the economic, political and cultural attainments of these neighbor nations."

The committee encouraged departments, particularly in the border states, Puerto Rico, Mexico, and Panama, to enhance friendly relations with Pan-American nations, while the national organization looked to Latin America for an increased number of posts. Considerations of national defense were coupled to those of mutual understanding and development when the Legion took a strong position for the construction of international highways to Alaska and Central America. In 1943, at Omaha, the Legion felt that the Good Neighbor Policy was "no longer a party policy, but a national policy." The Legion recognized that the inter-American program should not be a temporary arrangement, valid only for the duration of war, but a matter of continuing importance. The Legion discerned future threats to "justice, freedom and democracy," after evaluating the objectives and methods of the Soviet Union and international communism. In 1947 Commander Paul H. Griffith called together representatives of posts in the Caribbean and Latin America to discuss how communist ideology and propaganda might be more effectively countered and "to implement in that part of the world our fight against communism." The conference stressed the importance of "informational and cultural" activities of the State Department. Finally the Legion volunteered to provide American tourists with instruction in methods on how to conduct themselves "so they will make friends for the United States." While the State Department did not go along with this proposal, it devoted attention to these general objectives.

The Legion became a foremost civilian organization in promoting understanding and "hemisphere solidarity." The Good Neighbor Policy of the United States, promoted by The American Legion and a number of other civilian organizations, achieved solid results in World War II. Latin-American countries supplied three thousand critical war materials. Besides providing bases and information concerning the enemy, there were Latin-American countries engaged militarily—Mexico, Brazil, Cuba, Colombia, and Venezuela. The wartime alliance with our southern neighbors has continued with the exception of certain areas subverted by communist activity. In 1952 and 1953 the Legion in its conventions indicated an unrelieved concern with the "complete political, economic and military solidarity of the Western Hemisphere."

Even into the war years amounts contributed by The American Legion to its child welfare activities mounted. In Kansas City in 1942 the Child Welfare Division reported that The American Legion had been responsible for fifty million dollars reaching 5,900,000 children, and that 90 per cent of those children were in family homes. In twelve months the Legion, the Auxiliary, Forty and Eight, and Eight and Forty had expended a total of $2,789,440 in emergency financial aid to over half a million needy children. Emphasis on the well-being of the whole child led to recommendations and assistance to state training and industrial schools to change these institutions from penal agencies to places for the retraining and education of children adjudged delinquent. The Legion took the lead in a nationwide volunteer campaign to prevent juvenile delinquency through the formation of coordinated community "councils." Within a short time Legion findings, published in a booklet, had been adopted by thirty state training schools. Even the Child Welfare program was interpreted in terms of national defense by the Legion. It continued to emphasize that the security of the nation "depends upon the individual family home," that children with strong bodies and "unwarped minds are needed as the basis for future good citizenship."

The Endowment Fund for the purposes of child welfare and disabled veterans' care had been maintained in a sound financial position through the difficult years of the 30's. What losses it suffered had been recovered by mid-1945 when the fund's principal stood at over $5 million. It had yielded more than $3,250,000. The Legion considered a second endowment fund in 1943 to sustain the work for Americanism. This was delayed by the war and reconversion programs. In 1945 the national endowment of reserve and restricted funds, special trusts and minor revolving funds amounted to almost $10 million. The Legion's National Headquarters occupied a memorial building in Indianapolis. Its Washington Headquarters occupied offices in an old mansion.

The general tone of the wartime Legion conventions was a steadfast resolve to lay waste the tyranny of Hitler and of the Japanese imperialists. This was in harmony with the general national strategy being formulated in Washington. At last, the Legion could say with some assurance of fulfillment: Build up armed might to meet any contingency, adopt laws to put the resources of the nation behind the war effort, enforce a high degree of military training for the nation's young men, ensure against work stoppage, protect industry and agriculture from sabotage, look after the wants of the nation's fighting men and the needs of their families, prosecute the war to a successful conclusion without false economies, and make provisions for those who will return from the war and for the widows and orphans of those who will not.

After the Battle of Midway, the Japanese were in a defensive position. At Guadalcanal the Marines and Army took the initiative and the Navy managed at a terrible price off Savo Island and in "Iron Bottom Sound" to maintain them. Further bloody battles to drive back the enemy began. Although the United States was committed to give first priority to the European war, gradually strength in the Pacific grew. From Australia and Pearl Harbor came the forces that drove west along the Guadalcanal–New Guinea axis under General MacArthur—remembered by such names as New Georgia, Lae, Bougainville, Hollandia, Biak, Morotai. Simultaneously, forces under the command of Admiral Chester W. Nimitz drove across the central Pacific from the Gilbert Islands with Tarawa in November, 1943, through the Marshalls, including Kwajalein and Eniwetok, through the Marianas with Saipan and Guam in mid-1944, to Peleliu.

But long before these shattering victories were possible, when the Pacific winds straightened few American or British ensigns, U.S. submarines began to slash into enemy supply lines. They were to be the most lethal weapon in hamstringing and then strangling the Japanese economy.

Through much of 1942 the Atlantic, long a harrowing gauntlet which laden merchantmen "ran" at agonizing, slow-motion speeds, had become a burial expanse for sailors, ships, cargoes, and the hopes of an early defeat of the Axis. To correct this situation the Americans, British and Canadians improved antisubmarine operations. Shipyards turned out Liberty and then Victory ships, warships and auxiliaries required to beat the submarine menace, the multitude of vessels needed to launch amphibious operations that in sheer magnitude and inventiveness dwarf description. American farms produced food to feed the armies and a large part of the world, factories poured out the vast array of war's requirements. By late 1942 sufficient men were trained to mount an operation across the Atlantic.

The Axis adventure in North Africa was caught in a huge crusher which began to close as General Montgomery's hardened Eighth Army, replenished by huge quantities of U.S. equipment, routed Rommel at El Alamein in October 1942. The following month the Western jaw moved as "Torch" in Morocco. The largest overseas expedition in history, composed of U.S. forces, made landings at Casablanca and drove across Africa to meet with the British six months later to capture 250,000 German and Italian soldiers on Cape Bon.

In the spring of 1943 Commander Roane Waring and National Defense Chairman Warren H. Atherton flew to the North African battlefront on a comprehensive inspection tour. This supplemented the customary coverage by Legionnaires of military installations and maneuvers in the United States and frequent consultation with military and civilian personnel conducting the day-to-day defense and foreign policies of the nation. Although this trip was authorized by General Marshall, subordinate commanders shuddered at the idea of a civilian report from Africa. The bloody engagement at Kasserine Pass was over, and Generals Clark and Patton were moving ahead. Publicity of casualties would be most unfortunate, many Army men thought. Waring and Atherton toured the battle area and when they returned gave frank and truthful accounts of their observations and conclusions, including a statement by Waring to the effect that casualties at Kasserine Pass had been "terrific." It is clear to us today that many military men harbored an obsessive distrust of civilians. But Waring spoke in many cities, and General Marshall realized that his observations were important and beneficial. In 1944 Commander Warren H. Atherton covered the Pacific war areas. The fourth wartime Commander, Edward Scheiberling, fulfilled the heavy schedule assumed by most National Commanders.

Roane Waring is remembered as a "fighting national commander" who stumped the country "pounding home to all citizens their duties on the home front and their obligations to support our fighting men with every ounce of strength." Waring was intensely devoted to liberty and the economic principles that gave the United States strength. He warned against those who would destroy free enterprise, initiative and decision:

> We see evidence on every hand of people in America who have sold themselves on the theory of some other form of government. The winning of this war demands that we make every sacrifice to bring this war to a quick and victorious finish. All restrictions, all regulations, yes, all regimentation that is necessary to accomplish this fact, the American people will gladly submit to. Crushing taxes, longer hours of work, denial of luxuries and comforts speed the day of victory. We willingly make these sacrifices. In making them, however, in submitting to bureaucratic regulations, regimentation and wartime restrictions, we do it—we must do it, with the expressed understanding that it is done as a war necessity. . . . Let us keep in mind that a nation no longer self-governing by the ballots of its people

cannot set an example for the peoples of other countries. A nation with its own liberty gone can never free other nations.

Following victory in North Africa, Allied forces assaulted Sicily, then commenced the heartbreaking campaign up the Italian boot. Salerno and Taranto in September, 1943, and Anzio in January, 1944, led to the fall of Rome in June. Terrible fighting in the mud, wet and cold lay ahead to the north as GI's, sailors and airmen pounded and overtook objectives and Britain became an armed camp for an assault on "fortress Europe." During 1943 the Army, Air Corps and the RAF bombed Germany on a gigantic scale and greatly reduced Axis war production while eliminating most of the *Luftwaffe*.

American soldiers and airmen struggled tenaciously in China and Burma while the Red Army engaged in massive offenses against the German Armies on the Eastern Front.

On June 6, 1944, Overlord was set in motion, the result of prodigious planning and effort. An awesome array of ships moved to position off Normandy as airborne divisions landed behind the beaches. Airmen and sailors prepared the way for the main assaults, pounding ground targets, mine sweeping, and driving their landing craft and ships onto the beaches. There the Allied foot soldier staggered, crawled and clawed his way through the Atlantic wall. To the waves of GI's it was hardly a neat textbook maneuver. It was an uneven affair, punctuated by stops and starts. Bitter, brutal fighting accompanied the Allied advances that lacerated German positions. Ingenious and massive Navy and Army methods landed more men, armor and all manner of paraphernalia on the beaches so that heavy infantry and armored thrusts punished the enemy divisions and pushed them back as air power continued its methodical tactical and strategic strikes. Great obstacles were overcome. Desperate German defenses were finally broken. And the enemy was compelled to withdraw on a wide front.

When asked by Berlin, "What shall we do?" General von Rundstedt, inflicting grave casualties on the Allies in his hopeless struggle in the west, replied, "Make peace, you idiots." He added, "What else can you do?" The nazis brushed aside this bold, sound comment. Insane orders became commonplace. Months of sanguinary struggle remained before victory.

The lot of Americans fighting toward Tokyo was no less brutal. In October, 1944, the Philippines were successfully invaded. The sea battles off the Philippines marked the end of the proud Imperial Navy's capacity to challenge the American advance. The fast carriers ranged at will and, after Manila was taken in February, 1945, Americans assaulted Iwo Jima and Okinawa in the drive toward the Japanese home islands. Every mile of sand and jungle had exacted a heavy price. And the Navy in the waters off these objectives suffered frightful losses to the kamikaze suicide planes.

Hitler chose to carry Germany's defeat to a Wagnerian finale. In the European war alone, twenty million soldiers, sailors and airmen perished. Add millions upon millions of civilians who met violent ends or extinction by starvation, extermination and disease. The enormity of the nazi tyranny can hardly be encompassed. Then consider the monumental loss of human life elsewhere in the world which bloats these awesome, unknown figures. The mind cannot comprehend the tragedy. For the suffering of war is beyond all computation.

In the Pacific the Allies were now posed to undertake the final defeat of Japan, cut off from her empire and pulverized by Air Corps and carrier strikes. But until the atomic weapons were used at Hiroshima and Nagasaki, it appeared certain that an invasion of Japan, costing millions of lives, would be necessary. Five days after the second atomic bomb was dropped, hostilities ended. Besides sparing millions the agony of invasion, the use of the bomb has perhaps another significance. This significance from a longer perspective may loom above the immediate military consequences of its use. World communism appreciates that the United States not only has an arsenal of nuclear weapons but in certain circumstances could be expected to use them. This in itself has contributed toward our stronger position in the world today and reduced instances of communist aggression.

And so the war ended. Millions of lives after the rumble of armor and the scream of Stukas broke the quiet of that September day in Poland, thousands of heartbreaking miles from Battleship Row, a document of surrender was signed by the Japanese in Tokyo Bay.

For The American Legion peace was to bring fresh challenges and many responsibilities to the war's veterans. ". . . These men who stood between what peace we know of and what might have been."

16

The GI Bill of Rights

FROM its inception in the minds of Legion leaders to its final approval by the President, the GI Bill of Rights must stand for all time as an example of major statesmanship. The broad concept originated in The American Legion, a member of the Legion wrote the bill, an employee of the Legion suggested its meaningful name, Legionnaires promoted it and handled its legal presentation, and a former Commander secured its unanimous approval in the Senate. It was the Legion's greatest single legislative achievement.

One need only review all earlier congressional devices to provide veterans' benefits from the Revolution on to grasp the import of this new concept in post-service compensation. Previously, legislation was largely in the nature of mere handouts. Some arrangements were generous; others, woefully inadequate. Some were inequitable; most, badly administered. None served adequately to realize the purpose of understanding the men who left private life, not only to risk life and health but to lose those precious years which mean so much in shaping a career in the world.

For wars are fought in the main by individuals in the flower of the young years. Pericles, in his immortal oration honoring the men who fell in the Peloponnesian Wars, said that to take these young people from Athenian life was like "taking the spring from the year." To take the young years from those who enter the military service for the indeterminate experience of war is to take the bright morning from the day. Some die. Others face life under the affliction of injuries or illness. Of those who return, many find their places taken by

those who remained at home. Their early training in a chosen voca-
tion has been denied them. Their education has been cut short. Those
who needed them have been deprived. After discharge they must
somehow find a place to earn a living. Many are compelled to change
the whole pattern of their lives. In countless instances their entire
future is blighted by that loss of time.

"The storied urn or animated bust" may excite remembrance and
the gratitude of some who know what war service has meant. Names
on lifeless bronze or stone are there as a reminder and dedication.
A badge of war service is too often a pallid distinction in a cold and
competitive world. For those who do not return no government can
call back "the fleeting breath." True compensation is in the hands
of God.

For those who returned from World War II, however, much could
be done beyond the devices of earlier legislation. It remained for far-
seeing and understanding leaders of The American Legion to grasp
the possibilities within the power of government to provide in the
form of benefits something of what had been lost to the soldier, sailor,
Marine, and coastguardsman. Moreover, this was accomplished not
after the guns were stilled and the last ragged cheers, but amid the
alarms and confusion of engulfing conflict. As the story of the inception, the writing and the enactment of the GI Bill of Rights unfolds,
it will be seen how this legislation met the hitherto unanswered question of reconstituting the lives of those who served.

In the early years of the Legion recognition of the government's
responsibility concerning unemployment led to enactment of measures
for the employment of veterans, for checking immigration and for
veterans' preference in government employment. There was also
Federal and state legislation for retraining the handicapped and for
aiding veterans in later life.

The inception of the GI Bill of Rights came after a protracted
Legion effort to provide a flat payment of up to $500 as mustering-
out pay. In September, 1943, the National Convention authorized a
special committee to develop an over-all program for the veteran
from the time of his discharge until his final rehabilitation and declared in various resolutions that any master plan should include
education and vocational training, employment aids, unemployment
compensation, home and farm loans, and a system of "furlough pay"

to cushion the transition back to civilian life. Obviously, Legionnaires were thinking beyond programs of earlier years.

The Legion faced two challenges: action to meet the immediate needs of veterans already discharged, and long-range planning for rehabilitation of all veterans. Initially, Commander Warren H. Atherton telegraphed requests to department service officers for records of men discharged for disabilities. On November 29, 1943, he presented the incredible records of 1,536 men who had been obliged to wait from three to eleven months before care and compensation was allotted them. "The list is far from complete," he said, "it is only a quick sampling. . . . The situation is all the more tragic because it is preventable." With an edge of anger he declared, "The report is a shocking indictment of lack of foresight and preparation for the inevitable casualties already here, and those yet to come . . . I should not like to face the wrath of eleven million veterans after this war if our treatment of their disabled has been as shabby, indifferent and lax as the story of the last two years would indicate." Citing several cases, he observed, "Having no other income, the disabled dischargee must rely upon financial assistance from private or charitable sources."

Although some 640 bills concerning veterans had been introduced, Congress failed to act. To avert a hodgepodge, the Legion took vigorous action. Commander Atherton pushed the stop-gap measure for mustering-out pay of up to $500. While the Senate passed the $500 bill, this proposal encountered frustration in the House. Representative May, chairman of the Military Affairs Committee, stalled. Atherton presented the Legion's case on a national radio hookup on December 14, saying, "Mustering-out pay must be made immediately. . . . Whether or not Congress does do that will mean the difference between a Merry Christmas and no Christmas at all to the men who have returned, sick and wounded, from the war fronts where they have been fighting to preserve a safe, free Christmas for every other American."

But there was no action. May departed for his Christmas in the Kentucky mountains. When he returned, lashed by adverse publicity by the press, particularly in stories by David Camelon of the Hearst newspapers, he put through a $300 bill and won his fight in conference. Thus the Legion was confronted with a serious defeat in its first effort to provide for the 600,000 servicemen already released.

For the larger task, however, "sweet are the uses of adversity." Now the Legion could put behind it the labor necessary for piecemeal legislation and dedicate itself to the larger concept. The fight was to last for seven months against formidable opposition. There was no doubt of the Legion's determination. "We didn't organize the American Legion to be a savings bank to finance a last man's club," Commander Atherton said. "The best way to use every dime in our treasury is in assistance to the veterans coming out of this war."

At a meeting of the National Executive Committee in November 1943, massive leadership was provided by John Stelle of Illinois. Stelle, a big, fighting bulk of a man, proposed a special committee to draft a bill for the readjustment of World War II veterans. Commander Atherton picked Stelle to preside over its deliberations. As a distinguished former governor of a great state, Stelle was eminently suited for the task. His special committee included Robert W. Sisson, Chairman of the National Rehabilitation Committee; Harry W. Colmery, past National Commander; Sam Rorex of Arkansas; W. B. Waldrip of Detroit; R. M. McCurdy, then Assistant City Manager of Pasadena; Maurice F. Devine, Chairman of the National Legislative Committee; and Lawrence J. Fenlon, Chairman of the National Employment Committee. Working at the committee's side were Francis M. Sullivan, the Legion's Legislative Director; T. O. Kraabel, National Rehabilitation Director; Bruce Stabbefield of the Rehabilitation staff; Carl Brown, Chief of Claims in Washington Headquarters; Jack Cejnar, Acting National Publicity Officer; and a task force including past National Commander Roane Waring, Lyon W. Brandon of Mississippi, James P. Ringley of Illinois, and Pat Kelly of Georgia.

From Stelle's active mind and relentless committee work grew the Servicemen's Readjustment Act of 1944. Hard, tedious days and nights of unremitting toil passed before the first draft was ready on January 6. It was not a hastily prepared measure. Educational provisions benefited by Legion conferences with leading educational groups; the title on loans with real estate, building and loan and financial associations and the FHA; and veterans placement and unemployment compensation with the Interstate Conference of Employment Security Agencies and the Unemployment Benefit Advisors. Team work, ardent threshing out of positions and judicious compromise made possible a final draft in a form the Legion could unreservedly promote. It was extraordinarily fortunate that Harry Colmery was a member of the committee. He was an able lawyer from Topeka, Kansas, and upon him fell the responsibility of drafting the technical terms in which the bill appeared. As John Stelle said:

"Harry Colmery jelled all our ideas into words."

The bill provided for: adequate hospitalization; prompt settlement of disability claims; review of discharges; mustering-out pay (eliminated following its enactment separately); educational opportunity; vocational and on-the-job training; an effective Veterans' Employment or Placement Service; readjustment allowances (unemployment compensation); loans to aid the veteran in purchasing a home, farm or small business; and concentration of all veterans' affairs in the Veterans Administration, which was to be given top priority, second only to the Armed Forces, in obtaining the personnel needed for efficient operation. This bill, the Legion emphasized, must be passed. Colmery made the following points:

> The American Legion proposed this bill first because we believe it to be the duty, the responsibility and the desire of our grateful people to see to it that those who served actively in the armed services in this war not only should not be penalized as a result of their war service, but also that upon their return to civil life they should be aided in reaching that position which they might normally have expected to achieve had the war not interrupted their careers. And second, we urge its enactment as sound national policy, for the good of the nation.

On the day after the Stelle Committee finished the first draft, Cejnar said, "It's a Bill of Rights." His sense of public appeal immediately stirred, he added, "That's it! The GI Bill of Rights!" This was an important stroke in securing the passage of the bill, for the phrase —short, easily grasped and generally descriptive—became a fighting slogan over the country.

The bill was introduced in Congress on January 10, 1944. Bennett Champ Clark, Chairman of the Veterans' Subcommittee of the Senate Finance Committee, sponsored it in the Senate with nine co-sponsors. After its nature was made known, there were enough co-sponsors to have passed the bill.

Meanwhile the Legion was mobilizing its forces to develop public support. Under Cejnar's direction, departments and posts stressed the bill's importance in every city, town and crossroads in America. Radio spots and motion picture "trailers" gained backing. News releases explained provisions. The press was quick to cooperate, and substantial support appeared on countless editorial pages. Sullivan and Sisson, in particular, went from door to door in the Senate and House office buildings to line up congressmen. When they found doubtful members, telegrams to the Legion's state officials urged development of grass-roots sentiment and expression. Of course there was some resentment about this pressure, and there were protests against the Legion "lobby." But, by whatever name it was called, this activity brought results. Other forces were at work favoring the bill. Since it so greatly emphasized the need for educational facilities for veterans, the educational institutions and associations took note. Dr. George F. Zook, President of the American Council of Education, representing twenty-one leading educational associations, told the Clark subcommittee:

> The United States government has a grave responsibility to offer educational advantages to the members of the armed services after this war. This is the least we can do for those whose education has been so rudely interrupted. In that respect, we agree emphatically with the provisions of this bill. Each man should be permitted to select the type of education he desires. It is important, too, that students be allowed to select their own requirements.

While many leading citizens gave the measure their approval, from various quarters came volleys of criticism and objections. Some educators prophesied that a large influx of ex-servicemen into higher education would dilute the quality of the graduate, dwarf the prestige of coveted degrees and turn quiet campuses into sprawling "educational hobo jungles." Among those who opposed the bill were cynics who apparently lacked a shred of faith in the men who fought their battles. The GI Bill would provide veterans an "all-time gravy train." Its home loans would erect "havens for deadbeats."

To meet Army and Navy objections to some provisions, particularly to a section establishing a board to review discharges, Stelle invited their representatives to Legion Headquarters in Washington. The conference lasted for more than six hours. At last the fifteen Army and Navy officers rose to go, saying, "We'll have to confer with our superiors."

"Gentlemen," Stelle said with anger, his fist pounding the table, "our understanding was that you would come here with authority to reach a decision. If I had known that you didn't have that authority, I wouldn't have wasted the time of my committee here tonight. The provisions we have been discussing are important to the men who have been fighting our battles. The American Legion proposes to see that this bill is passed, and passed as it stands."

The War and Navy Departments supported the bill.

A very serious example of opposition came rather unexpectedly from four of the smaller veterans' organizations—the Veterans of Foreign Wars, the Disabled American Veterans, the Military Order of the Purple Heart, and the Regular Veterans Organization. Their joint open letter to every member of Congress held that the GI Bill, as drawn, was too comprehensive, that aid for veterans should be limited to those who had suffered physical or mental handicaps by reason of military or naval service. It cautioned against "hasty and possibly unwise legislation." This opposition gave encouragement to recalcitrant congressmen, for they could claim that some of the veterans themselves opposed the proposed legislation. Through the good offices of David Camelon, a newspaperman covering the Legion fight, a meeting was held between the Stelle committee and a VFW committee headed by past National Commander Paul G. Wolman, whereby the VFW agreed to support the bill. The Legion committee agreed to the VFW suggestion of the insertion of the figure $500,000,000 in the section authorizing the VA to proceed with adequate hospital building.

Little by little, one by one, senators and representatives were won to the GI Bill's cause. There was astute direction in Washington, but Legionnaires at the department and post levels supplied the drive that gave the bill headway. After some slight amendments and gaining approval of senators with important followings who were sponsoring piecemeal veterans' measures, the bill was guided to the floor by Senator Clark. There he was able to show that all senators, with two exceptions, had endorsed the bill. Put to a vote, it passed unanimously.

The situation in the House, on the other hand, was not encouraging. John Rankin had a number of objections, and the bill languished in his committee. This delay stimulated further action. Telegrams went out to all department commanders. Legionnaires were now determined to bring about submission of the bill to the entire body of the House. National Commander Atherton designated the Legion's birthday, March 15, as "National Sign Up Day" for petitions urging adoption of the bill. Members of the House wanted the bill reported out, and Chairman Rankin rose to strike out at his tormentors: "This is the most far-reaching and most explosive bill ever to reach Congress. The Committee is not going to be stampeded into bringing out a half-baked bill. . . ."

Petitions flooded Washington. James P. Ringley and Larry Fenlon of Chicago were among Legionnaires across the land who did an outstanding job. Finally, Rankin's Veterans' Committee simply overrode his objections and its version of the bill, incorporating all fundamental provisions, was passed 387 to 0 on May 18. Since it differed in some details from the Senate version, protracted meetings of the Joint Conference Committee followed. A majority from each house was required for approval. While all senators were in accord, the House group was evenly divided. A difference on veterans' placement was the rub, with the Legion backing the Senate provision. The seventh House member, John Gibson, who was known to favor the Senate's position, was recovering from an illness in Georgia.

The bill's advocates now experienced a "cliff hanger." Friday evening, June 9, when the conference broke up, a representative said to Stelle: "John, we can't hold this thing together much longer. We've agreed to meet once more, at ten o'clock tomorrow morning. If we can't reach agreement then, the conferees will vote to report back to each house that they are unable to agree. The bill will be lost."

Gibson's presence was the only hope, since his proxy was not honored. With long-distance calls to Georgia delayed by five hours, Cejnar in desperation managed to contact the Atlanta *Constitution*'s night desk, which had an emergency telephone priority. Rewriteman Rolf Edmundson, briefed on the urgent situation, went to work. He learned that Gibson was traveling toward his home in Douglas, gained a Highway Patrol alert and obtained the cooperation of local radio stations in broadcasting appeals that Gibson call Washington, while the Douglas operator monitored Gibson's phone. Meanwhile Legion Headquarters in Washington acquired a plane priority from Undersecretary of War Patterson. Bill Westlake, Chief of Air Corps Public Relations, was located in California by the Los Angeles *Examiner*. The Waycross Air Base near Douglas was notified to cooperate. Its commanding officer had no plane available but knew of a commercial flight leaving Jacksonville, Florida, at 2:30 A.M. Dyson Wright, the *Constitution*'s night editor, finally contacted Gibson and commenced to relay instructions from Stelle after Gibson declared he was "ready to go." The Congressman had ahead of him a hair-raising night—the dash to Waycross, a high-speed trip of 150 miles to Jacksonville in an army car in less than three hours, the hurried flight to Washington, and a dramatic welcome from Legionnaires who awaited him. At 10 A.M. he made a spirited entrance at the conference and swung his weight behind the bill.

The deadlock was broken. The long fight was won.

A year after the GI Bill was signed by the President, the critical period for which it was wisely designed was close at hand. The days of the Third Reich which were to last for a thousand years had ended. Half of Europe surveyed a terrible devastation. The Japanese were reaching the end of their means of defense. In less than two months the long, brilliant, heartbreaking haul across the reaches of the Pacific ended in Tokyo Bay.

Now the mightiest military force ever assembled was encamped around the world, far from its homeland. As might be expected, American fighting men felt that their job was done and longed for the warmth of homecoming. Beyond their strong desire for release were calculations of what lay ahead. They wanted jobs, business opportunities, education, and the common pleasures. If it crossed their minds, many fretted about getting along until they could make their way in civilian life. Economists held out gloomy predictions about stupendous unemployment after the men began to return in force and the vast industrial machine began to convert. These predictions ran as high as nineteen million, with more conservative estimates at eight million. Few forgot that when mobilization began in 1940, a grim residue of the great depression remained. Millions stood in the lines of the unemployed during the Battle of Britain and while Hitler's legions swept through the Balkans.

Those who knew their history recognized that even in the most enlightened of civilizations demobilized soldiers and sailors could be a grave economic and social threat. One observer commented on this in discussing the rise of Hitler and Mussolini: "Veterans have written many a bloody page of history and those pages have stood forever as a record of their days of anger." To appreciate the scope of the challenge following World War II, consider that never in the spaces of a single year had so many Americans ended their jobs. The Army and Navy alone released 9,387,307. Tens of millions in war work sought peacetime jobs. Compare this with the great depression when eleven million were unemployed in 1933, less than the total World War II demobilization. While the average length of service of World War I veterans had been twelve months, that of World War II veterans was thirty months. Twenty years later the VA noted, "On the one side were all the ingredients for near national breakdown. On the other side was the GI Bill of Rights."

For lack of a plan, the humiliation and unmitigated hardship that visited the World War I veteran remains a national disgrace. Although only four million were demobilized after 1918, there were immediate hardships for most, prolonged displacement for some, and, when the waves of depression rolled across the country, a full measure of misery for hundreds of thousands who had served. Few who remember those years can divorce the image of the "veteran" from cold, hungry men in tattered khaki warming themselves in hobo camps along the nation's railroads, the ex-serviceman selling apples on a street corner or sidling up to a soup kitchen in old shoes repaired with cardboard. The destitute veteran was a familiar sight for two decades between the wars. It is accurate to say that the bonus was largely an illusion, since it came too late to be constructive. It was hardly a substitute for a sound, comprehensive readjustment effort. The long, frustrating struggle for the bonus and piecemeal veterans' benefits proved to be the blighted fruits of inadequate foresight and statesmanship in 1917 and 1918. The domestic economic problems of the earlier post-war period were less massive than those of the second, but they were more sticky and insoluble for want of experience, of a bold, imaginative and sound approach to veterans' affairs, of a realistic sense of national purpose, and of an organization endowed with both the power and determination to achieve expression of its specfic program in law.

Of course, the unfulfilled wants of the civilian economy, the energy and imagination of the industrial and business communities, the requirements of many nations abroad in averting chaos met through the Marshall Plan and Point Four, and our vital defense commitments contributed to a satisfactory transition from war to peace. Indeed, American performance disproved the fond Soviet predictions that capitalism in the United States would suffer a shattering breakdown within a decade.

But the immediate implementation of GI Bill provisions was of major importance. First, the majority of veterans received mustering-out pay of several hundred dollars. Though it never got the name, it was the equivalent of the bonus for which The American Legion has been so harshly criticized. It came immediately, however, not, as for the doughboy, several years later in a belated attempt to alleviate desperate conditions.

In important respects the GI Bill that the veterans of the first war formulated and moved through Congress with the energetic work of Senator Clark and Representative Edith Nourse Rogers for the veterans of the second world war was the antithesis of the bonus. For it served to put the ex-serviceman on firm ground where he could succeed in his society to a high degree of self-sufficiency and self-reliance.

For convenience consider six separate benefits of the bill: education and training; guaranteed loans; unemployment pay; job-finding assistance; military review of discharges; and top priority for the VA to build hospitals.

In education the bill authorized the government to pay for the tuition, books, fees, and subsistence of eligible veterans seeking higher education, educational training leading to employment, training on the job or training on the farm. Under its provisions 7,800,000 veterans—nearly half of all who served—participated. More than two million attended college, and 3,500,000, other schools. Veterans moved into 19,000 trade and technical schools and 2,600 college campuses. About 1,400,000 increased their skills in on-the-job training, and more than three quarters of a million combined classroom studies in successful farming with practical training on the farm. This unprecedented educational effort ranks the GI Bill with the Morrill Act, which created land-grant colleges. While it was designed to increase the training and knowledge of a generation of veterans, its utility and ramifications were and are as profound as any legislation in this century. Millions who would have flooded the labor market seized the opportunities of education, thus reducing the potential pressure of the jobless at a critical time. When they did enter the labor market, it was gradually, and most were prepared to make a greater contribution to their families and society.

The ex-serviceman as student demonstrated his capacity to justify his country's trust just as he had in the terrible adversity and trials of war. He fulfilled his obligation to the astonishment of cynics, among them Robert Hutchins, former head of the University of Chicago, who darkly forecast that the college-training provisions of the bill would make academic tramps of the veterans. By 1950, the major colleges reported that the GI Bill veterans had provided the best generation of college students in the nation's history. Veterans showed awareness of the value of education and appreciation of the opportunity to obtain it. "They brought an intentness of purpose to the classroom that brooked few fraternity pranks," one educator said. "Graduate-school atmosphere became a common feature of the undergraduate campus," said another.

Among those whose trades or professions were attained through aid of the GI Bill were: 450,000 engineers; 180,000 doctors, dentists and nurses; 107,000 lawyers; 243,000 accountants; 36,000 clergymen of all faiths; 17,000 writers and journalists; 711,000 mechanics; 383,000 construction workers; 83,000 policemen and firemen; 288,-000 metal workers; 138,000 electrical workers; 61,000 printers and typesetters; and 700,000 trained in business. The cost of this program of education and training has been $14.5 billion. Eighty per cent went directly to veterans in subsistence allowances. Nearly all of the remainder went for tuition and other training costs, and only five per cent for administration.

The contribution to economic, social and cultural advance is profound and continuing. Continuing because it and its Korean War counterpart imprinted a more serious and dedicated influence upon school life and led to greater emphasis upon adult education, did much to enable the country to meet the demands of an expanding economy and a higher technology, and promoted an atmosphere conducive to cultural endeavor.

The loan program is at this date the only provision of the original legislation still in force. The most important type of loans has been that which has enabled veterans to acquire a home. Of 5,268,000 loans made up to 1964, 4,966,000 were for homes. One-fifth of all single-family residences built since the end of World War II has been financed by the GI program for either World War II or Korean War veterans. Of the twenty-eight million home-owner properties (one to four dwelling properties) in the United States, 16,000,000 are mortgaged properties and about 22 per cent are financed by GI loans. This stimulus to the housing industry and the national economy has been enormous. For the building of homes is followed by purchases of new furniture, appliances and a host of items (from grass seed to dog houses) about which the uninitiated never dreamed. The growth of suburban areas requires more cars, school construction, highways and other public projects, and business locations convenient to residents of the new populated areas. It has been said that the landscape architect of post-war America has been the VA loan-guarantee officer.

Under provisions of the loan program, veterans were helped with 231,522 business loans and 70,097 farm loans. The total amount involved has been $43.7 billion. Of this, $22.7 billion has been in guaranteed or insured loans. Under a direct loan program, 175,000 loans in the amount of $1.8 billion have been made.

Veterans have proved good credit risks. More than two million GI loans have been repaid in full. These repayments amount to $13 billion. The percentage of defaults has been very low. In these the VA has had to make good the guaranty, although in many all or part of the money involved will eventually be recovered.

To tide the veteran over from discharge to reemployment, the bill provided $20 a week for a maximum of 52 weeks. It paralleled, in less amount, the nonveteran's unemployment insurance benefit. This avoided a repetition of the 1919 situation, when veterans were driven to charities. Between 1944 and 1949 nine million of 16 million veterans took 52-20 benefits for an average of 17.2 weeks, and less than one-fifth of potential benefits were claimed. Only one out of 19 veterans exhausted his 52 weeks of entitlement. The "gold brick" was in a small minority.

Finally, the VA won important wartime priorities to aid immediately in expanding its hospitals to meet the potentially high demand for beds. The bill made certain that veterans' claims were promptly filed and processed. Before the war's conclusion the War and Navy Departments were carefully reviewing discharges, since they were the key to GI Bill benefits.

Today the image of the veteran as a man whom society has passed by or a resident in the Old Soldiers' Home—spending idle days rocking on porches or telling lies around a hot stove—is fading. Gone altogether is the spectacle, familiar in the 1930's, of ragged bunches of ex-servicemen driven from town to town by vigilantes. The veterans of World War II and Korea have demonstrated their capacity to become successful and outstanding individuals and citizens. A Secretary of Labor declared ten years after its passage that through the GI Bill veterans have become "the best educated, the best trained, and probably the best occupationally adjusted group of people in the history of the United States." The Bureau of the Census has emphasized that the World War II veterans not only gained a significant educational edge over nonveterans but overcame a slight lead in earning power by increasing their income by 40 per cent to the nonveterans' 10 per cent in the four years after 1947. Dr. Amos Yoder has found that the GI Bill's impact on men listed in *Who's Who in America* has been impressive, and that by 1980 a striking 15 per cent of total listings will be its direct beneficiaries. He concludes:

> It seems clear that the GI Bill made an important contribution to our society by making it possible for a sizable percentage of talented men to obtain a higher education, which equipped them to become leaders in our society.

From a distance of two decades the proportions of The American Legion's bold concept and its implementation gain true dimension.

As the millions returned from the armed services to civilian life, the Legion was prepared to welcome them. In 1942 the question of opening Legion membership to World War II veterans arose. All departments and posts considered its aspects prior to the Kansas City convention, where delegates decided overwhelmingly in favor of rallying new veterans to the Legion's ranks. While some felt that a new generation of veterans would submerge those who had served in the first world war, most recognized their inclusion as an opportunity to enlarge the Legion's influence and to advance its principles and programs. Opening membership to a long-established organization with important traditions to those who had served in the greatest of the Republic's wars "to preserve the national interest and to defend liberty and justice throughout the world" would maintain the supremacy of The American Legion as a veterans' organization. Legion administration, property, experience, and programs would give the younger veteran and his family a greater opportunity to serve the nation and community in peace.

Delegates decided that their action should be an offer, not a solicitation. Congress promptly amended the Legion's charter, making World War II veterans eligible to membership after honorable discharge or after the termination of hostilities. The Legion refused to recruit, although other veterans' organizations did so. Occasional declarations of political and economic groups favoring new societies for World War II veterans caused some annoyance.

The drive for membership began after September 2, 1945. At the Chicago convention in November, two World War II veterans were elected Vice Commanders, and in December each member of the NEC had as a consultant a World War II Legionnaire.

The onset of World War II in 1939 had increased Legion membership to over one million for the first time since 1931. Steadily the number of Legionnaires rose to more than one and a half million in 1945. The number of posts increased to 13,043. In 1946 membership doubled to the all-time high of 3,326,556. The number of posts exceeded 15,000. While membership dropped below three million, the number of posts increased to an all-time high of 17,360 in 1950. Since, membership has remained above 2,500,000, with the number of posts suffering a relatively slight decline.

The rise challenged the organizational and physical facilities of The American Legion and led to expansion of the National Headquarters in Indianapolis, the enlargement of existing posts and the construction or acquisition of new sites in every state and territory and across the world on every continent where ex-servicemen resided.

The National Convention of 1946 drew more than 3,500 delegates, and preparation for a reorganization of the Legion's committee, commission and division structure was accelerated.

Again, a few years later, American Legion membership was opened to veterans of the Korean War. By that time, the National Headquarters had moved into its impressive new building on the War Memorial Plaza in Indianapolis. Past Commander and former Governor Paul V. McNutt and National Commander George M. Craig dedicated the structure that provided double the floor space of the Legion's previous headquarters.

Like the Legionnaires of World War I, Legionnaires of World War II and Korea had experienced the vicissitudes and requirements of war. Some had fought the nation's battles and had served in countries whose entire populations had been subjected to the extremity of "total war." They had seen the tragedy wrought by unspeakable tyrannies. Many had survived great ordeals. Death, wounds, the loss of comrades, fear, disease, the loneliness that envelopes battlefields and stands its watch on the high seas or at twenty thousand feet were no strangers to the GI, sailor, Marine, or airman. Others had endured the tedium and longing that accompanies extended duty in a hundred distant outposts and the vital support missions at home and abroad. As before, they came from every walk of life, social position, economic circumstance, religious, racial, and political background.

Legionnaires from World War II and Korea had served in every branch of the Armed Forces, in all grades and ranks, many highly expert in their military specialties. A large number have kept themselves informed of developments and requirements of the nuclear age and the cold war. Some remained in the service and have been valuable members. Others entered politics or government, where they have advanced those Legion positions which they endorse.

Most Legionnaires returned to their communities determined to advance in peace principles and ideals for which they served in war. Time has proved their qualifications to make the necessary contributions and willingness to do the work upon which the success of Legion programs depends.

In Changing Times

17

The Legion and the Cold War

THE American Legion's traditional distrust in and opposition to communism proved well grounded in the seven years following the defeat of Germany and Japan. During the war years the Legion, along with Americans generally, recognized a common interest with Soviet Russia to crush Hitler. But in its support of cooperation with the Soviet in war-making, it held fast to the conviction that communism was a fundamental and abiding threat. Elimination of Hitler, Tojo and Mussolini would not eradicate all the great tyrannies. Even before hostilities ended the Legion saw alarming signs in Soviet policy. It recognized that ultimately the struggle of the free world would be with communism—not only as a subversive conspiracy but as an aggressive, imperialistic threat as well. In this, the Legion's perception ran far ahead of that of American and British political leaders.

From the time of Hitler's invasion of Russia and "no-strings-attached" lend-lease to the faltering Red Army and desperate Russian population to the fall of Berlin the United States exacted few promises or guarantees from the Soviet Union. Even Churchill allowed his consuming hatred of the nazis to obscure his vision. Also, his nation was the beneficiary of U.S. aid, and hard words with the President would have impaired Anglo-American relations. Western political and military leaders and their peoples recognized the important war the Red Army was waging. But long-range provisions and eventualities that would follow victory received little hard attention, though Churchill had expressed fear of Russian domination in Eastern

Europe and late in the war suggested that General Eisenhower meet the Red Army as far to the east as possible.

Stalin's will held enormous sway, and he was insistent that the second front be launched in the west. As he cynically deceived his allies concerning "free elections," he gained spheres of interest in Europe and in the Orient for promises that were broken with the exception of an attack upon Japan, which came five days before the Pacific War ended. But for a few realistic diplomats whose observations were disregarded, Western politicians supposed that Stalin's purposes were as good as his word. Western political and military leaders translated this unfortunate, myopic optimism into the text and substance of military decisions. Throwing back the present enemy to geographical lines agreed to with the Russians was paramount and exclusive.

This low condition of high strategy blighted the fruits of victory in many areas. There were a few exceptions. One, the outcome in the Pacific against Japan, was due in large measure to General MacArthur's realistic grasp, prestige and righteous influence in the Pacific, backed by the brilliance of Admirals Nimitz, Spruance and others and the prodigious striking power of the Navy and Air Corps.

Yet, even there Stalin gained certain strategic islands and concessions on the Asian mainland. Our government, largely because of President Roosevelt's enormous political self-confidence, which was fed by a measure of naïve, fraudulent and radical counsel, made concessions to Stalin in a series of summit conferences culminating at Yalta. Stalin's every move, on the other hand, was directed toward enlarging the areas of Russian sovereignty and influence.

Most Americans shared the illusions of their leaders. And until the naked reality appeared, the Legion hesitated to assume an attitude which might seem too critical of the government. Further, details of agreements were disguised or soft-pedaled.

Russian armed might moved into and assumed control not only of areas conquered in battle but of those gained by concessions exacted from the Western powers. The tragedy was of global dimensions. So far as the government of the United States was concerned the fatal flaw was a stubborn naïveté prevailing at the very highest levels. At the time of the London conference of foreign ministers in 1945, John Foster Dulles, serving in an advisory capacity in the

State Department, spoke with his habitual frankness. In previous conferences between the great powers there had been statements giving the impression of complete harmony. But this did not exist. It was, he said, "a diet of soothing syrup." Of that London conference he observed:

> It was inevitable that the time would come when the Soviet Union would want to test us out. . . . We are at the beginning of long and difficult negotiations which will involve the structure of the post-war world. We are emerging from six years of war during which morality and principle have increasingly been put aside in the favor of military expediency. The war has now ended and, with that ending, principle and morality must be re-established in the world.

This was not to be. Rash actions would have to be undone. The hard knots tied with almost juvenile abandon were not to be slipped. Communism was never guided by democratic principles or acceptable morality in its relations with other nations. Roosevelt's chief adviser, Harry Hopkins, clung to the belief that Stalin was a great Russian nationalist and patriot, that it was absurd to regard his communism as prevailing over his nationalism, that he trusted the United States, and that our trust would not be misplaced with him. Many shared these naïve views.

The American Legion took an early lead in exploring courses of action open to the United States after victory and was instrumental in conditioning its large membership, represented in all facets of American life and thus highly influential, to the vast responsibility of world leadership. The days of isolationism were gone. Shortly after Pearl Harbor the Legion inaugurated programs at all levels to consider objectives for the peace. With the National Grange, AF of L, NAM, Elks, Knights of Columbus, B'nai B'rith, and the Masons of New York, a combined study for a program to end "the philosophy of isolation" and to promise a "world arrangement of nations to establish and maintain order" was followed. *The National Legionnaire* in the spring of 1942 declared:

> We cannot win the peace, we cannot provide assurance to our people against periodic repetition of our involvement in world catastrophes, unless we as a major nation recognize and assume

our responsibilities and take our position of leadership in organizing the world to establish and maintain order. . . . There can
be no assurance or permanent national security except through
world security.

After resolving that the United States should take "the lead in some
international association of nations" in the 1942 Convention the Legion, when schemes for a "federation of the world" drifted about like
New Year's Eve confetti, opposed the surrender of "national rights by
amalgamation or confederation."

During the critical war year 1943 the Legion, at its convention
in Omaha, called for American participation "in the establishment
and maintenance of an association of free and sovereign nations implemented with whatever force" would be necessary. Thus the Legion
had done much groundwork among its membership and, indirectly,
in tens of thousands of communities before the Connally and Ful-
bright resolutions were brought before the Senate and the House. The
Legion's continued emphasis upon an effective international organization was widely recognized. *The New Work Times,* for example, regarded the Legion's work as "further evidence that the tide of American opinion is running strongly and irresistibly in favor of the assumption by the United States of the leadership and responsibility
in world affairs which fall logically to a world power."

The Legion asked all posts to lead in the discussion of the organization which was to be proposed at the Dumbarton Oaks Conference.
Later it observed that adoption of a charter at the world security conference in San Francisco was the "foremost objective of the Legion."
It warned Americans against bluster or appeasement and concluded
its observations by saying that such an organization could only succeed
through "the utter good faith of its members." At San Francisco,
Commander Edward N. Scheiberling served as consultant to the
United States delegation, and when the charter appeared in the Senate, The American Legion advocated ratification.

In 1946 the Legion resolved that the UN charter should be
strengthened, that the people of every nation should determine their
own form of government and that the United States should resist at
home and abroad the spreading of "tyrannical totalitarian ideologies."
It condemned communist intervention in the affairs of many nations,

and it especially condemned the high-handed actions of Marshal Tito of Yugoslavia. This was among the first forthright, specific, post-war assertions of distrust of communist states. The tempo of Legion criticisms was destined to increase with the years. At New York in 1947 the Legion expressed its concern about the Far East, mentioning Japan, Korea and China. Thus, three years before the Korean War broke out, it warned our government of the potentially explosive situation on that peninsula and its belief that the United States should act accordingly. This warning proved futile in influencing U.S. foreign policy. Then, at its 1948 Miami convention, over which James F. O'Neil presided as National Commander, The American Legion's position on foreign affairs became still more pointed. Its resolution specifically mentioned the USSR:

> This policy (for world domination) has crystallized at Berlin. The deliberately inhuman and unjust blockade by the dictators of Soviet Russia has created an act of aggression which could easily kindle the flames of war.... We most emphatically support the stand which the United States has taken there against interference with our rights and duties. Berlin has become a symbol of resistance to communist aggression, and this resistance must be maintained resolutely, without appeasement, without bluster, without wavering. The Airlift is bringing encouragement to all of Europe and especially to those friends of liberty who live under the shadow of the Iron Curtain.

Against the dark background of Soviet maneuvering the Legion urged the creation of a system of cooperation among the nations of Western Europe, anticipating what evolved the following year—the North Atlantic Treaty Organization. Once more the Legion recommended all practicable assistance to free China, and it urged the fullest discharge of our national obligations to Korea and the Philippines. Its call for the strengthening of the diplomatic service marked the beginning of an emphasis on the serious shortcomings of the State Department.

At the Philadelphia convention in 1949 the adopted report of the Foreign Relations Commission commended the European recovery program but emphasized that military assistance was the prime necessity. In reasserting its concern about the Far East and the integrity of China, it suggested a regional pact of the nations in the Far East, presaging SEATO and other arrangements. It also expressed concern about maintaining the security of our atomic secrets.

Hopes for the UN, already dampened, were quickly altered as the East-West struggle deepened. Its effectiveness depended upon a concert of interests among the great powers, which was unattainable. The Security Council was enfeebled, and with the exception of the Korean action, which was made possible by the absence of the Soviet delegate, the United Nations was powerless if either the United States or the USSR considered its vital interests jeopardized. Consequently, as time passed, the General Assembly and the Secretary-General assumed greater importance. The principals in the East-West conflict came to rely upon treaties and regional alliances, permitted under the Charter, to fortify their positions, improve their economic policies and promote their political, moral and social values, since the UN was unable to resolve the irreconcilable differences between communist ambition and the aspirations of free men. The American Legion was regarded by prominent newspapers as "the first national organization to offer specific methods of how the Charter of the United Nations could be strengthened so that it would become an effective world authority." The Legion referred to the Security Council as a "perpetually hung jury" and proposed "tyranny-proof" amendments. First, removal of the veto in matters of aggression or preparation for aggression with the International Court of Justice empowered to make appropriate interpretations. Second, limitation of arms production with positive international inspection. And, finally, establishment of an effective world police force.

Eventually there was a change whereby the General Assembly assumed greater authority. At this time the Legion "condemned the failure of the State Department to deal adequately with the advance of communism" and deplored the presence in the State Department "of men well known to possess communist leanings."

The years 1950, 1951 and 1952 were deeply disturbing and significant in our foreign relations. Evidence of the seriousness and permanence of the communist menace accumulated, and the American people at last awakened to the imperative requirement of coming to grips with reality. The Soviet Union had abandoned all pretense. Her enmity toward the West was undisguised. What promises she had cynically given lay shattered, as useless to an orderly construction of affairs as a handful of bone dust to the paleontologist. She had turned the thumbscrews of tyranny on her satellites. She flagrantly exploited the encirclement of Berlin—an unnatural encirclement strangely agreed to by the United States and Britain in the alarm of war. The communist blockade of 1948 had been overcome only by the heroic and stupendous airlift. In the Far East, through gross ineptitude, miscalculation and sabotage of congressional intent, our policymakers had made it easier for communists to drive the Nationalist Chinese government to Formosa.

Wishful thinking and laxness had permitted our vast conventional striking power of 1945 to deteriorate, a condition to be considered shortly. While we held a monopoly of atomic and, later, a preponderance of hydrogen weapons, communist espionage was active and treason was afoot. As a result, Soviet Russia acquired essential secrets that facilitated building an atomic capability of her own. High in our government disloyalty had exercised alarming power. Revelations of treasonable activity shocked the public. The Alger Hiss case was a vivid reminder of slack supervision at the top. There were also the activities of Harry Dexter White, who had supplied Secretary Morgenthau with the benighted plan to reduce Germany to an agrarian economy—used by the nazis to harden their control over the German people and direct the war to its Wagnerian finale. A chilling column of individuals who had engaged in treason, espionage and perjury were marched through courts and across the front pages of every newspaper in the country.

This spectrum of mischief, ranging from naïve incompetence to treason, spurred the Legion's interest in foreign policy. From reaffirmation of its attitude toward communism, the strengthening of its Americanism programs and repeated warnings about defense, it moved in 1950 to more direct and pointed criticism of the government itself. Indeed, the militancy of the Legion provided leadership at a moment when wide discontent with our foreign policy was at its height. But this was not enough. Now came the tacit announcement that our defense perimeter did not include South Korea, coupled with the withdrawal of forces from that unhappy land. The way was clear for the Soviet Union and Red China to try the United States, to mount a North Korean attack aimed at driving the free world from northeast Asia.

In this context North Korean divisions, supplied with Soviet weapons and advice, invaded South Korea on June 25, 1950. President Truman acted immediately, and two days later the UN urged its members to join in the defense. Thus, armed aggression made prophetic the Legion's foreboding of earlier years about the Korean Republic on a Red continent and our Army's decline. Through the summer the North Koreans swept everything before them. Much of the American force was composed of green recruits—another instance of lack of attention to Legion warnings. Reorganization of the Armed Forces had stripped the Army of its tactical air support—a tragic blunder. Fortunately the Navy and Marines had flyers skilled in this mission, and their weight was soon to be felt. But time was required to put them over the fighting line.

Finally, their crude but effective logistics strained, the North Koreans were stopped by the Americans and ill-equipped ROK's deployed at the tip of the peninsula.

Then, with reinforcements of Marines, General MacArthur struck. Holding the enemy at bay, he launched the brilliant amphibious landing at Inchon. Defense Secretary Louis Johnson, former National Commander of the Legion, was one of the few military and civilian leaders who supported MacArthur's plan from the start. The enemy was caught in an audacious, unprecedented envelopment. Unsparing in their praise, the British Chiefs of Staff cabled MacArthur that the Inchon counterstroke "will rank amongst the finest strategic achievements in military history." Now American troops, with the Korean divisions and contingents from other nations, broke from the Pusan perimeter, north toward the jaw that hinged at Inchon. Within weeks the crossing of the 38th Parallel came. Victory seemed but a short time away.

As American casualty lists lengthened, the Legion met in Los Angeles in October. Commander George N. Craig and other speakers, among them General Marshall and Secretary of Defense Johnson, stressed the necessity for universal military training. Craig underlined President Truman's words to him: "If we had had it in 1947, we wouldn't be in the fix we are now." The Foreign Relations Committee made its strongest report to date. For the first time, in adopting this report, the Legion declared its lack of confidence in the present administration of the State Department. It recommended that all necessary steps be taken to reconstitute it. Further, it opposed the recognition of Red China by the UN and called for the continued defense of Formosa and the Philippines. Above all, it urged the UN to insist upon the occupation of all Korea and to enforce peace until a free election could be held.

Faced with another war in which Americans bled and died, the Legion was alarmed. The cold war had shifted to a new area of activity, in which a Soviet satellite assumed the communist offensive. The Legion placed the responsibility squarely on the Soviet Union and called for the American delegate to the UN to forward a resolution that further aggression in any part of the world "by Soviet Russia will meet the full force of retaliation" by UN authority, "including, if necessary, the release of atomic weapons on Soviet Russia."

A year later the Legion lashed at the Soviet Union and the satellite governments, declaring that they had scoffed at, ridiculed and in every way shown contempt, not only for the principles and ideals of the United Nations, but also for the basic human values of freedom, independence and human dignity. The Legion's resolution concluded: "The American Legion vigorously condemns all efforts to appease communism . . . in Korea, in China, in any other part of Asia or the Far East or elsewhere in the world."

It was a sunlit autumn of hope for troops driving toward the long northern border of Korea in 1950. But as the cruel winter blew down from Manchuria it brought with it hoards of Chinese regulars—fraudulently identified as "volunteers." By stealth some quarter of a million Red Chinese gained their jump-off positions and, in November, smashed into the forward UN and ROK units. Most intelligence earned a black mark. In swirling snow and frostbite cold, divisions reeled from the shock of field armies. For the soldier, Marine and flyer it was to be a deadly, bitter, frustrating ordeal. The State Department, target of the Legion only a few weeks before, transmitted its fear to the White House and press that an attack on the new enemy's marshaling points and logistics across the Yalu River would trigger Russian intervention and even more massive Chinese participation. Men on the line, falling back in rearguard actions or fighting their way to the sea, knew that, despite the dreadful slaughter of

Chinese, more were pouring south from untouched bases. In this "new war" they had yet to learn that their goal was not victory.

Now, by a skillful redeployment to a ragged line below the 38th Parallel, the enemy was checked, and MacArthur's new field commander, General Matthew Ridgway, went to the attack. The State Department, however, bane of every commander and negotiator who served in that heartbreaking war, maintained a tight control over military strategy. As Ridgway's offensive gathered momentum, Eighth Army troops took new heart from this leader who moved among them in battle dress. When the front surged north across the 38th Parallel, armistice negotiations began. Units were told to dig in. The years of patrols and listening posts began. Then General Douglas MacArthur's military career was rudely ended.

Since many of The American Legion's positions and those of General MacArthur were in harmony from World War I days, his dismissal and extraordinary address to the Legion in 1951 require attention. MacArthur's removal was the culmination of a bitter, longstanding series of differences between the General and officials in Washington. Ample evidence reveals that these officials had for years undercut or attempted to undercut MacArthur's sound and prophetic strategic views, his administration of occupied Japan, his steadfast enmity toward communism, his scorn for "appeasement and defeatism" in the Pacific and the Orient, and, finally, his insistence on "aggressive, resolute and dynamic leadership" as a requisite to victory as well as a requirement of prosecuting our obligations. To say that he was unaware that his outright statements ran contrary to official Washington policy or that he did not comprehend civilian control of the military is most naïve. MacArthur unquestionably knew that an expression of his views might lead to his dismissal, but perhaps felt his highest duty lay in alerting America to the fact that the immediate battle with communism was in Asia. History does not reveal what might have been. Truman has recently stated that an attack across the Yalu would have meant World War III. Many of his advisers agreed in 1951. However, many others felt the pragmatic Chinese and Russians would have avoided this at any cost, but felt the United States would not extend the war, even if given outrageous provocation. International communism guessed right. Now in the spring of 1951, MacArthur's broad, positive views not only grated the nerves of his old enemies but bruised the extended, delicate feelers of the British, the Indians and others anxious to consort with the Red Chinese for lucrative trade opportunities. His position on Formosa and the Chinese question was too much. The pressure and fears of the UN and the State Department and the advice of Secretary of Defense George C. Marshall stiffened President Truman's resolve. For he also felt MacArthur wanted to sit in the White House. The General's candor made his dismissal inevitable. In a callous, abrupt manner this proud man, who had so brilliantly administered Japan but showed grievous indiscretion in dealing with President Truman, was dismissed.

At the Legion Convention in October Commander Erle Cocke, Jr., dwelt upon the conflict in the Far East and called for clear-cut victory. However, the commanding feature of that convention was a major speech by General MacArthur. He had returned to a wildly enthusiastic homecoming and already had addressed Congress. In important ways, his words to the Legion were most impressive, for they were directed to the veterans of two great wars and to the nation. As a soldier, statesman and Legionnaire, he regarded the Legion as a defender of American ideals, an advocate of indispensable principles and an exponent of adequate military strength and sound foreign policy.

MacArthur pointed out how our military policy is interwoven with foreign and domestic policies and observed:

> To understand the general direction of our military policy we must therefore understand the animating impulses which guide our domestic and foreign affairs. Both, under the leadership now administering our government, have departed sharply from tradition and constitutional mandate.

Some of our political leaders, he charged, "under the influence of allies who maintain diplomatic ties with communist China, propose to yield the island of Formosa at an appropriate time to . . . international communism." This would break our island defense chain, threaten peace in the Pacific and ultimately endanger the security of our Pacific coast. He charged that his opposition to yielding Formosa and seating Red China in the UN wrecked secret plans to abandon that island. As a result, he said, there was violent reaction in Washington and Lake Success against him. MacArthur pointed out that the impact of a mistaken foreign policy requires us "in the midst of deadly war to soften our blows and send men into battle with neither promise nor hope of victory." The Chinese communists could have been removed as a threat to freedom in Asia. He dismissed the idea that Soviet Russia would have started a war against us in the face of our power and added ironically, "Since the end of the Second World War, without committing a single soldier to battle, the Soviet, aided by our political blunders, has gained dominion over territory and people without parallel in history."

Before the silent Legion delegates he turned his attention to Europe. There, he said, the United States must insist not only on a closer-knit Atlantic community for mutual defense but greater efforts on the part of European nations to contribute to mutual defense.

In an appeal to the Legion he observed:

> The American Legion, composed of men who know and detest war for the scourge which it is, is particularly adapted to stand guard over our heritage of American liberty. It must exercise unrelenting vigilance. It must ensure that neither political expediency, nor foreign infatuation, influence the expenditure of vast sums now under contemplation for freedom's defense.

In that October of 1951 the Legion's position was that of "Fighting to win" in Korea, if necessary by blockade of Red China, bombing communist bases and military concentrations in China or elsewhere, defense of Formosa, support of guerrilla operations in China, and support of Chinese organizations that would fight the Red Chinese.

At New York in 1952 the Foreign Relations Committee's report, adopted without amendment, was the most complete and specific in Legion history. The gloves were off. The State Department, it pointed out, had not taken adequate steps to block communist aggression and harbored among its own employees men of communist leanings. Hence, the President should "take immediate steps to dismiss the Secretary of State (Dean Acheson) and those in his department found lacking in the proper activation of their duty to their country."

The UN, the report stated, "has not proved to be an effective instrumentality for the guaranteeing of world peace in the present crisis," its administration permitting Russia and her satellites to paralyze any effective action. "Fundamental changes" were essential.

The Legion called upon the United States to strengthen NATO by military and economic aid to West Germany, improvement of relations with Spain and the settlement of the Saar and Trieste disputes; to take leadership in calling a conference of the Arab states to alleviate tension; to give them aid comparable to that already tendered to Greece, Turkey and Israel; and to conclude a Pacific mutual defense pact under the terms of the UN charter. The Bricker Amendment which came before the Senate in 1953 was anticipated in one section. The report recommended that foreign aid be limited to countries which are helping themselves and denied to those trading in supplies on our restricted list with Russia and her satellites.

The Korean War dragged on. The Armistice talks became a dialogue of monotony, punctuated now and then by irresponsible concessions directed by ukase from the State Department. Robert Murphy, first post-war ambassador to Japan, tells how he finally learned of the error of calculations in Washington. Murphy recalls that in 1951 Chairman of the Joint Chiefs of Staff Omar N. Bradley supported the State Department and opposed the MacArthur plan for complete victory. In 1952 General Mark Clark, Commander Far East, talked with Murphy many times. The fruitless negotiations should be broken off, Clark held, and a full-scale attack made to drive the communists from Korea. To leave Korea divided would amount to a "grave American defeat." But Clark, like MacArthur before him, was overruled. Murphy fully agreed with his proposals but points out, "Neither Clark nor I were policymakers." * Nor, it might be added, was the judgment of field commanders taken very seriously at the policymaking level.

When General Eisenhower became President he decided to follow Truman's policy of no-victory in Korea, though bringing the hostilities to a halt. Thus the fighting ground to a stop on this dismal note. The fruits of this deplorable ending were reaped by the communist world. Its propaganda has projected the arrangement as a victory over the Americans, with profound effect ever since. Months before, at its 1952 Convention, the Legion had called for a most intensive development of psychological warfare. This was precisely the

* *Diplomat Among Warriors,* New York, Doubleday & Company, Inc., 1964.

field in which international communism is accomplished and in which it has scored on the United States most tellingly on numerous occasions during the cold war. The American Legion, characteristically, was to continue to stress this neglected but essential phase of the enduring struggle with communism.

Since the Korean War, positions taken by the Legion at its annual conventions have reflected a consistency of purpose that runs far back—to the birth of the Legion in 1919. This is the more remarkable when these positions are contrasted with official U.S. policies and with the meandering flow of thought in opinion-forming media. It is true that official statements, made in confronting the capricious spokesmen for communism, may be shaped by diplomatic considerations, and are sometimes, of necessity, vague. But the nation is under no obligations to abandon consistency of principle in the interest of such parleying.

During the eight years of the Eisenhower Administration there were times of heavy strain, even, as Secretary Dulles expressed it, moments which approached the brink of war. There were periods when Soviet-American relations relaxed and a desperate yearning for peace overwhelmed earlier suspicions and the considered judgment of many Americans. But each hope for peaceful coexistence was soon darkened by unveiled intrigue, notorious incitement or arrogant threats by the Kremlin leaders.

The American Legion maintains that too often policy has merely been a response to the calculated plans of official communism. Visitors to the Soviet Union and to its satellites have returned with hopeful expressions of great changes in the communist system due to any of a number of factors—altered leadership, a good crop year, Western influence, disputes among communist states. Official comments, often moved by political expediency, have repeatedly emanated from the White House and State Department heralding the possibility of mutual accommodation. Specialized writers, ministers of the Gospel, scientists, businessmen, and members of the academic community have urged official relations with Red China and its admission to the UN. In the mixture has been an ill-conceived willingness to abandon national interests. Some of this spirit of acquiescence is due to a persistent internationalism which is a vital force among Americans, a desire for business profit, unquenchable optimism, and long-endured fatigue from living in the midst of alarms. There has also been the insidious penetration of our life, even of our official life, by a certain number of communists, communist sympathizers and those who foresee the ultimate decay of our institutions.

Throughout all these years of uncertainty, however, The American Legion has stood firmly by its earlier convictions. It has never modified its belief that international communism has a fixed policy to dominate the world, possibly without war but by war if that seems more expedient. Because of this, the Legion has consistently opposed any yielding of our sovereign independence, even by subtle and seemingly minor concessions. It has consistently warned the nation of perils presented by communists and communist sympathizers in our midst and emphasized our obligation to use our great influence and power to frustrate communist penetrations or takeovers in Africa, Latin America, the Near, Middle and Far East.

A survey of the positions officially expressed by Legion conventions, the reports of successive National Commanders, the Foreign Relations Committees, and the Commission on Foreign Relations reflects this insistence that fundamental principles be applied to emerging issues.

Up to 1960, the Foreign Relations Commission reported its comment and its proposed resolutions as a unified document. But beginning in that year the importance of foreign relations was recognized by a division of this commission into subcommittees on "General Resolutions," "Soviet Russia," "Far East," "Treaties and Agreements," and "Inter-American Affairs." Their reports have been more lengthy than the unified reports of earlier years and have reflected more attention by the Legion's organization to the growing complexity of critical issues throughout the world.

The Legion, during the cold war, has maintained that the UN, while its performance has been disappointing, is a useful forum. The 1953 Legion Convention noted that 1955 had been designated as the year for a reconsideration of the UN Charter and, in anticipation of this, directed the NEC to consider and recommend amendments. The Foreign Relations Commission created a subcommittee to work on and report appropriate amendments. However, the tenth anniversary of the United Nations passed without any serious consideration of the charter. The Legion from time to time has expressed its opposition to UNESCO and refused in any way to recognize this agency of the UN by naming a delegate to the United States Commission for UNESCO. Indeed it went further and urged Congress to repeal the laws creating the American Commission, and proposed an investigation of UNESCO activities. In successive years the Legion warned against the so-called Covenant on Human Rights and called upon the Senate to refrain from making any part of this covenant legally binding on the United States. Also, in several conventions it urged that the United States withdraw from the International Labor Organization. In recent years the Legion has maintained a wary and critical position toward the UN and especially several committees and organizations of which it is the parent.

Many Americans, including distinguished leaders in the legal profession, have been increasingly disturbed by a practice which reached considerable importance during the presidency of Franklin D. Roosevelt—that of "treaty-making by Executive agreements." In essence, the Executive Department concludes an agreement with a foreign government without confirmation by the Senate, and this agreement supersedes any Federal and state laws with which it is in conflict. In effect, such an agreement has the status and force of a treaty.

In 1953 the Legion adopted the following resolution:

> There is need for an amendment to the Constitution of the United States, which will assure that treaties, pacts, and agreements made on behalf of the United States, should not become operative as internal law of the United States without specific action of Congress. It is our considered judgment that Senate rules should be changed to provide that at least a two-thirds majority of a quorum of the Senate shall approve treaties. We definitely oppose any modification or waver of treaty terms by the Executive Branch of the government without the consent of the Senate.

In the same year Senator John W. Bricker introduced a constitutional amendment which would have met this demand. Protracted debate ensued which drew large public support as well as opposition. It was a source of regret to supporters that President Eisenhower opposed this amendment and was supported by the Secretary of State despite his earlier statements, and on a final vote the Bricker amendment failed of adoption in the Senate by one vote. The Legion, however, continued its demands for such an amendment over a period of years.

Under the Connally amendment the United States had reserved to itself the right to determine whether any case brought before the International Court concerned an international issue or whether it dealt with a purely internal concern of the United States. In the late 1950's certain internationally-minded people, including some senators, demanded that we abandon the Connally amendment. The Legion in 1959 adopted a resolution on this subject:

> We request that the Senate of the United States reject emphatically all efforts aimed at the impairing of the sovereignty of the United States through abandoning the present power of the American government to limit the jurisdiction of the World Court to purely international affairs.

In the determination of the zones of occupation and control of Germany in 1945, the United States and the British agreed to Soviet demands for not only a divided Berlin but a Soviet zone of occupation, extending like an enormous puddle far to the southwest and west of the Elbe—the river line where GI's had embraced Red Army soldiers only months before. The inhabitants of Berlin found themselves stranded in the middle of this puddle, their freedom of movement and sources of supplies a hundred or more miles to the west depending upon Soviet whim and U.S.–British determination. The Legion regarded this arrangement as a tragic mistake as the Soviet Union created the satellite state of East Germany. This partition gave rise to crisis after crisis, the most notorious being the denial of Western access to West Berlin which was met by the airlift in 1949. Repeatedly the Soviet has demanded a unified Germany, but always on its own terms. Consistently the United States has reaffirmed its treaty rights in West Berlin, free access thereto, and ultimate German unification only by the consent of the people of all Germany. More recently the communists have erected the Berlin Wall—stone by stone, barb by barb, sentry post by sentry post—an ugly, vivid sign of the Soviet intention to maintain a permanent division of the German

people. Like a saber scar this welt slashes through the city, separating
neighborhood from neighborhood, brother from brother.

In 1962, the Legion officially commended the President's expressed
determination to support West Berlin, to insist upon access to the city
and to resist any communist effort to impair our rights "either gradually or by force." Another Legion resolution denied that our rights
were subject to negotiation and asserted that the good faith of the
Russians must be demonstrated by tearing down the Berlin Wall. At
this convention the Legion also declared that "the attitudes and actions of Soviet Russia toward the people of the free world are those
of an enemy" and should be so regarded by the United States and
"other free world nations."

The year 1956 was a dark year in international affairs. Soviet
arms were required to smash the liberal uprising in Hungary, and the
continued presence of Red Army tanks rumbling through city streets
and along country roads made brutal suppression of those aspiring
to liberty complete. Most serious troubles in the Middle East cul-
minated in the Suez crisis. Nineteen fifty-seven was bound to be a
signal year for Legion attention to the international menace of communism. Its National Convention adopted strong resolutions concerning Hungary. National Commander W. C. Daniel made a personal survey of the Middle East and reported that the crisis in the
preceding year had been engineered by President Nasser of Egypt
acting as a tool of the Kremlin. He stressed the necessity for international action to solve the refugee problem in the countries adjacent
to Israel, and his concerns were reflected in the Foreign Relations
Commission's report. Convention resolutions declared opposition to
American aid to Soviet satellites and reaffirmed opposition to the
recognition of Red China and her admission to the UN.

The apprehensions expressed in 1957 were amply confirmed in
1958 when, in response to a call for aid, President Eisenhower
landed Marines in Lebanon, which averted a communist takeover in
that area. The 1958 Foreign Relations Commission's report commended this action. But the report repeated warnings about communism in the Middle East and again directed attention to Nasser's
designs. "The United States has never had a practical and realistic
policy for the Middle East," it complained. Prophetically, the report
pointed to the Panama Canal, and charged that Nasser had been

sending agents to Panama, no doubt for the purpose of aggravating anti-American sentiment.

The 1953 Convention mentioned the recent armistice in Korea, questioning the sincerity of the Red Chinese and North Koreans. In the event that the armistice failed to restore a lasting peace, a resolution called for the use of our "full military strength and might . . . to drive the Communist forces out of Korea and to establish a unified, democratic government" in that country.

Repeatedly in recent years The American Legion has opposed recognition of the tyrannical and aggressive government of Red China and its admission to the United Nations, demanded the preservation of the independence of Formosa and affirmed the responsibility of the United States to work toward preserving freedom and independence in Southeast Asia. At Dallas in 1964 Legion delegates considered neutralization of Southeast Asia a factor which would "favor communist China's objectives" and U.S. military and Naval forces "the major deterrent to Chinese expansionism." They resolved that the United States pledge its strong determination to combat communist activities in Southeast Asian countries. They also urged

> . . . the increased commitment of American forces and full employment of those military measures which promise early and complete destruction of the forces of aggression—both at the places of their attacks and at their sources of power as military judgment decides—in an effort not only to preserve freedom in Southeast Asia but also as a part of our world-wide commitments to the defense of freedom against Communist aggression.

Here the Legion's resolutions gained a measure of fulfillment when some months later, after abortive attempts at a satisfactory diplomatic settlement in Viet Nam, the Administration committed large forces in that continuing struggle and expanded U.S. military operations above the 17th Parallel.

The Legion has since been steadfast in supporting the firmest policies in blunting communist advances and in maintaining the position of the free world in that area.

World War II brought a renewed Legion emphasis on Latin America. In the midst of world conflict, the *Annual Reports* pointed out:

Toward our friends, and particularly toward those of the Americas, our policy is and will continue to be that of mutual helpfulness, fairness and good faith. We have no territorial ambitions, no desire for commercial domination anywhere.

The Legion's wartime Inter-American Affairs program made inter-American cooperation a major objective which is a continuing concern. In 1947 Commander Paul H. Griffith called a conference of posts of the Caribbean area and Latin America at Ancon, Canal Zone, which agreed upon

... a program looking toward closer cooperation with the duly constituted agencies of the Government of the United States of America and the governments of the various countries in which (Legion posts) are located, subject to the laws of those countries, and to offer all cooperation possible to the above-mentioned entities to combat communism.

Ancon Convention resolutions called for Congress to restore appropriations for the informational and cultural programs of the State Department, "dissemination of information on various phases of American life, the maintenance of libraries, the exchange of students, and other features ... to promote better understanding of democratic ideals and attainments," and provision that American tourists be given "instruction in methods of how to conduct themselves so they will make friends for the United States of America in the foreign countries visited. ..." Subsequently Inter-American Affairs centers were organized in seventeen U.S. cities and a Legion *Bulletin* published, —"Proposed Program of Inter-American Activities." This activity, strenuously carried on during the war, has been a valuable Legion contribution throughout the Americas to the present day.

However, the chill of the cold war was to penetrate many of our neighbors to the south, a fact of which Legionnaires are painfully aware. In 1958, a year before Castro became the master of Cuba, the Legion declared that "Any doubt of communist infiltration throughout Latin America has been completely dispelled" by the hostile attitude toward and attacks upon Vice President Nixon. In several Latin American countries the neglect of our government was blamed for this, and it was asserted that the defense of the Western hemisphere depended upon cooperative efforts of all American nations to check and curb communist activities, and that private investment, government loans and cultural exchanges should be encouraged and promoted as well.

Resolutions adopted at successive National Conventions reflect an intense and growing concern over the Castro regime, the establishment of Soviet military forces in Cuba and the violation of the Monroe Doctrine by this alien intrusion. The Legion's attitude is clear in a resolution adopted two weeks before President Kennedy's demand in October, 1962, for the removal of Soviet missiles and bombers from Cuba. It noted resolutions in 1960 and 1961 that "called upon our Government to take appropriate action and to use all means at hand to insure maximum support of any economic, psychological or underground measures to terminate the existing threat . . . by the Castro regime," and the USSR's boasts of "economic support and establishment of military, naval, air and missile bases and encampments . . . within ready striking distance" of Guantánamo Bay and the mainland of the United States. Since the government failed to heed these recommendations, "thereby increasing the danger to the security of our country, [since] each day of delay permits our communist enemy to become more strongly entrenched on our very doorstep [and] may one day be paid for in the blood of American boys," and since the United States failed to obtain effectual agreement (from the OAS) to maintain the security of the Western hemisphere, the Legion demanded that the government "unilaterally or in cooperation with other Western hemisphere countries impose every method at its command including the use of Armed Forces" and by assisting noncommunist Cubans "to put an absolute halt to any further build-up in Cuba of the communist expansion [and] to overthrow the Castro communist regime and enable the people of Cuba to establish their own non-communist government." The 1962 Convention also reiterated its position that the Monroe Doctrine is "vital and valid" and its enforcement "essential." The Legion declared its opposition to the extension of "any form of aid or trade, military, economic and otherwise, to any communist, communist-supported, communist-dominated or communist-affiliated nation or any nation unfriendly to the United States," restated its opposition to the continued trade between any nation of the free world and communist-bloc nations "to the detriment of the free world," and called for a reevaluation of our foreign aid program. These provisions have been emphasized in resolutions in more recent years.

In 1962 a long resolution opposed the U.S. proposal of general and complete disarmament at Geneva which "envisions a completely disarmed world except for a United Nations 'peace force' with all international disputes to be settled in accordance with the U.N. Charter." The Legion insisted:

> The national defense posture of the United States must remain unimpaired so long as there exists a threat to our security and freedom such as is now posed by the forces of international communism, and insists that the United States must at all times maintain a status of military preparedness commensurate with our national and international responsibilities, and must reserve to itself freedom of action in all matters respecting the national security.

With monotony, the Legion's recent disarmament resolutions have stressed the point, expressed clearly in Dallas in 1964:

> The American Legion opposes United States entry into any disarmament treaty or arms reduction agreement with any nation or group of nations unless such treaty or agreement includes enforceable provisions for inspection, and ironclad safeguards against cheating.

The 1963 Convention placed the Legion on record in support of the limited nuclear test-ban treaty, provided certain safeguards were met. Specifically, the convention urged the Senate to assure that the treaty would not in any way be considered a step toward the disarmament of the United States, or toward the surrender of our national sovereignty, and that the treaty would in no way serve to curtail our underground testing program or related weapons development, or otherwise interfere with our readiness for immediate resumption of atmospheric testing in the event of a violation of the treaty.

The Legion repeatedly warned against those who had suggested that the United States take steps toward surrendering our treaty rights in the Panama Canal Zone. In 1960 the Legion noted with "grave concern" that attempts had been made to "symbolize non-existent Panamanian rights" by hoisting the Panamanian flag in the zone. In 1962, the Legion took note of the fact that, despite an overwhelming opposition by vote in the House of Representatives, the President by executive order had permitted the display of the Panamanian flag over the Canal Zone and had also agreed to a consideration of treaty revisions. This the Legion strongly condemned.

The Foreign Relations Commission attempts to carry out convention or NEC resolutions as well as to make recommendations in keeping with the "controlling convention mandates." Staff work is handled by the Administrative Division under the Director of the Washington Office. Among its duties, the staff maintains liaison with the State Department and other agencies, including the proper committees of the Congress; informs Legion national officers of developments relative to the Legion program; prepares or assists in preparing informational data; coordinates headquarters' staff activities on foreign relations matters when there is overlapping of interest between programs (for example, between the Foreign Relations and the National Security Commissions); cooperates with the Legislative Division; represents the National Organization at various meetings and public affairs involving foreign relations; serves as the point of contact for other national organizations interested in foreign affairs; and assists the several departments and posts in the furtherance of their respective foreign relations programs.

The American Legion feels that its foreign relations program depends ultimately upon post support. In fact, if its positions are to serve the best interest of the United States, individual posts must continue to develop sound resolutions. Post efforts include close attention to foreign affairs and related legislation. Frequently post commanders and legislative chairmen coordinate appeals to members of Congress from individual Legionnaires. This method of exercising influence has been successful in foreign affairs as it has in other facets of Legion interest. *The American Legion Magazine, Advance* (a Headquarters' publication for post commanders), the *National Legislative Bulletin,* and department publications provide information on progress of Legion programs and relevant background reports. Post programs include discussion groups, speakers, documentary films, participation in foreign aid efforts, sponsoring of foreign tours, and independent action to help less prosperous countries. Medicine and bandages go to many needy areas from Legion posts.

The care and education of war orphans is an important underwriting function of some posts. For posts located abroad or near our borders with Canada and Mexico, activities that promote understanding and respect are numerous. While direct good-will activity is vital, posts not in a position to participate have donated many books to school and community libraries, sponsored essay contests on foreign policy topics and established scholarships for students desiring to enter the foreign service.

In 1958 the 40th Annual Report underlined Legion objectives and activities:

> One of the most difficult problems of this commission is to make foreign relations meaningful on Main Street. Over the years, a number of unusually successful activities have been carried out to accomplish this—the Tide of Toys of 1951, a Latin-American tour by picked American Legion Junior Baseball stars in 1956, participation in the People-to-People program in 1957 and 1958.

It is clear that the Legion's Foreign Relations Program is major in its proportions and manifold in its activities. The Legion believes it serves "to promote the organization's fundamental ideals and purposes." This program is woven into the national defense efforts of the organization. While it supports the UN and claims dedication to the achievement and maintenance of world peace, the Legion adheres to the "peace through strength" concept and is unalterably opposed to moves which might diminish national sovereignty or identity or invite any loss of national honor and self-respect. The Legion was in the van of the American maneuvers that established mutual defense arrangements—the NATO, SEATO, CENTO, and OAS treaties— since it was virtually the first powerful organization to appreciate the serious shortcomings of the UN. Throughout the cold war the Legion has been a moving force behind "the extension of economic aid to nations which have need of it and which show a willingness to join us in combating the spread of communism (e.g., the Legion backed such aid programs as the Marshall Plan for Europe, the Truman Doctrine for Greece and Turkey, the Eisenhower Doctrine for the Middle East, the Point Four Mutual Aid Program for underdeveloped areas, etc.)."

It is to the Legion's enduring credit that it has exercised through years of alarm, provocation and stress a steady leadership in meeting the challenges this nation faces. It has done this relentlessly, without abandoning principle or adopting expediency. It has done this when it was unpopular to do so, placing the interests of free men who strive to remain free alongside those of Americans. It has moved in the foreign relations field with a certain assurance and a breadth of understanding despite the fusillade of its worst critics and sworn enemies and the sniping of tinseled experts. There is no question that Legionnaires are responsible in some measure for the fact that public opinion is behind the United States' posture in the world today. As a leader of that vital ingredient in our position of free world leadership, the Legion boldly resolved in 1965 that the United States continue "to increase its efforts and its capacity to meet and repel communist aggression wherever it may occur." In 1966 the Legion held to its firm resolve that U.S. foreign policy remain steadfast in Viet Nam, implying that the national interest embraces support of freedom abroad, containment of communism and an implacable opposition to tyranny wherever it exists.

18

Organization—Source of Influence and Achievement

COHESIVE forces maintain human organizations. The mystic bonds of tradition, Duty, Honor, Country, comradeship, "pride in the Corps," mutual reliance in the performance of missions, leadership and discipline from the final authority of the nation run through strong military outfits like the cords of steel in reinforced concrete. Ties of friendship, companionship and collective enjoyment, as well as a sense of community responsibility and devotion to good works, keep club members together. And political parties exist through the desire of their members for office or influence, usually strengthened by shared beliefs about policy. In part, all the foregoing conditions bind together members of the Legion with the exception of a desire for public office.

But the real sentiment that has given the Legion such a long and vital life is belief in American ideals and principles which are embodied in its original statements of faith and objectives. For nothing short of such a nationally accepted consensus could hold together so many members so widely scattered and so varied in their interests and occupations. True, there is authority at the top of the Legion, but following the American principle of short terms with popular elections, the Legion has never been nor is ever likely to be the creature of a small group. The national organization has no disciplinary power except suspension and expulsion and no means of guidance except advice. The posts enter into a multitude of activities in which they exercise a right of selectivity. The Legion can never be a monolithic structure.

In the act of 1919, establishing the Legion's legal status, Congress declared The American Legion to be "a body corporate," with a corporate purpose:

> To promote peace and good will among the peoples of the United States and all the nations of the earth; to preserve the memory of the Great War of 1917–1918; to cement the ties of love and comradeship born of service; and to consecrate the efforts of its members to mutual helpfulness and service to their country.

By subsequent amendments eligibility for membership was extended to veterans of World War II and the Korean conflict. The original act describes the Legion to be nonpolitical and requires the Legion to report annually its proceedings and financial affairs. The annual National Convention of the Legion is its legislative body. Immediately after the close of a convention a full-time director moves to the city selected for the next meeting. He organizes and works with a local convention corporation, making all necessary arrangements. Before the opening date of the convention, a working staff from National Headquarters arrives and sets up a convention office. Every headquarters division is represented. Standing commissions and committees are summoned, among them the Resolutions Assignment Committee. It receives all resolutions offered for consideration by the Convention. Such resolutions may include constitutional changes, which must be filed with the National Adjutant in sufficient time for him to circularize them to all departments and members of the National Executive Committee well before the Convention meets. A two-thirds affirmative vote of the total authorized delegate strength is necessary to amend either the Constitution or the bylaws.

The authorized membership of the convention consists of five delegates from each department, and one additional delegate for each thousand members or major fraction thereof whose current dues have been paid to the National Treasurer. One alternate for each delegate is allowed. Delegates must be chosen at department conventions or in a manner specified by department constitutions. Each delegate is entitled to one vote, and in his absence his alternate casts a vote. In

1966 arrangements were being made to open membership to Viet Nam veterans.

Members of the National Executive Committee include National Vice Commanders, past National Commanders, the National Chaplain, and one National Committeeman from each department. An alternate committeeman serves in the absence of his NEC man.

Since the most important function of the convention is the adoption or rejection of resolutions, the Legion is very specific about how such resolutions reach the floor. Thus, if an individual wishes to have a resolution brought before the convention, he must first get his post to act upon it. If it is approved, the post then gets the department to pass upon it. And if it is germane to The American Legion, the National Adjutant will refer it to the convention. The Resolutions Assignment Committee assigns resolutions to the several convention committees, exercising great care in considering and clearing resolutions to avoid conflicts in convention action.

The National Commander, elected by the convention, is the executive head of The American Legion and serves but one term. It is interesting that despite this relatively rapid turnover a sound continuity can be maintained. This is largely due to the fortuitous organization of the Legion. The National Commander is authorized to enforce the provisions of the National Constitution and bylaws and also the expressed will of the National Convention. He is Chairman of the National Convention and of the NEC. He appoints all necessary commissions and committees, subject to ratification by the NEC.

Each National Commander, except for those of the very beginning, has had wide experience and, generally, is well known in the Legion. His service record includes commandership at the post level, departmental service, important committee assignments, and he has a broad familiarity with Legion programs and a deep devotion to Legion principles and objectives. His services as National Commander are frequently overshadowed by his accomplishments before and after this hectic time.

The National Commander enjoys the assurance that the business management of the Legion will go forward under a permanent staff headed by the National Adjutant, as discussed elsewhere. Commissions and divisions are charged with the responsibility of advancing the mandates of every convention. This frees Commanders to devote themselves to promote immediate programs by explaining them to Legionnaires, the public, the Congress, the President and his executive branch of government, and frequently to foreign nations. Each Commander and his family are subjected to an arduous year, in which he has the opportunity to devote his full energy and time as head of the Legion.

Commanders have come from every section of the country and have been members, some in high standing, of either the Republican or Democratic Party. They have ranked from private to colonel during their war service. Geographically, three have come from New England, four from the Prairie States, seven from the South, twenty from the large group of Midwestern States, seven from the Pacific Coast, one from the Southwest, and six from the Atlantic Seaboard.

Although all divisions at the National Headquarters carry out assignments for the National Commander, he is assisted by a travel aide, a secretary and an assistant secretary. Five elected National Vice Commanders, each representing a geographical area, act upon all matters referred to them by the National Commander.

The National Adjutant, appointed by the NEC, is the administrative head of the organization, and under his direct supervision are all of the administrative functions of the Legion. From his office at the National Headquarters in Indianapolis he supervises all administrative activities of the Legion and acts as secretary to the NEC and the National Finance Commission.

The National Chaplain, elected at the convention, is granted a good deal of freedom in the execution of his duties to promote the Legion's emphasis on religion. The National Treasurer, Judge Advocate and Historian perform duties implied in their titles. A national executive committeeman and one alternate from each department, elected for two years by department convention, serve on the NEC, and between National Conventions the executive power of The American Legion is vested in this body, which holds at least four meetings each year and publishes a record of its actions. Any effective action of the NEC must be the result of the formal adoption of a resolution.

A great deal of the responsibility for determining the policies and activities of the Legion rests upon commissions provided for in the Legion's By-laws:

Americanism
Child Welfare
National Convention
Economic
Finance
Foreign Relations
Internal Affairs
Legislative
Publications
Public Relations
Rehabilitation
Security

Commission members are nominated by the National Commander. The NEC then appoints them and assigns the duties and responsibilities of each commission. These commissions devise and propose programs, and report to the NEC or the National Convention. A commission has no administrative powers or duties, and what it proposes must be consistent with policies determined by the Conventions or the NEC.

Standing committees are assigned to the various commissions. These, too, formulate proposals and programs which may, if found acceptable by the commissions, pass on to the NEC or the Convention. These standing committees are, like the commissions, appointed by the NEC upon nomination by the National Commander and fit into the framework of the Legion outline on page 319.

Since the office of National Commander is one of great honor and authority, it attracts the service of men of high character and distinction and places a heavy burden on the individual chosen. His year's tenure is exhausting, almost consuming, sometimes verging on the frantic, and gives him limited time for reflection and attention to most important objectives. His calendar suggests that inordinate time is devoted to formalities and overexposure. While it is important to departments that the National Commander visit their states, this cuts into periods in which a Commander might achieve greater stature and more widespread appreciation and support of Legion positions and programs on the national level. His travel schedule is prodigious, his speaking engagements and appearances as a representative of the Legion in most states, and frequently abroad, sometimes resemble

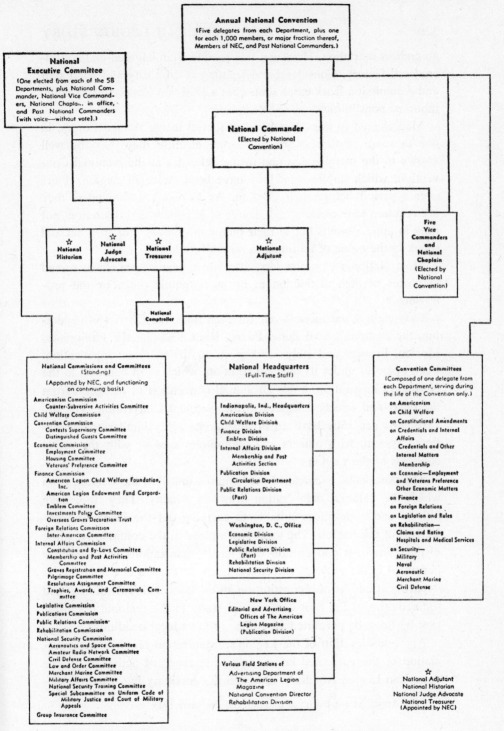

Annual National Convention
(Five delegates from each Department, plus one for each 1,000 members, or major fraction thereof, Members of NEC, and Past National Commanders.)

National Executive Committee
(One elected from each of the 58 Departments, plus National Commander, National Vice Commanders, National Chaplain, in office, and Past National Commanders (with voice—without vote).)

National Commander
(Elected by National Convention)

Five Vice Commanders and National Chaplain
(Elected by National Convention)

☆ **National Historian**

☆ **National Judge Advocate**

☆ **National Treasurer**

☆ **National Adjutant**

National Comptroller

National Commissions and Committees
(Standing)
(Appointed by NEC, and functioning on continuing basis)

Americanism Commission
  Counter-Subversive Activities Committee
Child Welfare Commission
Convention Commission
  Contests Supervisory Committee
  Distinguished Guests Committee
Economic Commission
  Employment Committee
  Housing Committee
  Veterans' Preference Committee
Finance Commission
  American Legion Child Welfare Foundation, Inc.
  American Legion Endowment Fund Corporation
  Emblem Committee
  Investments Policy Committee
  Overseas Graves Decoration Trust
Foreign Relations Commission
  Inter-American Committee
Internal Affairs Commission
  Constitution and By-Laws Committee
  Membership and Post Activities Committee
  Graves Registration and Memorial Committee
  Pilgrimage Committee
  Resolutions Assignment Committee
  Trophies, Awards, and Ceremonials Committee
Legislative Commission
Publications Commission
Public Relations Commission
Rehabilitation Commission
National Security Commission
  Aeronautics and Space Committee
  Amateur Radio Network Committee
  Civil Defense Committee
  Law and Order Committee
  Merchant Marine Committee
  Military Affairs Committee
  National Security Training Committee
  Special Subcommittee on Uniform Code of Military Justice and Court of Military Appeals
Group Insurance Committee

National Headquarters
(Full-Time Staff)

Indianapolis, Ind., Headquarters
Americanism Division
Child Welfare Division
Finance Division
  Emblem Division
Internal Affairs Division
  Membership and Post Activities Section
Publication Division
  Circulation Department
Public Relations Division
  (Part)

Washington, D. C., Office
Economic Division
Legislative Division
Public Relations Division (Part)
Rehabilitation Division
National Security Division

New York Office
Editorial and Advertising Offices of The American Legion Magazine (Publication Division)

Various Field Stations of
Advertising Department of The American Legion Magazine
National Convention Director
Rehabilitation Division

Convention Committees
(Composed of one delegate from each Department, serving during the life of the Convention only.)

on Americanism
on Child Welfare
on Constitutional Amendments
on Credentials and Internal Affairs
  Credentials and Other Internal Matters
  Membership
on Economic—Employment and Veterans Preference
  Other Economic Matters
on Finance
on Foreign Relations
on Legislation and Rules
on Rehabilitation—
  Claims and Rating
  Hospitals and Medical Services
on Security—
  Military
  Naval
  Aeronautic
  Merchant Marine
  Civil Defense

☆
National Adjutant
National Historian
National Judge Advocate
National Treasurer
(Appointed by NEC)

ORGANIZATION OF THE AMERICAN LEGION

an endless marathon. However, this routine is anticipated and considered satisfactory. Considerable delegation of authority and good staff and commission work eases somewhat a National Commander's enormous responsibilities.

Men elected to the office have all served in the Armed Forces, in one or more of three wars. To secure election they must be well known to the membership and to the delegates at the National Convention, which implies that they have been active in Legion affairs over a period before their election. As National Commanders they are required to exercise a high degree of judgment and discretion, not only in appointments but in their public utterances. For they act and speak in the name of an immense organization.

Most National Commanders, after their year's term, have served in places of high distinction in business, public office or the professions.*

Fifty-eight departments—one for each state, the District of Columbia, the Panama Canal Zone, Puerto Rico, Canada, the Philippines, Mexico, France, and Italy—link posts to the national organization. Each operates under its own constitution, which must conform to the National Constitution, holds an annual convention of delegates from the posts and selects delegates to the National Convention. The departments generally have an organizational setup similar to the national system, with officers and committees dealing with the major concerns of the Legion.

The posts have been called the "combat units" of the Legion, from which the national organization draws its vitality. They, too, have officers and committees suitable to carrying out the ideals and objectives of the Legion. The local post's place in the community, while distinct, involves cooperation with local organizations and authority permitted under national directives. Each post has a charter from its department and its own constitution and bylaws. This constitution and the activities of the post conform generally to the national organization but may be permitted variations to meet local conditions.

Any consideration of the Legion's organization requires an appreciation of the dedicated efforts and wide range of activities of The American Legion Auxiliary, although the Auxiliary has a unique his-

* See Appendix for listing of national officers since 1919.

tory of its own. Its association and cooperation in Legion affairs has been mentioned frequently in previous chapters. Today its membership is close to a million—mothers, wives, daughters, and sisters of Legionnaires, as well as women who have themselves served in the Armed Forces. Auxiliary units, as the name implies, aid and supplement the actions of Legion posts, departments and the national organization.

The Auxiliary's service in the rehabilitation and child welfare programs are most important. Women workers are mobilized in the thousands for voluntary work in hospitals. The Auxiliary also maintains contact with disabled veterans outside the hospitals, helping them and their families in many ways. Another important Auxiliary activity is the supervision and distribution of memorial poppies, made by disabled veterans. Twenty million poppies are distributed in the streets of cities and towns on Poppy Day, generally observed in the week before Memorial Day. This observance not only brings the Legion's interests before the public, but the contributions of those who take and wear the poppy help to sustain the rehabilitation and child welfare activities of the Legion locally and nationally.

The remarkable fact that emerges from a consideration of the organization of the Legion is its consistency of purpose and methods. This is a tribute not only to the wisdom and foresight of those who created the Legion so many years ago but to the vitality of its membership, its dedication to sound and practical public services, and the loyalty of its members. In those five decades the population of the nation has undergone enormous growth and a great shifting about. Revolutionary changes in the nation's economy, in political ideas, in certain frontiers of learning and knowledge, in the scope and nature of social problems, in communications and propaganda, in methods of influencing other nations, and in the position of the United States in the world are a continuing phenomenon of our twentieth century. New challenges stem from advances as well as disasters, from peace as well as war. Upheaval is a feature of our time—in prosperity, depression, worldwide conflict, and cold war. The industrial revolution is carried by awesome momentum through the twentieth century, scattering the generations, changing the contours of economic, social, religious, and political life. It becomes apparent that not only vigil but struggle in quiet ways and in violence is the lot of free men.

Any appraisal or understanding of The American Legion must consider its vitality and performance in this light. Obviously, the Legion has had to meet change and challenge from time to time within its organization. Most recently for Legionnaires there has been the painful controversy over the Forty and Eight Society.

Following World War II, serious concern over the eligibility clause of the Forty and Eight constitution arose. This subordinate organization of Legionnaires was long regarded as an honor society devoted to camaraderie, the more playful aspects of National Conventions and to a number of good works. Its constitution stipulated that members be "white males."

Since the Legion is a cross-section of our population drawing its membership from all nationalities and races, men and women who served honorably in our wars, it was inevitable that heated debate would center on the issue of exclusion for reasons of race. When the Forty and Eight leadership took no action over a period of years, the 1959 Convention unanimously adopted a report of its Constitution and By-Laws Committee which declared the "white" restriction to be illegal. The convention called on the Legion's executives to seek the "sympathetic support of the Forty and Eight" to remedy the situation. The Legion was condemned in some segments of the press for not having passed a stronger resolution.

Within weeks National Commander Martin B. McKneally named a special committee headed by James E. Powers to confer with a Forty and Eight committee. Representatives of the Forty and Eight adopted "a passive attitude." McKneally asked the NEC to correct the situation. He directed National Judge Advocate Ralph Gregg to prepare a review of the legal aspects. Gregg reported that the Forty and Eight could not invoke membership restrictions that went beyond the Constitution and charter of the parent organization. He added that the restriction was in violation of the Fourteenth Amendment of the United States Constitution and warned that both The American Legion and the Forty and Eight were liable to legal actions by state attorneys general. Already such action threatened in California, where the national Forty and Eight had suspended a voiture's charter. This Forty and Eight unit had taken in a Legionnaire of Chinese extraction.

The NEC debate went beyond the legal question to consider principle and adverse publicity. "How," asked one NEC-man, "can a subsidiary organization find members of this Executive Committee itself ineligible for membership?"

The NEC overwhelmingly passed a resolution giving Commander McKneally the power to use "any and all measures" to end the illegality. McKneally recognized his responsibility to see that action was taken and in stating his position said:

> I believe that The American Legion, composed as it is of veterans of three wars which were fought for the preservation of freedom and human dignity, should be in the forefront in promoting brotherhood and should be the leader in allaying prejudice.

On the basis of legal opinion, McKneally informed the Forty and Eight that its use of the name and emblem of the Legion was prohibited. This prohibition is still in effect. A year later, Commander William R. Burke resigned from the Forty and Eight and stated that it was for each Legionnaire to decide whether his loyalties would remain with The American Legion or with the Forty and Eight Society. In certain areas the Forty and Eight operates as before, and nationally it still puts Legion service and membership as a prerequisite to membership. The 1960 Convention found it inappropriate to allow the Forty and Eight to participate in Legion programs. National Adjutant E. A. Blackmore observed:

> This is a matter which has been painful for all of us. It is a matter which has caused us to disassociate ourselves from old friends and old comrades. It is a matter which is now a closed issue. In the future we in The American Legion must give our best efforts to the advancement of the fundamental programs of our organization.

Today, the Legion's powerful organization stands on a foundation of many lasting truths. Its structure, its ideals, its activities, and its promise rest upon that firm base. In full vigor, it looks with confidence to the capabilities of its organization.

19

Public Relations and Publications

I N a society such as ours a myriad of activities, movements, ideas, programs, products, organizations, and personalities vie for the citizen's attention, allegiance, or both. This condition is inseparable from a free political, economic and social system. And so The American Legion and Legionnaires throughout a long and varied history have always been engaged in "publicity." This has become a more difficult task as the years have passed. The new mass medium of television joins radio, the motion picture and newsprint to struggle for an audience. The automobile and modern highways bring the out-of-doors and many forms of recreation within reach of most Americans. A score of diversions seek to occupy our attention. We are subjected to the "fast sell." Advertising and promotion intrude upon our time. Was it T. S. Eliot who said we are "distracted from distractions"?

There has also been the growth in size, number and quality of newspapers and periodicals. In an age of specialization many talented men, in staying abreast of developments in their narrow fields, neglect the obligations of citizenship and fail to keep themselves well informed on subjects vital to the welfare of the nation and its people.

Consequently, The American Legion has shared the common problem of gaining the close attention of its membership and the public. And as the Legion is placing greater emphasis upon its community activities, it is important to consider its information and publicity efforts, since they will become more important if the Legion is to fulfill its ambitious part in American life. A brief account of its national publications and public relations efforts reveals an extraordinary dynamism and unique success considering the proportions of the fierce competition for public attention.

The Publicity Division in 1943 pointed out:

> Because of its nature as a volunteer organization, The American Legion has, from the days of the Paris Caucus of March 1919, relied greatly upon the medium of the printed word to distribute news of its activities to the entire membership. This has served also to provide instruction to men and women busy with the concerns of every-day life, so that their avocation, advancement of the aims and ideals of The American Legion, could be effected most thoroughly. From national, department, district, and post headquarters there has been distributed annually, day by day, week by week, and month by month, a numerous body of mimeographed and printed publications, pamphlets, and brochures designed to keep pace with the expanding programs of the Legion.

The American Legion Weekly commenced publication on July 4, 1919, on the proposition that "we need a magazine to inform and inspire the membership." Quickly, it proved to be a very difficult publishing venture, for it was without funds and without an experienced organization to guide it. Its editor and general manager, George A. White, recognized a shaky venture and accepted the unenviable challenge with reluctance. *The Weekly* was losing $20,000 an issue when a printers' strike made necessary an overnight shift to Washington. White informed Commander D'Olier that unless $40,000 was forthcoming within twenty-four hours, the magazine would be compelled to suspend operations. Publishers, accustomed to accepting heavy losses as an investment toward any profitable publication, advised D'Olier to hold on. The Commander advanced his own money and obtained other loans. In early 1920 White turned the affairs of *The Weekly* over to George D'Utassy, a Legionnaire and a notable publisher, who drew no salary. Marquis James, an old-fashioned, digging newspaperman, has said, "I was the entire editorial department for a few weeks." Harold W. Ross became editor, and John Tracy Winterich managing editor. D'Utassy led *The Weekly* from a $250,000 mire of debt to a $60,000 plateau of profit by 1922. Ross edited the magazine until 1924, when he moved on to a brilliant career as editor of *The New Yorker*.

A period of distinction followed in 1926 as the conversion from a weekly to a monthly brought about production savings. Contributors included men whose names occupy important places in American journalism and literature, some newcomers who were to leave their mark in the writing profession. James Montgomery Flagg and other distinguished artists provided many illustrations.

The Weekly and, after 1926, *The American Legion Magazine*, have experienced a powerful influence in American life, a fact over-looked by most students of the past half century. For these publications have gone into every Legion home, most public libraries, and tens of thousands of schools, thereby gaining a readership of considerable proportions. From 1919 content has been of interest not only to Legionnaires but to conscientious citizens as well. Space devoted to national and international topics generally far outweighs information of a strictly Legion character. The *Magazine* has been a forum for debate on important issues. It has been especially effective in presenting outstanding articles dealing with national problems, and over the years it has exposed conditions in government and national life that have in part been corrected due to pressure exerted by informed Legionnaires. Hence, it has been a journal of advocacy, "muckraking," if you like, entertainment, and information.

In 1935 the Legion dissolved The American Legion Magazine Corporation and created a Publications Commission to assume its duties. At that time the National Publicity Division commenced publication of *The American Legion Monthly,* a newspaper for distribution to all Legionnaires. After ten years it was combined with the *Magazine* and later discontinued. This caused a "serious problem of communicating with membership on program matters." Divisional publications multiplied, and in 1956 the NEC became concerned and directed the Public Relations Division to issue a monthly National News Letter for post commanders, department officials and other Legion leaders. Since it was primarily a "news vehicle," the National Headquarters' staff Committee on Publications decided that "greater emphasis on program information and stimulation called for a new type of publication," and in 1960 *The American Legion Advance* was launched, aimed primarily at the commanders of the almost seventeen thousand posts.

The National Legionnaire, a tabloid newspaper, commenced publication in 1936 with ten cents allotted to the magazine from the seventy-five cents of the national membership per-capita dues. It became a profitable venture, returning $500,000 annually by 1944, when newsprint was in short supply.

During the second world war the editorial policies of Legion publications turned to material of interest to servicemen and women. Free distribution in growing quantities was provided for those in the Armed Forces. The Legion considered this in keeping with their principles of service as well as a means of conveying the ideals and programs which it had long promoted to millions of young Americans, some of whom would become Legionnaires, and the vast majority, conscientious citizens.

In the period during and since World War II *The American Legion Magazine* had been fortunate in the high caliber of its publishers, James F. Barton and James F. O'Neil. It has remained the leading accomplishment of veterans in the field of publicity, for it is not a mere house organ but a national magazine of merit, dealing with American life in a comprehensive manner. Its pages testify to a fine staff and the broad democracy and tolerance exemplified in The American Legion. Both Barton and O'Neil have provided a dynamic leadership and restless devotion to this vital facet of the Legion. Today O'Neil is assisted by an imaginative editor, Robert B. Pitkin. O'Neil's service to the nation has been exemplary, paralleled by a surprising number of Legionnaires. His work in the Legion goes back to its early days. In the 1940's he served high in the military councils of the nation and was the Legion's National Commander in 1947–48. He has perseverance, an intense curiosity and courage to fight for principles in which he believes.

O'Neil heads an organization with editorial and advertising offices in New York, backed by a large Circulation Division in Indianapolis, where a staff of more than a hundred maintains individual membership records of 2,600,000 Legionnaires which require 20,000 changes of address a month. Conscientious effort has gained substantial non-member subscriptions.

The downward trend that struck magazine advertising and subscription revenue in 1958 stimulated measures to improve the *Magazine* and invoked strict economies. At that time the *Magazine* stood first among men's publications, tenth among monthlies and fifteenth in the entire magazine field. For four years the *Magazine* weathered a storm in which many venerable publications disappeared in waves of red ink.

By 1965 *The American Legion Magazine* was again thriving and the Publications Commission under Dr. Charles R. Logan was confident that it was moving to higher ground. At the commission's annual meeting in 1964 and again in 1965 the commission members were satisfied that the publisher, editor and the director of advertising had developed plans consistent with decisions of the commission. The *Magazine's* 56-page format and its objective to move to a 64-page format reveal a spirit of optimism grounded to achievement. The net gain of the *Magazine,* which goes to the General Treasury of The American Legion to help defray the costs of the expansive network of programs conducted and directed by the National Organization, was $166,322.78 in 1964. This brought the grand total to more than $11,000,000 since the *Weekly* was established in 1919, with only one red-ink year for the *Magazine,* and that in 1927, one year after the publication was converted.

The Commission and others connected with *The American Legion Magazine* frequently go back to the 1926 resolution:

> That there be no recession from the high standards thus established, and that it is the sense of this convention that *The American Legion Monthly* shall be built into an institution of public service, not alone for The American Legion, but for all America, which shall be one of the enduring monuments of this organization.

The primary duty of The American Legion Public Relations Commission and Division is to serve the other commissions and divisions to The American Legion in presenting "the best possible overall picture to the general public."

Ivy Lee, a pioneer of modern press relations, started a publicity department in 1919 with Thomas J. Ross in charge. For some time this establishment was a modest, often a one-man, operation. Both Marquis James and Fred Painton served in the first years, single-handed but with single-minded devotion. The Publicity Division, established in 1921, dealt "with what the Legion does and why, and with what it aims to do." In the days of financial stress that followed the Minneapolis Convention it was discontinued, only to be revived by George D'Utassy. The American Legion News Service became a department of the *Weekly* in 1920 but later came under the Publicity Division.

Gradually the Publicity Division expanded to include the National Speakers Bureau, American Legion Film Service and the editorial department of the *Weekly*. Marquis James was the first Director of Publicity; Humphrey Sullivan the second, in 1922, when the Film Service was made a separate division and the Speakers Bureau was consolidated with the Americanism Committee. In the 1920's the News Service was a news gathering and distributing agency, placing news of the Legion in ten thousand publications by 1923. Today it carries on the mission, described by James in 1922, of informing the public and expediting "the internal flow of information." The 1921 National Convention passed a resolution favoring a meeting of representatives of Legion publications at the Convention each year, and later The American Legion Press Association was formed. Its members are Legionnaires who as private citizens work in mass media, and are affiliates of post, district and department publications. Their association still provides valuable service for the public relations program.

Although "publicity and information" efforts during the 1920's and 1930's were at times disjointed, they did exert a positive force in the drive of the entire organization toward legislative and service objectives. A Legionnaire recently offered an example:

When the Legion came under fire in the early 1930's the Committee on Internal Organization gained adoption of a resolution to "launch a campaign to educate the public by proper newspaper and radio publicity to the actual facts concerning relief of World War veterans and their dependents." If the extensive legislation adopted by Congress on veterans benefits since can be taken as a measure this campaign has been successful. It continues today.

There is also some truth in the charge of some Legionnaires that for the first forty years the public relations record of the Legion lacked consistency, especially at the department level. In 1920 a Convention Committee on Publicity made a number of broad recommendations including one to all states to employ publicity directors, but after forty years only a relatively small number of departments had full-time public relations men. The annual National Public Relations Conferences, commenced in 1959, has since revived efforts to further this idea. Still other Legionnaires, in an organization where members feel that the privilege of "sounding off" is fundamental, regarded the task of gaining wide public support as hopeless, especially at certain times when the Legion was subjected to violent abuse. "We'll do what we feel is right and forget about trying to justify our position," they said.

Nineteen forty-four was a period of planning for the anticipated expansion of The American Legion, and the NEC recommended a Publicity Commission to replace the National Publicity Committee. The Public Relations Division, consisting of an acting director and two secretaries in Indianapolis and an assistant director in Washington, was expanded. The 1944 Convention urged that the National Public Relations Commission be composed of acknowledged experts in that field—a recommendation which has been followed. The Legion named a commission of eighteen members to guide news, radio and general public education about Legion matters, and Ray Fields of Oklahoma took on the job of PR director with the heavy responsibility of "explaining the Legion to veterans of World War II." Edward McGrail in the late 30's and early 40's had expanded the Division by establishing an office in Washington and staged many elaborate programs for nationwide radio. His assistant, Jack Cejnar, took over during the war years and carried on with limited help.

It was not until after World War II that public relations gained the great emphasis it enjoys today. Prior to that time many talented men followed the calling of publicity and information, but a public relations boom swept the country following 1945, when business and industry, enjoying the prosperity of the war years, had sufficient money to hire specialists in these fields to inform the public and to improve "the image" of a product or a corporation. Leaders of business and industry realized that ahead lay stiff competition, and they were convinced that advertising and the stimulation of desire for what they had to offer was a more important aspect of sound business conduct than before. Various groups included in their public relations programs emphasis on matters of broad public concern not specifically related to their products or services. Labor organizations, too, with bulging treasuries set out in ambitious ways to gain support and to influence public opinion concerning "the American way of life."

When the NEC made its major reorganization of National Committee structure in 1947, the PR Commission became one of twelve commissions under which all National Committee responsibilities were grouped. Since there were no committees to be assigned to the commission for "coordination and supervision," the 1947 reorganization made little change in its operation. Its inclusion as one of twelve commissions, however, did reaffirm the importance placed on this activity by the Legion's governing body. The Legion's PR Commission was charged with activating "a Publicity Division to handle all publicity and advertising matters pertaining to The American Legion." While this is a logical delegation of responsibility, it is one which could never be completely carried out because of the nature of the organization. Each commission and division in the national organization functions on a semiautonomous basis. But through the 1950's Legion leaders expended considerable effort to gain a more effective PR program and to instill in the membership a regard for its importance.

One of the periodic attempts to "beef up" the Legion's PR program came in 1956. Extensive study by the NEC reorganization subcommittee called for a considerable expansion of the PR Division and its responsibilities. National Conventions have adopted several of these recommendations—regular staff meetings, publication of the *American Legion Advance,* staff work to improve efficiency, economy and internal communications, and greater coordination among divisions and the Indianapolis, Washington and New York (Magazine) offices.

The PR Commission under James V. Demarest and the Division under James V. Day engaged in extensive promotion of the fortieth anniversary of The American Legion in 1959, hailed as "the most widely observed organizational birthday in history." The movie, *We Who Serve,* which gives highlights of the Legion story, was a notable success. When the convention met in 1959, 327 television stations of the nation's 521 had shown the film. The Legion estimates that between 25 to 30 million viewers saw *We Who Serve.* An illustrated brochure distributed to post commanders generated two thousand requests for bookings and purchases. The PR Commission felt that besides giving the public facts about the Legion, the movie proved its merit by giving Legionnaires "a deeper understanding of their organization and stimulating them to greater efforts at their posts." Public Relations Appreciation Awards, authorized by the NEC in 1959, extend recognition to agencies and individuals outside The American Legion rendering unusual service to the nation through the medium of public communications. Early American Legion Mercury Awards (now the Fourth Estate Award) were presented to Walt Disney, *U.S. News & World Report,* Advertising Council, Inc., the Hearst Newspapers, and the radio program "Lifelines."

The PR Division has always been important to a National Commander although frequently in the past it has been neglected by him. However, since World War II public relations have been recognized by virtually all Legionnaires as an indispensable function of their organization. The 1960's have seen the fulfillment of PR programs, activities and functions which, over the long haul, may gain for the Legion a new stature in American life and a significance it has never had.

In its long career The American Legion has had many shining moments and Legionnaires have felt the elation of great legislative victories as well as the enduring satisfaction of knowing that they have participated in successful campaigns that give strength, vitality and purpose to the nation's people. They have also felt the warmth of comradeship and of selfless giving to children in need of help and their disabled brothers. Yet all too often their organization has been viciously slandered or simply ignored. Millions of their fellow Americans have no conception of the vast amount of work Legionnaires have done, and even when coverage has been given certain programs, mention of Legion sponsorship is frequently avoided.

Perhaps the 1960's will be remembered by Legionnaires as the decade in which their organization achieved long-awaited, national recognition. Legion leaders have felt that such a development would not only increase and sustain membership but facilitate the tasks it has set out to do.

In C. D. DeLoach the Public Relations Commission in 1960

gained a chairman with exceptional insight into the workings of the
Legion, its relationships with other important groups in national affairs and the needs of the Legion during a period of profound change.
His position as Assistant Director of the FBI has given him a close
understanding of the practical aspects of many problems which both
the Legion and the FBI have shared for so many years. DeLoach,
gifted in his grasp of the importance of public relations, has impressed
many influential and sometimes suspicious newspapermen and others
prominent in mass media.

Recent directors—James V. Day, Charles J. Arnold and James
C. Watkins—besides conducting the affairs of their divisions, have
been called upon to travel throughout the country and to remote
parts of the world with the National Commander. In 1963 this involved Commander James E. Powers' trips to the Caribbean at the
height of the Cuban crisis, to Vietnam and to Guatemala. The PR
Director is harassed by much the same schedule.

In the 1960's, benefiting from a larger and more effective arrangement and, for the first time, volunteer workers in most posts, the
PR Commission and Division gained new plateaus of excellence.
Greater coordination with National Officers and divisions as well as
with other commissions and energetic promotion to get more complete and uniform press coverage produced results. A study of PR
activities over the years shows the vast improvement that has taken
place.

The first National Public Relations Symposium was held in the
spring of 1960; its main purpose was the strengthening of the PR
program in the field and the coordination of the total effort at all
levels of the organization. Top-flight newspaper, television and radio
personalities address these annual events.

Press coverage of Legion conventions and other gatherings increased considerably in the first half of the decade. The coordination
with other commissions and divisions is evident in the 1964 Annual
Report which points out the year's highlights:

> The National Commander's Public Relations Award for the De-
> partment producing evidence of an outstanding Public Rela-
> tions job during the year.
> The Commander's approval of a recommendation that each

Department be encouraged to enlist the services of trained public relations personnel.

The fourth annual Washington Mid-Winter Conference again proved an excellent news source, and in addition to our hometown news desk, which provided photographic and news story service to the delegates, there were some 20 video-taped and recorded interviews arranged by the Public Relations staff for Department officials with their Congressmen.

National Public Relations support to Regional Child Welfare Conferences and to the finals of the National Oratorical Contest.

News generated by the National Commander's joint appeal with the President of the American Legion Auxiliary for funds for the relief of Alaskan earthquake disaster victims.

The third annual Speech Guide for American Legion Speakers containing Legion program and policy information provided by the National Commander, commissions and divisions.

A program was inaugurated, containing helpful hints on how to make good PR out of given situations, and examples of how Departments and Posts have promoted news contacts.

These examples reflect Legion concern and aspirations regarding public relations. As a great organization that is rooted in American communities, its members recognize the importance of publicity. And their leaders express the conviction that only by committing the Legion to a broader, enlightened and dynamic public relations program can Legionnaires realize a satisfactory measure of achievement.

20

The Legion and the Community

AMERICANS enjoy an advantage which is found in very few places
in the world. We live in a classless society. We are born with
no inherited distinction of rank. The glory of America is that in principle it offers to all the opportunity to achieve whatever an individual's will and capacity earn for him. This man may inherit more
property than that man. But, in principle at least, the inheritance of
riches is a trusteeship imposing upon the owner the responsibility to
use what he has for the betterment of his community and his nation.
There are, to be sure, many disadvantaged by denied opportunity
because of where they are or what they are. But the collective will of
Americans through their governments and private effort has struggled through the generations to open the gates for advancement to all.

And so the Legion from its beginning, through its leaders, has
encouraged its members and posts to work with others to promote
the community's life and happiness. Members may wear the Legion
uniform and emblem, but they seek to form no special or privileged
class where they live. In fact, they are expected, because they are
organized, to do a little more than their share as citizens of the
community and the nation. They cannot stand apart from, or claim
more, or give less than their neighbors.

Whatever is the community's business is their business. Whatever
is designed for the general good they accept as their duty to promote.
And over the years, in innumerable communities, they have initiated
or entered into scores of common endeavors.

335

True, their major duty is to promote American ideals and patriotism. But the patriot is also the good neighbor. For the nation's health is preserved in the soundness and harmony of its parts.

Every post is expected to select and to promote at least one important community project every year. If it is the initiator of such a project, so much the better, for if it succeeds, the Legion has earned a new distinction.

More than two hundred different types of projects have been carried out by Legion posts. No community lacks room for improvement. From an array of unfinished or undone community projects the Legion post makes its selection and goes to work with other civic-minded people.

A practical step taken by many posts is to designate one of its members as "Community Service Chairman." He, with his committee members, selects a project which seems immediately desirable, and if there is no other community organization already at work, solicits assistance from non-Legionnaires. Such achievements add to the attainment of the community and promote local pride. Through the reaches of this big nation, a most familiar landmark is the sign which says, "This is a good place to live," or "This is a friendly city," or "This is a good location for new business." These are the expressions of the spirit and pride of the community. And you may reflect as you read these claims that in most cases an American Legion post has been doing its duty.

A list of suggestions for the local post's community activities is given by the Legion's Extension Institute:

> *Winter:* National high school oratorical contest, ice skating, coaster hills, boxing and wrestling, hobby contests, dances, forum discussions of community problems and study courses ... designed so that the greatest possible number of the community's people, young and old, will be reached.
>
> *Spring:* Legion Baseball, playground improvement and construction, tennis, badminton, volley ball court improvement or construction. Improve picnicking facilities. Construct outdoor broiling pits as well as tables, benches, etc. Organize a teen-age council so that the post may have the benefit of the teen-age groups' thinking in preparing a program for the summer.

Summer: Boys' State, Boys' Nation, bicycling, golf tournaments, hiking, concerts, street dances, summer camps and the development of swimming and wading pools.

Fall: County fairs and exhibits, educational facilities, educational entertainment courses, fall parties of varied types, return to school, safe driving.

The range of post activities covers almost every concern and interest in which American communities are engaged. The Community Service Committee surveys the community, notes its needs, and considers what is already under way to meet those needs by non-Legionnaires. When there is already a program for community betterment, it frequently puts its resources in manpower, and often its money, behind it. But while it may give active help in any number of community projects, the post is expected to select a special project to which it will give major attention.

In the many directives published at the national level of the Legion, supplemented by advisory bulletins and pamphlets from the department, posts are instructed about operations and reminded of the many community concerns to which they may direct programs. The posts are warned about selections. They are told to "go easy at first," to weigh their own capacities and resources; then, when they have decided upon a program, "Plan your program—work your plan—publicize the results."

One publication directed to the posts offers a long list of activities that includes projects and programs which have been successfully carried on:

Erection of safety signs and the promotion of safety programs.

Purchase and voluntary manning of an ambulance for communities without ambulance service.

The construction of an athletic field or the clearing of sufficient space to permit children of the neighborbood to engage in athletic activities.

Band Concerts conducted by many Posts during the summer months.

Beach and swimming pool facilities improved with a provision for necessary bath houses.

Beautification Programs in which the Auxiliary can participate. A number of projects such as highway triangles, memorial parkways, clean-up campaigns, etc., can be classified as a community-betterment program.

Parties and Christmas trees for the benefit of the underprivileged children of the community.

The cooperation of the churches may be secured in planning the public observance of any holiday. Easter Sunrise services have been held under Legion supervision.

A number of women's posts are furnishing either a community or a school nurse.

In many localities the management of the county fair has been taken over by a Post. The Auxiliary might well assist in arranging the displays of work pertaining to women.

Legion Posts are performing a real service to small communities without fire protection by organizing volunteer fire departments from their members. In several instances the Post has furnished fire-fighting apparatus for the volunteer firemen.

Providing flower boxes to crippled children's homes or other places where it is impossible for normal gardening pursuits to be followed.

Get-Out-the-Vote Campaigns are activities in which every Legion Post might well interest itself in securing a Legionnaire vote, regardless of partisan politics.

The establishment of a community golf course has been undertaken by many Posts throughout the country.

Through hobby contests recognition is brought to those individuals for accomplishments during spare-time activities.

Building or raising funds for the erection or maintenance of hospitals or provision of beds and other equipment needed.

Kindergartens—an activity ideally suited for the feminine members of a Post have been promoted, and, in many cases, no fee is charged.

The Post can do a real service to its community by inaugurating a learn-to-swim campaign to make the community safe from drownings.

Lights for Parks and Playgrounds have afforded citizens of their community an opportunity to further benefit from evening outdoor recreational activities.

By taking groups of schoolboys and girls to their shops and offices and telling them about their work, Legionnaires can give the youth of the community a clear idea of the opportunities existing in the specific lines of endeavor which, in turn, will assist the youngsters to make a wise choice in their life's works.

The furnishing of picnic tables and benches is a commendable project.

Many Posts have given their communities places where the younger children may play safely. Other Posts have provided supervision for the playgrounds from their membership.

A number of Legion Posts have organized their membership to serve as auxiliary police officers. Working with the established law-enforcement body of the community, they serve in many capacities. One of the primary functions is to protect school children at dangerous crossings.

The establishment of a skating rink or supervision of ponds and other public places for skating can be accomplished at small cost.

Almost all radio stations will contribute radio time as a public service if the Post will develop interesting programs on the affairs of the community.

Hundreds of Legion Posts are sponsoring schoolboy patrols.

Street Showers, a summertime activity for youngsters in congested areas, can frequently be arranged for with city officials if the Post's membership will supervise the activity.

Summer camps have been established on lakeside fronts owned by Legion Posts. In addition to the operation of such camps, Posts also sponsor underprivileged boys for summer camps.

A program for summer sports might include picnics, athletic meets or contests, various kinds of races, band concerts, etc.

Nothing will gain the good will of citizens in a sweltering inland town like the building of a community swimming pool.

Provision of tennis courts is an activity which can be carried out in connection with the public playgrounds or as a separate development.

Toys which have been broken or outgrown may be contributed by school children. These could be mended and painted by Post members, and distributed to the poor children of the city during the Christmas season.

A community wading pool for small children is a source of pleasure for the children and may be developed within the neighborhood or in the city park or playground.

Building ice-skating rinks and providing safe places for coasting, promotion of ice skating, skiing or bobsled parties are a few of the activities embodied in a winter sports program.

The Legion's concern with medical care, health and rehabilitation runs through all levels, from post to department and national organization, and is related to its constant watchfulness over government establishments for veterans and their dependents. At the community level, blood banks have been a vital service of the posts. In some instances the giving of blood for medical use has been consolidated at the state level, notably in Pennsylvania and Rhode Island. Simon Schneider, a New York postal worker who in 1960 was living in retirement in California, deserves mention, for by 1956 he had given eighty pints of blood for the care and health of his fellow Americans.

The American Legion sponsors two extraordinary activities for high school students—Boys' State and Boys' Nation—discussed in previous chapters with the Auxiliary's Girls' State and Nation. Today each department conducts a Boys' State, designed to provide training in the processes of government, political parties and legislative operations. The Legion maintains that this program is in keeping with the statement in its Preamble, "To Transmit to Posterity the Principles of Justice and of Freedom and Democracy." Maurice T. Webb, Americanism Director, explains, "In carrying out this program, The American Legion teaches thirty thousand boys annually fundamentals of government and transmits to these young men an interest in active participation in government at all levels." By 1965 almost half a million high school juniors and seniors had participated in Boys' State. Boys' Nation meets in Washington annually. Those who attend participate in lectures, "mock" conventions and a senate, as well as visits to places of national and historical interest in and around Washington. These programs have given to the nation young men and women dedicated to public service and aware of their civic responsibilities.

The Legion has vigorously supported two of our most vital community activities—the Boy Scouts and baseball. The ideals, nature and activities of the scouting movement are celebrated. Since its beginnings in 1910, the Boy Scouts of America has become a fundamental part of our national life. The Legion as early as 1919 pledged its support and in 1922 made it an integral part of its Americanism

Program. Under directives by the Americanism Commission, every post, district and department is urged to appoint a Boy Scout chairman. More than one out of four Legion posts sponsor a Boy Scout unit, and the number has grown year by year. An indication of The American Legion's continuing interest in the Boy Scout movement was the 1965 action to conduct a national conference of Department Boy Scout chairmen with the purpose of increasing sponsorship by the organization to more than five thousand units. This was inaugurated in connection with the Boy Scout's "Breakthrough for Youth" program.

Legion posts have always been active supporters of every form of community athletics, encouraged by the national and state organizations. For such activities are not only wholesome means of contributing to the individual Legionnaire's health and vitality, but organized games invoking physical vigor and skill are the means of bringing together the people in the community and providing links between the posts and their fellow citizens. Bowling, boxing, wrestling, roller and ice skating, and golf have been major interests among posts.

But baseball is the national game. It forms firm ties between the young and their elders. It not only engages people who play, but gives entertainment to innumerable others.

While numerous organizations sponsor youth baseball teams today, The American Legion claims the distinction of establishing this activity. Some five thousand Legion baseball teams from all departments enter competition each year. After the department champions are determined there are eight regional competitions and, then, the national finals. Aside from the hundreds of professional baseball players who have graduated from American Legion Baseball, hundreds of thousands of American men have learned the rudiments of fair play on American Legion diamonds.

The multitude of programs conducted by The American Legion and the Auxiliary, which include the 4-H Clubs, other national programs and numerous local activities, ensure a certain continuity, since their purpose is the early development of strong characteristics of leadership, self-reliance, character, and citizenship.

The expression in the Legion's Constitution, "For God and Country," has practical meaning in the many essentially religious observances in Legion activities. There has always been a place in the Legion's organization for chaplains at every level, and there is an opening and closing prayer in every official Legion meeting. Free institutions which recognize individual worth and responsibility had their far-distant origins in religious precepts. And the mission of the Legion in building character recognizes belief in God as a fundamental factor.

In 1951 the National Convention formally authorized a "Back to God" program. In 1963 this program was redesignated as "Service to God and Country," and various resolutions adopted at National Conventions have run counter to the trend in Supreme Court rulings against prayer in public schools.

The National Chaplain is responsible for stressing, without denominational discrimination, that the Legion and its members work everywhere to promote church membership, attendance and support. To plan practical programs and emphasize their application, he calls a meeting of chaplains once a year. And a Chaplain's Breakfast is a feature of every convention. Further, the Americanism Commission prepared and distributes a handbook, "Service to God and Country," which emphasizes and explains the spiritual activities of the Legion.

A major concern of every Legion post and of the national organization is child welfare. This work has a fine but uneven tradition in our history. Lincoln, anticipating in 1865 the end of four brutal years of war, spoke to the nation of the days ahead: "Let us strive on to finish the work we are in; to bind the nation's wounds; to care for him who shall have borne the battle and for his widow, and his orphan . . ." In the terms of his time an orphan was not a child without living parents. An orphan was any child denied the care and guidance of home life.

Long since, the United States has officially abandoned the name "orphan asylum." For it became clear that only a minority in such collective homes were without both parents. Most were children without a complete and healthy home.

Two generations of children have grown to maturity during the forty-seven years of the Legion's life. And in those generations the children of veterans have become a majority in their age groups. Prior to World War II, there were 42 million Americans under eighteen. Of these, 10 million were children of veterans. In 1965 there were 74 million U.S. children. Of these, more than half, or 42 million, were children of veterans.

The men and women who established the Legion and the Auxiliary recognized a timeless fact—that the most universal and helpless victims in war are the children of those called into the fighting services. There is not only the economic pinch with the breadwinner away. The home—its guidance and discipline—lacks the father's presence. For the postwar benefit of many of these and other children, the Legion dedicated itself through its organizational machinery to child welfare.

The present National Child Welfare Commission can trace its origins back to the assassination of the four veterans at Centralia, Washington, in 1919. The Convention in 1920 decided that the best memorial to those victims would be an institution to care for the children of veterans. Also, the Legion, soon occupied by its immense labors to provide care for the war's disabled, realized that the best institutional care of a veteran would be impaired if he were at the same time distressed and worried about his family. The importance of this was stressed by members of the Auxiliary, and through the efforts of its devoted women the Legion officially created distinct programs for child welfare. In 1924 the temporary committee became a permanent Child Welfare Committee, and in 1947 it became the present National Child Welfare Commission.

Early organized efforts to help children were experimental and somewhat primitive. Soon, however, patterns of social welfare were beginning to be revolutionized. The most important element in child welfare was not to put children together in institutions but to help maintain them in wholesome homes. Welfare services became more professionalized.

The Legion, while continuing its own activities through its own organization and with its own money, gave increased attention to a trend in government—to enter the welfare field directly. Thus, it threw its influence behind legislation dedicated to child welfare.

For a brief period in the 1920's the Legion set up and operated four "billets" for children of veterans. But Legion leaders soon realized that this could not be a sound answer to the problem. In 1928 the Legion withdrew its efforts to establish specific institutions of its own and turned to the collection and distribution of funds for home aid and the promotion of mothers' aid and mothers' pension laws in many states. Subsequently, the Legion backed the program of aid for dependent children in the Federal Social Security system. In 1946 and 1947 the Legion was the first to call attention to the need for helping the growing number of children whose fathers were studying under the GI Bill.

In a summary of the Legion's concern for child welfare, Randel Shake, since 1950 the National Director for Child Welfare, said:

> Many other legislative gains for children on both the Federal and state level have come about through the Legion's effort: in the field of adoption and guardianship; in the regulation of child labor; in the provision of increased benefits for disabled veterans with dependents; in the more effective laws dealing with desertion and non-support; in the speeding up of the investigative and certifying processes of departments of public welfare; in the provision of facilities for the care and education of handicapped children; in the granting of scholarships for children of deceased and disabled veterans; and in countless other aspects of child welfare.

Tangible activities for children have also been effected by the Legion through channels other than legislative. In 1945 the Legion and its Auxiliary made a $50,000 grant to a small, struggling organization, the American Heart Association, since grown to large proportions, and, in 1951, a grant for mental health. This was followed by the amalgamation of various organizations into the National Association for Mental Health. New concepts of treatment have been developed through the efforts of this private organization. Later, the Federal government established the National Institute of Mental Health, which provides large grants to various programs.

The American Legion joined with others in supporting the National Foundation for Infantile Paralysis. The "breakthrough" in the fight against this disease—a children's scourge—is now a matter of common knowledge, and many posts have vigorously promoted programs to bring their communities' children the great benefit of polio vaccine.

The Legion has also in recent years given attention to legislation designed to combat narcotics distribution and venereal disease.

In 1950, after years of effort by the Legion, Congress enacted legislation which provided social security benefits through Old Age and Survivors Insurance for 80,000 widows and orphans of World War II servicemen. Later, this same coverage was extended to those affected by the Korean war and, finally, military service was made a "covered occupation" for purposes of Old Age and Survivors Insurance coverage.

The Legion turned to the most lasting and effective approach to child welfare problems—prevention and research—by establishing The American Legion Child Welfare Foundation in 1954. This foundation makes grants for the expansion of knowledge concerning the problems of children and youth and for distribution of such knowledge to agencies dealing with children's problems. Typical of its grants have been provisions for the costs of police officers attending the Delinquency Control Institute at the University of Southern California, from which 710 have been graduated, and financial support to the National Hospital for Speech Disorders. From time to time Legionnaires and Auxiliary members receive a report of the foundation's activities, and response has been gratifying to those directing the program. Contributions have been substantial, many made as memorials to departed comrades.

Three basic principles have guided the Legion in the Child Welfare field:

1. *Preserve the integrity of the home:* Our American way of life has become increasingly complex, making the role of the parent more important than ever in the proper development of children. Although government, church, and private agencies provide many services for children and youth, there is no substitute for good parents. This is the reason The American Legion tries to preserve the integrity of the home.

2. *Maintain a "Whole Child" program:* This principle recognizes that a child's physical, mental, emotional, and spiritual needs are inseparable and of equal importance. A sound Child Welfare Program must be geared to satisfy all of these needs. Caution must be exerted to maintain an even balance among these basic components in order to avoid undue emphasis or specialization in our Child Welfare activities.

3. *Cooperate with and strengthen other sound organizations and agencies for children:* It is not the purpose of The American Legion Child Welfare Program to establish duplicating services

and assistance for children. Sound existing services for children should be supported by American Legion Posts and Departments and utilized whenever possible.

Under these principles, there are five fields of interest:

1. *Financial Assistance to Needy Children:* When families are broken by the vicissitudes of life or when placed in jeopardy by serious economic need, adequate financial assistance should be promptly available for children of such families, preferably in their own homes, or, if necessary, in foster homes.

2. *Health Services for Children:* Adequate health services should be available to all children to assure their physical, mental and emotional well-being.

3. *Protective and Social Services:* Protective and social services to meet the individual needs of children should be provided by the child's own family or other responsible sources, with government bearing the ultimate responsibility of maintaining needed protections and services which are not otherwise available.

4. *Education:* Opportunities for education—academic, vocational and religious—should be available to all children commensurate with their abilities and interests and the needs of society.

5. *Child Welfare Administration:* All services for children—financial, health, social and educational—whether administered by public or private agencies, should be promptly and equitably rendered by competent personnel.

The above five statements were drawn up by the National Child Welfare Commission after an extensive study of Child Welfare resolutions adopted by previous National Conventions and the National Executive Committee, and furthering these objectives, there have been three methods of operation:

1. *Legislation:* The American Legion supports new legislation and public appropriations at the local, state, and federal levels of government in accordance with mandates of the National Convention, National Executive Committee, and Department Conventions to the end that the needs of all children are met.

2. *Information:* The American Legion seeks to inform its own membership and the general public about the needs of chil-

dren and how these needs may be met. Information is provided Posts and Departments on how they may organize for sound and effective Child Welfare work.

3. *Direct Assistance:* The American Legion provides direct assistance and services to individual children of veterans when established sources are not available to provide for needs of veterans' children.

Year after year, the annual reports of the Legion record the amounts spent by the Legion and its affiliates on its child welfare programs. These yearly amounts are generally in excess of $7,000,-000. By 1965 such outlays since 1925 had totaled more than $200,000,000.

As an indication that there has been no slackening in the Legion's concern for children, long after the children of two world wars had grown up, the all-time high in total expenditures was registered in 1963—$8,648,000.

As with so many Legion activities, the National Headquarters urges dedication at the post level which cannot be measured in dollars and cents. Detailed and comprehensive suggestions were selected as specific objectives for 1964 by the National Child Welfare Commission: an active Child Welfare chairman in every post; post participation in efforts to curb juvenile delinquency; attention by posts and departments to mentally handicapped children; encouragement of youth employment and such programs as stay-in-school campaigns to reduce the number of high school dropouts; attention to legislation dealing with the physically abused child; and expansion of youth physical fitness.

A remarkable effort and expense is put forth at the national level in publications available to posts on these matters. To name a few: *Juvenile Delinquency—A Community Problem; Mentally Ill Children; Retarded Children; Why Stay in School?; Youth Employment;* and *Youth Physical Fitness.*

The American Legion's child welfare effort of more than four decades is a living testament to the ability of an organization of free men and women to adopt itself to evolving needs, while maintaining high principles and taking on increased responsibilities under those principles.

21

Rehabilitation

REHABILITATION of the veteran is officially regarded by The American Legion as a comprehensive service. In a narrow sense, the term means restoring or supplanting capacities which have been impaired by war. But it has come to mean, also, providing opportunities for those in need of a helping hand. Since the rendering of physical help and the extension of opportunity to the veteran who has served the nation and borne the shattering wound, the stress, the sacrifice or a disease in its campaigns are essential responsibilities of government, the Legion has undertaken to provide advice and a means of communication between the individual and appropriate agencies by which the government meets its obligations.

These services are important in modern societies, for government looms as a great, impersonal authority. While it may seek to bring its services to the individual, generally private efforts are necessary to guide the individual so that he may comply with laws and regulations concerning entitlement.

In the past, as city, state and Federal governments became larger and more complex, the citizen frequently relied upon political organizations to unsnarl his problems. In more recent and enlightened times other means of assistance grew which measurably eliminated politics in these contexts. Private and philanthropic agencies took over numerous services, for the individual continued to require guidance. Most citizens approach their institutions of government with perplexity mingled with fear. The awesome public buildings, the remote bureaucrats stifled by routine, impersonal authority, the confusion of laws, regulations and paper work—all exist in even the most humane governments.

For the veteran a complex of laws and institutions designed for his aid developed, many the result of Legion work, recommendation and pressure. The American Legion through its wide ramifications became the veteran's friend and advocate. Legion help came not only in guidance but in direct assistance. And at the center of Legion concern has been the physically disabled and the unemployed veteran.

In 1919, at its first National Convention, the Legion set up two committees to care for all matters relating to the needs of veterans and their dependents. Later, a Hospitalization Committee was created. But to avoid duplication of effort, the 1922 Convention merged all such activities under a National Rehabilitation Committee, in 1947 renamed the National Rehabilitation Commission. It also called upon the National Adjutant to see that all departments maintain a service director to assist veterans with their claims and to help them present these claims to the Veterans Bureau and other agencies. Consequently, a nationwide service to veterans developed.

The great increase in veterans and those who had lost their men in war brought about further legislation. Certain advisory boards were needed and were established to give professional direction to the commission, departments and posts of the Legion. One dealt with insurance, one with medical service and another with vocational training and education. In 1961 these advisory boards were discontinued when the commission was adequately staffed with professional help.

The Rehabilitation Commission operates under the direction of an executive body of twenty-one members. It has set up a series of committees in five areas to reach all departments and posts. The Rehabilitation Commission, since 1952 headed by a dedicated Legionnaire, Robert M. McCurdy, meets each year in Washington on the day preceding the opening of a four-day Annual National Rehabilitation Conference of the Legion. This is one of the central events in the Legion's year.

The program of the Rehabilitation Commission is defined in general terms and its operation, centered in Washington, requires a large staff. Since 1958 John J. Corcoran has served as director of this headquarters' division, ably headed by T. O. Kraabel for the preceding seventeen years. The functional activities of the division's staff are:

To carry out The American Legion's established policies with respect to the rehabilitation and welfare of war veterans and their dependents;

To maintain effective liaison with all agencies of government concerned with the administration of veterans' benefits;

To review and analyze continually the several benefit programs so as to detect weaknesses in their administration or deficiencies in their effectiveness;

To remain informed on developments in veterans' affairs generally, including related social and economic matters;

To analyze such developments in relation to the Legion's policies, with specific reference to their effect or possible effect on the several benefit programs;

To advise the Commission of any findings which appear to require policy determination or redetermination;

To inform all interested national officers and department officials of significant developments in veterans' affairs within the Rehabilitation Commission's jurisdiction, including a report on actions taken or contemplated on behalf of the Legion, and reference to any pertinent Legion position or policy;

To inform through Legion media and other means veterans and dependents generally of their rights to Federal benefits and services;

To cooperate with and in every possible way support department officials in the furtherance of their respective rehabilitation programs;

To provide the American Legion Auxiliary with all feasible assistance and encouragement in connection with its collateral national rehabilitation program;

To coordinate Rehabilitation Commission activities and programs with those of other commissions where there is overlapping or inter-divisional responsibility, and to advise the National Adjutant, the Directors of the Washington and New York offices, and the Directors of other divisions as indicated, of all significant rehabilitation staff activity;

To foster better public understanding of the several benefit programs for war veterans and their dependents, and of the Legion's position relative thereto, and to consult with the Director of the Public Relations Division concerning such matters.

It can be said generally that while the Rehabilitation Commission extends some immediate care of needy veterans, its major purpose is to serve as a channel through which veterans can communicate with various government organizations which under the law have responsibility for direct aid.

To finance both the child welfare and rehabilitation programs in part, the Legion in 1924 launched a nationwide campaign to raise an endowment fund of $5,000,000. It achieved this, and in 1945 increased it to $7,000,000. This was the only public drive ever made by the Legion for this purpose.

Much of the work performed by the rehabilitation staff is the often difficult task of securing background or historical information in order to serve the veterans' needs. It is in direct daily contact with the Veterans Administration and Department of Defense officials. While its representatives of the Field Service make periodic visits to VA offices, hospitals, and domiciliary homes, the commission divides its work into a number of specific programs: Claims, Legislative Program, Conferences, Information Service, Field Service, Voluntary Program (in which the Auxiliary plays a leading role), Junior Volunteer Program, Eyebank Program, and a Program for the Recognition of Outstanding Work.

The Legion endeavors, in cooperation with the VA's policy to establish a healthful association of the veteran patient with members of the community, to keep every veterans' hospital from being divorced from the surrounding community, for the disabled veteran must eventually live in normal civilian surroundings. The Legion volunteer service encourages communities to welcome afflicted veterans into their homes and activities.

The impact of The American Legion, largely through its rehabilitation services, upon the government's veterans' program, has been a profound and extraordinary achievement. Its legislative successes are hard won and, at times, endangered. In 1965 Legionnaires considered the proposal to close eleven VA hospitals and numerous other facilities, a blow to rehabilitation and veterans' care. The Legion had won a battle with the Hoover Commission and Veterans Administrator Omar Bradley some years before over a proposal which would have scattered responsibility for veterans among several government agencies and established a United Medical Administration. Concentration of veterans affairs in the VA was maintained, but again the Legion was involved in conflict over what it considers its first obligation. Donald E. Johnson, whose year as national commander was crowded with activity, including a tour of South Vietnam and a report to President Johnson, led the fight against the VA directive. He made it clear that "cross service" between the Public Health Service and the VA might lead to what had been defeated in 1949. At his side were Rehabilitation Chairman Robert M. McCurdy, Director John J. Corcoran, Legislative Chairman Clarence C. Horton, and Director Herald E. Stringer.

The Legion urged legislation to restore congressional control over policy affecting veterans and VA control over the operation of the veterans' programs, "usurped by the Bureau of the Budget." Consequently, the President appointed a special committee which recommended continuation of several hospitals, domiciliaries and regional offices, slated for closing. In 1966, as it awaited a presidential decision, the Legion continued its efforts to resolve the fundamental and long-range national policies involved.

Besides those Legionnaires mentioned in previous pages and the appendix, the Legion's rehabilitation work has been advanced by thousands in local posts, prominent doctors who have served as consultants and disabled men who have worked with amputee veterans. Among the latter have been Charles C. McGonegal, Herman Pfeffer and Walter Antoniewicz, all amputees themselves.

Closely related to the Legion's rehabilitation program is another, distinct effort which falls within the jurisdiction of the Economic Commission. It has to do with assistance to veterans in areas of employment, housing, agriculture, conservation, and loans. Its concern is with all veterans who need guidance in availing themselves of government provisions for economic help.

Since the end of World War II, the Federal government, along with the states and communities, has entered what is called welfare on a broad front. Dozens of Federal programs have been initiated, involving expenditures of many billions of dollars, now concentrated to a large extent in the Department of Health, Education, and Welfare and the Department of Labor. Woven into the laws creating welfare services are many provisions giving preference to veterans which the Legion has staunchly supported. In seeking to avail himself of government services, the American citizen faces a bewildering maze of bureaus and agencies.

Broadly speaking, the Economic Commission under Chairman John J. Flynn through its staff and committees on employment, housing and veterans' preference represents veterans and posts in matters under the jurisdiction of various Federal agencies. It disseminates information, keeps close contact with government agencies, and processes inquiries and claims of members and posts. The Economic Commission's staff and committees encourage and maintain an active employment program; work toward a sympathetic and effective administration of the Veterans' Preference Act and other laws relating to veterans' benefits; cooperate with Federal, state and municipal agencies to maintain an effective merit system; assist veterans in protecting their just employment and reemployment rights; secure preferential employment consideration for disabled veterans; continue a program of education among employers pointing out the economic wisdom of utilizing the residual abilities of the disabled; combat the discrimination against mature or older workers because of age; and urge the extension and improvement of unemployment coverage and benefits. The Employment Committee conducts a comprehensive program to assist posts in fulfilling responsibilities in these regards.

Because veterans have preference in the vast employment operations of the Federal government with its 2,500,000 civil employees, the Veterans' Preference Committee of the Legion maintains contact with Federal employing agencies to see that the law operates as intended and to keep Legion members informed about job applications.

Among other concerns of the Economic Commission are GI loans made by private lending institutions for innumerable authorized purposes guaranteed by the Federal government and administered by the Veterans Administration and loans for veterans financed by the Federal Housing Administration and the Farmers' Home Administration.

In all these operations the Economic Commission staff provides constant service to veterans by specific information, by checking into individual cases and by considering from time to time recommendations for new legislation and more effective administration of laws already enacted.

22

The Fight Against Subversion

EVER since the Tsarist regime disintegrated in 1916 and the Kerensky government manifested a temporary flash of new energy in World War I, recurrent waves of sympathy for revolutionary Russia have washed across the United States. Western democratic institutions did not survive in the bleak, backward regions of a land accustomed to autocracy and receptive to a new tyranny. After the bolsheviks seized power and uprooted what democracy had been instituted, they concluded the peace of Brest-Litovsk with Germany. American attitudes changed, for this so-called "peace" took Russia from the war and ceded great areas in Eastern Europe to Germany.

We are familiar with the facts that the Wilson Administration decided on a general policy of nonrecognition and A. Mitchell Palmer, Attorney General, instituted a vigorous attack upon communists in the United States. J. Edgar Hoover, then a young attorney in the Department of Justice, prepared a lengthy brief on communism. Liberal elements in the United States screamed about Palmer's "Red hunts," and an attack was made, probably by a revolutionary, on Palmer's life. Manifestations of violence were, however, incidental to the efforts of communists and their sympathizers in subverting the agencies of our government and in winning many people to their cause.

In the late 1920's, after Stalin had gained firm control of Russia, various economic "plans" were instituted. Despite the Soviets' ruthless methods, a good deal of liberal sympathy in the West showered their efforts. Some prominent Americans made visits to Russia and

355

came back with glowing accounts of what was happening there. In 1933 President Roosevelt recognized Russia, and fond hopes of mutual good will were accelerated. Soon after recognition the Soviets manifested the hard truth that they had no intention of living up to agreements.

Ominously, recognition made it possible for innumerable spies and propagandists to be installed in the Russian Embassy, Russian consulates and elsewhere. Earlier chapters discuss the Legion's unrelenting efforts to blunt the edge of subversion.

Throughout its history the Legion has stood firmly against communism, never wavering from its conviction that the United States must be alert to communist aims. This has been true in all the periods of appeasement and of pseudo-friendship with the Soviet Union and other communist states. Resolutions passed in the many conventions of the Legion have reiterated this position. The Legion's attitude has been that toleration of communism is not a true expression of traditional liberalism. It has held that discussions of domestic and foreign problems must permit certain differences of opinion but that there are broad areas of firmly held principles that are not debatable. Communism presents not only an attack on these principles but is in essence an international conspiracy dedicated to revolutionary changes in our institutions. Communism is not a partial departure from American principles and traditions. It is not in the political arena as just another political party. The concept that a communist party should be tolerated in the United States raises the serious question of whether a party which is designed to destroy our freedoms should be permitted to operate under our tolerant concept of liberalism.

However, the Legion has consistently taken the position that neither nationally nor in its posts should it exercise anything suggesting police power. It has therefore limited itself to alerting the appropriate government agencies to the danger and to its sponsorship of means by which subversion can be exposed and controlled. In part through the efforts of the Legion, there have been and are committees of Congress dedicated to the investigation of un-American activities. There have also been several such committees formed in states, notably in California and New York.

Following World War II some of the Legion's worst fears were realized. Men and women with a fanatical devotion, high intelligence and gifted backgrounds were actively working in high positions in the government and in our most secret defense developments as well as in other important areas of our national life. Betrayal of American and British scientific secrets by British and American citizens working as agents of the Soviet Union came to light. The activities of these people had gone on for a number of years undiscovered. There had been permissiveness which had placed persons of known communist leanings in high positions in a number of government departments, and, although numerous leaders of the Administration and the Democratic Party attempted to minimize the gravity of what communist espionage had achieved, the American public was shaken. It was a rough awakening for many who had become accustomed to the downgrading of the avowed intentions of the international communist movement.

The House Un-American Activities Committee and the FBI, as well as security organizations of government departments, energetically worked toward strengthening security and eliminating subversives from positions of public trust.

The situation was deplorable enough without the celebrated accounts that portrayed it as an even more widespread conspiracy. Some hysteria and irresponsible accusations gained notoriety. Responsible men and women realized that there had been laxity and carelessness among those charged with the security of the Republic, that betrayal and treason had walked the corridors of the Washington bureaucracy and that the national interest had been grievously damaged.

Once the frightening array of disclosures was made public, many of those whose sympathies had long been with the Soviet "experiment," whose fond illusions had misled them into convictions that the ideological chasm between the Free World and the communist bloc had shrunk to a crack in the freeway of international relations and whose most scathing indictments were reserved for the United States and American institutions, lashed out at what they described as mass hysteria and panic. Their behavior was familiar. It was reminiscent of reactions to public concern over communist and radical violence of the 20's.

Congressional committees have served and are serving an essen-

tial requirement of investigating and exposing subversive activities
and providing Congress with information upon which legislation is
based. But the enforcement of laws and the day-to-day watchfulness
so essential to our security falls largely upon the Department of Justice and the Federal Bureau of Investigation.

The relations of The American Legion with these agencies has been
continuous over many years. This is evident in the many appearances
of J. Edgar Hoover as a speaker at National Conventions, in the
presence of a number of Legionnaires serving in the Justice Department and the FBI and in a close liaison between the various agencies
of the Legion and the FBI. The Legion has passed resolutions
praising Hoover and the FBI. In turn, Hoover has repeatedly commended the Legion's support of American principles. In addressing
the Legion's 1962 Convention, he said:

> Today, The American Legion is more vigorous than ever in
> inspiring national loyalty and promoting national preparedness.
> You have never faltered in your dedication to and promotion
> of American ideals.

FBI accomplishments have merited many commendations by the
Legion. The FBI plays a major role in protecting the integrity of the
Federal government. In accordance with the Federal Employees Security Program it has the responsibility of checking its files for names
and fingerprints of government employees and applicants. Where allegations of disloyalty exist it conducts investigations to obtain facts
which interested agencies can use in deciding employment suitability.
Results of these inquiries go to appropriate government officials without opinion or recommendation.

Over the years the FBI has effectively penetrated the Communist
Party in the United States at all levels. By this access it has been able
to identify not only party members but communism's collaborators
in many areas of organized life. The FBI provided the vital evidence
by which members of the National Board of the Communist Party
were indicted and tried in 1949 and convicted under the Smith Act.
As a result of this sensational trial, Congress passed the Internal
Security Act of 1950. Under this Act and on the basis of a 660-page
FBI report, the Attorney General sought an order compelling the
party to register. After hearings, the Subversive Activities Control

Board issued such an order, and when it was not complied with, an indictment was obtained. A District Court conviction in 1962, which imposed a fine of $120,000, was reversed in the District Court of Appeals, and the Supreme Court denied a review. However, in 1965 the party was reindicted.

The position of the Legion concerning subversive activities is well expressed in a description of the Americanism Program by The American Legion's Extension Institute:

> 1. No Legionnaire and no private citizen enjoy any police or investigative authority. The American Legion is not an investigative or prosecuting agency. We cannot take the law into our own hands, no matter how provocative the situation. To do so would be to degrade The American Legion to the level of the communists.
>
> 2. As Americans we Legionnaires fully realize that it is not our mission arbitrarily to enforce or "sell" our forms of government or social organization on other peoples. Our interests and duty to our country begins and ends with repelling attempts of treasonable and misguided elements in our midst from instilling alien ideologies in America.
>
> 3. As a truly patriotic organization reserving to each member the sacred right of freedom of conscience, we are not opposed to orderly and democratic progress. The Constitution, our basic law, specifically provides in the American way for such progress. That traditional American principle must not be denied. The American Legion demands only that we shall proceed and progress in an orderly way, every member reserving to himself the inalienable right to support or oppose changes as he sees fit. The American Legion demands only that such changes and progress shall be accomplished in our own American manner by due process of law and not by violence, force, chicanery, or fraud.

Frequently, bitter criticism has showered not only congressional committees but the Legion because of its support of these agencies and its pronouncements. Leading congressional figures in investigations have been subjected to abuse by the press, radio and television, on campuses and street corners, in the pulpit and Congress, and in academic and artistic circles. Their names are uttered with contempt and derision. In part, the outcry against congressional investigations of communism has been due to a liberalism which mistakes the acceptance of subversion as a manifestation of mere dissent. But a considerable part of the criticism has been inspired by communists and their fellow travelers. Excesses appear on a subject so charged with emotion. These excesses have characterized not only the anti-anti-communists, but some individuals anxious to gain headlines through sensational, unsubstantial utterances and even some sincerely dedicated enemies of communism. A few Legionnaires have been zealots in expression and action in their fight against subversion. Such deviations from reason and common sense must be deplored. The overwhelming majority of Legionnaires do not indulge in nor do they condone such sedulity. Stupidity, avarice for publicity gained by irresponsible attacks, and blind, brawling assaults on leftist organizations are occasionally the source of deep embarrassment to departments and National Headquarters. Advice, suggestions and forthright instructions to refrain from linking the Legion with irresponsible attacks are usually followed, if not by individuals, then by posts. Noncompliance with the organization's constitution and bylaws can lead to expulsion.

The fact that hysterical men and zealots in the United States have unjustly accused their neighbors of sympathy for communism should not obscure truth. Communism has been and is a real and present peril to the national interests of the United States and her many allies. Communism is pledged and actively working to destroy her international influence and internal security. How many revelations must we have? What words must be spoken; what violence done? How often must men devoted to liberty hear the boast, "We will bury you!" hurled from the capitals of current tyranny or shouted from the cellars of conspiracy? The imperialistic foreign policy of the Soviet Union and her satellites and, more recently, Communist China has shown that they will not permit their neighbors to live in peace without threats to their independence and the liberties of their peoples. Communism's expansionism in Europe, the Middle East, Asia, Africa, and Latin America and its infiltration and subversion of governments and free institutions show that its purpose to dominate the world has been and is a virulent menace.

In the United States abundant evidence attests that communists have found their way into most Federal departments, into defense industries, scientific operations and labor organizations, into communications and the educational, religious, entertainment, and professional fields. No area of endeavor is impervious, no agency impenetrable. All this recommends the vigilance that The American Legion has encouraged over the years.

The overwhelming support of investigations in Congress and the states reveal that representatives elected by the people are aware that there is a constant danger from subversive influences.

The Legion's concern with and opposition to communism and other alien forces dedicated to civil and economic disorder and the subversion of our constitutional institutions has generally been a part of its Americanism program, and a special section of the Americanism Commission devotes its attention to subversive activities. In the international field the Legion maintains that the penetration of nations by communism and the promotion of revolutionary movements, together with hostile demonstrations against the United States, show that there has been no slackening in the intent of communist nations upon world revolution.

Despite certain decisions which indicate an overly anxious desire to protect dissent, the Supreme Court has validated the foregoing in a notable case in 1959. In *Barenblatt v. United States* (360 U.S. 109) the Court said:

> That Congress has wide power to legislate in the field of Communist activity in this Country, and to conduct appropriate investigations in aid thereof, is hardly debatable. The existence of such power has never been questioned by this Court, and it is sufficient to say, without particularization, that Congress has enacted or considered in this field a wide range of legislative measures, not a few of which have stemmed from recommendations of the very Committee whose actions have been drawn in question here. In the last analysis this power rests on the right of self-preservation, "the ultimate value of any society," *Dennis v. United States* (341 U.S. 494, 509). Justification for its exercise in turn rests on the long and widely accepted view that the tenets of the Communist Party include the ultimate overthrow of the Government of the United States by force and

violence, a view which has been given formal expression by the Congress.

On these premises, this Court in its constitutional adjudications has consistently refused to view the Communist Party as an ordinary political party, and has upheld federal legislation aimed at the Communist problem which in a different context would certainly have raised constitutional issues of the gravest character. . . . On the same premises this Court has upheld under the Fourteenth Amendment state legislation requiring those occupying or seeking public office to disclaim knowing membership in any organization advocating overthrow of the Government by force and violence, which legislation none can avoid seeing was aimed at membership in the Communist Party. . . . Similarly, in other areas, this Court has recognized the close nexus between the Communist Party and violent overthrow of government. . . . To suggest that because the Communist Party may also sponsor peaceable political reforms the constitutional issues before us should now be judged as if that Party were just an ordinary political party from the standpoint of national security, is to ask this Court to blind itself to world affairs which have determined the whole course of our national policy since the close of World War II, affairs to which Judge Learned Hand gave vivid expression in his opinion in *United States v. Dennis* (183 F. 2d 201, 213), and to the vast burdens which these conditions have entailed for the entire Nation.

Congress has not only indicated its awareness of the communist menace by majority support of its committee investigations, but has adopted into law a substantial number of the recommendations of these committees. Of 120 recommendations by the House Un-American Activities Committee between 1941 and 1960, 35 were enacted into law. A number of recommendations for action by the President and the Executive Departments resulted in Executive orders or directives.

A review of the Legion's resolutions adopted by its National Conventions shows that frequently these actions by government were anticipated, that the Legion firmly supported the investigations by congressional committees and their recommendations, and that, moreover, by its persistent legislative activities the Legion was influential in the adoption into law of the various committees' recommendations.

Through our representative institutions, law most frequently grows from an aroused public opinion. In creating this opinion out of which these investigations and the new laws arise, the Legion, more than any other American organization, has played a vital part. The posts and individual Legionnaires, informed by the publications and directives from their state and national organizations, have vigorously brought the communist issue to the attention of millions of Americans. Legionnaires, with the Legion's legislative service in Washington and in state capitals, have been an incalculable force in countering subversion and strengthening the knowledge of the people that their own and the liberties and interests of others are at stake and that their perseverance as active citizens of a Republic is required.

23

Positive Americanism

I N an unforgettable expression of political principle, Edmund Burke, America's staunch friend and defender in the British Parliament during our struggle for independence, said, "From Magna Charta to the Declaration of Rights, it has been the uniform policy of our Constitution to claim and assert our liberties as an entailed inheritance derived to us from our forefathers, and to be transmitted to our posterity."

Burke's deep comprehension of law as the companion of freedom induced him to use the word "entailed." For we cannot in honor and must not in practice dissipate or impair that legacy which has been given us by those who won it by their energies and blood. Each generation holds and preserves and cherishes liberties for the generations yet to come.

To maintain this hard-won inheritance the founder-statesmen of The American Legion emphasized Americanism. It is an expression which comprehends a variety of principles, approaches and activities. Indeed, it is so broad that it could be used to include all that the Legion means, or believes, or does. And so, in designating its various functions and activities, putting them in its various agencies, the Legion charges its Americanism program not only with teaching principles of our national life, but with many related concerns which affect national and community life. Americanism and the Legion's faith and good works in the restricted sense are the substance of this chapter. However, a number of related activities are described in other chapters.

364

The Constitution of the United States prescribes the Presidential oath of office. This oath requires that he shall not only "preserve" but "defend the Constitution of the United States." The Constitution of the United States in its broadest sense encompasses the entire body of principles which defines the national creed of all Americans. To "preserve" these principles implies a constant process of education in and an observation of these principles; to "defend" them implies a constant vigilance that alien philosophies inimical to them shall not take root in the United States.

The Legion recognizes this twofold responsibility—the one, to educate and impart to Americans their heritage; the other, to resist subversive influences and action.

From its beginnings The American Legion, through its officers, its commissions, its committees, its conventions, and its posts, has considered itself a strong exponent of a sound and progressive American nation. In its record of many years, this ideal has been stated in many forms and in numerous activities and declarations of principle. A high tribute which the Legion has earned rests upon consistency in defending and advancing these principles. For it has lived through great reconsiderations of national policy, vast changes in the form and habits of the nation, and fierce challenges.

The Legion was born of peril and sacrifices of a great war. And war endangers not only the lives of those who go into battle, the substance and even the existence of the nation, but the integrity and solvency of institutions essential to individual liberty. In war, the individual to a great extent yields his liberties and freedom of choice to authority. The protections afforded to the individual in peace are strained and often denied in the interest of national survival. Too often in the history of nations it has been difficult to regain these individual freedoms when peace returned. For there is always the threat, implicit in human nature, that some will seek dominance over others. And the individual who has offered his life, his fortune and his honor to assure a nation's survival will emerge with some of his personal freedom lost forever. It was the determination of those who formed the Legion in those distant months of 1919 that this manifestation of an impaired individualism should not prevail among Americans in the war's aftermath. Twenty-seven years later, when a stillness fell again upon the oceans and recent battlefields, Legionnaires were as determined as before that the individual should again move in the quests of peace free of the shackles imposed by war. But another malign menace arose, a challenge to liberties as monstrous as that of the defeated Axis. The period of the "cold war" began. This great world conflict in which so many governments and institutions have tottered and fallen has imposed upon some nations, peoples and individuals hardships, sacrifice and a stern discipline as great as those imposed during World War II. The unshouldered burden was quickly taken up again. Governments fell and new rulers of men emerged. Nations, gifted in culture and imbued with the fierce desire for liberty, were gripped by communist adventurers. The tragic spectacle was repeated from the shores of the Baltic to the Sea of Japan. A struggle for power occurred even within victorious free nations. To an extent, threats arose in the United States. Men determined to overthrow free institutions crawled from cellars and garrets into the light of notoriety. Others, equally dedicated, with a thick veneer of respectability and enjoying the advantage of what might be considered impeccable social and educational backgrounds, were found in positions of high public trust and professional esteem. And then there were those who advocated, under the aegis of Constitutional rights, forms of marxian socialism. The latter has been somewhat more benign, but in its ultimate projections offers a threat to be recognized. All this, The American Legion has maintained, requires that Americans be constantly reminded of their principles of liberty and the need to preserve them.

A vast economic collapse such as gripped so many Western nations in the early 1930's is a grim menace to individual liberty. For when men and women are impoverished and denied the opportunity for profitable work, when the streams of commerce dry up and the currents of trade cease to flow, desperation starts up. Liberty may be traded for the illusion of security. In the long ground swell of changing times the fainthearted abandon hope and, rudderless and aimless, drift into disillusionment and despair. In the 1920's and in the 1930's many were broached in these periodic troughs.

The American Legion recognized that such times presented an especially dangerous threat to youth who at the termination of school discipline entered what seemed an inhospitable world. Somehow youth must benefit from steady hands and organized effort. Toward youth lies the major thrust of the Legion's Americanism program. For the future will be shaped by these young people, for good or ill, and they will not believe themselves to be a "lost" or "sick" generation if given American opportunities and an awareness of their heritage and obligations. These programs are itemized in another chapter.

Perhaps the philosophy of Americanism, so often expressed in the Legion's statements of principle, can be summed up in a few simple propositions.

1. Paramount in all considerations of our national faith is the individual, his worth, his rights, and his destiny. The roots of his worth rest in religious traditions. Before God, each individual has direct and substantive value. And his belief in God gives him direct and unimpeded access to Divine authority through prayer and sacred observances.

2. Our concept of individual rights rises from this concept of individual worth. Our constitutional rights specify, in part, the individual's liberty to choose and, so far as he is able, to shape the course of his own life.

3. Long before there was an American nation there were communities. Individuals clustered together, drawn in part by ties they had known in the old world, in part by the necessity of mutual aid, cooperative labor and by the human need for companionship. Those who lived in these settlements of clustered homes and rude manufactories had ties with those who lived miles away on lonely farms. Rude forces of concern began, a division of labor appeared, religion taught fellowship under God, and governments took root based upon individual equality. The later imposition of forms of colonial government by a government across the sea laid the basis of what became state government. The persistent and undying vitality of our common life stems from these communities. And while Americans learned, as the generations passed, that wider relationships must follow means of transportation, commerce and communication, the community remained the vital center of our national life. The Legion's division into posts whose members are a part of neighborly living is recognition of this truth.

4. The American Revolution produced longer ties of relationship. The integration of individuals, communities and states into a national

unity was largely forced by the economic policies of George III and his benighted government in the mother country. The common cause of independence submerged sectional and community differences, frictions and jealousies, and, after several critical years, committees of correspondence in various states brought together representatives in Philadelphia and a Constitution was established, followed by a Bill of Rights.

5. Into the founding documents and agreements were either explicit or implicit the principles of order and liberty—the creation of enlightened minds over the centuries. These basic principles are behind the governmental institutions created when the nation entered upon its history.

This heritage, these basic principles and the recognition and dedication they require is regarded by the Legion as fundamental to Americanism.

It is important to note that while Americans after the Revolutionary War had none of the symbols of unity upon which the British nation rests, they were compelled to create their own in their own way to meet special and imperative needs. In speaking of the British nation, Disraeli said, "Individualities may form communities, but it is institutions alone that can create a nation." The institutions to which Disraeli referred were the Crown, the House of Commons, the Lords Temporal and Spiritual, and, at that time, the Empire. For the new American Republic all that was gone, like the wisps of smoke from the musketry at Bunker Hill. Lacking them, Americans created their own institutions and rooted them in human nature and common American life. Some were derived from our inheritance; some came later from custom and experience. By inheritance we have constitutional government, the supremacy of law, the consent of the governed, individual rights as against others and against government itself, a division of government power between the Federal government and the states and within the Federal establishment checks and balances among the Executive, the Congress and the courts. Thus an indivisible union of indestructible states. By custom and experience and common consent other principles emerge—the independence of the Supreme Court, the party system and measurable world responsibility. Implicit in our safeguards for the individual we have in America the almost unique principle of a classless society.

All of these national characteristics are embedded in many statements and resolutions of The American Legion as well as in its practical methods to foster and preserve them through Legion activities. The Preamble to the Constitution of The American Legion is its most notable expression of the American creed:

> For God and Country, we associate ourselves together for the following purpose: to uphold and defend the Constitution of the United States of America; to maintain law and order; to foster and perpetuate a 100 per cent Americanism; to preserve the memories and incidents of our associations in the great wars; to inculcate a sense of individual obligation to the community, state and nation; to combat the autocracy of both the classes and the masses; to make right the master of might; to promote peace and good will on earth; to safeguard and transmit to posterity the principles of justice, freedom and democracy; to consecrate and sanctify our comradeship by our devotion to mutual helpfulness.

The 1919 National Convention assumed responsibilities and objectives that remain today:

> We recommend the establishment of a National Americanism Commission of The American Legion, whose duty shall be the endeavor to realize in the United States the basic ideal of this American Legion of 100 per cent Americanism through the planning, establishment and conduct of a continuous, constructive educational system designed to:
>
> 1. Combat all anti-American tendencies, activities and propaganda;
> 2. Work for the education of immigrants, prospective American citizens and alien residents in the principles of Americanism;
> 3. Inculcate the ideals of Americanism in the citizen population, particularly the basic American principle that the interests of all the people are above those of any special interests or any so-called class or section of the people;
> 4. Spread throughout the people of the nation the information as to the real nature and principles of American government;
> 5. Foster the teachings of Americanism in all schools.

The Legion through its Americanism Commission and other agencies has elaborated these earlier definitions:

Americanism is a vital, active, living force. Americanism to The American Legion means peace, strength, the will and the courage to live as free men in a free land. It means a friendly hand to people everywhere who respect our institutions and our thinking. It is not a word, it is a cause, a way of life. . . . Americanism, as we in The American Legion know it, is patriotism—living for God and Country. It is unwavering loyalty to the United States as established under the Constitution. It is willingness to defend our form of government against all who would overthrow, change or misinterpret its principles. It is understanding of the functions of our government and respect for the traditions that brought it into being and the constitutional processes through which it lives. It is recognizing that the common good is paramount to the individual interests, with protection of the common good through prescribed legal procedures rather than the rules and whims of men.

Americanism is—an unfailing love of country, loyalty to its institutions and ideals; eagerness to defend it against all enemies; individual allegiance to the Flag; and a desire to secure the blessings of Liberty to ourselves and posterity.

Americanism is—complete and unqualified loyalty to the ideals of government set forth in the Bill of Rights, the Declaration of Independence, and the Constitution of the United States. It is respect for and ready obedience to duly constituted authority and the laws of the land. It is freedom without license, religion without bigotry, charity without bias or race hatred, love of Flag and a readiness to defend that for which it stands against every alien and subversive influence from without or within.

The Legion holds that these memorable sentiments, however exalted and heart-stirring, need constant care. Liberty must be affirmed by every generation. It must sometimes be won and rewon. As the older generations fade away, new and virile generations must accept and bear the burdens of free men and women. Through education in its broadest sense the Legion seeks to pass on this responsibility for the maintenance of American ideals from generation to generation.

In the practical application of the foregoing principles, two sorts of activities have been carried on by the Legion. The one is observances of a patriotic nature; the other, intensive education—especially of the young—to assure that the principles of free men may be understood

and become a primary factor in every American's mental and intellectual equipment. As we have seen, the Legion's concerns with these
two methods of providing love of and dedication to the nation and
its ideals began in its very early years. The latter became in large
part a responsibility of the Americanism Commission and is shared
down the line to the posts and individual Legionnaires. The American
Legion emphasizes that principles and objectives of its Americanism
programs are designed to:

> Cooperate closely with the National Education Association
> (NEA) and state and local education groups; with the National
> Congress of Parents and Teachers and state and local PTA or-
> ganizations; and with the U.S. Office of Education and other
> interested groups.
>
> Established teachers' salary schedules on a professional basis,
> adequate to attract and retain well qualified instructors in the
> teaching profession.
>
> Guarantee equalization of education opportunity free from
> federal control.
>
> Teach through American History, Civics, Geography, English
> and kindred subjects vital to the building of future citizenship.
>
> Instill in youth a love of country and the willingness to de-
> fend this land and its principles against all enemies.
>
> Establish supreme faith in American constitutional govern-
> ment and provide daily practice of such ideals in the school.
>
> Destroy false propaganda and eliminate the teachings of those
> who advocate changes in our way of life—opposing the original
> concepts laid down by our founding fathers. This can best be done
> by the best education of our children in a better knowledge of
> the American way of life.
>
> Teach children the problems involved in the ever increasing
> importance of international affairs.

American Education Week grew out of the revelation during World
War I that an alarming proportion of the American people were illiterate and physically unfit. Talks between the NEA and The American Legion led to its observance in 1921. The objective of American
Education Week is to acquaint the parents and all citizens of every
community with the achievements, aims and needs of their schools,
and the Legion holds, "No other agency is more vital to the well-

being of the nation than our school system," and that "no other cause is more deserving of special consideration" by Americans than this observance. The Americanism Commission prepares and distributes literature for the week fixed to coincide with Veterans Day in November. Of it the Legion observes:

> American Education Week is a great national institution in which American Legion posts participate. It is the responsibility of all citizens to help maintain good schools which build good citizens. The American Legion, throughout its history, has accepted the responsibility of giving all-out support to the schools, and it is in keeping with The American Legion's program of good citizenship for individual Legionnaires to give their schools all possible aid.

In 1964 the week's four co-sponsors selected the general theme, "Education Pays Dividends," and assigned seven supporting daily topics: ". . . in Better Human Relations; in Improved Earning Power; in Personal Fulfillment; in Good Citizenship; in National Economic Growth; in Better Communities; and in International Relations."

World War II produced a "crisis in education" which will linger into the late 1960's. Wartime marriages resulted in immense increases in enrollments in the grades and high schools during the 1950's. As these children grew up, the colleges felt the impact, and the Legion swung its resources and energy to face the problem. In the mid-1950's The American Legion's Scholarship Program outlined its objectives:

> 1. To help make it possible for any child of a veteran who has ability or desire, to receive an education beyond high school;
> 2. To encourage the membership of The American Legion and its affiliated organizations to take an active part in the development and maintenance of a school system that will serve the needs of *all* children at every level;
> 3. To encourage students to select careers where personnel shortages exist.

Policies established to accomplish these objectives are designated:

> 1. To explore and summarize existing scholarship sources;
> 2. To make known to potentially eligible children the sources of scholarships that exist;

3. To develop new scholarship opportunities for the increasing number of students who will reach college in the years ahead;

4. To cooperate with established organizations in the recruitment of students for careers where personnel shortages exist.

Today the Legion distributes its thirteenth edition of "Need a Lift?" —a valuable source of career and educational assistance information for qualified and interested students. Its "Guide for Parents and Students" is designed to serve in planning for future education and to "place a positive Americanism Legion program into homes throughout the community."

Other prominent Legion undertakings include the National High School Oratorical Contest, aimed at developing a deeper understanding of the Constitution and cultivating leadership, citizenship and the ability to think and speak clearly. From four thousand contestants in 1938 the competition now involves well over a third of a million students in most departments, at home and abroad. The American Legion School Medal Awards place emphasis on development of character and scholarship and are presented to a graduating boy or girl "at an impressionable age," on the threshold of "more extensive education" or entrance "into the bread-winning world." Winners, the Legion feels, will perpetuate "those fighting qualities and that love of country, that unselfishness, that high regard for truth and honor which have been displayed by our fighting men participating in the World Wars and in the Korean conflict."

More encompassing undertakings of The Americanism Program include:

> Constitution Week in September is intended by the Legion through its posts to instill the concepts of the Constitution "in the minds and hearts" of youth, and "to re-educate our citizens concerning the Constitution." The Legion considers this educational observance vital. "Today, there are groups, and even governments, which are denying the inalienable rights of men and are advocating the imposition of their ideologies by force and violence on democratic governments and free peoples. Thus, the preservation of the American system of government demands the militant support of all citizens. The guarantees of liberty, evolved from history and the experience of people, will continue to be maintained only by active vigilance of our people."

Citizenship Day, designated by Congress to commemorate the signing of the Constitution on September 17, 1787, and to recognize all who have attained the status of citizenship by coming of age or by naturalization, stems from a 1939 Legion resolution establishing Annual Citizenship Recognition Day.

Posts observe Bill of Rights Day, December 15, "since it is this document on man's rights which guarantees every individual personal liberty and safety, and the states their rights as states."

Ever since the high tides of immigration reached our shores late in the nineteenth century, there has been the problem of providing education in Americanism to the foreign-born, especially in great industrial centers. For years the Legion has worked, often in cooperation with the public schools, in presenting classes designed to assist aliens in acquiring the knowledge necessary to naturalization. The Americanism Commission has published literature for such needed instruction, and over the years the Legion has harbored strong attitudes toward the necessity of naturalization of immigrants.

Those who have come from alien cultures have brought fine gifts, as well as strong backs to these shores, but in some cases in the past they have arrived, accustomed to autocratic and tyrannical systems, only to be preyed upon by racketeers whose influence goes back to their native lands or politicians intent upon exploiting their ignorance, their initial poverty and loneliness. They should be made aware of the concepts of free men living under enlightened constitutional forms. They should be given the opportunity to learn English and to become participants in the American democratic process. They should, if they desire citizenship, be prepared to share the responsibilities and, occasionally, the great sacrifices that are a man's lot under liberty, if that liberty is to be preserved. Long ago, Legionnaires recognized that some new arrivals could not successfully shift for themselves. By helping them to realize something of the "American dream," Legionnaires could find satisfaction in knowing that these people had added to the fiber and strength of the nation.

Finally, in the realm of education, leaders and members of the Legion have kept a sharp eye on the content of education in public schools. Textbooks have been subject to examination by Legionnaires who exercised the right to point out what they considered deficiencies to school boards and administrators. Occasionally, this has been a

source of bitter controversy and recriminations. In the changes
in the interpretation of American history and civil government during
the past half century, serious departures from tradition have appeared
from time to time. New theories of education too often make light of
basic causes and effects in our history as they were formerly understood. Considerable evidence has accompanied charges of officers and
posts of the Legion that there are "distortions" designed to temper
the patriotic sentiments of the young. But it is not necessary to claim
that the United States has always been divinely directed, for those
who have directed our government are human beings prone to make
mistakes. However, the growth of the nation over the generations is
proof of the essential soundness of our course. The Legion, nationally
and locally, feels that it serves a high purpose in being alert to the
preservation of our tested traditions and assumes a reasonable position in attacking distortion.

Finally, the Legion engages in a practical application of its Americanism principles through observances of a patriotic nature. The Legion is responsible for the adoption of an official Flag Code, for
legislation making "The Star Spangled Banner" the national anthem,
and for establishing Armistice Day, November 11, as a national holiday, now celebrated as Veterans Day.

Two years after its establishment the Legion held one of its most
memorable and stirring conventions in Kansas City, an event that ri-
valed Victory Day in Paris. Present at the Convention with the President of the United States and Commander John G. Emery were
men whose names echo in history—"Black Jack" Pershing; Foch,
Marshal of France; the dashing Earl Beatty of the Royal Navy;
Jacques, hero of Belgium; Admiral Rodman of the U.S. Navy; the
blunt Lejeune of the Marine Corps; and Díaz, "Savior of Italy."
Some months before, the NEC recommended by resolution to the
President that America honor one of its unknown war dead. Legislation, introduced by two Legion members, made provision for a shrine
that is honored as hallowed ground beside Lexington, Concord, Constitution Hall, Valley Forge, and Gettysburg—the Tomb of the Unknown Soldier. On Armistice Day following the convention, the
Legion's distinguished foreign guests stood in the bleak November
day with celebrated and humble Americans at graveside in Arlington

Cemetery. Beneath the bare trees flew two flags, the Stars and Stripes and the emblem of The American Legion.

It was not until 1937 that Congress and the President officially designated Armistice Day as a national holiday after the Legion and its posts had secured such observance in thirty-six states. Wherever they are on that day, Legionnaires promote and participate in suitable observances of the end of World War I, and the National Commander often shares the forum at ceremonies at the Tomb of the Unknown Soldier. The Legion also adopted in memory of the more recent veterans dead Memorial Day, May 30, It had originally been a tribute to those who participated in the War Between the States. Wherever a veteran lies buried, a flag and a poppy decorate his grave on that day.

Observances are also made on Independence Day, Flag Day, Constitution Day, Armed Forces Day, and "I Am an American Day," with Legion members and officers in attendance. The Legion also promoted the permanent sentries arrangement at the Tomb of the Unknown Soldier, and in 1945 led the move to provide that an unknown soldier from World War II rest beside him. A third grave is there—the Unknown of the Korean conflict.

In more recent years the Americanism Commission has strongly recommended that communities establish living memorials—"war memorials created in the form of parks, recreation centers, community buildings, etc. . . . memorials that live will build a stronger and healthier citizenship."

But most moving is the awesome sight of crosses and Stars of David stretching away from the eye row on row near a hundred battle-grounds—from the Normandy beaches across Europe and Africa to Asia and the farthest reaches of the Pacific.

24

Defense in the Nuclear Age

A TENET of The American Legion is that successful conduct of
foreign policy must be supported by certain considerations
not the least of which is great military strength. This has been reemphasized since 1945. But The American Legion's national defense
concerns were not shared by most Americans at the close of war.
Haste in dismantling U.S. strength made a mockery of Legion
resolutions.

The war had nourished high hopes that mankind might enter new
vistas of realized aspirations. Morally, the United States had assumed
a leading role. But moral force can be a flimsy, tinseled thing—like
a Hollywood set—with little to give it durable persuasiveness. To with-
stand the buffeting of international politics and other realities of the
mid-twentieth century, moral force must be stanchioned, reinforced
and made secure.

Yet, in the giddy, exalted atmosphere of victory glorious motives
dispelled fears that aggression and tyranny might spring from fresh
quarters. When the Legion met in Chicago in the fall of 1945, America was already rushing back to policies followed so precipitously after
each of her wars. Families clamored for the return of their menfolk.
Domestic political considerations and wartime agreements dictated
withdrawal from large areas in liberated Europe. The GI's trudged
back over ground won at appalling cost to "zones of occupation." The
services dismantled divisions wholesale, inactivated great task forces
and grounded illustrious air wings. The gigantic, worldwide war-
surplus sale was on.

Notable and honest men magnified illusions of harmony and imagined a new birth of freedom for mankind. How, at the end of so much sacrifice, could there be further exactions against the manpower, substance, energy, and nerve of peoples so long at war?

This, despite the fact that for many nations the promise of peace and security was a guttering candle—a flame that could not sustain itself in the foul post-war atmosphere, close with acts and threats aimed at snuffing out liberty and self-determination.

In 1945 the Legion saw only disaster in America's course. Its resolutions were a catalogue for continued strength. This summary presents in some detail the Legion's policies of 1945, many of which have been reiterated over the years. It has strengthened, amended and specified its positions as it has viewed the onset and deepening of the cold war, and the increased responsibilities and commitments of the United States in the nuclear age.

The National Defense Committee, under S. Perry Brown, noted in 1945 the momentous happenings since the previous convention. It observed that Americans had adopted a familiar attitude—"All we want to do is to forget. . . . Predictions are being made that because of the development of the atomic bomb, war will never occur again because it would destroy mankind." The committee recommended continuation of the Legion's traditional espousal of a strong America. No matter what others might do, the Legion insisted that the United States should rely upon universal military training, a strong Army, Navy and Air Force, and an imaginative program for preparedness.

The committee held that the "only democratic foundation for adequate preparedness is in universal military training." Any appraisal of Legion effectiveness must underline the fact that, although conventions had adopted or reaffirmed resolutions for Federal legislation to provide for UMT, the Legion made no attempt to provide a specific plan or program until 1945. Commander Warren H. Atherton in 1943 had appointed a subcommittee under S. Perry Brown to formulate details for UMT. During 1944 this committee held more than eighty conferences with religious, educational, agricultural, and patriotic organizations and evolved its plan. By unanimous resolution, the 26th Annual Convention requested that Congress enact a UMT bill incorporating provisions that qualified young men receive twelve months of military training, integrated with academic education, and that at an age least apt to disrupt normal education and business life and for a reasonable period after training they serve in a component of the Armed Forces. This legislation would take effect upon expiration of the Selective Service Act. Congress showed little interest, and the National Defense Committee commenced an extensive campaign directed at the public. Legislative strategy talks in December, 1945, led to introduction of a bill, but Pentagon insistence on a full year's training smothered its chances.

The Legion had very nearly gone the route of effort and frustration on the subject. Legionnaires had carried the tattered UMT banner for a quarter of a century. Few imagined that ahead lay another decade on the tortuous trail toward congressional enactment of this Legion principle. A compromise bill in 1946 was voted out by the House Committee but met its end in the Rules Committee, although popular polls indicated 77 per cent of the people were favorable toward UMT. Bitterly, the Legion charged that political expediency had dictated its defeat. A 1948 redrafting of its bills without compromise gained but brief hearings in a Senate committee. The committee chairman in the House held Legion recommendations unnecessary.

By this time the United States had dismantled and withdrawn much of its striking power from Europe, while the Soviet Union was merely dissolving illusions about the shape of the peace, elbowing its armor and massed armies into position to subjugate Eastern Europe, concocting moves to extend further the frontiers of its tyranny. The Legion, haunted by past unpreparedness, spoke through *The National Legionnaire:*

> We must have peace-time conscription to keep up our commitments and carry on until a real peace is made—this has apparently been hard for average Americans to swallow and hard for Congress to accept as its duty in an election year.

Anger tinged the remarks of Legion spokesmen. Passage of UMT would have been certain but for "duty-shirking and political cowardice" of Senate and House leadership. National Commander James F. O'Neil, an experienced, shrewd and straightforward New Englander, and Legislative Representative Taylor bitterly blamed Republican House and Senate leaders for a "selfish and un-American procedure" in refusing to allow the bills to be reported. Congress "knows deep in its heart that this is the proper approach to security," O'Neil charged as he advocated a special session to enact the Legion's bill into law.

It was time to retire the old wheelhorse label "UMT," and the NEC determined that any subsequent manpower training bill would bear the title National Security Training Act. Nineteen fifty held bright prospects. There was Presidential approval for immediate enactment of a bill drafted jointly by The American Legion and the Department of Defense (DOD). The bill was reported, but President Truman's anticipated help was not to be had, and the Pentagon dropped the matter.

The legislative experience of 1951 was a close thing. In January, S.1, the Legion plan, was introduced. By legislative maneuver the DOD offered a substitute S.1, coupling NST with Selective Service and placing the entire program under military control. By unflagging effort the Legion gained changes which made the substitute acceptable, including a supervisory commission, a majority of its members civilians, to control training. The bill, adopted by large margins in both House and Senate, now came under the scrutiny of a Presidential Commission. Subsequently, Legion representatives appeared before congressional committees to submit recommendations for amendments for the commission's bill. However, opponents of military training for American youth were not idle. Through a parliamentary maneuver opponents in the House went into a Committee of the Whole and adopted amendments to defer substitution of NST while Selective Service operated and to limit the life of NST to six years. Seizing upon an opportunity when many House members were absent, the opposition put through a substitute measure for training in high schools. When the absent members returned, the Chair ruled out both the substitute and the amendment, forcing a vote on recommittal. Had not the amendment been ruled out at the last moment, a majority probably would have enacted NST. But, as in many things, the Legion was no amateur, no fragile advocate to be unnerved by defeat or checked by disappointment. Like an old pro it could keep punting and wait for a fumble.

The next big drive came in 1954, when Commander Seaborn P. Collins directed the NEC to draft and procure passage of an NST bill. Plans were made for drafting the legislation, introducing it and procuring adequate support from every department and post and every unit of the Auxiliary. Collins appointed a chairman in every department to secure letters, cards, telegrams, resolutions, and other communications from individual Legionnaires and posts to be forwarded to respective senators and congressmen at a time designated by Legislative Director James R. Wilson, Jr. The bill was ready in early December. In January it was introduced in Congress as S.2 by Senators Russell, Kefauver, Stennis, Symington, Jackson, Bridges, and Saltonstall, and in the House by Overton Brooks and Van Zandt. Hearings in the House centered upon the Legion's bill and an alternative dispatched from the Pentagon. Legislators who had reported their mail running heavily anti-NST found the trend abruptly reversed after the Security Division's signal. The subcommittee of the House Armed Services Committee embodied its recommendations in a bill by Representative Brooks which incorporated important provisions of the Legion's bill. Now the Legion put into effect operation "Reload," enlisting support from all its organizational levels. However, when the bill faced defeat because of a nonsegregation amendment, it was withdrawn.

Subsequently The American Legion and leaders of other organizations concerned with national security conferred with President Eisenhower and prevailed upon him to urge reconsideration and adoption of a Reserve Plan. The President fulfilled his task, and through concerted effort in 1955, H.R. 7000 carried in the House. The Senate passed a stronger bill, and in conference a compromise was developed which passed both houses in July. Today's six-month training program with subsequent availability is used by all services and is a direct outgrowth of the Legion's long efforts toward adequate manpower legislation.

At the 1945 Convention the Committee on National Defense listed national security demands:

    1. Unification of the Air, Army and Navy elements of our armed forces under a single command.
    2. Unification of world intelligence services in one highly trained corps.

3. Cooperation of the armed services and State Department in foreign affairs.

4. Maintenance of adequate stock piles of strategic materials.

Its resolutions included preservation of a powerful Merchant Marine, American Legion leadership in promotion of civil defense, the retention of a Navy sufficiently strong to "maintain the honor and security of the United States," greater Federal participation in aeronautics, a strong Army with powerful reserve components, continuation of officer training for all the services, and endorsement of the principle of a unified command of our Armed Forces with the Army, Navy and Air Force on an equal level.

National Commander Edward N. Scheiberling, after noting the increased size of the Legion, its new responsibilities to the country and its nationwide campaign to raise a fifteen-million-dollar Americanism endowment fund, discussed America's new world role in promoting peace by marshaling her splendid strength behind the efforts of the artisans of peacemaking:

> An impregnable America must be, therefore, the foundation upon which the world must build for its partnership of enduring peace, and it is the only basis on which America can plan her own security.

He ably presented the outlines of Legion effort for preparedness, and anticipated responsibilities in Legion activities mentioned in other chapters.

A lustrous group of speakers addressed the convention, among them Admiral Ernest King, British Air Marshall Sir Arthur Tedder, Admiral Chester Nimitz, prominent government officials, and civilian leaders.

It was not long after the first elation of victory subsided that indications became stronger that the Soviet Union was not going to act in good faith. It appeared that principles and the liberties of millions had been bartered away at the celebrated and notorious conferences with the leader of world communism, Joseph Stalin, and his henchman, Vyacheslav Molotov. Indeed, Western democracies and independent nations throughout the world were soon to find themselves in deadly jeopardy.

The American Legion as the most influential group concerned with defense matters outside the Federal government entered this period of uncertainty, conflicting views and unresolved strategies with a healthy awareness of the folly of defense cuts. Time was required for American illusions to dissipate concerning communist ambitions in the Far East and in Eastern Europe, a vacuum the Soviets had filled with all manner of military and political paraphernalia. Russian agreements made in the war years were callously broken. The iron hand of tyranny fastened upon peoples whose countries were occupied by the Red Army, and the fond hopes of self-determination became one of history's monumental daydreams. President Truman, Secretary of State Byrnes and, later, Secretary Marshall reacted. The United States had been the butt of Comrade Stalin's monstrous joke, and Truman in particular did not like it.

At the 1946 Convention, Fleet Admiral Nimitz pointed out to the delegates that the greatest naval power in history had shrunk to one-sixth its wartime size and indicated that it had almost reached its authorized peacetime complement. He spoke of the Navy as "a great safeguard against war." General Carl Spaatz spoke of the importance of air power and General Lewis B. Hershey, Director of Selective Service, warned of complacency and the fact that in armed strength "we have not retained the place in the world we occupied when The American Legion met in 1945."

National Commander John Stelle reemphasized former Legion positions, called for continued modernization of the Armed Forces, the maintenance of a wide network of air, sea and ground bases around the world and commended the policies set forth by the Legion's National Defense Committee. This was a twelve-point program rededicating the Legion to its traditional, progressive objectives. It gave special attention to the unification of the Armed Forces.

Although many of the Legion's objectives awaited future realization, reorganization of the Armed Forces came in 1947. The Legion established the National Security Commission which assumed all Legion activities in defense matters. Its responsibilities included the supervision and coordination of the following committees: Aeronautics (now Aeronautics and Space), Civil Defense, Merchant Marine, Military Affairs, Naval Affairs, and Law and Order. Today, there are, as well, committees on the Cold War, Amateur Radio Network and Uniform Code of Military Justice.

As James R. Wilson, Jr., Director of National Security Division, points out, two principal changes have greatly affected the operation of the commission under its chairman, William C. Doyle: first, the developments arising from the National Security Act of 1947, which has gradually invested greater responsibility in the Department of Defense; and second, the creation of "a National Security Division as an administrative arm to carry out the mandates of the American Legion in national security."

While the Standing Commission and Committees still meet four times a year, and while special committees delve into special problems, many of the appearances before the Congress and programs developed to fulfill mandates are now a staff responsibility.

During the pre-convention meetings and again during the National Commander's Conference top-flight military and civilian dignitaries brief the commission and committee members on the latest developments in our defense position and the national security in general. During these meetings the members also have the opportunity of visiting military installations.

Despite the dismal consequences of our wartime diplomacy and the swift pace of our reconversion, the United States was not destined to return to its traditional foreign policies. Now it became clear that the venerable powers of Europe could no longer ensure great tracts of territory from the menace of communism. The United States changed its foreign policy in revolutionary ways. The Truman Doctrine, which saved Greece and Turkey, and the Marshall Plan, which made the United States the main defender of independence in Europe, signaled a deep involvement in the problems of those nations desirous of self-government and marked the start of a program to contain communism. As the Iron Curtain had clanged down across Europe, Legion reservations were supported by a worldwide menace. International communism had not radically changed its ambition and objectives. In war it had merely been an arrested virus.

National Commander Paul H. Griffith declared to the Convention in 1947 that by poll of Legionnaires the national organization had backed the administration's programs abroad, "that the prime menace rests with the machinations of Moscow," that with enlarged international commitments the Armed Forces should be strengthened, and that "the Legion supported with all its legislative strength" ample funds for these purposes.

Secretary of the Navy James Forrestal's address gratified the Legion, since under the National Security Act objectives long sought by the Legion were to be realized, such as the National Security Resources Board which would establish reserves of strategic materials and make plans for the effective use of manpower and of the economy in wartime. It established a Munitions Board, the Research and Development Board, the Central Intelligence Agency, and a combined "War Council."

Still, the military requirements of the ambitious policy of containment and, later, the avowed capacity of "massive retaliation" were not adequate. In 1948 the Soviet closing of ground access to Berlin was overcome only by thirteen months of massive airlift.

As the Legion expended growing efforts toward defense in the years that followed, American military policies came to incorporate a variety of sophisticated weapons systems. These were deemed necessary to support the expanding system of alliances, including NATO, unilateral defense treaties and other regional arrangements.

In September, 1949, the Soviet Union exploded its first nuclear device. Meanwhile, in the Orient communism had gained mainland China and the 1950 communist assault on South Korea proved out the facts that international communism was prepared to use force to overwhelm independent nations and that the United States was not militarily prepared to respond decisively.

From 1945 to 1950, the Legion contended, "We again permitted the most powerful war machine in the world's history to waste away far below the level required to discharge our international responsibilities. The result was the naked communist aggression of Soviet Korea—a spectacle we earnestly trust will not soon be forgotten."

The Korean War has been discussed in some detail in the chapter entitled, "The Legion and the Cold War." From that conflict's impact, the Legion at last was realizing many of its national security objectives. Its support of a strong U.S. posture against tyranny was shared by a growing number of Americans who had given little thought to foreign policy or the military expenditures required.

Under the Eisenhower Administration the need for overwhelming nuclear striking power was recognized and fulfilled successfully.

Since, worldwide conflict has been avoided, brutal and stubborn conflicts burned or flared in numerous places. That the communists have curbed ambitions in many areas, the Legion maintains, is due to the "free world deterrent of a militarily strong America."

When it became evident that the communist movement was stepping up local military activities along the noncommunist perimeter, the Legion supported a buildup in conventional forces. By 1961 it was both gratified and apprehensive. The Legion praised action that added two divisions to the Army, but feared any reductions in the Army Reserve and the National Guard and failure to accelerate the RS-70 bomber and Nike-Zeus antimissile programs. Emphasis on the reserve components, which have in large measure been the sinew and fiber of all U.S. military operations in the cold war, should not be reduced. The Legion's appraisal of increasing "tensions in widely separated parts of the world" clashed with the Defense Department evaluations. The Legion felt that the nation required as a matter of discretion both Reserve effectiveness and size. This approach of balanced forces with highly diversified capabilities at first ran against Defense Department "counting house" methods. More recently the Defense Department has moved close to the Legion positions out of necessity.

It is well here to summarize the Legion's policies on various aspects of defense. The requirements of meeting aggression or the threat of aggression in the nuclear age have burdened the United States. They have demanded a wide variety of effort. The Legion recognized these requirements, studied them and made valuable contributions in meeting them.

As greater emphasis was placed on high-performance aircraft, missiles and the development of space technology, the American Legion broadened the purview of its Aeronautics Committee. It became the Aeronautics and Space Committee, which has repeatedly advocated expanded research and development "to assure that the United States will not be outstripped in the race for outer space." Since the USSR has continued its efforts in manned aircraft as well as missiles and space weapons, the Legion maintains that its thermonuclear capability "constitutes a critical menace to our very existence." The Legion supports research, development and production of manned airplanes and missiles to keep well ahead of obsolescence, highly motivated personnel, a vigorous aircraft industry, and the teaching of airpower and space technology in the schools. At Philadelphia in 1949, delegates resolved that an Air Force Academy be established. The Legion has also been most active at the community level in its aerospace endeavor, and also publishes *Aerospace Review*.

Resolutions adopted by the 1963 Convention typify the continuing Legion program. Of these, three called for increased United States aerospace power and a buildup in our deterrent and retaliatory capabilities. Specifically, the resolutions called for: (1) national recognition of the military space mission and priority development of required Air Force space capabilities with immediate emphasis on a manned orbital space station; (2) the continuation of a balanced mix of manned and unmanned strategic weapon systems sufficient to assure that United States strategic military superiority is perpetuated; (3) acceleration of the efforts to develop and produce an improved manned interceptor aircraft. Also, the committee called for strengthening the Military Air Transport Service, the "affirmation of our conviction of the capability of the Tactical Air Command" to prosecute its assigned missions anywhere on earth, and support of a strong Aerospace Educational Program.

Under the Eisenhower Administration the Strategic Air Command became an awesome global force. The Soviet belief that it would be used if communism moved against the West was the basis for its deterrent value. The Legion has consistently advocated up-to-date bombers for SAC.

Intermittent periods of complacency were shattered for the American public as the Soviet Union drove ahead in space technology. Sputnik was successfully launched in 1957. Military implications were clear, for the rocket used could also launch nuclear warheads. What has been called "rocket diplomacy" began, conducted by Soviet Premier Khrushchev unsuccessfully, first against the Eisenhower Administration and then the Kennedy Administration. From 1957, congressional appropriations urged by the Legion, the military and other responsible groups, made possible enormous strides in rocketry and its space and military applications.

The takeover of mainland China, U.S. commitment in defense of
Formosa, occupation of Japan, and the growing menace of communist expansion around the entire periphery of the communist orbit
made a costly variety of American means of response—advocated
by The American Legion since World War II—not only prudent but
necessary. This included a powerful Navy, Army, Reserve, Merchant
Marine and a satisfactory civil defense plan—all tailored to meet a
wide range of contingencies. All have been intensively studied and
promoted by the Legion with uneven degrees of success.

Let us consider them separately. The Legion through its Naval
Affairs Committee has been most progressive in its appreciation of
the enormous importance of sea power in fulfilling our commitments.
Its activities extend from testimony covering all convention mandates
by American Legion spokesmen to Defense Appropriations subcommittees to considerable effort at the post level. With an awareness
of the Soviet Union's huge submarine fleet and its programs of
merchant and naval ship construction, the Legion has urged the
building of fast carriers, nuclear propulsion, advanced antisubmarine
equipment and forces, Polaris submarines, and the wide assortment of
ships and landing craft that will keep the U.S. Navy a vital and invincible force, on, under and above all the world's oceans. The Legion's Naval Affairs Committee in a typical report after the fighting
in Korea began stated the following policy:

> That the safety of our essential trade routes and the maintenance
> of our communications lines have demanded a Navy adequate
> to the task. Control of the seas must be maintained if we are to
> protect areas of strategic importance.
>
> Korea has dramatically pointed out that our Navy must have:
>
> 1. Amphibious forces with which to transport troops to
> overseas positions and land them against opposition.
> 2. Carrier air forces as a highly effective mobile tactical
> air force at sea and in coastal areas distant from our own
> prepared air bases.
> 3. Surface fighting ships to support the amphibious forces
> and carrier forces, and to furnish gunfire support for amphibious landings.
> 4. Submarine forces of great power and a high degree of
> technological development.

5. Antisubmarine and naval reconnaissance forces, surface and air, capable of effectively covering the approaches to our coast and our essential supply lines at sea and under cover and supporting our ships. This to include an adequate "hunter-killer" group.

6. Supply ships and auxiliaries for the logistical support of all forces overseas, including the land armies and land air forces.

7. A Marine Corps maintained in numbers sufficient to assure a fighting force in readiness for any emergency.

8. An expanded naval and Marine Corps air arm for support of amphibious ground forces.

Only through training, the accumulation of a manpower Reserve and the stockpiling of material can our Navy maintain control of the seas. The excellent Reserve training program, facilities for training and training cruises have maintained a ready pool of naval manpower. The Navy's wholesome attitude toward its reservists has stimulated and held their interest.

Most recently, the Legion has been disappointed that the Defense Department has not recognized the critical problem of block obsolescence. Whereas the 1964 budget recommended 41 new ships, this was 29 short of the 70 per year a congressional committee had urged to avert a dangerous situation.

However, the Legion was gratified that with 41 Polaris submarines the Navy would have a launching capability of 656 missiles. The new 21-knot LST amphibious craft, capable of unloading tanks and heavy equipment to a beach, progress in development of missile ships, new electronic gear, ASW helicopters, a roll-on, roll-off cargo ship capable of carrying hundreds of tanks and trucks from port to port like the highly successful USNS Comet, the Fleet Rehabilitation and Modernization program, the request for survey ships to aid research in oceanography, additions to the Fleet of "antisubmarine submarines," a helicopter carrier, and new aircraft types for the Navy and Marine Corps gratified Legionnaires.

The Legion has felt that the Cuban blockade and naval operations in the nuclear age, particularly in combat situations in the Far East from the Sea of Japan to the Formosa Straits and South China Sea, fully justify its meticulous attention to naval matters.

The Security Commission in 1956 believed that in adjusting the emphasis of its military establishments, the United States should take full advantage of the latest technologies, including the power of the atom to deal decisively and quickly with aggression, to the end that it would supply sufficient strength to maintain peace in the world as a means of discouraging aggression:

> Our national security and the security of the remaining free nations of the world is increasingly threatened by the constantly growing menace of communist imperialism.

In order to win this new phase of war it became urgently and immediately necessary that our government and our dependable allies fully realize this danger.

The Legion believes:

> The most significant military development in recent years has been the substantial build-up of our conventional forces. Significant steps have been taken to achieve sufficiently powerful and mobile forces to prevent the steady erosion of the free world's position through limited wars and covert aggression. The concept of massive retaliation is no longer our sole tool of war and diplomacy. In its place the strategy of flexible response and measured retaliation has become a major factor in shaping our military posture.
>
> Of equal importance is the growing awareness that the biggest bang isn't necessarily the best ... the realization that all the super weapons in our arsenal have not been enough to prevent the steady nibbling at the edges of the free world and the political blackmail at the conference table which has since 1945 constituted the most active and constant threats to our security.
>
> The Defense Budget for Fiscal Year 1965, starting July 1, 1964, makes the first leveling off in Defense requests since the present administration started adding weapons and troops early in 1961. The three principal reasons given for the decrease of the military budget in 1965 are: first, the cost reduction program is beginning to have a major impact on budget requests, and second, Defense Department officials state that they are over the hump in the funding of the big missile systems and, third, DOD contends they have made good their FY 1964 funding of

many of the deficiencies that were found in equipment and supplies in the Army and the other services.

Defense strength will be largely unchanged, despite a cut of $1 billion in defense spending below the level for FY 1964. Some cuts will be found in nearly all items of weapons and equipment to be bought from industry. U.S. military aid abroad is also to be trimmed.

When manpower strength for 1965 was estimated, the Legion declared a million-man force would do much to enable the Army to carry out its responsibilities. It had been a leader in advocating improved weapons, the "pentomic structure" of divisions, proficiency in irregular warfare, and the procurement of long-range cargo and troop aircraft.

Recently the Legion observed:

> The need for modernization of our conventional forces has been recognized. Particularly notable is the continued expansion, training and equipping of the Army's special forces guerrilla warfare units to combat communist infiltration, subversion and self-styled "wars of national liberation." It is in this twilight zone of blurred, low-key violence that the decisive struggles of the next decade may well take place.
>
> The forward deployment of our forces, along with the prepositioning of supplies, ammunition and heavy equipment, also contributes heavily to providing the "stronger shield and sharper sword."

In 1962, National Commander Charles L. Bacon presented the Legion's opposition to proposed cuts in manpower and units of the Reserve Forces. Twelve years before, another National Commander, George N. Craig, had emphasized the importance of the National Guard and the Army Reserve in the Korean conflict, as did Commander Erle Cocke, Jr., a year later. Legion insistence upon strong Reserve Forces has met considerable frustration during Secretary of Defense McNamara's tenure, but developments in the Far East may strengthen the Legion's position.

The Merchant Marine, "the fourth arm of the service," has received detailed attention from The American Legion over many years. In 1962 the Legion reaffirmed its forty-year support of a strong, privately owned Merchant Marine, discussed in previous chapters. Its wide assortment of proposals, restated from year to year, have been designed to avoid "the huge outlays and sacrifices of time, lives and money" in times of emergency. Great frustration has been the Legion's lot in this endeavor. In mid-1963 the United States stood in ninth place in world standing of tonnage under construction—less than 5 per cent of the world total. The Legion and the Navy in appraising the defense readiness of our ocean shipping have maintained that there are "serious qualitative deficiencies" in sealift capacity. Nearly 90 per cent of U.S. dry-cargo ships are rusty World War II vintage vessels, and better than half of the U.S. tankers are the same. The American Legion maintains that a modern Merchant Marine is a necessary adjunct of national security and could be considered a sound financial investment if put on a competitive basis with foreign flag vessels. It urges use of private U.S. yards for building and maintenance. The Legion conducts informational programs and is in close contact with Merchant Marine leaders, just as it is with the Department of Defense, the military services, the Navy League on naval affairs, and the Association of the U.S. Army on military matters.

Long conscious of the nation's civil defense needs, the Legion has been a prime instrument in achieving the civil defense programs that we have today. This is especially true because of a working relationship with the Office of Civil Defense, the Office of Emergency Planning and the National Security Commission. The Legion coordinates and builds its program through its network of more than sixteen thousand posts. Programs singled out for top priority by the Legion in recent testimony to Congress included:

1. The Federal Shelter Survey, to identify, mark and stock shelter spaces.

2. The Federal Shelter Incentive Program to provide federal financial grants to institutions to build fallout shelters in schools, hospitals and welfare facilities.

3. Establishment of an improved warning system, attack-proof communications system and automatic radioactive fallout monitoring system.

4. Development of post-attack plans to provide for continuity of government and resource management.

Departments and posts are urged to set up National Security Commissions to assist in implementing the national program. These state and local groups have proved effective in forwarding many ideas to the national commission. They are active, too, in recruiting and supporting Reserve and National Guard components, sponsoring tours of defense installations, assisting in Light Duty, Rescue and Fallout Shelter programs, participating in The American Legion Blood Donor Program and promoting the National Aerospace Program, co-sponsored by The American Legion Civil Air Patrol and the National Aero-Space Education Council.

In 1964, National Commander Daniel Foley, after traveling 225,-000 miles, visiting every state and journeying to seventeen foreign countries, directed his convention remarks to the international scene, pointing out that the Legion felt that the defense of freedom in South Vietnam was essential to a defense of freedom in all Southeast Asia. He praised the President and his forceful positions.

The Legion has urged the Nation to be wary of changes in the "communist line," such as policies pursued by the Soviet Union under the terms coexistence and *détente*. It has emphasized the application of preponderant power in Viet Nam. Speaking to delegates at the Portland Convention in 1965, National Commander Donald E. Johnson pointed out:

> While we never have pretended to be experts on the situation in South Viet Nam, there is no question but what these top level briefings which were as complete as could be hoped for, and a first hand look at the battle arena and the work that our forces are doing there, have helped us to speak a great deal more authoritatively on behalf of the national security and foreign relations positions of The American Legion as adopted by our Dallas Convention.
>
> The policies of The American Legion in this respect are now largely the policies of the United States in that our Government, from President Johnson on down, has indicated to friend and foe alike that America stands prepared to fulfill her commitments to world freedom.
>
> During this past year we have seen a tremendous build-up of American forces in South Viet Nam, and I would remind you

once more of the wording of a foreign-relations resolution emanating from the Dallas Convention which said in part:

"The American Legion fully supports the continued assistance by the United States to the people and governments of South Viet Nam, Laos and Malaysia in countering aggression, and urges the increased commitment of American forces and full employment of those military measures which promise early and complete destruction of the forces of aggression—both at the places of their attacks and at their sources of power as military judgment decides. . . ."

The American Legion does not delude itself, nor would we mislead the American people into thinking there is any quick or easy solution to the difficult and dangerous problem of Viet Nam. Yet, we see no alternative to firmness, backed by strength, in dealing with Communist aggression in South Viet Nam or anywhere else in the world.

The Legion's firm stand on Viet Nam continued in 1966.

Thus the Legion fortuitously urged and fought for a strong America since the end of World War II. It recognized at that time that the United States is the only power militarily, industrially, financially, and perhaps morally that can provide the sort of global commitment required of Western thought and institutions in the gangland atmosphere that has descended upon many parts of the earth.

25

A Summing Up

THE panorama of national and world affairs, of American life and of American Legion endeavors over close to half a century may now be viewed with a sense of proportion and a degree of perspective. This tumultuous, revolutionary epoch has tried all the stays and fittings, all the skills and genius of the Republic.

In this period The American Legion has shown a great capacity for growth and what that growth entails—fuller recognition of its responsibilities, a finer skill in promoting its activities in the community and in its relations with government and an appreciation of the infinitely more complex society and world in which we live. This has required a growing understanding and perseverance as well as the virtues of considered judgment and constant resourcefulness.

One source of the Legion's power and influence is the nature of our democracy with its unique political institutions, the absence of hard class lines or a self-perpetuating ruling elite and the prominent role played by organized groups. The Legion is an example of that unusual American ability for solving problems through concerted, voluntary action. Legionnaires find that they can do this especially well in communities, states and the nation through their organization. In peace, men and women band together to improve conditions which concern them. And in time of crisis, when a remote Federal bureaucracy cannot inspire the full allegiance of citizens, there will be smaller units, made up of the citizens themselves, that will promote that necessary allegiance. The conduct of draft boards during World War II, their smooth operation and public acceptance of their decisions relied upon this principle. Legionnaires comprised a majority on most of these local units.

That the Legion survived its beginnings is a tribute to those who participated in its early deliberations. An appreciation of the danger of political affiliation prevailed, and the principle of nonpartisanship was established. Over the years most Legionnaires have guarded against embroiling the Legion in politics. This does not mean that the Legion has refrained from speaking out on public issues or avoided disputes. Its history is in part a stormy account of differences with Presidents, Administrations, the Congress, notable public figures, the press, and its avowed enemies. At times The American Legion has been the target of influential newspapers and journalists. It followed the lonely trail of unpopular causes, and sometimes despaired of winning more widespread support. But, increasingly, it came to recognize the importance of explaining its objectives. Today, Legionnaires are better informed and more articulate in expressing positions of concern to the Legion and to the Republic.

Within the Legion there have always been differences of opinion. Many Legionnaires disagree with convention resolutions and efforts of their national organization and officers in carrying out convention mandates. However, a capacity for compromise has averted divisive factionalism.

The Legion has managed to remain the most influential veterans' association in the world through a combination of fortuitous circumstances, decisions and leadership. Hard work, resourcefulness and the devotion of hundreds of thousands of Legionnaires and members of the Auxiliary have been the foundation for this achievement. That the Legion has attracted many veterans of World War II and the Korean conflict and may draw membership from veterans of the nation's cold war campaigns gives Legionnaires confidence that their traditions and programs will be carried on in the years ahead.

Like virtually all organizations, our two political parties and every individual in our society, The American Legion and its members have acted unwisely in the past and may do so in the future. These have been occasions when the Legion or Legionnaires have moved away from principles enunciated in their Constitution or, by commission or omission, have failed to live up to the standards and spirit that conform to the ideals of the Republic. Conscientious efforts have usually corrected the relatively few mistaken judgments and ill-advised courses on national, department and post levels.

Occasionally, posts and individuals have gained publicity by taking positions which are neither endorsed nor condoned by the national organization. This has sometimes involved the principle of freedom of speech, a small group opposing the appearance of a controversial speaker or, at times, the censure of a faculty member in a local school. Post, department and national commanders have intervened at such times to insure freedom of speech. There has also been infrequent use of the Legion, unauthorized and of limited scope, in partisan politics. Such activity has been quickly disavowed by the national organization and can lead to suspension of offending units. However, since an iron discipline does not run through the organization, the activities of certain posts and individuals have been an occasional source of embarrassment. Persuasion has generally corrected matters.

Legion disputes with newspapers have usually been of short duration, handled effectively by the NEC, commissions or the National Commander. Significantly, the Legion has fought for freedom of the press over the years. A notable example occurred in 1943 when Commander Waring put the weight of the national organization behind the Associated Press, under Federal antitrust attack, maintaining that the government was leaning too heavily on the Bill of Rights.

Frequently, there have been charges within the Legion that its leadership is often determined by the so-called king-makers. Indeed, in the Legion, as in most organized groups, certain individuals exercise great influence in the selection and promotion of men to high office. If this condition is to be changed, those who level the charges must work toward a greater influence within the Legion to promote their views.

While many Legionnaires have expressed the opinion that the Legion's destiny is in community activities, there is little likelihood that its influence in legislative matters, on administration policies and on public opinion will waste away. Achievements must be consolidated and guarded. Ability and judgment must not fall into disuse. For the nation relies upon the expression of opinions by individuals and organized groups in resolving its policies. This holds true for many

Legion activities, including its national security and foreign relations programs.

In its defense and foreign policy efforts the Legion has experienced many of its hardest reverses and most lustrous victories. Legionnaires have always contended that those who know war have an imperative obligation to look to the nation's defenses. The whole experience of war is theirs from defeats and triumphs, from anger and frustration brought on by stupidity, public apathy and the omissions of government to the exultation of national achievement. For most, war is not remembered as the movement of lines and positions on a map, nor casualties as figures on a piece of paper. The interruption of most veterans' lives was lived out in smaller events that may not have seemed to fit into a "big picture" at the time. The experience was often reduced to personal survival, the confines of boredom, a boiler room, a gun turret, a foxhole, or a listening post beyond the last barbed wire when the sweat ran cold down the ribs. Casualties were friends, gone or broken, the blood running through the fingers, the racking disease. But senseless confusion, waste, mud and cold, heat and sweat, loss and suffering, and tedious days and nights were leavened by comradeship, courage, unselfishness, and a sense of purpose. The bad and the good have given the generations of Legionnaires an incentive and basis for their unending endeavors to serve the Republic, their communities, the disabled, youth, the dispossessed, and the needy.

Perhaps it is too harsh to say that Americans have lost much of the spiritual strength, the patriotism, the initiative, and the toughness that is their heritage. It is true that cynicism is widespread. Failure of the public trust by those in high places arises. Individualism is often blighted by the craving for security. And many adults fail the nation's youth in numerous ways. Many Americans are embarrassed by the nation's achievements, wealth and ability to extend aid around the world to shore up the defenses of liberty. Others blush at the mention of honor, patriotism, national interest, and the imperishable principles set forth in the Declaration of Independence, the Gettysburg Address and other documents of American history.

Still, young Americans on the firing line today disprove the expectations of the pessimists and cynics among us. They astonish their enemy, schooled to believe that Americans are "decadent and soft."

This does not mean that all is well. There is room for vast improvement. The testing will continue for years to come, for our adversaries are capable in all types of warfare—conventional, irregular, political, propaganda, and cultural. And there are hidden traps and camouflaged snares and dangers, not of any enemy's doing but products of our own shortcomings. However, there is reason for hope. Most Americans are made of sterner stuff than the stereotype their critics never tire of depicting, and, increasingly, individuals and groups are working to strengthen America at the local level. As one astute Legionnaire noted:

> Today our emphasis centers more and more on the community, now that so many national goals related to the disabled of our wars, the veteran, national defense, and other objectives are on the statute books and supported by the people. Community service is the backbone of our success.

Thus, Legionnaires and other citizens in civic groups serve the nation. The work of individual Legionnaires and posts in thousands of American and overseas communities has been, and continues to be, a vital force in our common life. Wars take a terrible toll, and all too often fail to achieve the purposes and ideals for which they are fought. But the Legion, born in the aftermath of a world conflict, reinforced by World War II and the Korean War, turned its energies to the endless battles of peace—against apathy, social decay, delinquency, the neglect of those who are in need, and forgetfulness of national ideals. This struggle is never won, but the line can be held and advanced. And on that line Legionnaires have stood firmly, a force for the good life for all.

Formidable challenges are at our elbow, and awesome trials of masked duration await us. Yet we are not the progeny of fearful men. Great causes endure. Great words are indelible. What honor, what faith, and what strength we have sustain us and oblige us to pass these things on to posterity. So long as we keep this trust as individuals and through free institutions, among them The American Legion, the Republic shall remain steadfast. We will persevere and we will prevail.

Appendix

NATIONAL COMMANDERS

Five men who presided as Temporary Chairmen or Chairmen at Paris and St. Louis Caucuses in 1919 were voted titles of past National Commanders: Henry D. Lindsley, Tex., 1919; Milton J. Foreman, Ill., 1921; Bennett Champ Clark, Mo., 1926; Theodore Roosevelt, Jr., N.Y., 1949; and Eric Fisher Wood, Pa., 1955.

Franklin D'Olier, Pa.	1919–20	Roane Waring, Tenn.	1942–43
Frederick W. Galbraith, Jr., Ohio		Warren H. Atherton, Cal.	1943–44
	1920–21	Edward N. Scheiberling, N.Y.	
John G. Emery, Mich.			1944–45
	6-14-21–11-2-21	John Stelle, Ill.	1945–46
Hanford MacNider, Ia.	1921–22	Paul H. Griffith, Pa.	1946–47
Alvin M. Owsley, Tex.	1922–23	James F. O'Neil, N.H.	1947–48
John R. Quinn, Cal.	1923–24	S. Perry Brown, Tex.	1948–49
James A. Drain, Wash.	1924–25	George N. Craig, Ind.	1949–50
John R. McQuigg, Ohio	1925–26	Erle Cocke, Jr., Ga.	1950–51
Howard P. Savage, Ill.	1926–27	Donald R. Wilson, W.Va.	1951–52
Edward E. Spafford, N.Y.	1927–28	Lewis K. Gough, Cal.	1952–53
Paul V. McNutt, Ind.	1928–29	Arthur J. Connell, Conn.	1953–54
O. L. Bodenhamer, Ark.	1929–30	Seaborn P. Collins, N.M.	1954–55
Ralph T. O'Neil, Kans.	1930–31	J. Addington Wagner, Mich.	
Henry L. Stevens, Jr., N.C.			1955–56
	1931–32	W. C. (Dan) Daniel, Va.	1956–57
Louis A. Johnson, W.Va.	1932–33	John S. Gleason, Jr., Ill.	1957–58
Edward A. Hayes, Ill.	1933–34	Preston J. Moore, Okla.	1958–59
Frank N. Belgrano, Cal.	1934–35	Martin B. McKneally, N.Y.	
Ray Murphy, Ia.	1935–36		1959–60
Harry W. Colmery, Kans.	1936–37	William R. Burke, Cal.	1960–61
Daniel J. Doherty, Mass.	1937–38	Charles L. Bacon, Mo.	1961–62
Stephen F. Chadwick, Wash.		James E. Powers, Ga.	1962–63
	1938–39	Daniel F. Foley, Minn.	1963–64
Raymond J. Kelly, Mich.	1939–40	Donald E. Johnson, Ia.	1964–65
Milo J. Warner, Ohio	1940–41	L. Eldon James, Va.	1965–66
Lynn U. Stambaugh, N.D.	1941–42		

AMERICAN LEGION AUXILIARY
NATIONAL PRESIDENTS

Mrs. Lowell F. Hobart, Sr., Ohio
1921–22
Dr. Kate Waller Barrett, Va.
1922–23
Mrs. Franklin Lee Bishop, Mass.
1923–24
Mrs. O. D. Oliphant, N.J.   1924–25
Mrs. Eliza London Shepard, Cal.
1925–26
Mrs. John William Macauley, Wis.
1926–27
Mrs. Robert Walbridge, Mass.
1927–28
Mrs. Boyce Ficklen, Ga.   1928–29
Mrs. Donald Macrae, Ia.   1929–30
Mrs. Robert Lincoln Hoyal, Ariz.
1930–31
Mrs. Frederick C. Williams, N.Y.
1931–32
Mrs. S. Alford Blackburn, Ky.
1932–33
Mrs. William H. Biester, Jr., Pa.
1933–34
Mrs. Albin C. Carlson, Minn.
1934–35
Mrs. Melville Mucklestone, Ill.
1935–36
Mrs. Oscar W. Hahn, Neb.
1936–37
Mrs. Malcolm Douglas, Wash.
1937–38
Mrs. James Morris, N.D.   1938–39
Mrs. William H. Corwith, N.Y.
1939–40
Mrs. Louis J. Lemstra, Ind.
1940–41
Mrs. Mark W. Murrill, Mass.
1941–42
Mrs. Alfred J. Mathebat, Cal.
1942–43

Mrs. Lawrence H. Smith, Wis.
1943–44
Mrs. Charles B. Gilbert, Conn.
1944–45
Mrs. Walter G. Craven, N.C.
1945–46
Mrs. Norton H. Pearl, Mich.
1946–47
Mrs. Lee W. Hutton, Minn.
1947–48
Mrs. Hubert A. Goode, Ore.
1948–49
Mrs. Norman L. Sheehe, Ill.
1949–50
Mrs. Willis C. Reed, Okla. 1950–51
Mrs. E. A. Campbell, La.   1951–52
Mrs. Rae Ashton, Utah   1952–53
Mrs. Harold S. Burdett, N.Y.
1953–54
Mrs. Percy A. Lainson, Ia.
1954–55
Mrs. Bowden D. Ward, W.Va.
1955–56
Mrs. Carl W. Zeller, Ohio 1956–57
Mrs. J. Pat Kelly, Ga.   1957–58
Mrs. Charles W. Gunn, Ore.
1958–59
Mrs. Alexander H. Gray, Tenn.
1959–60
Mrs. Henry Ahnemiller, Wash.
1960–61
Mrs. J. Howard McKay, Pa.
1961–62
Mrs. O. L. Koger, Kans.   1962–63
Mrs. Luther D. Johnson, Neb.
1963–64
Mrs. Walter W. Andrews, Ala.
1964–65
Mrs. Walter H. Glynn, Ind. 1965–66

NATIONAL VICE COMMANDERS

1919–20
Allan A. Tukey, Neb.
Joyce S. Lewis, Minn.
Alden B. Chambers, Mass.
Wm. B. Follett, Ore.
James O'Brien, Cal.

1920–21
John G. Emery, Mich.
Thomas Goldingay, N.J.
Claudius G. Pendill, Wis.
J. G. Scrugham, Nev.
E. Jackson Winslett, Ala.

1921–22
George L. Berry, Tenn.
Raymond O. Brackett, Mass.
H. Nelson Jackson, Vt.
Charles H. Kendrick, Cal.
John A. McCormack, Colo.

1922–23
Edward J. Barrett, Wis.
Watson B. Miller, D.C.
E. E. Cocke, Ga.
Robert O. Blood, N.H.
C. P. Plummer, Wyo.

1923–24
Ira Thurman Mann, N.C.
F. Ryan Duffy, Wis.
Celora M. Stoddard, Ariz.
Lester F. Albert, Ida.
Wm. B. Healy, Pa.

1924–25
Frank McFarland, Cal.
Eugene Armstrong, Conn.
A. L. Perry, Panama, C.Z.
Wm. Stern, N.D.
Peyton H. Hoge, Jr., Ky.

1925–26
Joseph Y. Cheney, Fla.
Hughes B. Davis, Okla.
Vincent A. Carroll, Pa.
Raymond B. Littlefield, R.I.
Judge J. A. Howell, Utah

1926–27
J. G. Sims, Tenn.
C. Thomas Busha, Jr., Mont.
Dr. John G. Towne, Me.
John E. Curtiss, Neb.
Stafford King, Minn.

1927–28
John T. Raftis, Wash.
Ralph T. O'Neil, Kans.
Paul R. Younts, N.C.
Dan Spurlock, La.
J. M. Henry, Minn.

1928–29
Lawrence E. McGann, Jr., Ill.
George W. Malone, Nev.
E. L. White, Conn.
Miller C. Foster, S.C.
Walton D. Hood, Tex.

1929–30
Milt D. Campbell, Ohio
John J. Dugan, Del.
Frank Schoble, Jr., Pa.
Morton M. David, Colo.

1930–31
Dr. Neal D. Williams, Mo.
Dr. James A. Duff., W.Va.
Harry B. Henderson, Jr., Wyo.
Bert S. Hyland, Vt.
Roland B. Howell, La.

1931–32
Richard F. Paul, Mass.
Harold L. Plummer, Wis.
Forrest G. Cooper, Miss.
Roy L. Cook, N.M.
Frank N. Brooks, Wash.

1932–33
Russell Meadows, Ariz.
Robert D. Flory, Neb.
Wm. E. Easterwood, Jr., Tex.
John J. Maloney, Me.
Chas. A. Mills, Fla.

1933–34

Chas. R. Mabey, Utah
R. L. Gordon, Ark.
Miguel Munoz, P.R.
Ed Carruth, Kans.
Chas. L. Woolley, R.I.

1934–35

Daniel J. Doherty, Mass.
Harold J. Warner, Ore.
John K. Kennelly, N.D.
Milo J. Warner, Ohio
Quimby Melton, Ga.

1935–36

Raymond F. Gates, Conn.
Dr. W. E. Whitlock, Fla.
Oscar W. Worthwine, Ida.
Dr. F. Whitney Godwin, Va.
Louis R. Probst, Wyo.

1936–37

Salvatore A. Capodice, Cal.
Leo A. Temmey, S.D.
Leonard Sisk, Tenn.
J. Fred Johnson, Jr., Ala.
Jack Crowley, D.C.

1937–38

Drury M. Phillips, Tex.
Phil M. Conley, W.Va.
Harry M. Johnson, Mont.
James F. Daniel, Jr., S.C.
James R. Mahaffy, Hawaii

1938–39

Edward J. Quinn, Me.
Charles W. Crush, Va.
Earl T. Ross, Nev.
James T. Crawley, Miss.
Henry C. Oakey, Wis.

1939–40

Leo E. Ray, N.H.
Charles Q. Kelley, D.C.
Matthew J. Murphy, Ill.
James B. Fitzgerald, Md.
H. Elwyn Davis, Colo.

1940–41

Erwin A. Froyd, Wyo.
James L. McCrory, Neb.
Harold P. Redden, Mass.
Edward R. Stirling, Pa.
Alcee S. Legendre, La.

1941–42

W. C. Sawyer, Ariz.
Wm. DeLacey Allen, Ga.
Charles E. Booth, W.Va.
V. M. Armstrong, Ind.
John F. Sullivan, Vt.

1942–43

John T. Batten, Ala.
Fred G. Fraser, D.C.
Arthur J. Connell, Conn.
Herman H. Lark, Mo.
Jefferson Davis Atwood, N.M.

1943–44

Martin V. Coffey, Ohio
E. A. Littlefield, Utah
Roy L. McMillan, N.C.
Edward A. Mulrooney, Del.
Hector G. Staples, Me.

1944–45

Bascom F. Jones, Tenn.
Frank E. McCaffrey, R.I.
Dan McDade, Ore.
Ray S. Pierson, Kans.
William P. Shadoan, Ky.

1945–46

R. Graham Huntington, N.J.
Fred Laboon, Kans.
Sam L. Latimer, Jr., S.C.
Dudley Swim, Ida.
Jeremiah Twomey, Mass.

1946–47

Richard C. Cadwallader, La.
Joseph W. Brown, N.H.
Edward J. Sharkey, Cal.
Ernest H. Dervishian, Va.
Martin B. Buckner, Mich.

1947–48

Albert A. Cree, Vt.
Myron R. Renick, W.Va.
Joe W. White, Ga.
Richard B. Ott, Wash.
L. W. Barns, S.D.

1948–49

James Lane, Ala.
Leonard W. Moody, Ark.
James Annin, Mont.
Edward J. Kelly, Conn.
Walter E. Alessandroni, Pa.

1949–50

Frank E. Lowe, Me.
Dr. D. R. Perry, N.C.
Dave H. Fleischer, Mo.
J. E. Martie, Nev.
Milton G. Boock, Minn.

1950–51

Joe H. Adams, Fla.
Herbert J. Jacobi, D.C.
Felix Pogliano, Colo.
Lewis K. Gough, Cal.
Frederick C. Bramlage, Kans.

1951–52

Adolph F. Bremer, Minn.
Frank R. Kelley, Mass.
Thomas E. Paradine, N.Y.
Oscar B. Rohlff, Wyo.
Audley H. Ward, S.C.

1952–53

William Ralph Bourdon, Ariz.
Lyon Wright Brandon, Miss.
Wilbur C. Daniel, Va.
Harry V. Groome, N.J.
J. Addington Wagner, Mich.

1953–54

John A. High, N.H.
Dr. Deward H. Reed, N.M.
Truman C. Wold, N.D.
Herbert M. Walker, Pa.
Thomas W. Bird, N.C.

1954–55

Leonard L. Jackson, La.
Patrick H. Mangan, Jr., Vt.
Howard C. Kingdom, Ohio
Dr. Carl J. Rees, Del.
Robert L. Shelby, Utah

1955–56

Guy O. Stone, Ga.
John H. Van Horn, Alaska
L. Everett Page, Tex.
James V. Day, D.C.
Gilman H. Stordock, Wis.
William J. Holliman, D.C.

1956–57

J. Edward Walter, Md.
Gaylor M. Brown, Ia.
Carl R. Moser, Ore.
John F. Stay, Pa.
George T. Lewis, Jr., Tenn.

1957–58

William A. Cottrell, Hawaii
Ramon R. Guas, P.R.
Harry W. Miller, W.Va.
Lee A. Lemos, R.I.
Isadore E. Levine, Ind.

1958–59

C. D. DeLoach, D.C.
John W. Collins, Pa.
James B. Kerrigan, Mo.
Robert Charles Smith, La.
James C. Bangs, Ida.

1959–60

Nate V. Keller, Minn.
Willard W. Brandt, N.D.
A. Layman Harman, S.C.
Charles C. McGonegal, Cal.
Corydon T. Hill, Cal.
William A. Brennan, Jr., Ind.
Frank Gianotti, Minn.

1960–61

George K. Walker, Mass.
James M. Wagonseller, Ohio
Vincent J. Maxheim, Ia.
Dr. Harry H. Kretzler, Wash.
R. C. Godwin, N.C.

1961–62

Walter W. Barnard, Mont.
Edward T. Hoak, Pa.
Wilson H. Morrison, Mich.
J. Milton Patrick, Okla.
Edward Wysocki, N.J.

1962–63

Claude A. Hamilton, S.D.
Paschal C. Reese, Fla.
Harold D. Beaton, D.C.
James W. Doon, N.H.
Victor F. Whittlesea, Nev.

1963–64

Garland D. Murphy, Jr., Ark.
Earl D. Franklin, Jr., Colo.

Harry Wright, Mex.
Emilio S. Iglesias, Vt.
George Emory Sipple, Wis.

1964–65

Edward H. Lynch, Jr., Conn.
Joseph Paul, Mich.
Herbert D. Black, S.C.
Ward W. Husted, Wyo.
David Aronberg, Ky.

1965–66

A. R. Choppin, La.
William J. Rogers, Me.
William E. Galbraith, Neb.
Soleng Tom, Ariz.
Robert O. Phillips, P.I.

NATIONAL ADJUTANTS

Lemuel Bolles, Wash.
                          11-13-19–2-1-24
Russell G. Creviston, Ind.
                          2-1-24–7-31-25
James F. Barton, Ia.
                          8-1-25–9-15-32
Frank Edward Samuel, Kans.
                          11-14-32–7-25-43

Donald G. Glascoff, Mich. (acting)
                          7-27-43–9-23-43
Donald G. Glascoff, Mich.
                          9-23-43–1-31-48
Henry H. Dudley, Neb. (acting)
                          2-1-48–5-5-48
Henry H. Dudley, Neb.
                          5-5-48–7-1-56
Emil A. Blackmore, Wyo. 7-1-56–

ASSISTANT NATIONAL ADJUTANTS

Russell G. Creviston, Ind.
                          1919–2-1-24
No Record   2-1-24–4-4-25
James F. Barton, Ia. 4-4-25–8-1-25
No Record   8-1-25–1-15-26
Frank E. Samuel, Kans.
                          1-15-26–11-14-32
Harold L. Plummer, Wis.
                          10-1-32–2-15-40
Donald G. Glascoff, Mich.
                          4-22-40–7-27-43
Henry H. Dudley, Neb.
                          10-1-43–2-1-48

Robert R. Poston, Tex. (acting)
                          2-1-48–5-1-48
Robert R. Poston, Tex.
                          5-1-48–2-14-49
Joe E. Rabinovich, N.D.
                          5-1-48–11-7-49
William E. Sayer, Jr., Ind.
                          10-24-49–12-31-52
Emil A. Blackmore, Wyo.
                          1-5-53–7-1-56
Robert E. Lynch, Colo.   7-1-56–

NATIONAL JUDGE ADVOCATES

Robert A. Adams, Ind.   1919–27
Scott W. Lucas, Ind. 1927–6-24-31
Robert A. Adams, Ind.
                          6-24-31–9-24-31

Remster A. Bingham, Ind.
                          9-24-31–34
James A. Drain, Wash.   1934–35
Ralph B. Gregg, Ind. 1935–7-8-60
Bertram G. Davis, N.Y.   7-8-60–

NATIONAL CHAPLAINS

Thomas H. Wiles, Colo.   1919–
Rev. Francis A. Kelly, N.Y.
1919–20
Rev. John W. Inzer, Tenn.
1920–21
Rev. Earl A. Blackman, Kans.
1921–22
Rev. Wm. P. O'Connor, Ohio
1922–23
Rev. Ezra Clemens, Minn.
1923–24
Rev. Joseph M. Lonergan, Ill.
1924–25
Rev. Wm. E. Patrick, Cal. 1925–26
Rev. Joseph L. N. Wolfe, Pa.
1926–27
Rev. Gill Robb Wilson, N.J.
1927–28
Rabbi Lee J. Levinger, Del.
1928–29
Rev. George F. Kettell, D.D., N.Y.
1929–30
Rev. Jos. N. Barnett, Wis. 1930–31
Rev. Harris A. Darche, Ill.
1931–32
Rev. Irwin Q. Wood, Ia.   1932–33
Rev. Robert J. White, Mass.
1933–34
Rev. Dr. Park W. Huntington, Sr.,
Del.   1934–35
Rt. Rev. Msgr. Thomas D. Kennedy,
Mo.   1935–36
Rev. Bryan H. Keathley, D.D., Tex.
1936–37
Rev. Fr. Frank J. Lawler, Ill.
1937–38
Rev. Jerome L. Fritsche, Neb.
1938–39
Msgr. Patrick N. McDermott, Ia.
1939–40
Brigadier Wm. G. Gilks, Tex.
1940–41
Rev. Frederick J. Halloran, N.J.
1941–42

Dr. Paul Def. Mortimore, Wash.
1942–43
Rev. John F. McManus, Kans.
1943–44
Rev. DeWitt C. Mallory, Fla.
1944–45
Rt. Rev. Msgr. Edward J. Smith, Ia.
1945–46
Rev. Arthur L. Rustad, Minn.
1946–47
Rev. Fr. Frank L. Harrington,
Mont.   1947–48
Rev. Thomas Grice, Cal.   1948–49
Rev. Fr. Edward J. Carney. O.S.A.,
Mass.   1949–50
Rabbi David Lefkowitz, La.
1950–51
Rev. Olaf G. Birkeland, Wis.
1951–52
Rev. Father John E. Duffy, Ohio
1952–53
Dr. Tom B. Clark, Okla.   1953–54
Rev. Albert J. Hoffman, Ia.
1954–55
Rev. Joseph MacCarroll, N.J.
1955–56
Rev. Bernard W. Gerdon, Ind.
1956–57
Rev. Feltham S. James, S.C.
1957–58
Rt. Rev. Msgr. John J. Twiss, Mass.
1958–59
Rabbi Robert I. Kahn, D.H.L., Tex.
1959–60
Rev. Wm. H. Moss, Tenn. 1960–61
Father Robert G. Keating, Conn.
1961–62
Rabbi Albert M. Shulman, Ind.
1962–63
The Rev. John J. Howard, Va.
1963–64
Rev. Fr. Morris N. Dummet, La.
1964–65
Rev. Alfred C. Thompson, N.Y.
1965–66

NATIONAL TREASURERS

Gaspar G. Bacon, Mass.
      11-13-19–12-20-19
Robert H. Tyndall, Ind.
      12-20-19–10-18-27
Bowman Elder, Ind.
      10-18-27–11-20-33

Neal Grider, Ind.
      11-20-33–11-1-34
James A. Drain, Wash.   1934–35
John R. Ruddick, Ind.
      1935-7-13-45
Neal Grider, Ind.   7-13-45–58
Francis Polen, Ind.   1958–

NATIONAL HISTORIANS

Eben Putnam, Mass.   1920–33
Thomas M. Owen, Jr., Ala.
      1933–48
Monte C. Sandlin, Ala.   1948–53
Robert T. Fairey, S.C.   1953–57

Mrs. Charles A. (Emily) Herbert,
   N.J.   1957–60
Glenn B. Hoover, Ia.   1960–61
Earl D. Young, Colo.   1961–62
H. Armand deMasi, Italy   1962–64
Harold A. Shindler, Ind.   1964–

NATIONAL SERGEANTS-AT-ARMS

Lewis P. Fields, Tex.   1927–28 *
No record   1928–29
William A. Carey, Mass.
      1929–30
Don Pierce, Kans.   1930–31
William D. Browne, Ore.
      1931–32
Henry Rhode, Ill.   1932–33
No record   1933–34
Rowan Howard, Tex.   1934–35
Ed I. Lindsay, Ia.   1935–36
Frank H. McFarland, Kans.
      1936–37
Richard A. Morrissey, Mass.
      1937–38
Andy Viland, Wash.   1938–39
John G. Dunn, Mich.   1939–40
Val Ove, Wis.   1940–41
William D. Browne, Ore.
      1941–42
Paul Dague, Pa.   1942–43
John E. "Jack" Short, Cal.
      1943–44
Edward F. O'Neill, N.Y.
      1944–45

George A. Dustin, Ill.   1945–46
Fred G. Fraser, D.C.   1946–47
Edward F. Humer, Fla.   1947–48
Richard C. Gusman, Tex.
      1948–49
John W. Webster, Ind.   1949–50
Thomas L. "Doc" Jennings, Ga.
      1950–51
Robert E. Lester, W.Va.
      1951–52
Harry E. Engelund, Cal.
      1952–56
C. Howard Larsen, N.Y.
      1956–60
Harry E. Engelund, Cal.
      1960–61
Kenneth Cruse, Mo.   1961–62
C. Howard Larsen, N.Y.
      1962–63
Frank C. Momsen, Minn.
      1963–64
C. Howard Larsen, N.Y.
      1964–65

* Have no record prior to 1927–28.

FÉDÉRATION INTERALLIÉE DES ANCIENS COMBATTANTS

Legion Officers

President

Thomas W. Miller, Del., 1925
Edward L. White, Conn., 1932

U.S.A. Vice President

Cabot Ward, France	1921–22	Lamar Jeffers, Ala.	1931
H. Nelson Jackson, Vt.	1923–24	Frank D. Rash, Ky.	1932
Roy Hoffman, Okla.	1925	Charles Hann, Jr., N.Y.	1933
Lemuel Bolles, Wash.	1926	Louis Johnson, W.Va.	1934
Henry D. Lindsley, Tex.	1927	Robert J. White, Mass.	1935–37
L. R. Gignilliat, Ind.	1928	Nathaniel Spear, Jr., Pa.	1938
E. Arthur Ball, Ind.	1929	F. Whitney Godwin, Va.	1939
Julius I. Peyser, D.C.	1930		

DIRECTORS OF DIVISIONS AND SECTIONS AT NATIONAL HEADQUARTERS, INDIANAPOLIS, INDIANA

Americanism

Garland W. Powell, Md.
(1923–1924)
Frank C. Cross, Md.   (1925–1927)
Dan Sowers, W.Va.   (1927–1930)
Russell Cook, Ind.   (1930–1934)
Homer L. Chaillaux, Cal.
(1934–1945)
Elmer W. Sherwood, Ind.
(1945–1946)
W. C. "Tom" Sawyer, Ariz.
(1947–1950)
Allen B. Willand, N.Y.
(1950–1953)
Lee R. Pennington, D.C.
(1953–1956)
C. A. "Bud" Tesch, W.Va.
(1956–1963)
Maurice T. "Spider" Webb, Ga.
(1963–   )

Child Welfare

John W. Gorby, Ill.   (1925–1926)
Miss Emma C. Puschner, Mo.
(1927–1950)
Randel Shake, Ind.   (1950–   )

Emblem

E. O. Marquette, Ind.
(1924–1945)
Carlos A. Morris, Ind.
(1945–1957)
James S. Whitfield, Mo.
(1957–   )

Field Service

Jack M. Oakey, Colo.
(1943–1954)
Nicholas Lynch, Jr., N.Y.
(1954–   )

Finance
(National Comptroller)

Glen D. Crawford, Ind.
(1920–1960)
Robert R. Fleming, Ind.
(1960–   )

Membership
Charles M. "Chuck" Wilson, Ill.
                        (1949–1957)
George W. Rulon, N.D.
                        (1957–1961)
C. W. "Pat" Geile, Ind.
                        (1961–   )

Publicity
Fred C. Condict, Mo.
                        (1921–1922)
   and again from   (1928–1934)
Frederick C. Painton, Ind.
                        (1923–1928)
Harold K. Philips, D.C.
                        (1934–1937)
Edward McGrail, W.Va.
                        (1937–1945)
   (with military leave from 1942 to
1945)

Public Relations
(formerly Publicity)
Raymond H. Fields, Okla.
                        (1945–1949)
Edward F. McGinnis, Ill.
                        (1949–1954)

Publications
James F. Barton, Ia.   (1932–1950)
   (Manager and Director)
Irving N. Larson, Ind.
                        (1950–1959)
Dean B. Nelson, Va.   (1959–   )

Librarian
Mrs. Verna B. Grimm, Wash.
                        (1925–1957)
Thomas V. Hull, Ind.
                        (1957–   )

DIVISION DIRECTORS AT NATIONAL HEADQUARTERS, WASHINGTON, D.C.

Economic
Elbert H. Burns, Ill.   (1947–49)
Ralph H. Lavers, Mass. (1949–54)
Clarence W. Bird, Vt.   (1954–   )

Legislative
John Thomas Taylor, Penn.
                        (1945–49)
Miles D. Kennedy, N.Y.
                        (1949–62)
Clarence H. Olson, Mont.
                        (1962–64)
Herald E. Stringer, Alaska
                        1964–   )

Rehabilitation
Watson Miller, Md.   (1923–41)
T. O. Kraabel, N.D.   (1941–58)
John J. Corcoran, N.Y. (1958–   )

Public Relations
(formerly Publicity, continued
      from 1954)
George J. Kelly, Va.   (1955–56)
James V. Day, Me.   (1956–61)

Charles J. Arnold, Ind.   (1961–63)
James C. Watkins, Md.   (1963–   )

National Security
Milton D. Campbell, Ohio
                        (1942–1948)
Martin B. Buckner, Mich.
                        (1948–1952)
James R. Wilson, Jr., Pa.
                        (1952–   )

Foreign Relations
Under direction of Director of
   Washington Office

Director of Washington Office
Paul Griffith   (1935–44)
Elbert H. Burns   (1944–46)
Leonce R. Legendre   (1946–51)
William F. Hauck   (1952–   )

NATIONAL EXECUTIVE COMMITTEEMEN

Alabama

Crampton F. Harris	(1919–20)	E. R. Wren	(1930–32)
E. Jackson Winslett	(1920–21)	Rufus H. Bethea	(1932–34)
Frank M. Dixon	(1921–22)	Catesby R. Jones	(1934–36)
Walter E. Bare	(1922–25)	Dr. Francis Marion Inge	
Mathew H. Murphy	(1925–26)		(1936–44)
M. E. Frohlich	(1926–28)	George L. Cleere	(1944–50)
Headley E. Jordon	(1928–30)	Hugh W. Overton	(1950–)

Alaska

George A. Getchell		Ralph R. Reeser	(1932–34)
	(1919–May, 1920)	John A. Talbot	(1934–36)
Walter B. King	(May–Oct., 1920)	Anthony E. Karnes	(1936–38)
Harold F. Dawes	(1920–21)	Clyde R. Ellis	(1938–39)
Homer G. Nordling	(1921–22)	Roland H. Stock	(1939–48)
N. R. Walker	(1922–23)	Walter B. King	(1948–50)
John A. Talbot	(1923–25)	Perry S. McLain	(1950–52)
Dayton W. Stoddard	(1925–26)	John H. Van Horn	(1952–54)
Nicholas Nussbaumer	(1926–28)	Perry S. McLain	(1954–56)
Howard J. Thompson	(1928–30)	Herald E. Stringer	(1956–64)
David Adler	(1930–32)	George Petrovich	(1964–)

Arizona

Clifford C. Faires		John H. Moeur	(12-31-29–34)
	(3-11-20-9-29-20)	Irving A. Jennings	(1934–2-3-40)
Andrew P. Martin	(1920–21)	W. C. "Tom" Sawyer	
Bert H. Clingan	(1921–22)		(2-3-40–8-24-40)
Duane Bird	(1922–23)	William R. Bourdon	(1940–42)
John P. Greeway	(1923–24)	Al N. Zellmer	(1942–46)
George V. Hays	(1924–26)	William R. Bourdon	(1946–48)
A. J. Dougherty	(1926-2-15-28)	John R. Stille	(1948–56)
W. V. DeCamp		Calvin R. Sanders	(1956–60)
	(2-15-28–8-23-28)	Soleng Tom	(1960–54)
W. Paul Geary	(1928–12-5-29)	Ralph A. Watkins, Jr.	(1964–)

Arkansas

Thomas A. Jackson		Robert L. Gordon	(1931–33)
	(2-24-20–3-26-20)	Oran J. Vaughan	(1933–35)
Frank B. Nelson		Charles Q. Kelley	(1935–37)
	(3-26-20–8-27-20)	James H. Graves	(1937–39)
Joseph F. W. Morrison	(1920–21)	Sam Rorex	(1939–46)
Dr. L. J. Kosminsky	(1921–23)	Jordan B. Lambert	(1946–47)
J. Robert Reichardt	(1923–25)	Guy Hendrix Lackey, Sr.	
Frank D. Clancy, Jr.	(1925–27)		(1947–49)
O. L. Bodenhamer	(1927–29)	Harry G. Miller	(1949–51)
Frank D. Clancy, Jr.	(1929–31)	Leonard W. Moody	(1951–53)

Sam Rorex   (1953–55)   Marshall Blackard   (1961–63)
Dr. Garland D. Murphy, Jr.   Claude B. Carpenter, Jr.
                         (1955–59)   (1963–65)
Abe J. Davidson   (1959–61)   Ulys. A. Lovell   (1965–   )

California

Walter K. Tuller   (1919–20)   Joseph S. Long   (1938–40)
Charles H. Kendrick   (1920–21)   Thomas J. Riordan   (1940–42)
Buron R. Fitts   (1921–22)   Leon V. McCardle   (1942–44)
John R. Quinn   (1922–23)   Leon E. Happell   (1944–46)
Seth Millington, Jr.   (1923–24)   William P. Haughton   (1946–48)
George J. Hatfield   (1924–26)   Edward W. Bolt   (1948–49)
Nathan F. Coombs   (1926–28)   Harry L. Foster   (1949–52)
Philip Dodson   (1928–30)   Jack F. Ahern   (1952–54)
Frank N. Belgrano, Jr.   (1930–32)   William R. Burke   (1954–56)
Bertrand W. Gearhart   (1932–34)   Malcolm M. Champlin   (1956–58)
Homer L. Chaillaux   Alfred P. Chamie   (1958–60)
                    (1934–1-22-35)   John J. Flynn   (1960–62)
Clifton A. Hix   (1-22-35–36)   Roscoe T. Morse   (1962–64)
Warren H. Atherton   (1936–38)   A. Lee Oder   (1964–   )

Canada

Howard Bird   (1923–24)   Clarence M. Simpson   (1934–36)
William H. Wardwell   (1924–26)   Paul G. Hinder   (1936–40)
Christian A. Thomson   (1926–28)   Clarence M. Simpson   (1940–52)
Carl B. Cooper   (1928–30)   John B. Finucane   (1952–62)
Harry J. Bohme   (1930–31)   Francis S. Kaszas   (1962–64)
W. N. Millar   (1931–32)   Forrest Monner   (1964–   )
Albert C. Doyle   (1932–34)

Colorado

Erskine Reed Myer, Jr.   James P. Logan   (1939–41)
                (2-15-20–9-1-20)   John R. Decker   (1941–43)
Harry A. Sullivan   (1920–22)   Ben C. Hilliard, Jr.   (1943–45)
Wilkie Ham   (1922–25)   Trevor P. Thomas (1945–7-30-47)
Orla A. Garris   (1925–27)   Albert F. Cruse   (7-30-47–9-1-47)
Raymond M. Sandhouse   John C. Vivian   (1947–4-26-48)
                         (1927–29)   Albert F. Cruse   (4-26-48–6-5-49)
Earl E. Ewing   (1929–31)   Leo J. Crowley   (1949–51)
Kenaz Huffman   (1931–33)   Albert F. Cruse   (1951–53)
Howard E. Reed   (1933–35)   William R. Egan   (1953–61)
Wilbur M. Alter   (1935–37)   Robert B. Grauberger   (1961–   )
H. Elwyn Davis   (1937–39)

Connecticut

Justus J. Fennell   (1919–21)   Eugene P. Armstrong   (1925–27)
Thomas J. Bannigan   (1921–22)   Harry C. Jackson   (1927–31)
Justus J. Fennell   (1922–23)   Kenneth F. Cramer   (1931–33)
E. L. Barlow   (1923–25)   Anson T. McCook   (1933–34)

Edward L. Newmarker	(1934–35)	Raymond F. Gates	(1941–45)
Sydney A. R. Finer	(1935–37)	Herbert L. Emanuelson	(1945–47)
William J. Miller	(1937–38)	Arthur J. Connell	(1947–53)
Arthur L. Baldwin	(1938–39)	Joseph G. Leonard	(1953–)
J. Fred Collins	(1939–41)		

Delaware

Thomas W. Miller	(3-25-20–28)	George Ehinger	(1948–50)
J. Alexander Crothers	(1928–29)	Samuel S. Fried	(1950–52)
Earl Sylvester	(1929–30)	Dr. Carl J. Rees	(1952–54)
John J. Dugan	(1930–34)	William J. B. Regan	(1954–56)
Herman H. Hanson	(1934–36)	Charles A. Burrous, Jr.	(1956–57)
Howard T. Ennis	(1936–38)	Harry S. Zerby	(1957–58)
Edward A. Mulrooney	(1938–40)	Garland D. Bloodsworth	
George D. Hill	(1940–42)		(1958–60)
John R. Fader	(1942–44)	Morris Wasserman	(1960–62)
William E. Matthews, Jr.		Dr. Park W. Huntington	
	(1944–46)		(1962–64)
Samuel Green	(1946–48)	Charles E. Jackson	(1964–)

District of Columbia

E. Lester Jones	(3-24-20–9-27-20)	William J. Holliman	
James A. Drain	(1920–22)		(1954–2-24-56)
John Lewis Smith, Sr.	(1922–23)	Robert A. Bunch	
Watson B. Miller	(1923–24)		(2-24-56–7-21-56)
Paul J. McGahan	(1924–30)	James D. Hill	(1956–58)
John Lewis Smith, Sr.	(1930–36)	John J. Finn	(1958–60)
Joseph J. Malloy	(1936–48)	Harold D. Beaton	(1960–62)
Owen C. Holleran	(1948–50)	Frederick H. Livingstone	
James D. Hill	(1950–52)		(1962–64)
Lee R. Pennington	(1952–53)	Allyn C. Donaldson	(1964–)
David E. Kisliuk	(1953–54)		

Florida

Dr. Davis Forster	(3-3-20–22)	Herbert R. Dyer	
Joseph Y. Cheney	(1922–25)		(5-21-34–10-26-34)
H. Neil Kirkman	(1925–29)	Joseph S. Clark	(1934–44)
Charles A. Mills	(1929–33)	Sam S. McCahill	(1944–46)
J. A. Franklin	(1933–5-21-34)	E. Meade Wilson	(1946–)

France

Francis E. Drake	(1920–21)	Sedley C. Peck	(1952–60)
R. Emmet Condon	(1921–23)	Dana W. Lyman	(1960–62)
S. Prentiss Bailey	(1923–36)	Sedley C. Peck	(1962–)
James L. McCann	(1936–52)		

Georgia

Eugene Oberdorfer, Jr.	Quimby O. Melton (1935–37)
(2-24-20–8-21-20)	Edward F. O'Connor, Jr.
Sam A. Cann (1920–22)	(1937–39)
Asa W. Candler (1922–25)	J. Pat Kelly (1939–41)
Terrell W. Hill (1925–27)	Hoyt C. Brown (1941–43)
Manton S. Eddy (1927–7-5-30)	Jackson P. Dick (1943–47)
Charles P. Graddick	Guy O. Stone (1947–54)
(7-5-30–11-10-30)	James E. Powers (1954–62)
Edgar B. Dunlap (11-10-30–33)	J. S. "Jack" Langford (1962–63)
Quimby O. Melton (1933–34)	W. D. Harrell (1963–)
James D. Gould, Jr. (1934–35)	

Hawaii

Leonard Withington	James Tice Phillips (1941–42)
(3-3-20–10-30-21)	James R. Mahaffy (1942–43)
John R. Galt (1921–22)	Kennett W. Dawson (1943–44)
Walter F. Dillingham (1922–23)	P. L. Murphy (1944–45)
Adna G. Clarke (1923–27)	Orvel T. Shonk, Sr. (1945–49)
James R. Mahaffy (1927–33)	Earl L. Holman (1949–51)
Adna G. Clarke (1933–35)	Orvel T. Shonk, Sr. (1951–53)
Harold C. Hill (1935–37)	Philip M. Corboy (1953–57)
Robert E. Kries (1937–39)	Wallace C. S. Young (1957–)
Harry F. Cooper (1939–41)	

Idaho

George E. Edgington	Gardner B. Parsons (1942–44)
(2-24-20–7-19-20)	James C. Bangs (1944–46)
Oscar W. Worthwine (1920–21)	William T. Marineau (1946–48)
E. W. Sinclair (1921–23)	Bert Weston (1948–50)
Charles A. Robins (1923–24)	Elbert S. Rawls (1950–52)
James Harris (1924–25)	Sidney E. Smith (1952–54)
Samuel E. Vance, Jr. (1925–28)	Harry R. Harn (1954–56)
Frank Estabrook (1928–30)	Andrew F. James (1956–58)
David L. Bush (1930–32)	John Hawley Atkinson (1958–60)
Harry Benoit (1932–38)	Peter B. Wilson (1960–62)
O. C. Wilson (1938–40)	Douglas D. Kramer (1962–64)
Alfred W. Shepherd (1940–42)	Bernard F. Gratton (1964–)

Illinois

Milton J. Foreman (2-23-20–22)	Edward A. Hayes (1931–33)
Horatio B. Hackett (1922–23)	James P. Ringley (1933–34)
Charles W. Schick (1923–12-2-23)	Charles C. Kapschull (1934–35)
S. L. Nelson (12-2-23–25)	Paul G. Armstrong (1935–39)
Howard P. Savage (1925–27)	Karl B. Nash (1939–41)
Ferre C. Watkins (1927–29)	William F. Waugh (1941–43)
David L. Shillinglaw (1929–31)	John H. Stelle (1943–45)

James P. Ringley	(1945–47)	Michael J. Healy	(1957–59)
Leonard W. Esper	(1947–49)	Omar J. McMackin	(1959–61)
John S. Gleason, Jr.	(1949–51)	Charles C. Shaw	(1961–63)
Douglass D. Getchell	(1951–53)	John H. Geiger	(1963–65)
Perce F. Brautigam	(1953–55)	Karl Yost	(1965–)
S. William Ash	(1955–57)		

Indiana

Dr. T. Victor Keene	(2-23-20–21)	Charles Patriot Maloney	
Oswald Ryan	(1921–22)		(1945–47)
Bowman Elder	(1922–27)	George N. Craig	(1947–49)
Paul V. McNutt	(1927–28)	Harry E. Fitch	(1949–51)
Frank M. McHale	(1928–29)	Vincent F. Kelley	(1951–53)
Raymond S. Springer	(1929–31)	John C. Wilson	(1953–55)
Dr. A. C. Arnett	(1931–33)	Lawrence H. Hinds	(1955–59)
Glen R. Hillis	(1933–35)	Ferd S. Badt	(1959–61)
Isadore E. Levine	(1935–43)	Arthur M. McDowell	(1961–63)
V. M. Armstrong	(1943–45)	Dr. Fred N. Daugherty	(1963–65)
		Robert L. Kuntz	(1965–)

Iowa

Daniel F. Steck	(2-23-20–21)	Fred E. Keating	(1943–45)
John H. Kelly	(1921–23)	Gaylor M. Brown	(1945–49)
Dr. R. J. Laird	(1923–25)	Paul A. Tornquist	(1949–53)
Maurice P. Cahill	(1925–27)	Theodore E. Murphy	(1953–55)
Volney Diltz	(1927–29)	Ward M. Loftus	(1955–57)
Ray Murphy	(1929–33)	Donald E. Johnson	(1957–61)
Wm. J. O'Connell	(1933–35)	John W. Moore	(1961–63)
Leo J. Duster	(1935–39)	Ward M. Loftus	(1963–2-7-65)
Ray O. Garber	(1939–41)	Robert H. Lounsberry	
Morris Y. Kinne	(1941–43)		(2-15-65–)

Italy

Edward R. Warner McCabe		Amerigo Vitelli	(1946–52)
	(1-8-27–11-14-27)	H. Armand deMasi	(1952–62)
Mrs. Julia Woodruff Wheelock		Sexon E. Humphreys	(1962–)
	(1927–46)		

Kansas

William F. Kurtz	(2-23-20–20)	Myron C. Miller	(1930–32)
W. W. Holloway	(1920–21)	Rex M. Montgomery	(1932–34)
R. C. Meek	(1921–22)	Leslie E. Edmonds	(1934–36)
Wilder S. Metcalf	(1922–23)	Ed. Morgenstern	(1936–38)
Jay H. Bracken	(1923–24)	Oscar Renn	(1938–40)
Dr. C. C. Hawke	(1924–26)	Sam Brolund	(1940–42)
W. D. Reilly	(1926–28)	Everett C. Garrison	(1942–44)
Braden Johnston	(1928–30)	McCulley Ashlock	(1944–46)

Harry W. Woods	(1946–48)	Ora D. McClellan	(1956–58)
Walter Reed Gage	(1948–50)	Harold J. Hollis	(1958–60)
Verner C. Smith	(1950–52)	Keith D. Brecheisen	(1960–62)
Guy E. Holt	(1952–54)	Robert J. Kubat	(1962–64)
Dale L. Duncan	(1954–56)	Virgil L. Lehr	(1964–)

Kentucky

Emmet O'Neal	(9-13-20–21)	John F. Hagner	(1949–51)
Maurice K. Gordon	(1921–22)	Garland G. Bryant	(1951–53)
Emmet O'Neal	(1922–25)	Charles M. Blackburn	(1953–57)
Frank D. Rash	(1925–4-19-46)	Darrell B. Hancock	(1957–61)
William P. Shadoan	(4-28-46–47)	Robert W. Anderson	(1961–63)
G. Lee McClain	(1947–49)	Kenneth Fern	(1963–)

Louisiana

Bret W. Eddy	(2-23-20–20)	Ernest L. Hawkins	(1937–39)
T. Semmes Walmsley	(1920–21)	Joseph A. Partridge	(1939–43)
Oswald W. McNeese	(1921–22)	J. Perry Cole	(1943–45)
Clarence J. Bourg	(1922–23)	Joseph Emmett Snee	(1945–49)
Gus Blancand	(1923–25)	Leonard L. Jackson	(1949–51)
Joseph L. McHugh	(1925–27)	Claude B. Duval	(1951–53)
Dan W. Spurloch	(1927–29)	Dr. Arthur R. Choppin	(1953–57)
Charles E. McKenzie	(1929–31)	Albert V. LaBiche	(1957–63)
Sam H. Jones	(1931–35)	Henry B. Clay	(1963–)
T. Ray Mobley	(1935–37)		

Maine

Albert Greenlaw	(1919–28)	Paul J. Jullien	(1946–48)
Edward S. Anthoine	(1928–30)	Hector G. Staples	(1948–50)
Dr. John G. Towne	(1930–32)	Fred A. Clough, Jr.	(1950–52)
Albert Beliveau	(1932–34)	Peter A. Thaanum, Jr.	(1952–54)
Basil H. Stinson	(1934–36)	James V. Day	(1954–55)
John J. Maloney, Sr.	(1936–38)	Ralph M. Merrow	(1955–58)
Raymond E. Rendall	(1938–40)	Anthony J. Rumo	(1958–60)
Edward J. Quinn	(1940–44)	William J. Rogers	(1960–65)
Llewellyn C. Fortier	(1944–46)	Maurice R. Parisien	(1965–)

Maryland

Henry S. Barrett	(1919–20)	John W. Jennings	(1934–38)
David John Markey	(1920–22)	J. Bryan Hobbs	(1938–42)
H. Findley French	(1922–23)	Godfrey Child	(1942–48)
E. Brooks Lee	(1923–24)	Harry S. Allen	(1948–52)
John Carmichael	(1924–25)	Frank T. Powers	(1952–54)
J. Moses Edlavitch	(1925–28)	J. Edward Walter	(1954–56)
Asa Needham	(1928–32)	David L. Brigham	(1956–64)
Caesar L. Aiello	(1932–33)	John A. Matthews	(1964–65)
Alex T. Grier	(1933–34)	H. Laird Roeder	(1965–)

Massachusetts

John F. J. Herbert	(2-5-20–20)	Richard F. Paul	(1930–31)
James T. Duane	(1920–21)	Stephen C. Garrity	(1931–32)
Charles H. Cole	(1921–22)	James P. Rose	(1932–33)
William H. Doyle	(1922–23)	Stephen C. Garrity	
Clarence R. Edwards	(1923–24)		(1933–12-26-43)
Leo M. Harlow	(1924–25)	Harold P. Redden	(3-1-44–47)
Francis J. Good	(1925–26)	Tracy A. Dibble	(1947–51)
William McGinnis	(1926–27)	Frederick L. Mellin	(1951–55)
John W. Reth	(1927–28)	Charles N. Collatos	(1955–59)
Dr. William H. Griffin	(1928–29)	Gabriel T. Olga	(1959–)
John J. O'Connell	(1929–30)		

Mexico

Leigh H. Rovzar	(1920–23)	Walter S. Sollenberger	(1940–46)
P. B. Holsinger	(1923–4-12-26)	Robert E. Feike	(1946–48)
R. H. Hudgens		Roscoe B. Gaither	(1948–52)
	(4-12-26–11-18-27)	Andres J. du Bouchet, Jr.	
Will S. Link	(11-8-27–28)		(1952–57)
Donald Lee McCuen	(1928–30)	William J. Seibert	(1957–60)
Walter S. Sollenberger	(1930–37)	Norbert W. Schmelkes	(1960–64)
John Welsh	(1937–38)	Harry Wright	(1964–)
Harry W. Berdie	(1938–40)		

Michigan

Fred M. Alger, Sr.	(1919–20)	David V. Addy	(1938–41)
Alton T. Roberts	(1920–21)	Carl H. Smith	(1941–43)
Paul A. Martin	(1921–23)	W. Bea Waldrip	(1943–45)
Dr. Robert B. Harkness		Herman F. Luhrs	(1945–47)
	(1923–24)	Lawrence C. Knox	(1947–49)
Dr. C. V. Spawr	(1924–25)	Guy M. Cox	(1949–51)
John F. Roehl	(1925–26)	Earl F. Ganschow	(1951–53)
J. Joseph Herbert	(1926–27)	Arthur H. Clarke	(1953–55)
Harold G. Edwards	(1927–28)	Robert G. Mathieson	(1955–57)
Willis M. Brewer	(1928–29)	R. Gerald Barr	(1957–59)
Ray Charles Conlon	(1929–31)	Thomas Roumell	(1959–61)
Raymond J. Kelly	(1931–33)	Donald J. Smith	(1961–63)
Leslie P. Kefgen	(1933–35)	William J. Clarahan	(1963–65)
John W. Gilmore	(1935–37)	John M. Carey	(1965–)
Don L. Beardslee	(1937–38)		

Minnesota

Arch H. Vernon	(1919–20)	John M. Henry	(1925–27)
Dr. A. A. Van Dyke	(1920–21)	Rufus R. Rand, Jr.	(1927–29)
R. A. Rossberg	(1921–22)	Dr. J. J. Morrow	(1929–31)
Z. L. Begin	(1922–23)	Earl V. Cliff	(1931–33)
Frederic D. McCarthy	(1923–25)	Gerald V. Barron	(1933–35)

William R. Mitchell	(1935–37)	Carl L. Lundgren	(1953–57)
Lloyd B. Kolliner	(1937–39)	Daniel F. Foley	(1957–63)
Michael F. Murray	(1939–43)	Eugene V. Lindquist	(1963–)
Roy T. Anderson	(1943–53)		

Mississippi

Alexander Fitzhugh	(8-18-20–21)	Adrian H. Boyd	(1938–46)
Dr. Ira L. Parsons	(1921–22)	Fred W. Young	(1946–48)
Winfred C. Adams	(1922–23)	H. Kirk Grantham	(1948–50)
Kenneth G. Price	(1923–24)	Robert D. Morrow	
Curtis T. Green	(1924–26)		(1950–1-16-55)
Leon F. Hendrick	(1926–27)	Ralph M. Godwin	
Ben F. Hilbun	(1927–28)		(1-31-55–7-13-55)
Ernest Waldauer	(1928–30)	Rollins S. (Polly) Armstrong	
Wm. A. Schmitt	(1930–32)		(1955–56)
Forrest G. Cooper	(1932–36)	Ralph M. Godwin	(1956–)
James T. Crawley	(1936–38)		

Missouri

Albert Linxwiler	(1919–20)	Charles L. Brown	(1938–42)
Jerome F. Duggan	(1920–21)	William B. Stone	(1942–50)
J. Pearce Kane	(1921–22)	Truman Ingle	(1950–54)
Bennett C. Clark	(1922–23)	James B. Kerrigan	(1954–56)
Herbert R. Booth	(1923–24)	Elmer W. Kuhlman	(1956–58)
Carl G. Schrader	(1924–25)	William J. Kenney	(1958–60)
Harry W. Castlen	(1925–26)	William H. Cain	(1960–3-21-62)
Dr. Neal D. Williams	(1926–30)	Buel A. Baclesse	
Herman H. Lark	(1930–32)		(3-21-62–7-29-62)
George Fiske	(1932–34)	Roy L. Carver	(1962–64)
Hal S. Beardsley	(1934–36)	James F. Kerr	(1964–)
Al J. Haemerle	(1936–38)		

Montana

Robert K. West	(1919–20)	Ory J. Armstrong	(12-12-40–41)
Charles E. Pew	(1920–21)	William H. Reif	(1941–43)
Wm. G. Ferguson	(1921–22)	Frank E. Flaherty	(1943–45)
C. Thomas Busha, Jr.	(1922–23)	George M. Gosman	(1945–47)
Loy J. Molumby	(1923–25)	Edwin O. Orleman	(1947–49)
N. J. Gilliland	(1925–26)	John B. C. Knight	(1949–51)
Charles L. Sheridan	(1926–27)	Victor O. Overcash	(1951–53)
Harry M. Johnson	(1927–28)	Walter W. Barnard	(1953–55)
Herbert Kibler	(1928–29)	Grover C. Schmidt, Jr.	(1955–57)
Dan B. Noble	(1929–31)	W. Charles Wallace	(1957–59)
James A. Livingston	(1931–32)	John S. Wulf, Jr.	(1959–61)
Arthur F. Lamey	(1932–35)	Russell W. Lindborg	(1961–63)
Hugh N. Marron	(1935–37)	Neil Shepherd	(1963–65)
Clarence H. Olson		William A. Lindsay	(1965–)
	(1937–12-12-40)		

Nebraska

Edward Patrick McDermott		Fred B. Winter	(4-14-36–38)
	(1920–21)	Clinton Brome	(1938–4-24-46)
Earl M. Cline	(1921–23)	John E. Curtiss	(4-24-46–5-22-60)
Frank Warner	(1923–24)	Lyman Stuckey	(7-27-60–8-28-60)
Samuel W. Reynolds		Stanley M. Huffman	(1960–62)
	(1924–1-22-35)	Edward T. Foster	(1962–64)
Golden P. Kratz		William E. Galbraith	(1964–65)
	(1-30-35–4-14-36)	Robert W. Lowry	(1965–)

Nevada

J. G. Scrugham	(2-27-20–22)	George W. Malone	(1930–32)
George W. Malone	(1922–23)	A. C. Grant	(1932–34)
Thomas J. D. Salter	(1923–24)	Ioannis A. Lougaris	(1934–38)
Earl T. Ross	(1924–26)	Dr. J. Dayton Smith	(1938–40)
Joseph G. Allard	(1926–28)	Ioannis A. Lougaris	(1940–46)
E. H. Hursh	(1928–30)	Thomas W. Miller	(1946–)

New Hampshire

Orville E. Cain	(2-24-20–20)	William J. Johnson	(1945–47)
Reginald C. Stevenson	(1920–21)	James W. Doon	(1947–55)
Dr. Robert O. Blood	(1921–22)	Eli A. Marcoux	(1955–57)
Orville E. Cain	(1922–29)	Floyd J. Daley	(1957–61)
Maurice F. Devine	(1929–41)	Raymond F. Mudge	(1961–)
James J. Doyle	(1941–45)		

New Jersey

Philip J. Ehrhardt	(1919–20)	John Grimshaw, Jr.	(1927–29)
Leonidas Coyle	(1920–21)	Herbert H. Blizzard	(1929–31)
Joseph D. Sears	(1921–22)	Theodore R. Crichton	(1931–33)
Harry C. Kramer	(1922–23)	Frank A. Mathews, Jr.	(1933–35)
A. Eugene Pattison	(1923–26)	William G. McKinley	(1935–)
Philip Forman	(1926–27)		

New Mexico

Bronson M. Cutting	(1919–20)	H. C. Neuffer	(1937–40)
Herman G. Baca	(1920–21)	Edwin G. Hobbs	(1940–41)
John W. Chapman	(1921–22)	Charles Morgan	(1941–43)
Joseph C. Wallach	(1922–25)	Edward C. Smith	(1943–47)
E. P. de Bujac	(1925–27)	Joseph H. Kirkpatrick	(1947–49)
Aud E. Lusk	(1927–29)	Reed Mulkey	(1949–57)
Jesus M. Baca	(1929–31)	James A. Tadlock	
Roy L. Cook	(1931–33)		(1957–10-21-57)
Herman G. Baca	(1933–34)	Dr. Deward H. Reed	
Ollie A. Davis	(1934–35)		(10-31-57–7-10-64)
Edward L. Safford	(1935–37)	W. Peter McAtee	(7-10-64–)

New York

William J. Donovan	(2-24-20–20)	Edward J. Neary	(1933–35)
W. R. Pooley	(1920–21)	Robert E. Minnich	(1935–39)
Ralph K. Robertson	(1921–23)	Jeremiah F. Cross	(1939–44)
Donald C. Strachan	(1923–25)	William N. Lewis	(1944–45)
Albert L. Ward	(1925–27)	Leo V. Lanning	(1945–57)
William M. Leffingwell	(1927–33)	Louis E. Drago	(1957–)

North Carolina

David J. Whichard, Jr.	(2-23-20–20)	J. Erle McMichael	(10-20-33–34)
		Louis G. Ratcliffe	(1934–40)
Wade H. Phillips	(1920–21)	Wm. Bryan Booe	(1940–6-15-46)
Dan S. Hollenga	(1921–22)	Claude S. Ramsey, Sr.	
Cale K. Burgess	(1922–23)		(6-15-46–2-24-47)
Miss Alice S. Gray	(1923–24)	Robin S. Kirby	(1947–54)
Thomas W. Bird	(1924–26)	R. C. Godwin	(1954–56)
George K. Freeman	(1926–29)	W. Austin Gresham	(1956–58)
E. Jack Edwards	(1929–30)	Tim T. Craig	(1958–62)
Wm. T. Joyner	(1930–10-20-23)	Wm. Dudley Robbins	(1962–)

North Dakota

James M. Hanley	(1919–20)	Fred A. Kraemer	(1923–24)
C. L. Dawson	(1920–21)	Francis Blaine Streeter	(1924–25)
M. H. Sprague	(1921–22)	William Stern	(1925–1-1-64)
Philip R. Bangs	(1922–23)	Patrick T. Milloy	(1964–)

Ohio

F. W. Galbraith, Jr.	(3-12-20–20)	Martin V. Coffey	(1944–48)
John R. McQuigg	(1920–24)	Don W. Schoeppe	(1948–50)
Lucian Kahn	(1924–26)	Aaron J. Halloran	(1950–52)
Milo J. Warner	(1926–29)	Rossiter S. Williams	(1952–54)
George E. Denny	(1929–32)	Clarence W. Whitemyer	
Paul M. Herbert	(1932–34)		(1954–56)
Thomas W. McCaw	(1934–36)	James M. Wagonseller	(1956–58)
William S. Konold	(1936–38)	Edward J. Sklenicka	(1958–60)
James R. Favret	(1938–40)	Merle F. Brady	(1960–64)
Eli A. Jensen	(1940–42)	Alec J. Blair	(1964–)
James V. Suhr	(1942–44)		

Oklahoma

Roy V. Hoffman	(2-23-20–21)	Jack A. Porter	(1937–39)
Robert B. Keenan, Sr.	(1921–22)	Hugh Askew	(1939–41)
William S. Key	(1922–23)	Dr. Ambrus B. Rivers	(1941–49)
Wm. L. Eagleton, Jr.	(1923–25)	Dr. Charles W. Hoshall	(1949–51)
Gilbert S. Fraser	(1925–27)	Ike E. Crawford	(1951–55)
Edward L. Allison	(1927–29)	Preston J. Moore	(1955–58)
Raymond H. Fields	(1929–35)	H. Coleman Nolen	(1958–61)
Wm. G. Stigler	(1935–37)	Gene Hassman	(1961–)

Oregon

Dow V. Walker	(2-25-20–20)	Willard J. Chamberlin	(1939–41)
George A. White	(1920–22)	E. L. Knight	(1941–43)
Charles W. Erskine	(1922–23)	Oral E. Palmateer	(1943–45)
Dr. E. B. Stewart	(1923–25)	Hugh A. Bowman	(1945–47)
Charles J. Johnson	(1925–27)	Alfred P. Kelley	(1947–49)
Vic MacKenzie	(1927–29)	David Blakeman	(1949–51)
Ben S. Fisher	(1929–30)	B. E. "Kelly" Owens	(1951–53)
Vic MacKenzie	(1930–31)	Hollis C. Hull	(1953–56)
Sidney S. George	(1931–37)	Karl L. Wagner	(1956–65)
George L. Koehn	(1937–39)	William Stevens	(1965–)

Panama, C.Z.

Fred DeVeber Sill	(1920–26)	Thomas F. Sullivan	(1944–46)
Theodore M. Drake	(1926–28)	LeRoy Schick	(1946–50)
Fred DeVeber Sill	(1928–32)	Nelson W. Magner	(1950–56)
Osborne E. McKay	(1932–34)	Claude E. Campbell	(1956–60)
Theodore M. Drake	(1934–36)	Raymond G. Bush	(1960–62)
Osborne E. McKay	(1936–38)	George A. Black, Jr.	(1962–64)
Fred DeVeber Sill	(1938–40)	Raymond G. Bush	(1964–)
Osborne E. McKay	(1940–44)		

Pennsylvania

Albert J. Logan	(2-24-20–20)	Vincent A. Carroll	(1932–37)
David J. Davis	(1920–21)	J. Guy Griffith	(1937–42)
Joseph H. Thompson	(1921–22)	Harry K. Stinger	(1942–52)
Wm. B. Healey	(1922–23)	William L. Windsor III	(1952–54)
J. Leo Collins	(1923–27)	Walter E. Alessandroni	(1954–65)
Lucius McK. Crumrine	(1927–30)	Daniel A. Drew	(1965–)
Charles A. Gebert	(1930–32)		

Philippines

Whipple S. Hall	(1920–23)	Gailey B. Underwood	(1951–52)
No record	(1923–24)	Andrew R. McKelvie	(1952–54)
Harry J. Morgan	(1924–25)	Jose J. DeGuzman	(1954–56)
Harry D. Cranston	(1925–27)	Bernard L. Anderson	(1956–58)
Harrison S. Kerrick	(1927–33)	Robert O. Phillips	(1958–60)
Forrest E. Williford	(1933–34)	Jose J. DeGuzman	(1960–62)
Harrison S. Kerrick	(1934–36)	Robert O. Phillips	(1962–63)
Frank Parker	(1936–46)	Jose J. DeGuzman	(1963–64)
Benjamin F. Ohnick	(1946–48)	Robert O. Phillips	(1964–65)
Marc A. Stice	(1948–51)	Charles A. Park	(1965–)

Puerto Rico

Harry F. Besosa	(1922–23)	Noah Shepard	(1928–29)
Athos W. Besosa	(1923–26)	Dr. Juan Lastra Charriez	
Harry F. Besosa	(1926–27)		(1929–35)
Manuel Font	(1927–28)	Harry L. Hall	(1935–37)

Manuel Font   (1937–39)   Ramon Rafael Guas
Dr. J. H. Font   (1939–41)   (1953-4-12-55)
Ignasio Saavedra   (1941–43)   Alejo Rivera Morales
José Cantellops   (1943–47)   (4-12-55–7-17-55)
Charles H. Julia   (1947-3-14-49)   Ramon Rafael Guas   (1955–57)
Vincente Reyes Fitzpatrick   Osvaldo Rivera   (1957–59)
                             (1949–53)   Gilberto M. Font   (1959–   )

Rhode Island

G. Edward Buxton, Jr.   (1919–20)   William Beehler   (1937–39)
William P. Sheffield, Jr. (1920–21)   Frank E. McCaffrey   (1939–43)
L. H. Callan   (1921–22)   Edward H. Ziegler   (1943–45)
Thomas J. H. Peirce   (1922–23)   Chester A. Follett   (1945–47)
Bertram W. Wall   (1923–29)   George Andrews   (1947–49)
Raymond B. Littlefield (1929–31)   Arthur E. Marley   (1949–51)
Charles L. Woolley   (1931–33)   Lee A. Lemos   (1951–53)
Bertram W. Wall   (1933–35)   John A. Ryer   (1953–   )
Ralph S. Mohr   (1935–37)

South Carolina

J. Monroe Johnson   (1919–22)   James F. Daniel, Jr.   (1945–51)
Thomas B. Spratt   (1922–23)   W. J. McLeod, Jr.   (1951–52)
J. Monroe Johnson   (1923–35)   Dr. Roland Hoyt Fulmer
Miller C. Foster   (1935-1-24-36)   (1952–53)
George D. Levy   (1-24-36–41)   E. Roy Stone, Jr.   (1953–   )
Sam L. Latimer, Jr.   (1941–45)

South Dakota

M. L. Shade   (2-25-20–20)   Turner M. Rudesill
Fred B. Ray   (1920–22)   (1941-4-10-44)
J. H. Williams   (1922–23)   Claude A. Hamilton
Dr. G. G. Cottam   (1923–27)   (4-10-44–6-18-44)
Walter H. Burke   (1927–29)   Carroll H. Lockhart   (1944–49)
Frank G. McCormick   (1929–30)   Claude A. Hamilton   (1949–57)
Dr. Carle B. Lenker   (1930–37)   Earl E. Hoelscher   (1957–63)
R. A. Schenkenberger   (1937–41)   Glenn R. Green   (1963–   )

Tennessee

Harry S. Berry   (1919–21)   David N. Harsh   (1946–48)
Phil B. Whitaker   (1921–22)   Halbert Harvill   (1948–50)
L. Jere Cooper   (1922–23)   George A. Caldwell   (1950–52)
Dr. Samuel T. Parker   (1923–24)   Bert B. Barnes, Jr.   (1952–54)
John G. Sims, Sr.   (1924–26)   Rev. William Henry Moss
Oscar L. Farris   (1926–28)   (1954–56)
Roane Waring   (1928–30)   John J. Duncan   (1956–58)
Adam B. Bowman   (1930–32)   George T. Lewis, Jr.   (1958–60)
Prentice Cooper   (1932–34)   Walton D. Griffin   (1960–62)
Roane Waring   (1934–42)   William S. Todd   (1962–64)
Bascom F. Jones   (1942–44)   Whit S. LaFon   (1964–   )
Dr. Nat H. Copenhaver   (1944–46)

Texas

Claude V. Birkhead	(2-24-20–20)	George E. Broome	(1934–36)
John S. Hoover	(1920–21)	Dr. Wm. F. Murphy	(1936–38)
R. G. Storey	(1921–22)	Dr. William J. Danforth	
Charles C. Ingram	(1922–23)		(1938–46)
Jay A. Rossiter	(1923–24)	James M. Caviness	(1946–48)
Ben J. Dean	(1924–26)	H. Miller Ainsworth	(1948–50)
Wayne B. Davis	(1926–28)	H. J. Bernard	(1950–54)
Yorick D. Mathes	(1928–30)	Albert D. Brown, Jr.	(1954–58)
Ernest C. Cox	(1930–32)	Joseph L. Matthews	(1958–62)
Scott Reed	(1932–34)	J. Walter Janko	(1962–)

Utah

Baldwin Robergson	(2-25-20–20)	William J. Higbee	(1941–43)
Murray W. McCarty	(1920–22)	Allison Bills	(1943–45)
John E. Booth	(1922–23)	J. Harry Hickman	(1945–47)
Dr. B. W. Black	(1923–25)	Francis J. Springer	(1947–49)
John E. Booth	(1925–27)	Robert L. Shelby	(1949–51)
Ray L. Olson	(1927–29)	Ferris R. Thomassen	(1951–53)
E. A. Littlefield	(1929–31)	Victor J. Bott	(1953–55)
Joseph E. Nelson	(1931–33)	William Sutter	(1955–57)
Darrell T. Lane	(1933–35)	Doran T. Duesler	(1957–58)
Harry T. Reynolds, Jr.	(1935–37)	P. Clark Cheney	(1958–63)
Norman L. Sims	(1937–39)	William E. Christoffersen	
Otto A. Wiesley	(1939–7-10-40)		(1963–)
Spencer S. Eccles	(7-10-40–41)		

Vermont

Dr. H. Nelson Jackson	(1919–20)	Clarence S. Campbell	
Redfield Proctor	(1920–21)		(1-22-55–57)
John F. Sullivan	(1921–23)	Harry O. Pearson	(1957–59)
Jack Crowley	(1923–28)	J. Raymond McGinn	(1959–61)
Dr. H. Nelson Jackson	(1928–36)	Edward H. Giles	(1961–63)
Bert S. Hyland	(1936–37)	Simon J. Godfrey	(1963–65)
Dr. H. Nelson Jackson		Ray Greenwood	(1965–)
	(1937–1-14-55)		

Virginia

John J. Wicker, Jr.	(2-23-20–21)	Robert B. Crawford	(1935–37)
Robert T. Barton, Jr.	(1921–22)	Wilmer L. O'Flaherty	(1937–39)
Dr. J. F. Lynch	(1922–23)	Gates R. Richardson	(1939–41)
Edward E. Goodwyn	(1923–25)	Randolph H. Perry	(1941–43)
John J. Wicker, Jr.	(1925–27)	W. Catesby Jones	(1943–7-9-44)
Henry M. Taylor	(1927–29)	Chapman K. Hunter	(1944–45)
Nelson C. Overton	(1929–31)	Fred C. Buck	(1945–47)
Roby C. Thompson	(1931–33)	Ferdinand Clinton Knight	
Dr. F. Whitney Godwin			(1947–4-26-49)
	(1933–35)		

Fred W. Higgason   Dr. G. Hunter Wolfe
                (5-25-49–8-6-49)   (3-15-52–53)
Lemuel W. Houston   (1949–51)   Lemuel W. Houston   (1953–57)
W. Marshall Geoghegan   L. Eldon James   (1957–65)
                (1951–3-13-52)   Dr. Thomas H. S. Ely   (1965–   )

Washington

Louis H. Seagrave   (2-27-20–20)   Dr. Theodore J. Rasmussen
Paul Edwards   (1920–21)   (1945–47)
Charles S. Albert   (1921–22)   Jack M. Baldwin   (1947–49)
Dewitt M. Evans   (1922–23)   N. P. Peterson   (1949–51)
L. B. Donley   (1923–25)   John F. Shrader   (1951–1-19-53)
Edward H. Faubert   (1925–27)   N. P. Peterson   (2-1-53–8-15-53)
Stephen F. Chadwick   (1927–29)   Frank O. Sether   (1953–55)
Zola O. Brooks   (1929–31)   Loris A. Winn   (1955–57)
Harold B. King   (1931–33)   Ralph E. Goodrich   (1957–59)
John J. O'Brien   (1933–35)   Langford W. Armstrong
Frank N. Bruhn   (1935–37)   (1959–61)
William J. Conniff   (1937–39)   W. A. "Wally" Carpenter
E. C. Knoebel   (1939–41)   (1961–63)
George E. Flood   (1941–43)   Russell I. Grob   (1963–65)
Charles A. Gonser   (1943–45)   Aiden F. Russell   (1965–   )

West Virginia

Louis Johnson   (2-24-20–22)   Hubert S. Ellis   (9-5-35–5-7-36)
Andrew E. Edmiston, Jr.   Edmund L. Jones   (5-7-36–39)
                      (1922–23)   W. Elliott Nefflen (1939–4-14-46)
Spiller Hicks   (1923–25)   Stanley C. Morris (4-16-46–47)
James H. McGinnis   (1925–27)   Dr. P. E. Kercheval   (1947–57)
Robert B. McDougle   (1927–34)   Leonal O. Bickel   (1957–   )
Robert E. O'Connor
                (1934–9-5-35)

Wisconsin

Harold S. Crosby   (2-23-20–21)   Frank L. Greenya   (1940–42)
Edward J. Barrett   (1921–22)   Harvey V. Higley   (1942–44)
F. Ryan Duffy   (1922–10-15-23)   James R. Durfee   (1944–46)
James H. McGillan (10-15-23–24)   William F. Trinke (1946–1-18-48)
Vilas H. Whaley   (1924–26)   William R. Kenney (1-18-48–50)
Harold L. Plummer   (1926–28)   Charles L. Larson   (1950-52)
Frank J. Schneller   (1928–29)   Kenneth L. Greenquist (1952–54)
Delbert J. Kenny   (1929–30)   Gordon W. Roseleip   (1954–56)
Marshall C. Graff   (1930–32)   George Emory Sipple   (1956–58)
Dr. C. H. Dawson   (1932–34)   William J. Haese   (1958–60)
John J. Burkhard   (1934–36)   Lloyd J. Berken   (1960–62)
George R. Howitt   (1936–38)   Gilman H. Stordock   (1962–64)
Lawrence H. Smith   (1938–40)   James E. Mulder   (1964–   )

Wyoming

Harry Fisher	(2-24-20–20)	Chiles P. Plummer	(1936–40)
Fred W. Dralle	(1920–21)	George A. Johns	(1940–42)
Charles S. Hill	(1921–10-20-22)	Charles J. Hughes	(1942–44)
Chiles P. Plummer		T. T. Tynan	(1944–46)
	(10-20-22–11-29-22)	Oscar B. Rohlff	(1946–48)
Will G. Metz	(11-29-22–23)	Ward W. Husted	(1948–50)
W. J. Wehrli	(1923–24)	Valdemar S. Christensen	
Marshall S. Reynolds	(1924–26)		(1950–52)
Dr. Albert B. Tonkin	(1926–27)	Lyle E. Poole	(1952–7-10-54)
Harry B. Henderson, Jr.		Olin F. Jacquet	(7-10-54–54)
	(1927–30)	Ernest J. Goppert, Sr.	(1954–56)
Dr. W. W. Yates	(1930–32)	Floyd W. Bartling	(1956–60)
Louis R. Probst	(1932–34)	Charles B. Metz	(1960–)
George A. Heilman	(1934–36)		

CHAIRMEN OF NATIONAL COMMISSIONS AND COMMITTEES

AMERICANISM

Commission

Arthur Woods, N.Y.	1919–20	Jeremiah F. Cross, N.Y.	1938–39
Henry J. Ryan, Mass.	1920–21	Leslie P. Kefgen, Mich.	1939–40
Leonard Withington, Hawaii		James O'Neil, N.H.	1940–43
	1921–22	Robert J. Webb, Neb.	1943–46
No Chairman shown on National		James F. Green, Neb.	1946–50
Records	1922–23	A. Luke Crispe, Vt.	1950–51
John R. Quinn, Cal.	1923–24	James F. Daniel, Jr., S.C.	1951–53
E. K. Bixby, Okla.	1924–26	J. Addington Wagner, Mich.	
Arthur W. Proctor, N.Y.	1926–27		1953–54
Frank L. Pinola, Pa.	1927–29	James F. Daniel, Jr., S.C.	
Dan Spurlock, La.	1929–31		1954–11-30-59
Edward J. Neary, N.Y.	1931–32	Edmund G. Lyons, N.J.	
Hugh T. Williams, Va.	1932–33		5-15-60–60
Paul H. Griffith, Pa.	1933–34	Martin B. McKneally, N.Y.	
Ray Murphy, Ia.	1934–35		1960–61
Stephen F. Chadwick, Wash.		Charles F. Hamilton, Mo.	1961–62
	1935–38	Daniel J. O'Connor, N.Y.	1962–

CHILD WELFARE

Committee

George A. Withers, Kans.	1922–24	Wilbur M. Alter, Colo.	1934–35
(Orphans' Home)		Roland B. Howell, La.	1935–37
Mark T. McKee, Mich.	1924–27	Glen R. Hillis, Ind.	1937–39
Sherman W. Child, Minn.	1927–30	Ed Morgenstern, Kans.	1939–40
Edwin E. Hollenback, Pa.	1930–32	Lawrence H. Smith, Wis.	1940–41
Milton D. Campbell, Ohio		L. A. Williams, Wash.	1941–42
	1932–34	Harry C. Kehm, S.D.	1942–45
		David V. Addy, Mich.	1945–47

Commission

Ralph Heatherington, W.Va.
                       1947–48
David V. Addy, Mich.   1948–49
A. H. Wittmann, Pa.   1949–50
David V. Addy, Mich.   1950–51
A. H. Wittmann, Pa.   1951–52
Samuel S. Fried, Del.
               1952-3-21-53
David V. Addy, Mich. 3-21-53–53

George Ehinger, Del.   1953–56
David V. Addy, Mich.   1956–57
Maurice T. Webb, Ga.   1957–58
Arthur W. Wilkie, Ind. 1958–59
Percy A. Lemoine, La.   1959–62
Garland D. Murphy, Jr., Ark.
                       1962–63
David V. Addy, Mich.   1963–64
Morris "Bob" Nooner, Jr., Ill.
                       1964–

CONVENTION

Committee

Samuel Reynolds, Neb.	1924–25
M. S. Eddy, Ga.	1928–29

  (France Convention Investigating
  Committee)

Vincent A. Carroll, Pa.	1934–35
James P. Ringley, Ill.	1935–40
Leo J. Duster, Ia.	1940–1-31-43
David N. Harsh, Tenn.	1943–46

Commission

Vincent A. Carroll, Pa.	1946–51
Frank E. Brigham, Fla.	
	1951–8-4-52
Joe H. Adams, Fla.	8-7-52–53
Harry L. Foster, Cal.	1953–54
Joe H. Adams, Fla.	1954–55
Harry L. Foster, Cal.	1955–56
Joe H. Adams, Fla.	1956–6-2-59
Harry L. Foster, Cal.	6-25-59–59
James V. Demarest, N.Y.	1959–60
Harry L. Foster, Cal.	1960–61
James V. Demarest, N.Y.	1961–

ECONOMIC

Henry D. Lindsley, Tex.   1920–21
  (War Risk and Compensation)

Unemployment Committee

Roy Hoffman, Okla.	1921–22
Maurice K. Gordon, Ky.	1922–23

National Employment Commission

Howard P. Savage, Ill.	1930–31
Henry L. Stevens, Jr., N.C.	
	1931–32

*National Veterans Employment
Committee*

J. Bryan Hobbs, Md.	1935–36
Forrest G. Cooper, Miss.	1936–37
Jack Crowley, Vt.	1937–41
Lawrence J. Fenlon, Ill.	1941–47
Spence S. Boise, N.D.	1947–51
John L. Connors, Conn.	1951–53
Joseph S. McCracken, Pa.	1953–56

National Employment Committee

Frank O. Sether, Wash.	1956–57
J. Edward Walter, Md.	1957–60
Elmore R. Torn, Tex.	1960–62
Wm. J. Chisholm, Colo.	1962–

ECONOMIC COMMISSION

Lawrence J. Fenlon, Ill. 1947–53
Wilbur C. Daniel, Va. 1953–54
Norman A. Johnson, Miss.
  1954–55
Adolph F. Bremer, Minn. 1955–56
Stanley M. Huffman, Neb.
  1956–58

Everett Richaud, La. 1958–59
Robert H. Hazen, Ore. 1959–60
George T. Lewis, Jr., Tenn.
  1960–61
Almo J. Sebastianelli, Pa. 1961–63
John J. Flynn, Cal. 1963–

FINANCE

Committee
deLancey Kountze, N.Y. 1919–20
Milton J. Foreman, Ill. 1920–22
Wilder S. Metcalf, Kans.
  1922–11-1-34
Samuel W. Reynolds, Neb.
  11-1-34–35
John Lewis Smith, Sr., D.C.
  1935–36
Samuel W. Reynolds, Neb.
  1936–47

Commission
Samuel W. Reynolds, Neb.
  1947–49
William J. Dwyer, N.Y. 1949–55
Harold P. Redden, Mass. 1955–65
Churchill Williams, Iowa 1965–

FOREIGN RELATIONS

Committee
Franklin D'Olier, Pa. 1921–22
Herbert R. Booth, Mo. 1923–24
  (Permanent Peace Committee)

Commission
H. Nelson Jackson, Vt. 1924–25
Thomas A. Lee, Kans. 1924–25
  (World Peace Committee)
H. Nelson Jackson, Vt. 1925–26
Henry D. Lindsley, N.Y. 1926–28
  (World Peace & Foreign Relations)
Lemuel Bolles, N.Y. 1928–31
  (World Peace & Foreign Relations)
Darrell T. Lane, Utah 1931–32
  (World Peace & Foreign Relations)
H. Nelson Jackson, Vt. 1932–34
  (World Peace & Foreign Relations)

Robert J. White, Mass. 1934–37
  (World Peace & Foreign Relations)
Darrell T. Lane, Utah 1937–39
  (World Peace & Foreign Relations)

Committee
Wilbur M. Alter, Colo. 1939–40
Harry A. Sullivan, Colo. 1940–46
Anson T. McCook, Conn. 1946–47

Commission
Anson T. McCook, Conn. 1947–48
Leon Happell, Cal. 1948–49
William Verity, Ohio 1949–50
Donald R. Wilson, W.Va. 1950–51
Rogers Kelley, Tex. 1951–57
Addison P. Drummond, Fla.
  1957–59
Emilio S. Iglesias, Vt. 1959–63
Thomas E. Whelan, N.D. 1963–

INTERNAL AFFAIRS

Commission

Wm. B. Stone, Mo.	1947–48
H. Miller Ainsworth, Tex.	1948–49
William J. Lowry, Conn.	1949–51
Ralph A. Johnson, Va.	1951–53
Charles L. Larson, Wis.	1953–54
George T. Lewis, Jr., Tenn.	
	1954–Sept., 1956

Addison P. Drummond, Fla.	
	Sept., 1956–57
Herbert J. Jacobi, D.C.	1957–61
George T. Lewis, Jr., Tenn.	
	1961–62
Herbert J. Jacobi, D.C.	1962–

LEGISLATIVE

Committee

Gilbert Bettman, Ohio	1920–21
Daniel Steck, Ia.	1921–22
Wayne Davis, Tex.	1922–23
Aaron Sapior, Ill.	1923–24
O. L. Bodenhamer, Ark.	1924–25
Hugh K. Martin, Ohio	1925–26
Scott W. Lucas, Ill.	1926–27
Donald C. Strachan, N.Y.	1927–28
John H. Sherburne, Mass.	1928–29
Ferre C. Watkins, Ill.	1929–30
Harry W. Colmery, Kans.	1930–32
J. Ray Murphy, Ia.	1932–33
Raymond J. Kelly, Mich.	1933–34

Vilas H. Whaley, Wis.	1934–35
Robert W. Colflesh, Ia.	1935–37
Frank L. Pinola, Pa.	1937–39
Irving A. Jennings, Ariz.	1939–41
Maurice F. Devine, N.H.	1941–45
Wm. H. Doyle, Mass.	1945–47
Robert W. Colflesh, Ia.	1947–48
Thomas W. Miller, Nev.	1948–49
Elmer W. Sherwood, Ind.	1949–50
Jerome F. Duggan, Mo.	1950–55
Herman F. Luhrs, Mich.	1955–56
Jerome F. Duggan, Mo.	1956–62
Clarence C. Horton, Ala.	1962–

NATIONAL SECURITY

Committees

AERONAUTICS

Reed G. Landis, Ill.	1922–26
Gill Robert Wilson, N.J.	1926–27
Rufus R. Rand, Jr., Minn.	1927–28
No Aeronautics Committee	
	1929–32
Edward V. Rickenbacker, N.Y.	
	1932–33
John Dwight Sullivan, N.Y.	
	1933–34
Howard C. Knotts, Ill.	1934–35
Dudley M. Steele, Cal.	1935–36
W. W. Arrasmith, Neb.	1936–38
David S. Ingalls, Ohio	1938–39
John Dwight Sullivan, N.Y.	
	1939–40

Norman M. (Pat) Lyon, Cal.	
	1940–43
Carlyle E. Godske, Wis.	1943–44
John Dwight Sullivan, N.Y.	
	1944–46
Edward V. Rickenbacker, N.Y.	
	1946–47
Roy B. Gardner, Ohio	1947–50
Roscoe Turner, Ind.	1950–58
Wm. J. Danforth, Tex.	1958–61
Roscoe Turner, Ind.	1961–

CIVIL DEFENSE

G. Lee McClain, Ky.	1941–46
Niel R. Allen, Ore.	1946–57
Ray A. Pierce, Tex.	1957–58
William L. Weiss, Mo.	1958–59

David Aronberg, Ky.

1959–10-6-64

Ray C. Stiles, Ia.   10-6-64

Stacey A. Garner, Tenn.   1964–

MERCHANT MARINE

S. Perry Brown, Tex.   1941–43

Ray O. Garber, Ia.   1943–48

Albert B. Stapp, Ala.   1948–49

Jimmy Phillips, Tex.   1949–50

Henry C. Parke, N.Y.   1950–

MILITARY AFFAIRS

Wade H. Hayes, N.Y.   1920–21

D. John Markey, Md.   1921–22

Wm. P. Screws, Ala.   1922–23

Milton J. Forman, Ill.   1923–24

George E. Leach, Minn.   1924–25

Milton A. Reckord, Md.   1925–26

John R. McQuigg, Ohio   1926–27

Edward L. Logan, Mass.   1927–28

J. Arthur Lynch, Ga.   1928–29

No committee   1929–44

Ed. J. Zable, Wyo.   1944–45

A. D. Welsh, Mo.   1945–47

Omar J. McMackin, Ill.   1947–49

A. D. Welsh, Mo.   1949–53

William S. Todd, Tenn.   1953–54

William C. Doyle, N.J.   1954–62

Edwin R. Bentley, Fla.   1962–

NATIONAL DEFENSE

Roy Hoffman, Okla.   1926–28

Albert L. Cox, N.C.   1928–29

C. B. Robbins, Ia.   1929–31

Albert L. Cox, N.C.   1931–32

Milton A. Reckord, Md.   1932–33

Amos A. Fries, D.C.   1933–34

Thomas H. Healy, D.C.   1934–35

Edward J. Neary, N.Y.   1935–36

J. O'Connor Roberts, D.C.

1936–38

Warren H. Atherton, Cal. 1938–43

Michael J. Kelleher, Mass.

1943–44

S. Perry Brown, Tex.   1944–47

NAVAL AFFAIRS

Edward E. Spafford, N.Y.   1920–25

Thomas Goldingay, N.J.   1925–26

Edwin Denby, Mich.   1926–27

Charles Schick, Ill.   1927–29

Sam Long, Tex.   1941–42

Arthur F. Duffy, N.Y.   1942–47

Paul Dever, Mass.   1947–48

Arthur F. Duffy, N.Y.   1948–54

Emmett G. Lenikan, Wash.

1954–

NATIONAL SECURITY COMMISSION

S. Perry Brown, Tex.   1947–48

Erle Cocke, Jr., Ga.   1948–50

Bruce P. Henderson, Ohio

1950–52

Thomas E. Paradine, N.Y.

1952–53

Seaborn P. Collins, N.M.   1953–54

Bruce P. Henderson, Ohio 1954–55

Will F. Nicholson, Colo.   1955–57

Robert H. Bush, Ia.   1957–59

Addison P. Drummond, Fla.

1959–61

Robert H. Bush, Ia.   1961–62

William C. Doyle, N.J.   1962–

PUBLICATIONS

Commission

Milo J. Warner, Ohio   1940–41

Lynn U. Stambaugh, N.D.

1941–42

Roane Waring, Tenn.   1942–43

Warren H. Atherton, Cal. 1943–44

Claude S. Ramsey, N.C.   1944–45

Roland Cocreham, La.   1945–47

Vilas H. Whaley, Wis.   1947–48

  (Publication Committee)

James F. O'Neil, N.H.   1948–50

John Stelle, Ill.   1950–57

Donald R. Wilson, W.Va.   1957–61

Edward McSweeney, N.Y.

1961–63

Charles R. Logan, Ia.   1963–

PUBLIC RELATIONS

Publicity Committee

E. H. Risdon, Cal.	1926–29
Karl W. Detzer, N.Y.	1929–30
C. W. Motter, Neb.	1930–32
Jack R. C. Cann, Mich.	1932–34
Lawrence W. Hager, Ky.	1934–35
C. W. Motter, Neb.	1935–36

Publication & Publicity Committee

Darrell T. Lane, Utah	1936–37

Publishing & Publicity Commission

Harry T. Colmery, Kans.	1936–37
Daniel J. Doherty, Mass.	1937–38
Stephen F. Chadwick, Wash.	1938–39
Raymond J. Kelly, Mich.	1939–40

Publicity Commission

Glenn H. Campbell, Ohio	1944–45

Public Relations Commission

Glenn H. Campbell, Ohio	1945–47
George A. Bideaux, Ariz.	1947–48
Frank J. Becker, N.Y.	1948–49
Herman Luhrs, Mich.	1949–52
Arthur J. Connell, Conn.	1952–53
Thomas E. Paradine, N.Y.	1953–54
W. C. Daniel, Va.	1954–55
James V. Demarest, N.Y.	1955–56
William R. Burke, Cal.	1956–58
James V. Demarest, N.Y.	1958–59
C. D. DeLoach, D.C.	1959–

REHABILITATION

Committee

Abel Davis, Ill.	1919–21
Albert A. Sprague, Ill.	1921–22
Joe Sparks, S.C.	1922–23
Watson Miller, D.C.	1923–35
Daniel J. Doherty, Mass.	1935–36
Earl V. Cliff, Minn.	1936–37
Walter J. Krisp, Pa.	1937–38
William F. Smith, Pa.	1938–39
Earl V. Cliff, Minn.	1939–40
John H. Walsh, Mass.	1940–43
R. W. Sisson, Ark.	1943–44
Robert M. McCurdy, Cal.	1944–47

Commission

W. Rex McCrosson, N.J.	1947–48
John H. Walsh, Mass.	1948–49
Robert M. McCurdy, Cal.	1949–51
Earl V. Cliff, Minn.	1951–52
Robert M. McCurdy, Cal.	1952–

Index

Index

Names of individual Legionnaires are not included in the index. National officers, officers of the FIDAC, directors of divisions and sections, national executive committeemen, chairmen of national commissions and committees, and national presidents of the Legion Auxiliary are listed in the appendix.